The Digitization of Healthcare

Loick Menvielle • Anne-Françoise
Audrain-Pontevia • William Menvielle
Editors

The Digitization of Healthcare

New Challenges and Opportunities

Editors
Loick Menvielle
EDHEC Business School
Nice Cedex, France

Anne-Françoise Audrain-Pontevia
Université du Québec à Montréal
Montréal, Canada

William Menvielle
Université du Québec à Trois-Rivières
Trois Rivières, Canada

ISBN 978-1-349-95750-7
DOI 10.1057/978-1-349-95173-4

ISBN 978-1-349-95173-4 (eBook)

This Palgrave Macmillan imprint is published by Springer Nature
The registered company is Macmillan Publishers Ltd.
The registered company address is: The Campus, 4 Crinan Street, London, N1 9XW, United Kingdom

For Annick Braley and Elyane Leclerc-Braley

Preface

When digital is revolutionizing medical practices!

IT has infiltrated the health sector and it is now beginning to have a growing influence on both doctors and patients. More than a passing trend, the health sector is undergoing a revolution which could change the way doctors and patients relate. While some companies may be adopting these changes for their own benefits, the digital revolution could be extremely positive for all of us.

Today, the eHealth market is worth more than US $250 billion, with an encouraging prospect of between 10 and 25% growth according to PwC (2015). Some medical actors see this emerging market as a consequence of new uses of technologies. eHealth is seen as a solution to care access issues, but not only this. It will give patients with chronic diseases the possibility to manage their illness. For healthy individuals, eHealth can provide a preventive approach, especially with self-monitoring apps, which are arousing more and more interest from Google, Apple, Facebook, Amazon (GAFAs).

First studies and projects comparing the economic efficiency of conventional health models to the connected health model tend to find in favor of the latter. For example, in the Mein Herz study (French Health Ministry, 2014), savings are substantial, costs related to patient hospitalization are reduced by almost 50%, and the overall cost of support for patients is reduced by 25%. Furthermore, the connected health model has a strong impact on hospital resources, particularly concerning medical staff whose number could be reduced by up to 25%. Connected health has also shown its effectiveness in reducing patients' readmission rate, by a significant 40% of the average length of hospitalization per patient. It seems that the connected health model could fundamentally change the process of delivering healthcare. The savings could improve other aspects of the health system both in Western and emerging countries.

The substantial savings generated by this new approach could contribute directly or indirectly to find answers to current questions of many countries both in Western and emerging countries.

WHO has put eHealth at the heart of their strategic plan? Given the way people use IT, mhealth is in a good position, particularly in emerging countries, to play an important role in delivering access to care and diagnosing sickness earlier. It can also be used to verify the origin of medication just by sending an SMS or using a QR code—especially useful for the African continent where fake drugs are causing a lot of deaths.

We are faced with major challenges, but the outlook is mainly positive. However, connected health technology must in no way devalue the relationship between healthcare providers and patients. On the contrary, it should be used to support this relationship, promoting the well-being of the sick while facilitating the process of caregiving.

The number of health apps developed for smart phones are estimated at more than 100,000. But, in addition to these virtual apps, there are devices that also exist using Web 2.0 to improve the lives of people who suffer, more or less, from unpleasant diseases. Three researchers interested in health marketing offer an overview of some major innovations that could enhance everyday life in the near future, while also mentioning limits or precautions for using some of them.

These are the themes and data presented in this work. Moreover, we examine a little deeper some certain realities that surround us or that already exist during the course of our lives, whether we are a patient who is aware of his/her health or a professional in the medical world. As many concerns are raised, we now should carry out a review to present answers to a few major legitimate questions that people ask:

How can we define eHealth or connected health?

It is the application of information technology to the health field, from medical records to telemedicine, and also mhealth with the development of connected objects. Nowadays, it is already a reality and a growing sector. Throughout the world, one Internet user out of two (almost 1.5 billion people) already uses a health app, and it has certain consequences. The research we conduct in partnership with two universities in Canada shows the changes in the relationship between patients and caregivers; this relationship has been enhanced through information exchange. Similarly, patient groups help the sick to renew broken social bonds that were affected by disease.

Is connected health a major economic issue as well?

We used to say that health is priceless, but it does have a cost. It is estimated that health spending will be multiplied by three by 2050 only for chronic care. Population aging will also result in a significant increase in expenditure. Considering only chronic diseases (cancer, diabetes, etc.), it represents nearly ¾ of current health expenditures. To fully weigh up economic issues related to chronic diseases, by 2030 there will be nearly 500 million people with diabetes worldwide, which will represent the equivalent of US $680 billion in healthcare expenditures... In this context, how to ensure a sustainable model, and the access to universal healthcare as well? How to treat patients effectively at a lower cost? eHealth provides answers both in Western and emerging countries, and it is necessary to consider this issue very seriously; hence, this is first outstanding conference in this field.

How eHealth can contribute to reducing costs?

By promoting prevention and a better monitoring of patients. We can readily understand it in developed countries where it is very easy to promote connected health incursion via the Internet. Regarding developing countries, this connected health issue is critical. In Africa and in India, telediagnosis is developing through mobile phones, which is widely used. It is possible, for instance, to perform remotely vision tests from a simple smart phone. Likewise, we can struggle against counterfeiting which kills thousands of people all over the world by controlling drug selection through cell phones. eHealth also ensures better monitoring of prescriptions and thus increase the effectiveness of treatments.

Is there any misgivings from patients regarding the development of eHealth to potential intrusion in their private lives?

Generally, patients are quite positive about eHealth, often because it makes that easier for them and it contributes to their well-being, but we must admit that confidence related to personal data is a crucial issue. However, for certain chronic illnesses, technical developments take precedence over individuals' concerns. Nowadays, diabetics have simple-to-use tools to monitor their blood sugar level. In Japan there are already many robots, and they are well considered; it is the case of Paro that looks like a plush baby harp and that efficiently stimulates people with Alzheimer's disease. eHealth also contributes to keeping the elderly at home because of apartments equipped with sensors and humanoid robots that provide monitoring and security, such a great expectation from them.

Is eHealth revolution still at its beginning?

Medical robotics and telesurgery are experiencing a significant development. The first remote surgery, called "Lindbergh operation," was successfully performed in 2001 by the Professor Jacques Marescaux's surgical team located in New York on a patient being hospitalized in Strasbourg. Frenchmen potential does exist and it is very encouraging particularly at a time when we sometimes face weak economic conditions... Institute of Chemical Technology (ICT) is creating values and will help create new technologies related to healthcare, but do not worry, sick people will always remain a priority in the relation with caregivers.

This book is written to a wide audience that has a common interest, and it is to be informed on health matters and ICT.

- It will please the computer scientist that will see a potential development of new apps for smart phones, to better help the care consumer to be aware of his own body.
- It will help the legislator to make better guidelines in regulating online medical practices by contributing to law, directives, and standards.
- It will allow the ethicist to better appreciate what users do with medical data and also with health information provided by Internet users that consult forums or online communities.

- It will help the sick person to better understand its rights, its involvement in this complicated and changing medical world, and will help him understand how data may be used.
- It will provide some guidance to general practitioners and medical specialists by showcasing best practices in the "online" medical field.
- Finally, this book will help every kind of person that is curious as well to find out more about connected health.

Overview of the content

This book that is about eHealth is cut up into five major parts, each covering a major theme and combining many chapters.

Part I contains four original contributions. Chapter 1 invites us to view an online healthcare market presentation by mainly presenting concepts that define this new paradigm. After having explained the situation, the author also specified new challenges that must be taken into account and possibly be overcome by eHealth system. The author describes in an original way challenges that healthcare must focus on and puts into perspective challenges that have affected art world because of Cubism, which became a revolutionary approach.

Chapter 2 makes us reflect on mobile health and health platformization (mhealth). Through the tool they always have on hand, that is to say smart phone, consumers instantly search information on their apps in a preventive and proactive way, giving them an additional sense of control on illness and a new role within the health system. In this new economic reality relying on demand, the authors show how mobile health recreate our healthcare system, which is creating value.

Chapter 3 shows that at the moment digital apps are in full bloom and at the moment of telemedicine, the economic model of the traditional health system (funded by public or private insurances) cannot ensure its fulfillment. The author therefore has questions regarding which model is most operational and viable to finance its achievements and consider the idea of an independent financing.

Chapter 4 deals with eHealth from another financial point of view. This contribution tends to show that the traditional funding system is not suitable for this new eHealth paradigm and that this reality should push all actors of society closely or remotely involved in healthcare to an additional responsibility. In this context, eHealth is an opportunity to redesign traditional funding models and establish bases for an approach implying a greater accountability of individuals and fostering a stronger empowerment of people toward their own health.

Part II of this book drew on new challenges underlying medical practice. In Chapter 5, the authors analyze the effect of digital interventions from the perspective of the citizen, health professional/policy maker or the population. This chapter will develop these concepts with examples and challenge the Web Science and Medicine 2.0 communities to develop new tools, to enable the triangulation of data to understand end-user interaction with the Web and thus identify new integrated strategies for preferable health outcomes.

Chapter 6 focuses on the usefulness, effectiveness, and impact of online health communities. While some indicators are commonly used, others have never been studied, as the link between use of online health communities and health impact on users. This is mainly the backdrop of their thinking that is mostly based on the need to better assess effects and impacts of online health communities.

Chapter 7 presents the virtual collaborations between medical professionals and the issues involved to contribute to a better medicine. This chapter describes the use of e-tools by medical professionals, their information exchanges and the knowledge thus generated and used.

As part of a study on an online health community, the authors of Chapter 8 tried to understand relationships between particular characteristics of those community users (interactions with other, user profile, and so on) and their attitude toward contributions of others and their intention to contribute as well to those online health communities.

Part III deals with eHealth and the current challenges it should consider.

The purpose of Chapter 9 is to explore the development and challenges raised by mhealth, especially mobile health for diabetics. This chapter emphasizes the importance of patients' communities especially for a chronic disease like diabetes.

Chapter 10 is about digital social networks development in the medical field. The authors support their thinking through concrete examples from major actors of the pharmaceutical and hospital fields. The authors suggest a model that measure the social impact of social media use for actors of the medical world.

Reflective thinking of Chapter 11 is about confidence related to eHealth. The future of medicine is shifting to a patient-centric model. NHS Grampian's No Delays concept uses video on demand to provide clinicians to make personalized patient postcards to patients. This chapter explores trust and provenance issues arising from healthcare delivered via the Internet and how the end-user engages with the technology rather than the wishful hope of "building it and they will use it."

A reflection about eMental health is presented in Chapter 12. Starting from the perception of the general public toward mental health, this contribution gets the credit to outline the organization and issues that should be taken into account to integrate mental health in the virtual world. This chapter aims to determine and discuss challenges and directions for eMental health research and practice based on current evidence of attitudes toward eMental health in the general population.

Chapter 13 is based on the study about online patient communities. The authors analyzed sick and healthy users in online patient communities regarding the impact of using those communities on the relationships between those individuals and their doctors.

The fourth part of this book is devoted to the concept of mobile health (mhealth).

Chapter 14 deals with matters relating to the protection of medical data and raises questions about the way sensitive data can be viewed, shared, and processed. This societal evolution will require healthcare information systems to make a giant leap toward the cause of empowering the "data subject," in building and sharing an acceptable "quantified self."

The theme concerning online communities that are devoted to mental health issues is covered in Chapter 15. Through mobile tools (phones, pads, notebooks, and so on), we can now reach people suffering from health problems, including mental health. This chapter examines this theme by providing a profile of challenges and opportunities related to it.

Chapter 16 combines eHealth and smart phones by outlining how those new tools affect traditional consultations and how new apps give greater weight to patients that are better informed and at the center of their own health decisions.

The use of new technologies in the healthcare sector has increased considerably in recent years, especially in terms of developing potential benefits of virtual reality. Chapter 17 is concerned about the way online personal trainers can have significant physical and psychological impacts on patients suffering from diseases needing regular physical activity for their well-being.

To conclude this part, Chapter 18 explores the adoption and absorption of virtual, increased, and diminished reality in the health field. It analyzes the evolution, the advantages and disadvantages, as well as providing perspectives, on the future growth and impact of these innovations in the healthcare sector.

The fifth part of this book talks about the new paradigm that the health field should adopt in a digital era context.

Reflecting Chapter 1, Chapter 19 concludes its analysis by describing how eHealth can be considered as a new business model related to economy, based on an improvement in the service delivery regarding healthcare, and a reduction in health costs.

Chapter 20 presents the cyberattacks the health sector can suffer from. Because of ICT massive development and a significant use of digital apps, hackers have a growing interest toward medical data and the exploitation that can be done. The authors describe the motivations of potential hackers and precautions that organizations managing online health apps can take to prevent it.

In Chapter 21, the author highlights legal and juridical problems related to information technologies use in the health sector. She describes how those laws are defined, which are based on the way each country perceive its healthcare system. This legal part leads to ethical and human issues, which are covered in Chapter 22, a vital approach of the reflection related to eHealth. The authors present several thoughts concerning telemedicine, which will be used as a basis for a wider reflection related to eHealth.

Chapter 22 completes the fifth part and the book. It outlines a vision of countries that are innovative and precursory concerning remote healthcare (United States, Canada, France, and Norway) and it presents as well the various forms of health and ICT combination: mobile apps, telehealth, telemedicine, and their variants. Those forms are reviewed and many examples are presented in this chapter.

Acknowledgments

A special thanks to Loick Menvielle for his particular investment in this project, who managed this project, contacted the authors for the book, compiled information, and prepared this manuscript.

This project also benefited from the collaboration of numerous authors that are at the top of one or more chapters. They should therefore be thanked for their original contributions by bringing new visions about subjects as eHealth, mHealth, telemedicine, or telehealth.

Lastly, we also wish to thank our publisher, Palgrave Macmillan, for its belief and its support for this project, particularly Madeleine Holder.

Contents

Notes on Contributors

Nathalie Angelé-Halgand is Associate Professor at the School of Medicine at Nantes University, where she is Head of the Department of Health Services Management and member of LEMNA research group (http://www.lemna.univ-nantes.fr). She is a scientist in charge of a network research program labeled TCS, which she launched in 2012. Their members are health clinicians, CEOs and researchers from various backgrounds worldwide with PhD students. This program received recognition from the Maison des Sciences de l'Homme Ange Guépin in 2012 and 2015 and is hosted by the research foundation of Montpellier Research Management (http://fondation-entreprendre.edu.umontpellier.fr/programmes-dactivites/axe-innovation-sante/chaire-innoveresante). It aims at redesigning health care services organization, regulation and funding in the Anthropocene taking ground on the care cycle concept, and on fiscal commons applied to public services. Her research interests and publications include New Public Management reform's health and public services funding, performance management in hospitals and universities, and more recently issues raised by Global e-Health and e-Learning in higher education and their impact on equity, and the modalities by which the public services could be revisited.

Anne-Françoise Audrain-Pontevia is a professor of marketing at ESG-UQAM (Écoles des Sciences de la Gestion—Université du Québec à Montréal). As an expert in services marketing, her research focuses on relationship marketing. A second field of research deals with health care and eHealth management. Her research appears in numerous academic marketing journals and international conferences. She also works as a consultant.

Dr. Jennifer Apolinário-Hagen (née Machado Apolinário) is a qualified psychologist, doctor in natural sciences in medicine (dr. rerum medicinalium), certified health counselor and currently working as research associate on her habilitation project at the FernUniversität in Hagen (Institute for Psychology, Department of Health Psychology, Hagen, Germany).

David Barrett is an assistant professor of operations management at the Ivey Business School and Executive Director of the Ivey International Centre for Health Innovation. David is also a Certified Management Accountant and a member of the Chartered Professional Accountants of Canada. His research is focused on the organizational factors that influence the successful adoption of Lean Management in health care.

Dr. Silvia Cacho-Elizondo is Associate Professor of Marketing and Academic Director for In-Company Programs at IPADE Business School in México. She has been lecturer and guest lecturer in several business schools in France, Spain and Mexico. Her professional career started as Research and Commercial Engineer at the Mexican Electric Research Institute (I.I.E.). She has also gained professional experience working for Procter & Gamble and collaborating with *e-Medicis*, a French start-up specialized in mobile health services. Furthermore, she has offered consultant services and strategic coaching to different companies in France and Mexico.

Dr. Cacho-Elizondo earned her PhD in Management with a major in Marketing at HEC Paris (France), her thesis analysed: "The impact of online services on the consumer-brand relationship". She also holds a M.Sc. in Marketing & Strategy (Université Paris-IX Dauphine, France), an MBA (IPADE Business School, México), a MSc in Management of Technology (Sussex University, United Kingdom) and a bachelor degree in Electronic Systems Engineering (ITESM Campus Monterrey, Mexico).

Her research interests include: Consumer-Brand Relationships, Consumer Behaviour, CRM, Innovation Adoption, Management of Technology, Online & Mobile Services, eHealth, and CSR. She has published in: *Journal of Retailing and Consumer Services, Journal of Health Marketing Quarterly, International Journal of Technology and Human Interaction, ISTMO, International Business Research Journal, International Journal of Hospitality Management, American Journal of Management*, among others.

Thomas M. Chen studied computer science at Purdue University. Thomas has extensive experience as a research assistant and software developer. He has worked in the private sector at companies such as General Electric and Global Context. Thomas has worked in General Electric and Global Context, and he has also made public contributions through collegiate Hackathons and Devpost.

Jean-Philippe Cobbaut is Professor of Medical Ethics at the Catholic University of Lille where he runs the Center of Medical Ethics. As lawyer and philosopher, he is interested in the ethical issues raised by modern medicine in a practical perspective and analyses the impact of the evolution of contemporary medicine on the role of caregivers, organizations and public policies.

Grant P. Cumming is an Honorary Professor with the University of the Highlands and Islands and Honorary Senior Lecturer with the University of Aberdeen. He is a consultant Obstetrician & Gynaecologist in NHS Grampian and is a cofounder of Health Web Science.

Aude Dufresne is honorary and associate professor at University of Montreal's communication department. She is the director of the LRCM research lab in multimedia communication. Her research portfolio spans a large range of publications with expertise in Human Computer Interaction, Artificial intelligence and the neurosciences and collaborations with the Canadian Spatial Agency.

Nina Duque is a doctoral student in communication studies at the University of Quebec in Montreal. She is a research assistant in the Health Communication Research Center ComSanté-UQAM, a member of the Research Chair on Digital Technology Uses and Changes in Communication, and of the Laboratory of Computer-Mediated Communication.

Linda Eftychiou is a graduate of the Bachelor of Health Studies Program at York University in Toronto, Canada. She is currently a candidate for Master's of Public Health at the Imperial College of London in England. Her current research interests include mHealth, Health VCs, Social Determinants of Health, and Health Policy, most specifically in regards to their relation in Mental Health Care as disease/illness prevention and health promotion tools.

Christo El Morr is a Health Informatics researcher at the school of Health Policy and Management at York University. His cross-disciplinary research covers health informatics and management. His research interests focus on Health VCs, e-Collaboration, particularly in the domain of Chronic Disease Management and health promotion: Peripheral Arterial Disease, Kidney Diseases, and Mental Health. He also has research interests in Global eHealth and equity, Hospital Patient Services and Patient Quality of Care (e.g., readmission patterns). He has published books, chapters, and articles in these areas. He received funds from the Ontario Center of Excellence (OCE) and the Canadian Institute for Health Research (CIHR) and is a Research Scientist at North York General Hospital. In 2016, he received recognition as York University Research Leader.

Victor-Ernesto Garcia, MBA is Product Manager within the Ericsson Chief Innovation Office in Silicon Valley. Prior to this role, Victor has been in several strategy, business development and technical leadership roles across the globe with firms such as Colgate, Deloitte Consulting and, more recently, as part of the Ericsson Excellerate Global Leadership Program, which he joined in 2012. Victor holds a Bachelor Degree in Computer Systems Engineering from Universidad Panamericana and an

MBA from IPADE Business School, both in Mexico. When not working, Victor is an amateur photographer and tennis fan.

Tara French is a Research Fellow at the Institute of Design Innovation, The Glasgow School of Art, tackling health and social care challenges using Design Innovation approaches. Tara holds a PhD in Psychology and has expertize in salutogenic, participatory approaches for health and wellbeing.

Sergio Gago-Masague works as a project scientist with specific expertise in medical informatics at the University of California at Irvine. His research focuses on human-computer interaction and information technology. His projects target the design and development of applications and networked systems to enhance usability, emotional interaction, and artificial intelligence.

Thierry Garrot is Associate Professor in the Business Administration Institute of University of Nice Sophia Antipolis. He is involved as co-leader in a French research project called TCS (http://tcs.hypotheses.org). This project aims at giving foundations to a new health care regulation system by concealing performance and solidarity between health professional and patients (or citizens). It lies on a Care Cycle Based Performance Management System including tariffs and a series of indicators relating to care quality, patient safety, waiting lists and access. He is President of the French Digital University for Business, Economy and Management (Aunege, http://www.aunege.org). He is a full member of the GRM's research team.

Heidi Gilstad is a postdoc and project manager at the Health Informatics Research Group, Department of Neuroscience, Faculty of Medicine, NTNU, The Norwegian University of Science and Technology, Trondheim, Norway. Her research interests are health communication and information exchange, eHealth literacy, eHealth monitoring and discourse analysis.

Roger C.M. Ho, MBBS, DPM, DCP, Gdip Psychotherapy, MMed (Psych), MRCPsych, FRCPC, is an associate professor and consultant psychiatrist at the Department of Psychological Medicine, National

University of Singapore. He graduated from the University of Hong Kong and received his training in psychiatry from the National University of Singapore. He is a general adult psychiatrist and in charge of the Mood Disorder Clinic, National University Hospital, Singapore. He is a member of the editorial board of Advances of Psychiatric Treatment, an academic journal published by the Royal College of Psychiatrists. His research focuses on mood disorders, psychoneuroimmunology, and liaison psychiatry.

Jamie Hogg is a GP and clinical lead for modernization in NHS Grampian. His interest is in the Internet as a trusted resource for patients and works with specialist teams to develop electronic postcards. He is the clinical director for Healthfit Digital—a spin out company developing this resource.

Eva Kahana who has done PhD (University of Chicago), is Distinguished University Professor and Robson Professor of Sociology, Nursing, Medicine, Applied Social Sciences and Director of the Elderly Care Research Center at Case Western Reserve University in Cleveland, Ohio. She has published extensively in the areas of stress, coping and adaptation of the aged, disability and heath care consumer proactivity.

Kyle J. Rose is the founder of Delta PM Diabetes, and is passionate about diabetes advocacy with over 10 years of research, development, sales, and marketing expertise. He earned his BS in Chemical Engineering from Cornell University and his MBA from INSEAD in France and Singapore. He enjoys speaking regularly at diabetes conferences around the world. Kyle joined INSEAD's Health Care Management Initiative as EiR Visiting Faculty after having previously served as presenting faculty at the Stanford University School of Medicine and College of Engineering BioDesign Program. Kyle divides his time between the United States and Europe and speaks regularly to medical and patient communities around the world. Other affiliations include Advisor at INNODIA (International consortium under the EU Innovative Medicines Initiative), Steering Committee: EU Patient-Medtech Dialogue, Member of American Diabetes Association, Union Sports et Diabète (France), and Fédération Française des Diabétiques (Rhone Alpes, France).

José-Domingo Lázaro Álvarez, MBA is Chief of Entrepreneurship Academy within the Panamericana University in Guadalajara (Mexico). Domingo holds a MPA from King Juan Carlos University (Spain) and a MBA from IPADE Business School (Mexico). Prior to this role, Domingo has been in business development and technical leadership roles across the globe.

Guann-Pyng Li is a professor at the University of California, Irvine, with appointments in Electrical Engineering and Computer Science, Chemical Engineering and Materials Science, and Biomedical Engineering. He also serves as Director of two research institutes at Irvine: The California Institute for Telecommunications and Information Technology and the Integrated Nanosystems Research Facility.

Alain Loute is Assistant Professor at the Catholic University of Lille. Recently he has published *La sagesse pratique face aux tensions des éthiques du care*, in Les ateliers de l'éthique/The Ethics Forum, vol. 10, n° 3, 2015, p. 13–28 and co-edited with L. Carré, *Donner, reconnaître, dominer: Trois modèles en philosophie sociale*, Lille, Septentrion, 2016. His research interests include the ethics of care, narrative ethics, ethics of technology, e-health and telemedicine.

Joanne S. Luciano, Ph.D., is a Visiting Associate Professor at Indiana University. She is internationally recognized for knowledge technologies that enable the integration of research artifacts to address global health concerns. She cofounded the field of Health Web Science in *Health Web Science* (2014) to study the role of the Web in the health-care ecosystem.

Douglas McKendrick is an Honorary Senior Lecturer with the University of Aberdeen. He is a consultant Anaesthetist in NHS Grampian with a special interest in peri-operative medicine, patient-centric clinical audit, digital health pathway formulation, and Health Web Science.

David Manset holds a PhD in Model-Driven Engineering of Distributed Computing Infrastructures for Biomedical Research, from the University of the West of England in Bristol, and an Executive Master in Business Administration from the Geneva School of

Economics and Management, specialized in crypto-currencies and their applications in new funding models. He is the CEO of gnúbila France a French data privacy company, and President and CEO of cerebro GmbH, a Swiss brain data scientist service company. David Manset punctually acts as an independent expert for the European Commission and the United Nations on ICT and eHealth related matters. Over the last decade, he architected important European and international Big Data platforms in eHealth and biomedical research. His work and team were awarded at major events in the field, such as the International Exhibition of Inventions of Geneva, in Switzerland, in 2007 (Gold Medal); Europe's largest conference on Information and Communication Technologies in 2008 and 2013 (ICT Best Exhibit 1st Prize); and more recently made it 2nd at the United Nations ITU Global SME Award competition in Bangkok, in November 2016.

Loick Menvielle is an Associate Professor at Edhec Business School and collaborates closely with searchers from Quebec University Network (Canada) and Columbia University (USA). He is the author of numerous academic publications and interventions for both academic and professional congress. He was consulted by the Haute Autorité de Santé (French National Authority for Health) as an expert concerning the digitalization of health. His current research projects deal with innovation in the health-care sector, impact of IT and patients communities on the way of delivering care and their consequences on patients' perception and attitudes.

François Meurgey has garnered deep expertise in Strategic Marketing and Market Access in the biopharmaceutical industry and has led operational teams across cultural and language lines. He was Director of Global Marketing for Prozac at Eli Lilly (1997–1999) and Senior VP, Global Marketing at UCB (2003–2007). He has been closely involved in the management of four blockbusters (Prozac, Zyrtec, Keppra and Cimzia) at various stages in their lifecycle, and has developed successful go-to-market strategies for top-tier pharmaceutical companies as well as small biotechs. He has been an independent consultant since 2007, and is currently Chief Marketing Officer of ASIT biotech, a late stage biotech company focusing on novel allergy immunotherapy products. François Meurgey holds an MBA from the Stern School of Business at New York University.

William Menvielle is an associate professor in marketing at the University of Quebec at Three-Rivers. He got his doctoral degree in Business Administration from this university. He has published chapters, articles, conference papers, and books, including the famous "Marketing," adapted from the original book, written by Grewal. His researches center around online consumer behavior. He received funds from the University of Quebec Network (FODAR) and grands from Fonds de recherche du Québec—Société et culture (FRQSC).

Jean-Christophe Mestres is the European Technical Leader for Healthcare and Life Sciences Solutions at IBM. Belonging to the Global Healthcare Center of Excellence sitting in Nice, he has been involved in several solution designs since 2001. Jean-Christophe Mestres was a Healthcare Technical Expert for ITU/WHO (International Telecommunication Union/World Health Organization) he has been involved in the design of a new tool called "DHAK" (Digital Health Accelerator Kit). The aim of this "kit" is to facilitate the development and the deployment of eHealth services in countries.

Bertrand Monnet is a professor at Edhec Business School and is the chairholder of the Edhec Chair "Management of Criminal Risks." He is the author of several articles about crimes committed against companies. He is an expert for television and radio channels. He conducts investigations in many countries on criminal risks topics: Columbia, Nigeria, Sierra Leon.

Florence Millerand is a full professor in the Department of Public and Social Communication at the University of Quebec in Montreal (UQAM). She is a member of the Interuniversity Research Center on Science and Technology, chairholder of the Research Chair on Digital Technology Uses and Changes in Communication, and codirector of the Laboratory of Computer-Mediated Communication.

David Molik a Scientific Informatics Developer, is a Systems Administrator, a Software Engineer, and a Computational Biologist. His work involves the problem of computational access to scientific software and resources. He is interested in how technology affects health care.

Christophe Pascal is an associate professor and director of the Institute for Education and Research in Healthcare and Social Service Organizations (IFROSS), Jean Moulin University, Lyon, France. He got his doctoral degree in management from this university, having successfully defended a dissertation about process management in hospitals. His research interests are organizational innovation, new organizational forms (virtual and physical networks and teams, hospital systems ...), and their impacts on patterns of care and the way health care is delivered.

Sandrine Prom Tep is an assistant marketing professor at the Business and Administration School of University of Quebec in Montreal. She teaches interactive marketing courses at both the graduate and undergraduate levels and focuses her electronic marketing research interests on online consumer behavior (e.g., UGC and Web 2.0) and the cutting edge notion of "social usability."

Matthieu Salvadore is Marketing Lecturer in the University Paris I Panthéon Sorbonne. He has completed his PhD in Marketing on smartphone uses and their consequences on consumer behavior (developing a relational model of antecedents and consequences of smartphone uses). He has collaborated on several projects with startups and public health institutions, such as mobile contactless applications for drugstores or serious games for children, intended to prevent domestic risks.

Sylvain Sénécal is fulltime professor at HEC Montreal Business School marketing department. He is the holder of the RBC Financial Group Chair of E-commerce and co-director of the Tech3Lab. His research and teaching expertise centers around Internet marketing, online consumer behavior, and the neurosciences. He has published in major research publication venues such as the *Journal of Business Research, International Journal of Electronic Business*, and *Computers in Human Behavior*.

Andrew D. Scarffe is a researcher at the Ivey International Centre for Health Innovation at the Ivey Business School. His research explores the opportuntiy for the globalization of health care through international agreements amongst Ontario Academic Health Science Centres. His current research is predominiantely focused on international health systems management, performance, and the concept of health security.

Pierre Simon, Ex-President of French Society of Telemedicine. He was the founder of the *Société Française de Télémédecine (SFT)* in 2006, became president from 2010 to 2015, and ex-president since 2016. He was General Counsellor for Health Care Facilities to the Minister of Health from 2007 to 2009. He is co-author of official report about "The role of telemedicine in the organization of care" (November 2008). He was hospital practitioner in nephrology from 1974 to 2007, Head of nephrology Unit (1975–2007), president of Medical Board (2001–2007), and president of Regional Medical Board (2004–2007). In addition to his medical training (MD in 1970, Specialist in Nephrology and Anaesthesiology in 1975), he is also a lawyer of Health (Medical Law degree in 2002).

Alexander D. Smith is a researcher at the Ivey International Centre for Health Innovation at the Ivey Business School. His research focuses on value-based health care management, with an emphasis on supply chain optimization and standardization.

Françoise L. Simon is a Professor Emerita at Columbia University and Senior Faculty at the Mount Sinai School of Medicine. She also manages her own international consulting group. Her teaching focuses on graduate and executive programs. She won the Chandler Award for Commitment to Excellence from the Columbia Business School. Prior to joining the Columbia faculty, Dr. Simon was a Director of Arthur D. Little, and developed a global strategy practice serving clients in the Americas, Europe, and Asia. Previously, Dr. Simon was a Principal of Ernst & Young, where she led a strategy practice in the health and consumer industries in the USA, Europe, and the Caribbean.

Christine Thoër is a full professor in the Department of Public and Social Communication at the University of Quebec in Montreal (UQAM). She is a member of the Research Center on Health Communication ComSanté-UQAM, and of the Laboratory of Computer-Mediated Communication.

Philippe Very is a professor of strategy at Edhec Business School and is head of Faculty, Management and Strategy. He was also awarded Robert Reynolds distinguished lecturer, University of Denver. He is the author of numerous academic publications in top-ranked journals and has also written eight books and a lot of book chapters. He has been elected president 2009–2010 of the French Academy of Management (AIMS). His current research projects deal with economic crime and with mergers and acquisitions.

Lina Williatte is a law teacher at the Law Faculty of the Catholic University of Lille, where she runs a Master 2 in Health Law. She also develops an important research activity in the domain of digital health. As such, she is part of the restrained offices of national and international erudite medical societies in her capacity as specialized legal expert, societies in which she takes part in the process of enactment of the norm in this regard. She is also a Lawyer at the Lille Bar. Main partners in her firm, she is specialized in Digital Health and offers an activity of accompanying to the health professionals and industrialists who use the new technology to improve the medical care.

Melvyn W.B. Zhang, MBBS, DCP, MRCPsych, is an associate consultant in psychiatry. He is an adjunct research scientist with the Centre for Healthcare Innovation and Medical Engineering, National University of Singapore (NUS). He graduated from the National University of Singapore and received his postgraduate training at the Institute of Mental Health, Singapore. He has a special interest in the application of Web-based and smartphone technologies for education and research and published extensively in this field. He is a member of the editorial board of the Journal of Internet Medical Research (Mental Health) as well as an associate editor for mHealth for BMJ Innovations.

List of Abbreviations

ANSM	Agence Nationale de Sécurité du Médicament et des Produits de Santé: National Agency for the Safety of Medicines and Health Products
AV	Augmented Reality
BPS	Biopsychosocial model
C2C	Consumer-to-consumer
CBT	Cognitive behavioral therapy
cCBT	Computerized cognitive behavior therapy
C^n	Community, co-development, communication, crowd wisdom, co-production, collaborating, co-creation
CSP	Code de la santé publique
CT	Computed tomography
CVD	Cardiovascular disease
Dallas	Delivering Assisted Living Lifestyles at Scale
DC&ET	Developing Countries' & Economies in Transition
DH	Digital health
DR	Diminished reality
e-awareness	eMental health awareness
ECG	Electrocardiography
e-discharge	Electronic discharge
EEG	Electroencephalogram
eHEALS	eHealth Literacy Scale
eHealth	Electronic Health
EHR	Electronic Health Record

eMental health	Electronic mental health
EMR	Electronic Medical Records
e-prescription	Electronic prescription
e-referral	Electronic referral
ET	Embodied Trainer
eWOM	Electronic Word-of-Mouth
FDA	US Food and Drug Administration
FOV	Field of view
GAFA	Google, Apple, Facebook, Amazon
GHT	Groupement Hospitalier de Territoire - Territory of Hospital Groupings
H	Health
HAS	Haute autorité de Santé
Health VC	Health Virtual Communities
HIPAA	Health Insurance Portability and Accountability Act
HIS	Hospital Information Systems
HMD	Head-mounted display
HON	Health On the Net
HWO	Health Web Observatory
HWS	Health Web Science
iCBT	Internet-based cognitive behavior therapy
ICD	International Classification of Diseases
IoT	Internet of Things
IRB	Institutional Review Board
ITU	International Telecommunication Union
IVR	Immersive Virtual Reality
LMIC	Low- and middle-income countries
mhealth	Mobile health
MIDI	Musical instrument digital interface
m-mental health	Mobile mental health (applications)
MRI	Magnetic resonance imaging
MVC	Mobile virtual community
NCD	Noncommunicable disease
NIVR	Nonimmersive virtual reality
NST	Nasjonalt senter for Samhandling og Telemedisin
OC	Online community
OECD	Organization for Economic Co-operation and Development
OHC	Online Health Community

P4	Medicine predictive, participatory, preventative and personalized medicine
PAC	Picture Archiving and Communication (system)
PBA	Person-based approach
PDAS	Personal digital assistant
PHR	Personal health record
PPS	Prospective payment system
RCT	Randomized controlled trial
RE-AIM	Reach Effectiveness Adoption Implementation Maintenance
RHA	Regional Hospital Agencies
ROI	Return on investment
SAMU	Service d'Aide Médicale d'Urgence: Emergency medical assistance service
SDG	Sustainable development goals
SDG3	Sustainable Development Goal N°3 (related to Healthcare)
SOVC	Sense of virtual community
TAM	Technology acceptance model
T-Health	Healthcare delivered via television
TRA	Theory of reasoned action
TTL	Tromsø Telemedicine Laboratory
UGC	User-generated content
UTAUT	Unified theory of acceptance and use of technology
VC	Virtual communities
VCoP	Virtual communities of practice
VCP	Videoconferencing psychotherapy
VHC	Virtual health communities
VR	Virtual reality
WHO	World Health Organization

List of Figures

List of Tables

Part I

Digitalization of Health-Care Overview and Outlook of a Promising Sector

1

State of the Art of Health Care: The Cubism Period

Jean-Christophe Mestres

Today's health sector is digital. This is a fact. From x-rays and magnetic resonance imaging (MRI) to computed tomography (CT) and ultrasound scans and much more, there is no question about it. In fact, virtually, all medical-imaging content today is high-tech and fully digitalized (x-ray film, e.g., is used less and less frequently). In 2012, research firm Frost and Sullivan predicted that, by 2016, medical imaging data in the USA alone will cross the one exabyte mark—one million terabytes (Frost and Sullivan 2012).

Biological analysis laboratories, equipped with robots, are generating increasing amounts of this digital information. For example, "the European Bioinformatics Institute in the United Kingdom, which is part of the European Molecular Biology Laboratory and one of the world's largest biology-data repositories, currently stores 20 petabytes (20,000 terabytes) of data and backups about genes, proteins and small

J. Mestres (✉)
IBM, Global Healthcare Center of Excellence, Nice-Paris, France
e-mail: MestresJ@fr.ibm.com

© The Author(s) 2017
L. Menvielle et al. (eds.), *The Digitization of Healthcare*,
DOI 10.1057/978-1-349-95173-4_1

3

molecules. Genomic data account for 2 petabytes of that, a number that more than doubles every year" (Marx 2013).

Hospitals and other institutions account for another large piece of the overall digital picture, using information technology to manage patients' administrative and medical files.

A report from EMC and the research firm IDC (Dec. 2014) offers a few imaginative ways at visualizing the health information proliferation, anticipating an overall increase in health data of 48 percent annually. The report pegs the volume of health care data at 153 exabytes in 2013. At the projected growth rate, that figure will swell to 2,314 exabytes by 2020. To paint a picture, the authors of the report suggest storing all of that patient data on a stack of tablet computers. By the 2013 tally, that stack would reach nearly 5,500 miles high. Seven years later, that tower would grow to more than 82,000 miles high, bringing you more than a third of the way to the moon! (Health Data Archiver 2015)

However, a question remains: "Is it digitally *efficient*?" That is the question we will now try to answer. But first, we need to set the scene, and try to understand the way all the different components fit together; like a cubist painting, everyone will see what they want to see, even if it is not the artist's vision.

1.1   What Is Digital Health?

A number of concepts are used today to define the term "digital health," or at least some aspects of it. Our intention here is not to provide an exhaustive list of definitions but, rather, to provide the most common ones, and determine if they have limits and what they are.

1.1.1   Historical Components of the "Digital Cube"

To make sure we have a common understanding, in this chapter we define the term "digital health" as, "the use of information technology/electronic communication tools, services and processes to deliver health-care services or to facilitate better health."[1] When viewed in that light, it is clear the health-care sector has been using such components for a long time.

To understand what currently exists, we can follow a hypothetical patient, John Doe, in his care journey and see how he interacts, directly or indirectly, with various digital systems.

John is a 50-year-old male who works in an office and enjoys skiing occasionally. One day, he has an accident on the slopes and is rushed to the nearest hospital.

In the ambulance, John is connected to various devices that record his vital signs onto a portable computer. This recording, which is partly automated to avoid major errors, is known as an emergency medical record. In certain cases, this system can be connected to the hospital and information exchanged with the hospital's back-end system.

Once he reaches the emergency room, John is registered and triaged and, because his condition is not immediately life threatening, he is put on hold to wait for the next available doctor.

This registration process is carried out using through the facility's *hospital information system.* These are among the oldest computerized systems used by hospitals and clinics. They are the hospital equivalent of what other sectors would call enterprise resource planning or business process–management software, which is used mainly to manage accounting, human resources, and other non-medical functions.

John is diagnosed with a broken leg and is sent to the imaging department so that his doctor can gain a better understanding of the problem. The radiologist takes the requested pictures and writes an image report. The images and the report are linked together and recorded.

These images may be recorded in the hospital's *radiology information system,* which itself may be associated with specific modalities (e.g., x-rays, CTs, MRIs). In addition to recording the images, the radiology information system may link them to metadata (image descriptions), as well as to the radiologist's report.

---

[1] Infoway: https://www.infoway-inforoute.ca/en/what-we-do/digital-health-and-you/what-is-digital-health

Depending on the provider and the homogeneity of the modalities within the hospital, several radiology information systems may be used within the same institution. In some cases, the hospital may have a *picture archiving and communication (PAC) system*, which archives all of a patient's imaging records in the same digital location.

PAC systems are designed to be "modality results consolidators," providing a single unified view by patient. For example, to make a single diagnosis, a physician may order x-rays, an ultrasound, and a CT scan. As a result, the doctor expects to have all of the images available as a "single view," that is, without having to access diverse systems.

Because the reason for John's fall is not clear, further tests are requested by the doctor, including some blood analysis. The emergency department nurse takes a blood sample from John and sends it and the doctor's requisition to the hospital laboratory. The laboratory analyzes the samples and records the results in their system.

Like the radiology information system, a *laboratory information system* captures the data generated by the biological analysis equipment. The system then consolidates the information into a single report where the laboratory biologist enters his or her interpretation of the results.

After reviewing the laboratory reports, the doctor determines that John collapsed due to hypoglycemia brought on by exertion, and diagnoses him with diabetes. The doctor records all of this information to build a medical history.

The digital tool used for this purpose is called an *electronic medical record*, which is the medical equivalent of an enterprise resource planning information system. This type of record enables a doctor to manage a patient's medical file electronically. In each medical case, the doctor will be able to create "events": stepping stones in the patient's treatment.

An electronic medical record may include links to medical images and laboratory results. It can also enable the generation of drug prescriptions (e-prescriptions) and "e-referrals" to specialists. Usually, an electronic medical record communicates with the institution's hospital information system so that invoices for any recorded medical procedure or treatment can be generated for the patient or public/private insurer.

As John leaves the emergency department after being treated, his doctor gives him a prescription. John brings the prescription to the nearest pharmacy, which the pharmacist reviews. The pharmacist then checks for possible drug interactions before giving John the medication.

A *pharmacy information system* enables pharmacists to better manage the dispensing of medication. For example, such a system can check for drug interactions and adverse events and manage the direct billing of insurers. It can also be linked with automated dispensing and packaging equipment and may include specific tools such as personalized drug management (e.g., for chemotherapy drugs).

John has also been told to make an appointment with his family doctor (general practitioner) so that a plan for his long-term care can be put in place.

During the appointment, John's doctor uses a *practice management system* to record all of John's medical events to keep track of John's care.

Going through this story, you may have noticed something: few—if any—of these systems are connected (some hospitals have a degree of integration that enabled through products produced by companies like SAP, Epic, and Cerner).

Some countries have developed a very advanced concept known as the electronic health record. However, there is much disagreement about the definition of "electronic health record" versus "electronic medical record," with some literature not making any distinction between the two.

To avoid confusion, in this chapter we are using the definition of electronic medical record as described earlier, that is, a digital record of a patient's medical treatment.

On the other hand, an *electronic health record* is a consolidated patient dossier containing the data generated by all of the information systems (e.g., emergency medical records, general practice systems, radiology systems, and information systems used by laboratories and pharmacies) involved in the treatment of a patient—even for diverse pathologies.

Countries that adopt this model could, without special effort, ensure that all of the actors involved in a patient's care have access to all of the information they need—according to access rights decided by the patient. This enables those caring for the patient to implement a "full care" plan.

Even if the concept of electronic health records is not well known, it will be soon, as this digital tool is about to be widely implemented.

1.1.2 The Need to Think Outside the (Hospital) Cube

Over the next few years, the health-care sector will be facing a number of challenges, including the following:

1. A decrease in the number of physicians:

   With a recent report from the Association of American Medical Colleges estimating the US could lose as many as 100,000 doctors by 2025, primary care physicians are already in short supply, particularly in rural areas, according to a *MarketWatch* report. Some 65 million Americans live in what's "essentially a primary care desert," said Phil Miller, of the physician search firm Merritt Hawkins. In fact, in about one-third of states, only half or less of patients' primary care needs are being met. (Finnegan 2016)

2. *An increase in the number of patients*, mainly due to increases in life expectancy:

   Globally, life expectancy has been improving at a rate of more than 3 years per decade since 1950, with the exception of the 1990s. During that period, progress on life expectancy stalled in Africa because of the rising HIV epidemic; and in Europe because of increased mortality in many ex-Soviet countries following the collapse of the Soviet Union. Life expectancy increases accelerated in most regions from 2000 onwards, and overall there was a global increase of 5.0 years in life expectancy between 2000 and 2015, with an even larger increase of 9.4 years observed in the WHO African Region. (WHO 2016)

3. *An increase in health costs* associated with the need to decrease the health care budgets: "PwC's Health Research Institute projects the 2017 medical cost trend to be the same as the current year—a 6.5% growth rate" (PwC 2016).[2]

---

[2] PwC Behind the numbers 2017: http://www.pwc.com/us/en/health-industries/health-research-institute/behind-the-numbers.html

One proposed solution to these challenges is to provide health services remotely, supported by ICT. However, as requirements and technologies have changed over time, the original concept—of connecting two points through one secure electronic channel—has been replaced with the idea of providing and receiving multi-channel data from and for multiple profiles (medical and non-medical).

This multi-channel view will require more than one digital solution. The following list is not intended to be exhaustive; rather, it is meant to take into account the most widely used and widely known concepts.

If we want to talk about the precursor to "remote health care," we need to talk about *telemedicine*, which is a method of providing medical services remotely using ICT solutions. Generally, this kind of approach assumes there is a medical doctor at one end who is able to provide a tele-consultation. At the other end is someone who has a minimum medical background, although not necessarily.

This system is usually structured as a point-to-point communication using a private network (for security) and a proprietary protocol (to increase the quality of sound and images). However, it is not necessary for the remote health-care practitioner to have visual contact, or even to formally speak to the patient. (For example, vital signs can be obtained without seeing or listening to the patient.)

Therefore, due to the limitation of the system, a number of Web-based digital services have rapidly developed. These are known as *eHealth* (electronic health) services. In this category, we find services like the following:

- e-prescriptions, where physicians prescribe drugs using an electronic system that is also available to pharmacists;
- e-referrals, where physicians can use an electronic system to refer a patient to a specialist (in this case, the specialist could be initially identified and referred through a private channel); and
- e-discharges, where the hospital uses an electronic channel to send the discharge summary to the patients, family doctors, or other actors.

In all of these cases, there is no specific solution or product associated with the service; rather, it is a way to operate differently using technology that can be located either inside an organization (intranet) or outside it (Internet or extranet).

As a result of further technological evolution and innovation, a new set of *mHealth* (mobile health) solutions has been created that use mobile devices (e.g., smart phones, tablets) and software (applications or "apps") to provide secure access to health-care data. Such technology is not limited to end users located in different geographic regions; it can also be used by medical staff navigating between services or wards within a single hospital (or other institution), providing them with mobile solutions that enable them to have continuous access to authorized data without having to change devices or workstations.

Until now, virtually all of the health-related technologies that have emerged in the areas of telemedicine, eHealth and mHealth still require human interaction through a graphical user interface. Another set of technological solutions, however, commonly known as the *Internet of Things* (IoT), refers to the addition of network connectivity to objects, buildings, devices, and other items.

In the health-care sector, for example, IoT solutions can collect data from sensors spread over a specific territory, from a single residence to a large geographic region. Given that external parameters such as temperature, air quality, and humidity can have an impact on health, these sensors can be used to provide information about the factors affecting an individual's environment. Connected to automatic alert mechanisms, these systems can, for example, be used to warn someone with a certain medical condition when critical factors are reached. "The many uses of the systems and products that connect to the Internet of Things (IoT) are changing business in numerous industries. Patients and providers both stand to benefit from IoT carving out a bigger presence in health care" (SearchHealthIT.com 2016).

1.1.3 The Overflowing Cube

Based on what we know is already happening, it is easy to understand that a major problem currently facing health-care professionals is the sheer volume of available data. Therefore, the question is, "How can we process this volume without losing any vital information?"

The answer is the concept of digital health, which also takes into account a new reality that has followed in the wake of the sector's technological revolution. In effect, the fundamental paradigm has evolved from one that is doctor-centric (where everything was done for the doctor or medical staff, while the patient was considered secondary), to patient-centric. Notably, that paradigm does more than make the patient the principal focus; it also asks patients to be active participants in their own health management.

As a result of that shift, health-care professionals found that clinical information alone is inadequate, and that other types of information—including genetic, social, family history, psychiatric—are needed.

The determinants of health are defined as, "The range of personal, social, economic, and environmental factors that influence health status" (ODPHP 2016).[3] Today, we can clearly say that such data (McGovern 2014) can be divided into three categories:

- **Clinical:** These data are currently managed by the systems described earlier (hospital, laboratory, and radiological information systems; mHealth; telemedicine; etc.) Such data represent only 10% of the determinants of health, about 0.4 terabytes (400 gigabytes) of data per person per lifetime.
- **Genetic:** These data are starting to be used in the field of "personalized medicine," although information about usage remains largely anecdotal.

> Today, personalized medicine, informed by a molecular understanding of disease, has brought new classification systems as well as more effective preventive and therapeutic interventions. Personalized medicine is 'a form of medicine that uses information about a person's genes, proteins, and environment to prevent, diagnose, and treat disease' (National Cancer Institute 2011). (Offit 2011)

These data represent 30% of the determinants of health or, in technological terms, six terabytes of data per individual, per lifetime.

---

[3] Healthy people 2020: https://www.healthypeople.gov/2020/about/foundation-health-measures/Determinants-of-Health

- **Exogenous**: The remainder of an individual's or patient's data represents 60% of the determinants of health; in other words, 1,100 terabytes of data per person per lifetime.

Therefore, it clearly appears that digital health is the new technological concept that will need to deal with the new challenges the determinants of health will present. In particular, how do we manage this huge amount of data? Or, in other words, how will we manage the "big data" paradigm in health care?[4]

To better understand this concept, Gartner analyst Doug Laney posited a theory in 2001. In a MetaGroup research publication, Laney introduced the concept of the 3Vs. "3 V data management: Controlling data volume, variety and velocity.[5]" Currently, the literature has increased the model up to 6 Vs (Normandeau 2013), but the consensus appears to be that digital health strategies should be aimed at finding technical solutions that are based on a 4Vs vision:

- **Volume:** Big data implies enormous volumes of information. At one time, all data was created by people; now, data is also generated by machines and networks, and human interaction with sensors or systems like social media. Therefore, the volume of data to be analyzed is massive.
- **Variety**: This refers to the many sources and types of data, both structured and unstructured. We used to store data from sources like spreadsheets and databases. Now, data comes in the form of emails, photos, videos, monitoring devices, PDFs, audio files, medical reports, medical image metadata, etc. This variety of unstructured data creates problems in terms of storage, mining, and analysis.
- **Velocity**: The velocity of big data refers to the pace at which data flows in from sources like business processes, machines, and networks, and from human interaction with things like social media sites,

---

[4] Big data is defined as extremely large data sets that may be analyzed computationally to reveal patterns, trends, and associations, especially relating to human behavior and interactions.

[5] Laney 3 Vs: https://blogs.gartner.com/doug-laney/files/2012/01/ad949-3D-Data-Management-Controlling-Data-Volume-Velocity-and-Variety.pdf

mobile devices, etc. The flow of data is massive and continuous. If researchers and businesses can handle the velocity, this real-time data can help them make valuable decisions that can provide strategic competitive advantages and return on investment.

- **Veracity**: This refers to the biases, noise, and abnormalities in big data. This raises a question, "Is the data that is being stored, and mined meaningful to the problem being analyzed?"

1.2 Is it Just a Question of Disorganization?

Due to the structure of the sector (lot of verticals), the amount of available technologies (including emerging ones arriving almost every day), and the amount of generated data, the meaning behind the title of this chapter becomes clear: In effect, the global picture looks very much like a portrait from the cubist period where all the elements are there, but not in their expected place.

Earlier, we reviewed some of the basic definitions that can help us better understand the digital environment in the health-care sector. However, even if there are some complex processes and a vertical structure, it seems that complexity is used more as an excuse than an insurmountable problem. Therefore, we will try now to understand why, for this specific sector, digital transformation looks like cubist painting.

1.2.1 Health Care: A Big World in a Small Word

Like the overuse of the word "green" in recent years, everyone these days is constantly referring to "health" or "healthy." A car becomes a healthy car, food is tagged as (at least) healthier than before (e.g., a new recipe). Thus, as an individual, if you want to understand exactly what "healthy" means, it becomes a bit of a nightmare. How, then, do we make it more understandable? The answer was alluded to earlier in the discussion of the theory of the V4s. However, the purpose of this publication is not to describe every element of the health-care sector from A to Z. Better to focus on determining what kind of data should be considered for inclusion in the digital health paradigm.

Even if that list of data will never be fully completed, it would still need to address how to manage, in an era of digital transformation in health care, the following data categories:

1.2.2 Data from Doctors and Medical Staff, Including Hospital and Mental Health Workers

This set of information is composed of the various types of data coming from medical devices or medical applications, which breaks down into two commonly accepted categories: "Structured data," provided mainly by applications and medical devices (representing 20% of the total available data), and "unstructured data" (coming from sources such as doctors, nurses, and radiology and laboratory reports, and representing about 80% of the available data, not all of it in electronic form).

1.2.3 Data from Social-Health Services and Affiliates

Almost all of the information used in the social-health sector is unstructured and composed of two types. In the first, we find rules, recommendations, and regulations applicable to specific, defined profiles. The other type contains information about the individual, some of which (mainly personal information) are electronic and structured, while the majority is composed of unstructured data in the form of reports and analyses.

1.2.4 Data from Utility Providers (e.g., Water, Electricity)

The information from these providers is important for the health-care sector for diverse reasons. First, they inform on the safety of the consumption of the service provided (e.g., polluted water). They also provide information on the status of the individual. For example, in some countries, such as France, an energy provider can know when a patient is undergoing hospital-type care at home better than the hospital itself (unless the hospital is overseeing that in-home care). They can also provide information on potential risks based on the service consumption patterns. For example, in an experiment in Bolzano in Italy, researchers were able to detect when some residents appeared to be in the early stages of Alzheimer's disease by analyzing their water consumption (which was more erratic than the "normal" pattern). The data from such operations are structured (mainly numbers), but need to be filtered or analyzed to reveal useful health-care insights.

1.2.5 Data from Mobile Devices, Apps, and Sensors Set Up by Medical or Social Staff

The information collected through these channels faces various challenges or inhibitors. The first such challenge relates to their structure. The data captured is mainly structured, with some unstructured information (mainly comments) stored in the solution back-end, which is not broadly accessible. The second challenge relates to the veracity of the data, as the information is captured through ICT components that are easily obtainable on the Web and lack any medical controls.

1.2.6 Actors' Roles and Strategies

As we have already said, the health-care sector is composed of different actors who do not always have the same objective; sometimes, they may have opposing goals, with each actor developing their own strategy aimed at reaching their particular objectives. However, it is interesting to note that all of these actors, at a certain point in time, are using more or less the same data to achieve their strategy. Therefore, we can create a basic list of actors as follows:

1.2.7 Patients

Before being a patient, the targeted person is an individual with loved ones. Therefore, his strategy in life is centered on his own interests, meaning (from a health-care point of view) he has a need to receive the best advice to ensure that he stays healthy, preferably with a minimum of constraints, no cost, and dedicated services. Some individuals may be willing to pay a little bit more to reinforce this healthy quest. However, even if that is true of most people in general, at an individual level, goals and preferences will vary. Some will prefer more constraint, but less cost. Others will prefer the reverse. Some will prefer to ignore all advice or warnings. To summarize, we would say that the patient's (individual's) strategy is very self-oriented (with the exception of concerns aimed at family members), which means they will be looking for a minimum of constraint in terms of treatments, institutional spending, and rules (private or public).

1.2.8 Doctors and Medical Staff

In the health-care ecosystem, there are a lot of different actors labeled "doctors and medical staff." At this stage, it is important that we not focus on their primary mission and strategy, which is "taking care of the patient and caring for him anywhere, at any time."

Rather, we are looking at this group as falling into two main categories: the public sphere (public servants) and the private for-profit sector. Public servants deliver a service to patients that, strictly speaking, can be provided without adding additional value. Conversely, private sector actors may propose unnecessary services to patients solely to generate more profit.

1.2.9 Pharmaceutical Companies

These companies are key, as they provide the raw material to cure patients. They have a high economic impact on the market and can even influence public policy, such as when a government decides not to add a manufacturer's drug to the official/approved formulary, which means it will not qualify for reimbursement. Such companies also decide which diseases they will research and develop drugs for, and which diseases they will ignore (e.g., rare diseases).

1.2.10 Medical Manufacturing Companies

From electrocardiogram machines and insulin pumps to prosthetics, many medical devices have been available in the marketplace for a long time and, as a result, are a common and accepted part of the system. But now, new devices are emerging that do not fit into the traditional definition of a medical device. As a result, they often end up falling into a legal desert that regulatory agencies are only now starting to look at.

1.2.11 Payers

Like medical staff, health-care payers also fall into two categories: the public sector (i.e., mainly national "single payer" insurers covering the reimbursement of drugs and medical activities), and private insurers that provide up to 100% of what the public insurer does not cover.

Public payers, because they decide what drugs and medical procedures will be covered, also play a regulatory role. (Exactly what procedures are covered can vary wildly between countries; gestational surrogacy, as just one example, may be reimbursed in one jurisdiction and banned in another.)

The private payer's approach is based on risk management, which can look a lot like gambling. For example, the payer might assume (bet) that among 10 insured people, only one will need reimbursement, and that person's claim will total only one third of what the 10 have paid in premiums. The problem with such a model is sustainability. As the population ages, fewer people are available to become new subscribers, while the risks (insurance claims) are increasing. Where this model is still active, a new approach will need to be found to continue providing everyone with equal access to health care.

1.2.12 Governments

In addition to their role as both service provider and payer, governments are the legal entities that create or alter laws to support health-care practices that are beneficial and ethical, and respectful of human rights. Their targeted goals are to ensure a healthy population, limit/reduce health-care costs, and support improved health-care practices. To accomplish this, governments need to put mechanisms in place that are capable of measuring whether or not their goals are being realized.

1.2.13 Differing Perspectives

As we have shown, one of the major problems within the health-care sector is there are a large number of actors with very different—and even opposing—perspectives. Thus, there is no consistency of approach; each participant acts according to their own objectives and particular point of view and level of knowledge. Each creates their own definition of continuity of care, and how such care will be provided.

One of the best examples of knowledge disparity came into sharp relief in 2015, when a solution provider for a national insurer/payer happened to notice that health-care providers were referring to ICD-9 or ICD-10 codes. "We should get some information about that," he said. Of course, virtually anyone working in health care understands that ICD stands for the World Health Organization's *International Classification of Diseases*, which has been the standard diagnostic tool for epidemiology, health management, and clinical purposes (World Health Organization 2016) for decades. ICD-10 (i.e., the 10th edition of the standards) was first published in 1992. In other words, more than 20 years later, some decision-makers are unaware that such widely accepted health-care standards exist.

The fact that one person lacks basic knowledge does not, of course, mean that everyone in an entire sector is similarly oblivious. However, there are still many basic "disconnects" between the various actors. For example, one European country (that will remain nameless) received several grants to help modernize its health-care system: One for e-prescriptions, one for e-referrals, and one for modernizing the national insurance system. The problem is that each was developed and presented as separate projects, with no communication between them.

Unfortunately, such "silo" funding is not uncommon; funding models around the world use a similar approach, i.e., they fund a specific project, not an integrated piece of a bigger picture. In the absence of governments with the right knowledge (and the will), major health-care projects—from systems integration applications to user portals—will remain separate and distinct, implemented again and again in difference places, using the same disconnected components.

Some countries, however, are finding their way toward a holistic approach to digital services. Estonia, for example, has developed a true e-government infrastructure where services are provided using shared technology and existing components are reused or adapted as needed. This came about because Estonia chose to take an "enterprise architecture" point of view. This involves starting with an initial "frame" that is bigger than necessary, which makes growth that much easier: every time a new service is required, the first step is to understand what can be used/reused from within any part of the current architecture. Only then are decisions made about what needs to be built or added, and what standards need to be in place to deliver the required service to citizens.

In this type of model, any usable infrastructure components that may have been developed for a previous project (say, a technological upgrade to the tax collection system) can be repurposed for any other type of need, such as digital health services.

1.2.14 Toward a Common Utopia

Because of the number of actors and (often opposing) perspectives at play in today's health-care marketplace, the entire process is reactive: an event occurs, a person is affected, and care is provided and paid for.

Now, imagine a system where, instead of reacting, we anticipate. A system where personal health forms part of an overall picture that is constantly adjusted throughout a person's lifetime. A system where the right services are provided for an appropriate price that is decided by facts, not by placing bets on people's health.

References

"Determinants of Health," *Office of Disease Prevention and Health Promotion*, accessed August 30, 2016, https://www.healthypeople.gov/2020/about/ foundation-health-measures/Determinants-of-Health.

Finnegan, Joanne, "Primary Care 'Deserts' Leave Patients without Physicians," *FierceHealthcare*, April 4, 2016, accessed August 30, 2016, http://www. fiercehealthcare.com/practices/primary-care-deserts-leave-patients-without-physicians.

"Health Data Volumes Skyrocket, Legacy Data Archives on the Rise," *Health Data Archiver*, July 24, 2015, accessed August 30, 2016, http://www.healthdataarchi ver.com/health-data-volumes-skyrocket-legacy-data-archives-rise-hie/.

Marx, Vivien, "Biology: The Big Challenges of Big Data," *Nature* 498, no. 7453 (June 13, 2013): 255–260.

McGovern, Laura, George Miller, and Paul Hughes-Cromwick, "Health Policy Brief: The Relative Contribution of Multiple Determinants to Health Outcomes," *Health Affairs*, August 21, 2014, accessed August 30, 2016, http://healthaffairs.org/healthpolicybriefs/brief_pdfs/healthpolicy brief_123.pdf.

"Medical Cost Trend: Behind the Numbers 2017," *PwC*, accessed August 30, 2016, http://www.pwc.com/us/en/health-industries/health-research-insti tute/behind-the-numbers.html.

Normandeau, Kevin, "Beyond Volume, Variety and Velocity Is the Issue of Big Data Veracity," *insideBIGDATA,* September 12, 2013, accessed August 30, 2016, http://insidebigdata.com/2013/09/12/beyond-volume-variety-velo city-issue-big-dataveracity/.

Offit, Kenneth "Personalized Medicine: New Genomics, Old Lessons," *Human Genetics* 130, no. 1 (July 2011): 3–14, doi: 10.1007/s00439-011-1028-3.

TechTarget, "A Guide to Healthcare IoT Possibilities and Obstacles," **SearchHealthIT.com**, accessed August 30, 2016, http://searchhealthit.tech target.com/essentialguide/A-guide-to-healthcare-IoT-possibilities-andobstacles.

"U.S. Medical Imaging Informatics Industry Reconnects with Growth in the Enterprise Image Archiving Market," *Frost & Sullivan*, November 1, 2012, accessed August 30, 2016, http://www.frost.com/prod/servlet/press-release.pag?docid=268728701.

World Health Organization, "International Statistical Classification of Diseases and Related Health Problems, 10th Revision," 2016, accessed August 30, 2016, http://apps.who.int/classifications/icd10/browse/2016/en.

2

Reshaping Health Care Through mHealth: Lessons from the On-Demand Economy

Andrew D. Scarffe, Alexander D. Smith
and David Barrett

2.1 Introduction

In most sectors, it is normal and encouraged to look at other industries for innovative opportunities, inspiration, and growth. In the modern technology-enabled world, many of these inspirations are coming from fast-growing technology companies. Participate in any of today's industry conferences or university business courses, and you will likely hear at least one individual who affirms that they have invented, or conceptually designed, a platform that will "uberize" industry X, Y, or Z. While the original platform refers to a vehicle ride-sharing program, "to uberize" has become a verb that describes enabling new provider-to-consumer interactions that leverage underutilized assets to achieve seemingly instant access to a product or service. Technological innovations like "Uber" have changed consumer behavior and have enabled almost immediate fulfillment of consumer demand through the rapid provisioning of goods and services.

A.D. Scarffe (✉) · A.D. Smith · D. Barrett
Ivey Business School, Western University, Ontario, Canada
e-mail: ascarffe@ivey.ca; asmith@ivey.ca; dbarrett@ivey.ca

© The Author(s) 2017
L. Menvielle et al. (eds.), *The Digitization of Healthcare*,
DOI 10.1057/978-1-349-95173-4_2

It is now possible to stand on a corner of an unfamiliar city and, in the palm of your hand, locate all of the restaurants within a desired proximity while simultaneously accessing the most recent consumer reviews. Unquestionably, the advent of digital/mobile technology is rapidly changing the ways in which we interact with the physical environment around us.

At the heart of many new consumer-focused technology companies are new economies focused on convenience and access for the consumer. The "on-demand economy" is a rapidly emerging market where consumer demand and the corresponding supply are converged instantaneously. On-demand economies are often adopted in conjunction, or used interchangeably, with other new economies such as the "sharing economy," which enables consumers to share underutilized assets, and the "marketplace economy," where consumers are able to submit highly customized orders to the market to get exactly what they want. Examples of technology featuring the on-demand economy can be found in most industries, including user platforms such as: Uber, Airbnb, Lyft, Car2Go, UShip, Push for Pizza, etc. (Maselli et al. 2016, p. 2; Frenken et al. 2015; The On Demand Economy 2016). Regardless of interpretation, it is important to note that the on-demand economy has three essential components:

1) the sharing economy (i.e., temporary access to underutilized assets between consumers);
2) auctions or contests (i.e., receiving a service after conducting a competitive bid); and
3) a product-service economy (i.e., business-to-consumer relationships)

(Maselli et al. 2016, p. 2; Frenken et al. 2015).

2.2   From the On-Demand Economy to Health Care

According to Price Waterhouse Coopers (PWC) (2015), "44 percent of US consumers are familiar with the [on-demand] economy [i.e., approximately 90 million people] ... [and] 19 percent of the total US adult population has engaged in a sharing economy transaction" (PWC 2015, p. 8). Further, "the five key sharing sectors—travel, car-sharing, finance, staffing and entertainment—have the potential to increase [their] global revenues from roughly $15 billion today to around $335 billion by 2025" (Maselli et al. 2016, p. 3). This on-demand economy relies heavily on the growing connectivity that global consumers now have with one another, through mobile technology and the digital marketplace to conduct business. Globally, smartphone ownership rates are rising at an incredible rate; the median smartphone ownership rate is 68% across all advanced economies and 43% across all countries (Pew Research Centre 2016). For example, in the Canadian population, 68% own a smartphone (which is expected to grow in the coming years) with an average of 19 apps [i.e., applications] per consumer (Catalyst 2015). This demand is only likely to increase as people become more accustomed to having information, products, and services available to them through mobile technology and their associated applications.

In the health-care sector, adoption of on-demand economics has been relatively slower. The emergence of mHealth (i.e., mobile health) and eHealth (i.e., electronic health) platforms have started to take advantage of concepts from the on-demand economy, but adoption is often inconsistent and insular. What is unique about the health sector is the consistent and ubiquitous demand for health care and health systems in virtually every region, province/state, country, and economy around the world. There are near limitless domestic and international opportunities for health care and sophisticated health systems to embrace facets of the on-demand economy to enhance the levels of service and value delivered to users.

On-demand economics and mHealth technologies hold tremendous opportunity for health care to digitalize and incorporate itself into individuals' everyday routines through media, such as mobile applications (apps) or online programs (Elias 2015). These concepts could potentially change a culture of reactionary and passive consumer use of health systems to one that is preventative, proactive, and empowers the patient, while at the same time returning value to the greater health system.

2.3   Current State: Emerging mHealth Technologies

To date, there are over 165,000 mHealth apps available on the Apple iTunes and Google Play app stores; "in the case of iOS apps, the number [of] available [apps] has increased more than 100 percent over the past two years" (IMS Health 2015, p. 1). The myriad of opportunities for mHealth and the corresponding on-demand economy are shaping how consumers (e.g., patients, health-care providers, and/or health systems) access and manage care.

For consumers, the majority of the mHealth apps found on these platforms (e.g., iOS, Android, etc.) focus on the areas of: wellness, diet, and exercise; nearly a quarter of the other mHealth apps focus on disease and treatment management (IMS Health 2015, p. 1). In an environment where health systems are increasingly pressured to provide "patient-centered care", these consumer apps provide an opportunity to empower the consumer to take control of their own health and wellbeing. For example, Apple Inc. has embedded a health app feature in their iOS devices which can help track health data related to: body and vital measurements, fitness and nutrition levels, reproductive health metrics, and sleep patterns. Patient centered care is facilitated though other apps such as: "Uplift," "Pager," "Revere Care," "Knock," etc. In each of these examples, the app connects patients to care providers (e.g., physicians, nurses, personal support workers, etc.) to provide home-based care; the concept is based on geographical location and proximity to health-care providers who are willing to do home visits and is similar to the Uber model of consumer demand being instantly fulfilled by available supply in close proximity.

From the perspective of the health-service provider, there are a variety of different apps that assist in the clinical decision-making process to help improve patient care. In one study of over 3,300 US physicians, "56 percent reported [that] they currently use apps in their clinical practice" (Franko and Tirrell 2012, p. 2), for which the same respondents reported that apps that were of greatest utility to them for the purposes of:

textbook/reference material, classification/treatment algorithms, and general medical knowledge (ibid.). In general, these apps are designed to complement the pre-existing model of care, allowing for instant access to the most up-to-date medical information. One example of an app that is used to improve clinical decision-making is the app "UpToDate". UpToDate is an app that provides, "regularly revised, evidence-based monographs on topics in adult internal medicine, pediatrics, and obstetrics and gynecology" (Isaac et al. 2012, p. 86; Fox and Moawad 2003). UpToDate, through leveraging elements from the on-demand economy, has been associated with: shorter lengths of stay for hospitalized patients, lower risk-adjusted 30-day mortality rates, and increased quality performance (Isaac et al. 2012). Other apps like "Figure 1" leverage lessons from sharing economies by promoting the education and collaboration of health professionals through the sharing of clinical experiences and photographs on a platform similar to that of "Instagram" (Falk 2015; iTunes 2016; Neporent 2015); the platforms allow clinicians to share new and compelling cases as well as solicit feedback and advice from other active users.

At a global health system level, mHealth is helping to serve underserviced populations and low-resource settings situated predominately in rural settings. In fact, "among the 45 countries in the African region, only 23 are able to finance health care at a minimal target of at least US$44 per capita recommended by WHO [World Health Organization]" (Mehl et al. 2014, p. 6). This dearth of resources creates an opportunity for low-cost mHealth solutions to support or sustain large elements of a region's health system. Even in many remote, underserved communities, there are developed telecommunications infrastructures and the availability of low-cost cell phones; globally, more people have access to cell phone technology than they do access to proper sanitation systems (UN News Centre 2013). As opposed to operating out of brick and mortar locations and/or training and dispatching health professionals to live in remote communities, the proliferation of telecommunications technology allows for remote monitoring and tracking of patients at a significantly reduced cost. Even for communities with limited cellular data connectivity, many of the services offered fall under the classification of teleHealth, which can be a hybrid of both the mHealth and eHealth platforms and achieve similar results of remote patient monitoring without requiring cellular data connectivity. Many of the services offered through these platforms (i.e., mHealth and eHealth) to these communities include: "video and other conferencing, transmission of computed tomography (CT) images, and computer-assisted or Web-based provider-patient communication systems" (Kaplan 2006, p. 2). These services are often offered where an in-state health-care provider, from a larger urban center, can remotely manage, monitor, and track their virtual patients.

From all perspectives, these apps, and their integration in our everyday life through mobile technology, have an innate ability to collect large amounts of data about our day-to-day routines, which consequently can help inform, or better understand, a person's health profile. They also serve as an excellent platform to increase collaboration amongst health service providers and offer important bedside assistance with respect to clinical decision-making. Individually, mHealth technology is changing the way patients, providers, and systems are interacting with health care. However, there is a disconnect from achieving system value as mHealth is predominantly targeted towards individual users/stakeholders rather than the system as a whole. The on-demand model found in health care is only constructive at a system level if all stakeholders subscribe to, and use, mutually compatible programs. For example, from a system perspective, there is no mechanism for an individual who wears a "Fitbit" to walk into their health provider's office and have their activity data from the last month downloaded into meaningful information that can be leveraged by their health service provider. This begs the question, as we continue to leverage the on-demand economy through mHealth technology, what will an integrated, system-oriented structure look like and how can it be achieved?

2.4   Future State: Integrated System-Level Adoption of mHealth

With the emergence and continued growth of mHealth and eHealth platforms, it is almost certain that the landscape of health systems will shift along with them. Because health care, in comparison to other industries, is often a laggard in adopting new technology, the certainty of this shift is foreshadowed through the evolving landscapes of other sectors (e.g., hospitality, banking, education, etc.), particularly as they embrace facets of the on-demand economy. But how does a system respond to the opportunities of mHealth and the on-demand economy in a way that benefits the entire health system? This section of the chapter highlights examples, through the lens of system stakeholders, as to how mHealth could continue to positively impact the health-care landscape for patients, while increasing value to the greater health system.

From a patient lens, there is an abundance of mHealth platforms that allow patients to access health service providers when and where they wish to access them. One of the challenges is that not only do these solutions only work when both the patient and the provider subscribe to the same platform but also in many instances, the patient and provider must reside in the same province or state due to regulatory or billing limitations. As patients become more inherently transient, and providers are more readily available through mHealth platforms, health systems need to reconsider their policies for who can provide care and in what settings. For example, a practitioner who resides in Ontario, Canada, and provides virtual mHealth consultative services to a patient in Alberta, Canada, is (assuming equal levels of ability and training) as competent at delivering this service as a practitioner who resides in Alberta; regardless of the geographic location, the user experience for both the patient and practitioner is near identical. Alternatively, when thinking about the future of primary care, which is currently largely hospital or clinic based in many countries, mHealth could make it possible to revert back to the community method of delivery and provide home care visits; ultimately allowing practitioners to abandon costly physical brick and mortar infrastructure and operate more like an Uber model of care. These types of mHealth adoptions have the potential to benefit all system stakeholders; patients through preferred home-based care; providers through lower infrastructure overhead costs; and health systems through lower care delivery costs and greater patient value generation.

When envisioning how the on-demand economy and the mHealth industry could begin to transform how health service providers interface with the health system, we can look to platforms like Airbnb for important insights into sharing underutilized capacity. Consider the case of surgical specialists—surgeons are given hospital privileges which grant them permission to operate in a particular hospital (or network of hospitals). It is often falsely believed that there is more demand for surgical operating room (OR) time than there is supply (i.e., availability of ORs); the prevailing belief is that this perceived lack of supply is what limits the amount of surgical procedures performed. However, in fact the problem may be that by implementing a policy of granting "hospital privileges," we are hindering our own ability to deliver care, by limiting the systems agility and responsiveness in relation to the system capacity. For example, in Canada, "OR space is not the bottleneck for performing more surgical procedures . . . [in fact] physical space is available without looking beyond normal working hours" (CIHI 2015, p. 11). In fact, it was estimated that, "at a national level, the OR occupancy rate was 70%, meaning that 30% of the time between the hours of 8 a.m. and 4 p.m. [i.e., normal working hours], ORs were not occupied by patients or being prepared and cleaned" (CIHI 2015, p. 11). This challenge of locating and utilizing idle capacity is not unique to health care; the same challenge exists in other industries, like commercial kitchens and retail settings. Learning from the Airbnb model, health care could identify a way to maximize available capacity within the current system and within current OR hours to increase occupancy rates. This is not to suggest that physicians or hospitals should start selling OR time to the highest bidder, but rather reflects the conceptual premise of Airbnb and other platforms (e.g., "Kayak," "Expedia," etc.) that are adopting sharing economics by identifying vacancies and allowing users to self-select times that fit conveniently with their schedules; ultimately, benefiting both the vendor (i.e., hospital) and the customer (i.e., physician).

Another example of underutilized health system capacity relates to the usage of medical equipment and supplies. This challenge of managing physical resources, again, is not unique to health care. For example, an entrepreneurial chai company, "Chaiwala Chai", needed a certified commercial kitchen to produce their natural chai blend, but at the time of their inception, did not have the product demand, or access to capital, to justify investing in the infrastructure of a commercial kitchen. Instead, they rented/borrowed access to a commercial kitchen, which would otherwise be vacant, to fulfill their need, benefiting both their own personal business and the business that was able to share their commercial kitchen; Chaiwala Chai, as a result of their success, has since purchased their own commercial kitchen to meet the consumer demand for their product. In health care, a US company, "Cohealo", is maximizing the shared economy model to share non-emergency medical equipment that is often costly and underutilized between hospitals within a network of hospitals (Verel 2014). The same strategy of embracing the shared economy could be used across health systems to share demand for some of the more costly items found in a hospital setting.

Lessons from the sharing economy can also help to overcome barriers to care in many developing countries and economies in transition (DC&ET), by leveraging intellectual and physical resource from developed countries to share knowledge and delivery of health care through low-cost virtual solutions. As a society, particularly in Canada, tremendous financial resources have been invested into education as well as research and development of health-related technologies, devices and products; investments that are not possible to the same extent in DC&ET. As a result of Canada's highly educated population, Canada has been fortunate to create highly sophisticated health systems; their educational advantage also positions Canada as a world leader with respect to trained expertise and capacity for the generation of new knowledge from post-secondary institutions. In comparison, in many DC&ET there are massive health human resource shortages; globally there is an estimated shortage of more than four million health professionals (Chen et al. 2004). It is also estimated that, "70 percent of the world's population—4.5 billion people—live in the emerging economies of Asia, the Middle East and Latin America...where essentially all regulations and standards are created from scratch as their systems develop" (Crone 2008, p. 117, 119). Further, within these emerging economies, "life expectancy is increasing, as are the number of consumers with the means and willingness to pay out-of-pocket for one-time, life-transforming interventions like cardiac surgery, joint replacement, cosmetic surgery and bariatric surgery" (Crone 2008, p. 117). While life expectancies, as well as financial prosperity, are increasing in many DC&ET, there are often few opportunities to access the graduate, postgraduate, and medical educations that are required to develop sophisticated health systems (Crone 2008); it may even be that it is economically advantageous for these countries to seek consultative services for subspecialties rather than develop them in-state. This leaves a tremendous opportunity to leverage Canadian expertise and experience, in the spirit of the sharing economy, to aid in the creation of developed health systems within these DC&ET (Romanow 2002). From the perspective of developing health system capacity abroad, it is not advisable for Canadian health providers to be providing one-on-one patient consultation through mHealth platforms, as this reduces a systems ability to develop sustainable, in-state, capacity. With that said, there is the opportunity for Canadian expertise to provide case consultation to health care providers from DC&ET; this would allow for underdeveloped, or undertrained, health-care providers in resource-limited settings to consult with providers with substantial training or expertise in a particular subspecialty. The type of arrangement could prove to be mutually beneficial for both parties if there was a nominal fee associated with this type of provider consultation. Similar consultative models have been established in the agricultural industry. For example, "Thomson Reuters has developed a promising monthly service for farmers who earn an average of $2,000 a year. For a fee of $5 per quarter, it provides weather and crop-pricing information and agricultural advice. The service reaches an estimated 2 million farmers, and early research indicated that it has helped increase the incomes [of the farmers]" (Porter and Kramer 2011, p. 8). If a similar model were to be established between a resource-limited setting and the Canadian health system, Canadian knowledge and expertise would be able to assist in the development of capacity abroad, while at the same time providing additional funding to the Canadian system that could be reinvested domestically to enhance patient care.

2.5 Moving Forward: Promoting Successful Adoption of mHealth

The benefits of on-demand economics and mHealth technologies in relation to their potential impact on global health systems are well-accepted; it is also clear that this is a trend which will continue to grow and spread. The pivotal question, in relation to the prosperity, sustainability, and success of future health systems, will be whether funders (e.g., governments and insurers) are able to embrace the opportunities of mHealth and the on-demand economy in a proactive way.

Despite the proliferation of health apps, there is a systemic problem with mHealth and how apps interface with the greater health system. In fact, 40 percent of health apps have fewer than 5,000 downloads, and 36 apps account for nearly half of all downloads (IMS Health 2015), meaning that despite the continual emergence of new apps, the vast majority of apps are failing to embed themselves, as constructive contributors, to health systems. But why are these apps failing? Generally speaking, mHealth apps experience an inability to scale for two main reasons: (1) content (e.g., single issue, static vs. dynamic content, non-compliance with regulatory policies or best practices, etc.), and/or (2) single stakeholder focus and siloed value chains.

When exploring the challenge of content to broaden adoption and usage within mHealth platforms, there are number of issues. Often, mHealth apps are designed to address a single health matter; for example, the wearable app "Neuton" is designed to track and notify family members of an epileptic episode of loved ones, and the app "Pillow" was created with the intention of measuring and tracking sleep quality. The challenge for the end user is that to get a representational snapshot of their health status, the patient must navigate through multiple platforms and deduce which information is relevant to their current or desired health status. In Canada, trends suggest that users are selecting to limit the number of apps they subscribe to as the number of apps per user has fallen from 26 in 2014, to 19 in 2015 (Catalyst 2015). Another challenge with the content of mHealth apps is how the content is created (i.e., statically vs. dynamically). Many mHealth platforms are created with the intention of providing acute information to the end user; however, because new research and standards of best practice often take considerable time and effort in development, the content remains static. The challenge with static content, particularly on single issue platforms, is that once the user has answered their question, they are unlikely to return to that platform, unless they have another related question, as the user retains the information they learned on their initial inquiry; ultimately rending the app obsolete until it is used again. This is in contrast to content that is created dynamically and continually refreshed, either through active users (e.g., "Facebook", "Twitter", "Instagram", etc.) or platforms (e.g., "New York Times", "Travelocity", etc.), giving the user new content and experiences upon every login. The generation of dynamic content is also supported on mHealth platforms that track user information dynamically, like fitness apps that record daily step counts (e.g., "Fitbit", "Nike Fuel", "Pebble", etc.), which ultimately have a higher sustained rate of users (IMS Health 2015).

The larger challenge with mHealth solutions is that they often exclusively deliver value to a single stakeholder and infrequently reciprocate value across the value chain, ultimately leading to a siloed and fragmented value chain. As previously highlighted, mHealth is only constructive if all parties subscribe to, and use, mutually compatible programs, which ultimately comprises a platform's ability to deliver value within the value chain of health systems. Successful adoption of mHealth platforms in any type of environment (be it regional, provincial/state, national, or international) requires embracing the concept of shared value to ensure that all parties (i.e., patients, providers, and systems) benefit from the adoption, thus enabling scale. This is a pivotal concept when establishing sustainable, on-demand, mHealth within health systems. When talking about the value chain in health care, it is important that future mHealth solutions be able to identify and fulfill the value requirements of multiple stakeholders on issues such as: energy use and logistics, resource use, procurement, distribution, productivity, and location. By identifying the different value propositions of future mHealth solutions from the vantage point of multiple system perspectives (e.g., resource use, productivity, location, etc.), we will find new ways to innovate and unlock new economic, and societal value that our system has previously overlooked.

2.6   Conclusion

Ultimately, as the on-demand economy continues to embed itself in our society and culture, it is important, particularly in socialized health systems, for governments to respond accordingly and proactively. Governments can proactively support mHealth research, innovation, and commercialization that embrace sharing principles to facilitate scale. It is important that we consider not only the current state but the opportunities for future development of health systems through mHealth, and to grow and expand markets. We should not overlook the opportunity to share intellectual capacity with those regions that require it the most, in return of nominal individual investments that, collectively, could have a significant impact on the way health systems operate. Above all, we will only be successful in transforming health care and the way patients, providers, and systems interact with each if we develop platforms that mindfully and purposefully consider how their functionality can add value to multiple system stakeholders.

With that said, there is a tremendous opportunity for mHealth to completely revolutionize not only the way patients interface with the health system and how health-care providers deliver care, but also how governments and regions dynamically interface with each other with respect to the organization and structure of health resources and services. The opportunities to empower patients to take an active role in their day-to-day health management, promote unprecedented levels of professional collaboration among health professionals, breakdown geographical boundaries of clinical care, and develop fully integrated and collaborative systems are all possible as a result of the recent advances of mHealth and on-demand economics.

References

Catalyst (2015). With growth comes change: The evolving mobile landscape in 2015. *Catalyst*. http://catalyst.ca/2015-canadian-smartphone-market/. Accessed May 20, 2016.

Chen, L., T. Evans, S. Anand, J. Boufford, H. Brown, M. Chowdhury, M. Cueto, L. Dare, G. Dussault, G. Elzinga, E. Fee, D. Habte, P. Hanvoravongchai, M. Jacobs, C. Kurowski, S. Michael, A. Pablos-Mendez, N. Sewankambo,

G. Solimano, B. Stilwell, A. De Waal, and S. Wibulpolprasert. (2004). Human resources for health: Overcoming the crisis. *Lancet*, 364(9449), 1984–1990.

CIHI (2015). Exploring occupancy through administrative data: A test case using operating rooms. *Canadian Institute for Health Information*. https://secure.cihi.ca/estore/productFamily.htm?pf=PFC2846&lang=en&media=0. Accessed May 20, 2016.

Crone, R. (2008). Flat medicine? Exploring trends in the globalization of health care. *Academic Medicine*, 83, 117–121.

Elias, J. (2015). In 2016, users will trust health apps more than their doctors. *Forbes*. http://www.forbes.com/sites/jenniferelias/2015/12/31/in-2016-users-will-trust-health-apps-more-than-their-doctors/#17bc1da2d5f6. Accessed May 20, 2016.

Falk, W. (2015). What will the "sharing economy" mean for health care? *HealthyDebate*. http://healthydebate.ca/opinions/sharing-economy-health-care. Accessed May 20, 2016.

Fox, G., and N. Moawad. (2003). UpToDate: A comprehensive clinical database. *The Journal of Family Practice*, 52(9), 706–710.

Franko, O., and T. Tirrell. (2012). Smartphone app use among medical providers in ACGME training programs. *Journal of Medical Systems*, 36(5), 3135–3139.

Frenken, K., T. Meelen, M. Arets, and P. Van De Glind. (2015). Smarter regulation for the sharing economy. *The Guardian*. https://www.theguardian.com/science/political-science/2015/may/20/smarter-regulation-for-the-sharing-economy. Accessed May 20, 2016.

IMS Health (2015). IMS health study: Patient options expand as mobile healthcare apps address wellness and chronic disease treatment needs. *IMS Health*. http://www.imshealth.com/en/about-us/news/ims-health-study:-patient-options-expand-as-mobile-healthcare-apps-address-wellness-and-chronic-disease-treatment-needs. Accessed May 20, 2016.

Isaac, T., J. Zheng, and A. Jha. (2012). Use of UpToDate and outcomes in US hospitals. *Journal of Hospital Medicine*, 7(2), 85–90.

iTunes (2016). Figure 1—Medical cases for healthcare professionals. *iTunes*. https://itunes.apple.com/us/app/figure-1/id645948529?ls=1&mt=8. Accessed May 20, 2016.

Kaplan, W. (2006). Can the ubiquitous power of mobile phones be used to improve health outcomes in developing countries? *Global Health*, 2(9), 1–14.

Maselli, I., K. Lenaerts, and M. Beblavy. (2016). Five things we need to know about the on-demand economy. *CEPS Essay*. https://www.ceps.eu/system/

files/CEPS%20Essay%20No%2021%20On%20Demand%20Economy. pdf. Accessed May 20, 2016.

Mehl, G., L. Vasudevan, L. Gonsalves, M. Berg, T. Seimon, M. Temmerman, and A. Labrique. (2014). Harnessing mHealth in low-resource settings to overcome health system constraints and achieve universal access to health. *Oxford University Press.* https://cdn2.sph.harvard.edu/wp-content/uploads/ sites/17/2014/04/Mehl-2014.pdf. Accessed May 20, 2016.

Neporent, L. (2015). Figure 1 app is like an "instagram for doctors." *ABC News.* http://abcnews.go.com/Health/figure-app-instagram-doctors/story? id=30160402. Accessed May 20, 2016.

Pew Research Centre (2016). Smartphone ownership and internet usage continues to climb in emerging economies. http://www.pewglobal.org/2016/ 02/22/smartphone-ownership-and-internet-usage-continues-to-climb-in-emerging-economies/. Accessed September 9, 2016.

Porter, M., and M. Kramer. (2011). Creating shared value. *Harvard Business Review.* https://hbr.org/2011/01/the-big-idea-creating-shared-value. Accessed May 20, 2016.

PWC (2015). The sharing economy. *PricewaterhouseCoopers LLP.* http:// www.pwc.com/us/en/industry/entertainment-media/publications/consu mer-intelligence-series/assets/pwc-cis-sharing-economy.pdf. Accessed May 20, 2016.

Romanow, R. (2002). Building on values: The future of health care in Canada. *Commission on the Future of Health Care in Canada.* http:// publications.gc.ca/collections/Collection/CP32-85-2002E.pdf. Accessed May 20, 2016.

The On-Demand Economy (2016). Companies. *The On-Demand Economy.* https://theondemandeconomy.org/participants/. Accessed May 20, 2016.

UN News Centre (2013). Deputy UN chief calls for urgent action to tackle global sanitation crisis. *UN News Centre.* http://www.un.org/apps/news/ story.asp?NewsID=44452&Cr=sanitation&Cr1=#.VznrmWZUMpn. Accessed May 20, 2016.

Verel, D. (2014). Can Cohealo bring the sharing economy to hospitals? *MedCity News.* http://medcitynews.com/2014/10/cohealo-uber-ride-shar ing-medical-equipment-sharing/. Accessed May 20, 2016.

3

Tapping the Full Potential of eHealth: Business Models Need Economic Assessment Frameworks

Christophe Pascal

3.1 Introduction

Among the many manifestations in the phenomenon of health-care digitalization, telemedicine are probably the oldest. In the broadest sense, it refers to the delivery of health-care services through the use of information and communication technologies in a situation where the actors are at different locations (Kidholm et al. 2012) or, according to the US Institute of Medicine, the use of electronic information and communication technologies to provide and support health care when distance separates the participants. Long before the appearance of Institute of Chemical Technology (ICT), doctors have sought ways to use their skills remotely. In 1897, the *Lancet* reported on using telephone to diagnose a child with

C. Pascal (✉)
Jean Moulin University, IFROSS, GRAPHOS, 18 rue Chevreul,
Lyon, F-69007 France
e-mail: christophe.pascal@univ-lyon3.fr

© The Author(s) 2017
L. Menvielle et al. (eds.), *The Digitization of Healthcare*,
DOI 10.1057/978-1-349-95173-4_3

croup, and around 1910, Dutch physiologist Willem Einthoven used the telephone to record electrical heart signals of hospital patients 1.5 km away. However, the beginning of "modern" telemedicine is generally regarded to date back to the 1960s, particularly through establishing a program network for teleconsultation and tele-education around the Nebraska Psychiatric Institute, as well as the development of many projects, mainly in the USA. Telemedicine failed to find a place in medical practice, and the wave of enthusiasm declined at the end of the 1970s as projects were halted due to lack of funding and interest. However, telemedicine continued to grow through research programs by specialized organizations that were faced with the problem of delivering care to people with limited or no accessibility to care: NASA, the US Army, Antarctic Survey Stations, offshore oil exploration rigs. In the late 1980s, the launching of a Norwegian program entitled "Access to Health Care Services" revived interest in the wider use of telemedicine, supported by advances and lower-cost technology. This initiative marks the beginning of an uninterrupted period of development, which has accelerated over the past decade (Darkins and Cary 2000; Pascal et al. 2002; Dinesen et al. 2016).

If this enthusiasm reflects the magnitude of the expected benefits, telemedicine applications, however, are struggling to move through the project stages due to a lack of a solid demonstration of their impact on the health-care system. Traditional economic assessment frameworks recommended by health-care authorities are poorly adapted to the specificities of this new way to practice medicine. In this context, multidimensional assessment frameworks can help to better assess the added value of telemedicine, even if they are not themselves exempt from certain limitations.

3.2 Promises to Financing: Assessment as Prerequisite

3.2.1 A Favorable Context for Telemedicine

In recent years, telemedicine has experienced a resurgence of interest based on three main causes:

- The aging population: Increased life expectancy is accompanied by an increased prevalence of chronic diseases (diabetes, cancer, respiratory diseases, etc.) and the potential number of elderly populations with disabling conditions. The treatment of these diseases and disabilities requires regular monitoring to detect and, if possible, anticipate changes in their health status. Transportation barriers are important because they can lead to a deterioration of chronic disease management (Kidholm et al. 2012; Syed et al. 2013). As these populations often have difficulties with mobility, transportation reduction is a central issue.

- Medical demography: As the demand for care is constantly increasing, particularly because of the aging population, the ability to access medical services within a reasonable time becomes an issue in many Western countries. These difficulties particularly affect rural areas, which often have the largest elderly populations. This is exacerbated by the phenomenon of medical specializations, which requires the intervention of several different medical specialists to treat the same patient. The grouping of physicians in group practices or patient-centered homes improves their productivity and thus their availability, but it increases the distance from patients and the transportation time. Policies for transferring tasks to nurses and other health-care professionals are intended to relieve doctors of some duties to make them more available, but the effects are currently still quite minimal.

- Increasing health-care costs: Most developed countries are facing a continuous increase in health-care costs, using up very large portions of the gross domestic product (GDP). Financing these expenditures is a major concern because they are increasing faster than national wealth, leading to increased taxes, fees, and insurance premiums, having to give up other expenses, and/or go into debt. Funding also affects the competitiveness of companies and the purchasing power of individuals. The causes of this increase are multi-factorial: They are largely related to the extension of the definition of health care, which leads to continuously expanding the spectrum of interventions and their funding. The aging population and the consequences of this described above also play a large part. It also follows the rising cost of pharmaceutical and technological innovations in a system characterized by diminishing returns. Finally, some of these costs are linked to the organization of health-care production, which is not efficient or not efficient enough, and which needs to be reengineered.

3.2.2 Expected Significant Benefits

On paper, the expected benefits of telemedicine provide particularly attractive answers to these challenges, in terms of quality of care, accessibility, and cost (Bashshur 1995).

In terms of quality, the ability for doctors to easily and frequently communicate with each other using tele-expertise or teleconsultation methods helps maintain and develop their knowledge as well as their individual and collective skills. From the patient's perspective, especially for chronic conditions, the gain is based on improving the continuity of care, defined as the degree to which a series of discrete health-care events is experienced as coherent and connected and consistent with the patient's medical needs and personal context (Haggerty et al. 2003). Telemedicine fosters improvements in the continuity of information by making necessary information available to all stakeholders, continuity in management by planning and triggering interventions in a coordinated and complementary manner, and relational continuity by creating virtual teams around the patient.

Improving population health is also highlighted when telemedicine allows large-scale treatment protocols to be used, without which they may not have existed. The implementation of telemedicine services for stroke thus facilitates the care of cerebrovascular accident (CVA) patients in hospitals that lack neurologists, and improves the chances of recovery without patient recurrence.

Accessibility is closely linked to the continuity and quality of care: If the patient does not have access to care, continuity will be broken, and it is likely that his/her health will be degraded. Similarly, if a doctor does not have timely access to advice or assistance from his/her colleagues, this can lead to inappropriate decisions or improper actions. It is measured in terms of time and cost. Remote medical practice reduces unnecessary transportation costs. It also affects time-sensitive availability by reducing the time to receive advice or a medical procedure through two main mechanisms: Creating virtual pools of doctors who can consolidate their time to respond quickly, and automating the monitoring and alert processes which would release doctors from their usual tasks to focus their activity on problematic medical conditions.

Finally, reduced cost is a regular argument for promoting telemedicine. This is most often presented from the perspective of the health-care system and society, highlighting transportation costs and hospitalizations that are avoided by better continuity and quality of care and optimizing the use of medical resources.

3.2.3 A Specific and Binding Business Model

Despite these promises, the use of telemedicine is still underdeveloped. In Europe, it is mainly limited to projects funded by governments, which are often related to geographic regions and smaller populations.

This underlines the specificity of the telemedicine business model: unlike other economic sectors, the health-care sector is based on a complex system of payments, or reimbursements, which typically do not ultimately come from the consumer, but rather from a third party. In most Western countries, health-care expenses are mainly covered by health insurance companies and/or national health systems. This is why patients are often very reluctant to pay out-of-pocket costs for new services that they see as helpful gadgets. Any service that is reimbursed must scientifically demonstrate its ability to meet new health-care needs (clinical safety and effectiveness), or meet existing ones in a more cost-effective way. The value proposition of a telemedicine service must therefore include both the individual perspective and an aggregated perspective of the insured population. It is traditionally popular with funders in terms of clinical benefits return compared to expenses. In a way, the business model of a telemedicine application must take into account not only the return on investment (ROI) for the owners but also the ROI for the health-care system.

Consequently, authorities are reluctant to finance large-scale telemedicine interventions since there has not been a solid demonstration of their benefits in relation to their cost. Permanently reimbursed telemedicine procedures are still scarce, and the inclusion of new procedures requires long negotiation processes. For their part, the care producers and manufacturers cannot develop telemedicine services since a sustainable funding model has not been established. The dissemination of telemedicine is thus faced with the problem of the chicken or the egg: The formulation of a sustainable business model requires financing of insurance systems, and insurance systems require scientific demonstration of telemedicine's efficiency before including it in their reimbursement plans. This situation stresses the importance of economic assessment of telemedicine to develop business models and tap into the full potential of the digitalization of health care.

3.3   Applying Economic Assessment to Telemedicine: Limitations and Challenges

3.3.1 A Brief Review of Methods

The economic assessment frameworks that are recommended by insurance systems for telemedicine resort to generic evaluation methods developed in health economics as a decision aid, mainly in the pharmaceutical field. They are divided into four categories (Fig. 3.1).

Cost-minimization analysis (CMA): This type of analysis compares the costs of several treatments or technologies for which clinical outcomes are identical. This method is not only particularly attractive because of its apparent simplicity but also because it is intuitively easy to understand by decision-makers, since "cheapest is the best." Evidence of clinical equivalence is the Achilles heel of this method, because it is often treated lightly by evaluators who prefer to focus on the cost calculation. This is why economists are very suspicious of this kind of study (Briggs and O'Brien 2001). Ideally, clinical evidence must be

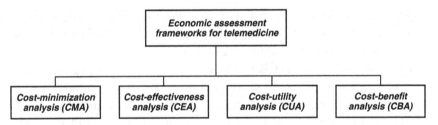

Fig. 3.1 Economic assessment frameworks for telemedicine

based on dedicated randomized clinical trials (RCT) or, if not possible, on a review of RCTs already conducted, which should be interpreted with caution. The comparison should not only include primary results but also secondary results, which may reveal significant differences in terms of safety, cost, or convenience (Jones et al. 1996). These differences may be significant enough to interfere with clinical results. This need for prior evidence of clinical equivalence makes it impossible to achieve a prospective evaluation of new technology based on a CMA.

Cost-effectiveness analysis (CEA): This method compares interventions or technologies that differ both in their cost and effectiveness. Patient outcomes are reported in nonmonetary terms such as blood glucose levels, reduction in wound size, anxiety, or pain levels. They are compared with the resources to be used to improve a unit as much as the committed result. For example, the cost-effectiveness study of wireless telemonitoring of continuous positive airway pressure (CPAP) treatment for Sleep Apnea syndrome reductions uses reductions in systolic blood pressure as a primary clinical outcome and the cost per millimeter of lowered mercury as measures of economic value for this treatment.

This approach is appropriate only if interventions or comparable technologies entail a change in the nature of the condition, and are conducted on similar patients in terms of disease and biological characteristics.

Cost-utility analysis (CUA): In this type of analysis, the outcome for the patient is represented by a composite indicator that combines the quality and length of life, measured in terms of Quality-Adjusted Life Years (QALY) or Disability-Adjusted Life Years (DALYs). It is then possible to calculate a cost per year of healthy life. This method compares interventions or technologies that produce different benefits, such as surgery compared to mammography.

Cost-benefit analysis (CBA) adopts a more overall perspective. It is a systematic analysis of one or more methods or programs for achieving a given objective and measuring both benefits and costs in monetary units (Aday and Begley 1993). CBA deals with what economists call allocative efficiency: It can determine whether a program is worth doing, in the sense that its benefits are greater than its costs.

These last three methods have developed considerably over the past 20 years to measure awareness of the need to control the increase in public spending in general, and in particular health-care expenditures. They are now the gold standard, and all health insurance systems require them to include new treatments or devices in their reimbursement plans.

3.3.2 Facing the Challenges of Complexity and Innovation

The results of such studies conducted in the field of telemedicine are contradictory: Some reports that telemedicine is cost-effective, others not. It is difficult for health-care authorities to use them because they often have significant methodological limitations that do not allow the production of valid and generalized results (Wootton 2012; Bergmo 2009).

These results portray the challenges for evaluating telemedicine. These challenges are financial and conceptual.

From a financial point of view, given the necessary investment budgets, telemedicine experiments are not sufficient to conduct large-scale projects. Because of this, the number of patients included is too small to produce statistically strong results. For the same reason, the duration of clinical studies rarely exceeds one or two years, as the clinical benefits are expected in the medium term, particularly in the case of monitoring chronic diseases (Alexander et al. 2008).

From a conceptual point of view, there are two types of challenges.

The first set of challenges relates to the measurement of outcomes and, more broadly, what economists call the utility function. Generic measures of quality of life such as QALYs are not sensitive enough to measure the small changes in health statuses produced by telemedicine. The use of measurement scales specific to a disease, such as cancer and heart disease, for example, is an alternative, but it prohibits comparison with programs whose QALY measurement uses other scales. On the other hand, the benefits of telemedicine are various and involve many actors. As part of the traditional economic evaluation methods, the need to choose a primary clinical outcome leads to neglect or underestimation of other clinical outcomes. More broadly, it asks the question of non-medical outcomes of telemedicine, which are potentially numerous and important, such as improving accessibility, skills transfer, and strengthening the sense of security.

The second set of problems relates to the nature of telemedicine. Originally, the economic evaluation methods were developed for the pharmaceutical sector. While it is relatively easy to isolate and specify the precise clinical and organizational conditions for the delivery of drugs through protocols and procedures, it is quite different for telemedicine (Campbell et al. 2000).

Telemedicine is an ICT-enabled innovation, but is not limited to technological innovation. It is primarily an organizational innovation (Schumpeter 1983) under new care production methods and the realization of new work organization. The impact of this innovation is the result of changes produced by the interaction between the technology and the organizational, professional, regulatory, and cultural system in which it occurs. In this perspective, telemedicine can be regarded as a plan of action as defined by Foucault (Foucault 2001; Agamben 2007), that is, "a decidedly mixed bag featuring discussions, institutions, architectural arrangements, regulatory decisions, laws, administrative measures, scientific statements, as well as philosophical, moral, and philanthropic propositions." In this plan, the communication technique tool is only one of the connections to a system of interactions (Engeström 2000) involving broader subjects (doctors and nursing users, actual or potential patients), a set of rules that govern the division of labor, and a community (community health workers of an establishment, territory, or specialty) that have a targeted purpose (the objective pursued by each telemedicine application). The impact of introducing a single telemedicine service will be different depending on the local form taken by the plan of action. This plan is particularly complex since telemedicine services by definition involves the interaction of several organizational entities that have their own structuring, practices, workflow, and funding models. Telemedicine applications can thus be considered as complex interventions (Campbell et al. 2000; Shiell et al. 2008), that is, interventions made up of various interconnecting parts between which the nature, intensity, and effects of causal links are difficult to establish and reproduce.

These characteristics make it very difficult to generalize the findings of telemedicine evaluations. While economic studies usually use a randomization of patient characteristics, this should be done on the organizational characteristics of the plans. The description of these organizational characteristics is often overlooked in health-care economic evaluations. When approached, it suffers from a lack of a clear organizational analysis framework from a scientific point of view.

One final challenge occurs based on the rapid evolution of ICT. These technologies are still immature, and the benefits of certain advancements or developments may not be taken into account because they were not expected. In particular, harmonizing information exchange standards allows an increased sharing of communication and equipment infrastructures. These economies of scope are difficult to predict and lead to over-estimating future operating costs. The invention of new uses for current users is also difficult to predict.

Therefore, the object to be evaluated, telemedicine, is a moving target. The timeline for conducting these studies are too long for these developments, which often makes the findings of studies obsolete upon publication.

3.4   Toward Multidisciplinary Evaluation Models

To overcome these limitations, much work has been done to provide a more comprehensive evaluation framework integrating more than just economic measurements.

3.4.1 Health Technology Assessment Models

The concept of Health Technology Assessment (HTA) is included in this perspective, defined for the first time in 1978 in the USA by the Office of Technology Assessment. This concept has quickly been very successful and is used by many national agencies, federated within a network of over 55 members in 32 countries and established in 1993.

HTA's activities are based on a model that covers 9 areas or "domains" to evaluate. Each domain is divided into topics, and each topic is divided into one or more issues, which are the questions to ask to assess a technology. The combination of a domain, a topic, and an outcome constitutes an evaluation component.

The scope of this approach is particularly broad, since it covers "any intervention that may be used to promote health, to prevent, diagnose or treat disease, or for rehabilitation or long-term care. This includes the pharmaceuticals, devices, procedures and organizational systems used in health care."[1] In fact, the generic model has been declining for a small number of technologies, primarily medical and surgical treatments, but also diagnostic and pharmaceutical technologies.

Based on a project funded by the European Union in 2009, Model for Assessment of Telemedicine (MAST) is an extension of the HTA model. Its goal is to establish a common model for evaluating telemedicine in Europe. Like HTA, it aims to provide decision support to the different stakeholders confronted with the question of investment choices in telemedicine: governments, insurers, institutions, and professional companies (MedCom and Telemedicine 2010; Kidholm et al. 2012; Ekeland and Grøttland 2015) (Fig. 3.2).

It uses basically the same domains as the HTA model, with two differences:

- A set of preliminary questions ("preceding considerations") is added, to determine whether to engage in the evaluation and the potential

---

[1] INAHTA (International Network of Agencies for Health Technology Assessment) (October 8, 2013). HTA glossary. HTAi.

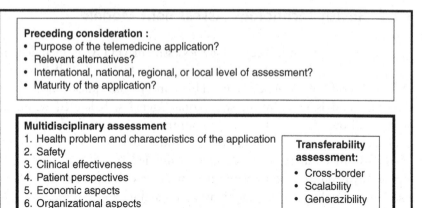

Fig. 3.2 Model for assessment of telemedicine evaluation framework

strength of this assessment. They focus on the main limitations in medico-economic assessments, in particular the project scale and its regulatory, financial, and technological maturity.

• The importance of the subject of the generalization is affirmed by the creation of a "transferability" domain, which includes issues already present in the HTA, related to the external validity and generalization of results.

3.4.2 GEMSA[2] Model

Appearing almost at the same time, the GEMSA method shares the same goal as MAST. It takes into consideration five axes of synthesized analysis, each by a central question (Le-Goff-Pronost and Picard 2011):

• Strategy: "How and what will the project contribute to resolving a clearly identified public policy in the health and social fields?"

---

[2] Grille d'Evaluation Multidisciplinaire Santé Autonomie—Multidimensional Evaluation Grid for Health and Autonomy.

- Technology, technological, and industrial expertise: "Are the type and extent of innovation brought by the solution defined, understood, and in accordance with professional and standard requirements? Is the developer of the solution credible and able to implement and deploy the solution?"
- Organization: "What are the benefits of the solution to the overall functioning of the users within the framework of their assignments?"
- Quality: "Does the service rendered by the solution to professionals, patients, and their support groups have the characteristics required in terms of quality, usefulness, and satisfaction for meeting their fundamental needs?"
- Economics: "Is the project economically viable and does it generate new economic activity?"

As shown in Table 3.1. (Le-Goff-Pronost and Picard 2011), these axes intersect and regulate domains already studied in MAST. The aspects studied are mostly the same, except for the technological dimension that is more developed in GEMSA and is not limited to safety, and also the quality dimension, which puts more emphasis on the concept of use and the value for the patient. The two grids use both quantitative and qualitative measures. In particular, the organizational impacts focus largely on semi-structured interviews and process descriptions (work flow and patient flow), as well as sociocultural and ethical considerations. This pluralism of measuring provides a more detailed understanding of the impacts, but it is problematic when it comes to comparing several telemedicine interventions.

Table 3.1 Domains of Health Technology Assessment

1. Health problem and current use of technology (CUR)
2. Description and technical characteristics of technology (TEC)
3. Safety (SAF)
4. Clinical effectiveness (EFF)
5. Costs and economic evaluation (ECO)
6. Ethical analysis (ETH)
7. Organizational aspects (ORG)
8. Patients and social aspects (SOC)
9. Legal aspects (LEG)

Both methods can be used either at the project design as a checklist, or after implementation.

Finally, the main difference between the two methods is the degree of standardization. The MAST Toolkit only suggests result measurement criteria examples for each domain (without going to the indicators), and it does not specify how the criteria should be used to produce a multi-criteria evaluation.

GEMSA offers a more formalized approach. Each axis is divided into sub-questions, which have proposed performance indicators with a measured value and a target value. The reliability and validity of the information used to populate these indicators is measured by a quality indicator of the process, which is qualitatively assessed on a 5-level scale. Each criterion is scored on a scale from 0 to 5, which then allows the use of multi-criteria decision methods. This approach allows the opportunity to compare multiple applications or views of various actors on the same application (e.g., patients vs. the establishment) (Table 3.2).

3.4.3 Perfectible Models

Even though both multidimensional models provide significant added value compared to purely economic assessments, they still have some limitations.

First, examining the economic aspects does not free them from traditional economic evaluation frameworks and their limits. An economic evaluation from a societal perspective is explicitly recommended by MAST, based on the methods presented earlier in this chapter. The subject is approached more diffusely in different GEMSA domains. Questions are designed to ensure that the actual benefits for public health are considered and that clinical studies have been conducted, and that the costs of the benefit are calculated. These assessments remain fundamentally microeconomic, and their generalization remains problematic in a macroeconomic perspective (Zamora 2013). Meanwhile, the two models recommend economic analysis from the institution's point of view. MAST recommends calculating the ROI from the expenses, income, and reimbursements (business case), while GEMSA goes further

Table 3.2 Coherence matrix between GEMSA and MAST

	Health problem and characteristics of the application	Safety	Clinical effectiveness	Patient perspective	Economic	Organizational	Sociocultural, ethical, and legal
Strategy	X						
Technology		X					
Organization			X				X
Quality and usage				X		X	
Economic aspects						X	

and focuses on the business model and its sustainability factors. The various addressed business model components are fragmented in different axes of the model, which does not promote a comprehensive understanding of its dynamics.

Reforming this model in a framework adapted to telemedicine, similar to the CompBizMod Framework (Peters et al. 2015) developed specifically for complex services, will allow the opportunity to better assess the model's consistency and sustainability (Fig. 3.3).

Dimension	Parameter	Characteristic			
Value proposition	Overall purpose	Prevention	Diagnosis	Therapy, curative	Therapy, palliative
	End consumer	Professional provider, physician (B2B)		Patient, relatives (B2C)	
	Partner network	A fixed set of other partners is involved	A flexible, competing set of partners is involved	No partners are involved, or if at all indirectly	
	Realization of benefits for the patient	By application		(if at all) indirectly	
Value co-creation	Portfolio role	One of several offerings in the same area	Complement offering	Singular, stand-alone offering	
	Contact with patient	Direct	Indirect	No	
	Domain-specific know-how	Not necessary	Necessary, provided by own employees/in-house	Necessary, requires cooperation with (external) domain experts	
	Required responsiveness	Immediate personal reaction	Automated immediate info forwarding, non-immediate personal reaction	Non-critical	
Value communication & transfer	Required means of communication*	No*	Platform (server, database)*	Measuring devices/ wearables & platform	
Value capture	Type of revenue	Transaction-based	Transaction-independent	Mixed	
	Paying entity	Health insurance	Patient	Other stakeholder	Mixed
	Cost drivers	Personnel costs		Equipment	
* Internet, telephone, mobile phone including mobile data are considered as given					

Fig. 3.3 The CompBizMod framework

On the other hand, the Achilles heel of these models is the question of organization. The proposed criteria for evaluating the organizational aspects in MAST focus on the quantitative description of patient flow, skills and training, information flow, organizational structure, culture, and management, but the suggested indicators are few and mainly qualitative. The GEMSA model not only studies the distribution of competencies and the improvement of information exchanges and coordination processes between professionals but it also stresses compliance with regulatory requirements in terms of delegations and responsibilities, as well as the support provided to users of the service in case of problems. However, it does not directly address the impact on structural components such as the number, size, and geographic distribution of units, nor the impact on transportation times. These differences clearly show the lack of consensus in how to address the organization determinants and the need for further research in this area. Considering that telemedicine is innovative, work on the organizational and behavioral factors for adopting innovations could be usefully mobilized for this purpose (Scott 1990; Damanpour 1991; Rogers 2003; May et al. 2007; Van Dyk 2014).

3.5 Conclusion

While traditional economic evaluations have many drawbacks, it is unlikely that health authorities waive these requirements given the financial pressure on health insurance systems. Multidimensional models can moderate the results and limitations of these assessments by incorporating other criteria, but they do not prevent them from being done. The demands of these economic evaluations are usually impossible to achieve during pilot phases of telemedicine projects and calls for a better integration of these evaluative constraints starting in the design phase.

While waiting to demonstrate the economic benefits retroactively once telemedicine services are widespread, business models must support these start-up phases by independent financing or they must be added to insurance financing. Widening the value proposition through the inclusion of telemedicine services in clusters of eHealth services to a larger and more lucrative range is certainly an interesting solution. During these design phases, multidimensional models can be of great use as guidelines to ensure that the key success factors are considered within the business model.

References

Aday, L. A., and C. E. Begley. 1993. *Evaluating the medical care system*. Ann Arbor, MI: Health Administration Press.

Agamben, Giorgio. 2007. *Qu'est-ce qu'un dispositif?* Paris: Payot & Rivages.

Alexander, Dobrev, Veli N. Tom Jones, Karl A. Stroetmann, Jörg Artmann Stroetmann, Anne Kersting, Narges Kasiri, Dainis Zegners, and Stefan Lilischkis. 2008. Sources of financing and policy recommendations to member states and the European Commission on boosting eHealth investment. European Commission DG INFSO & Media.

Bashshur, R. L. 1995. Telemedicine effects: Cost, quality, and access. *Journal of Medical Systems* 19(2): 81–91.

Bergmo, T. S. 2009. Can economic evaluation in telemedicine be trusted? A systematic review of the literature. *Cost Effectiveness and Resource Allocation* 7: 18.

Briggs, A. H., and B. J. O'Brien 2001. The death of cost-minimization analysis? *Health Economics* 10(2): 179–184.

Campbell, M., R. Fitzpatrick, A. Haines, A. L. Kinmonth, P. Sandercock, D. Spiegelhalter, and P. Tyrer. 2000. Framework for design and evaluation of complex interventions to improve health. *BMJ* 321(7262): 694–696.

Damanpour, Fariborz. 1991. Organizational innovation: A meta-analysis of effects of determinants and moderators. *Academy of Management Journal* 34(3): 555–590.

Darkins, Adam William, and Margaret Ann Cary. 2000. *Telemedicine and telehealth: Principles, policies, performances and pitfalls*. New York, NY: Springer Publishing Company.

Dinesen, B., B. Nonnecke, D. Lindeman, E. Toft, K. Kidholm, K. Jethwani, H. M. Young, H. Spindler, C. U. Oestergaard, J. A. Southard, M. Gutierrez, N. Anderson, N. M. Albert, J. J. Han, and T. Nesbitt. 2016. Personalized telehealth in the future: A global research agenda. *Journal of Medical Internet Research* 18(3): e53.

Ekeland, Anne Granstrøm, and Grøttland Astrid. 2015. Assessment of mast in European patient-centered telemedicine pilots. *International Journal of Technology Assessment in Health Care* 31(5): 304–311.

Engeström, Y. 2000. Activity theory as a framework for analyzing and redesigning work. *Ergonomics* 43(7): 960–974.

Foucault, M. 2001. *Dits et écrits II, 1976–1988*. Paris: Gallimard.

Haggerty, J. L., R. J. Reid, G. K. Freeman, B. H. Starfield, C. E. Adair, and R. McKendry. 2003. Continuity of care: A multidisciplinary review. *BMJ* 327(7425): 1219–1221.

Jones, B., P. Jarvis, J. A. Lewis, and A. F. Ebbutt. 1996. Trials to assess equivalence: The importance of rigorous methods. *BMJ: British Medical Journal* 313(7048): 36–39.

Kidholm, K., A. G. Ekeland, L. K. Jensen, J. Rasmussen, C. D. Pedersen, A. Bowes, S. A. Flottorp, and M. Bech. 2012. A model for assessment of telemedicine applications: Mast. *International Journal of Technology Assessment in Health Care* 28(1): 44–51.

Le-Goff-Pronost, Myriam, and Robert Picard. 2011. Need for ICTs assessment in the health sector: A multidimensional framework. *Communications & Strategies* 83: 87–108.

May, C., T. Finch, F. Mair, L. Ballini, C. Dowrick, M. Eccles, L. Gask, A. MacFarlane, E. Murray, and T. Rapley. 2007. Understanding the implementation of complex interventions in health care: The normalization process model. *BMC Health Services Research* 7(1): 148.

MedCom, and Norwegian Centre for Integrated Care and Telemedicine. 2010. MethoTelemed, Final Study Report, Version 2.

Pascal, Christophe, Eric Garcia, Stéphane Fraisse, and David Piovesan. 2002. La télémédecine, entre fantasme et réalité. *Santé et Systémique* 6(1-2-3): 321–336.

Peters, Christoph, Ivo Blohm, and Jan Marco Leimeister. 2015. Anatomy of successful business models for complex services: Insights from the telemedicine field. *Journal of Management Information Systems* 32(3): 75–104.

Rogers, Everett M. 2003. *Diffusion of innovations*, 5th ed. New York: Free Press.

Schumpeter, Joseph Alois. 1983. *Théorie de l'évolution économique: recherches sur le profit, le crédit, l'intérêt et le cycle de la conjoncture*. Translated by J.-J. Anstett. Paris: Dalloz.

Scott, W. Richard. 1990. Innovation in medical care organizations: A synthetic review. *Medical Care Research and Review* 47(2): 165–192.

Shiell, A., P. Hawe, and L. Gold. 2008. Complex interventions or complex systems? Implications for health economic evaluation. *BMJ* 336(7656): 1281–1283.

Syed, S. T., B. S. Gerber, and L. K. Sharp. 2013. Traveling towards disease: Transportation barriers to health care access. *Journal Community Health* 38(5): 976–993.

Zamora, Bernarda. 2013. *Strategic intelligence monitor on personal health systems, Phase 2.* Luxembourg: European Commission – Joint Research Centre – Institute for Prospective Technological Studies.

Van Dyk, L. 2014. A review of telehealth service implementation frameworks. *The International Journal of Environmental Research and Public Health* 11(2): 1279–1298.

Wootton, R. 2012. Twenty years of telemedicine in chronic disease management–An evidence synthesis. *Journal of Telemedicine and Telecare* 18(4): 211–220.

4

Digital Health Business Models: Reconciling Individual Focus and Equity?

Thierry Garrot and Nathalie Angelé-Halgand

4.1 Introduction

Digital health brings a disruptive advantage to patients by empowering them in a value co-creation process with health providers. This is reached by a Business to Consumer model. By doing so, digital health raises a main ethical issue that can be stated as follows: the patient should afford to be a digital health consumer; otherwise he/she cannot get access to it. This chapter contributes to address this issue by exploring digital health and identifying business models that may reconcile patient

T. Garrot (✉)
Université Côte d'Azur, Business Administration Institut of Nice, Research Group in Management (EA 4711), Nice, France
e-mail: garrot@unice.fr

N. Angelé-Halgand
School of Medicine & Research Centre in Management & Economics (LEMNA), Nantes University, Nantes, France
e-mail: nathalie.angele-halgand@univ-nantes.fr

© The Author(s) 2017   **59**
L. Menvielle et al. (eds.), *The Digitization of Healthcare*,
DOI 10.1057/978-1-349-95173-4_4

empowerment and equity. This leads us to propose a new typology of digital health business models.

The question of the financial balance of the health system is crucial for every country due to the on-going rise of expenses. The financial sustainability of Western health systems in the configuration allowing health services access for as many as possible is an increasingly debated issue. The Prospective Payment System (PPS)-driven regulation based on diagnosis-related group (DRG) fees has proved to fail both in containing health-care expenditures and in guaranteeing high-quality services as highlighted by Angelé-Halgand and Garrot (2014, 2015) for the French case. Researchers from various backgrounds try to address this issue by searching for disruptive innovation business models (Hwang and Christensen 2008) that would match the Anthropocene new deal characterized by increasing pressures put both on budgets and demand for care. In such a difficult context, Information Technologies (ITs) seem to bring a fruitful contribution as they promise to facilitate the development of better coordinated care models (Hunt 2013). Nevertheless, the issue is so complex than solutions that are based only on technology are likely not to be wholly satisfying: the resort to expertise in human and social sciences is required. Pointing out policies that pursue digitalization as a self-evident "solution" to problems in health care (Garrety et al. 2014) highlights the disruptive effects of national electronic health record systems on the production, ownership use and responsibility for health records. We aim at contributing to this debate by analysing a series of business models induced by digital health innovations and discussing their contribution to sustainable health accessible for as many as possible.

To do this, we first present a series of digital health innovations and propose to characterize them into those that relate to personalized health (1), those targeting community-based care providers (2) and those contributing to the performance management of healthcare delivery within a defined territory (3). We then analyse the business models associated to these digital health innovations to propose a typology of business models for digitalized health with a special attention granted to the financial impacts of each type (4).

4.2 Digital Innovations and Personalized Health Care

In line with patient-centred care, personalized medicine or mass customization in health institutions (Minvielle et al. 2014), some digital start-ups promise you to become manager of your health. This proposes to the patient to play the role of a general practitioner (GP) at home.

Ignilife is a Luxembourger start-up implicated in connected "health coaching". They propose digital solutions to coach people all day long to promote a healthy life. The software available on digital multi-support gives the opportunity to identify the patient's risk factors, for him/her to receive alarm for recommended exams or to follow a personalized program in nutrition, backache, sleep disorder, tobacco or stress. The company pretends to "help people become actors of their health". "Get your health under control" is its disclosed target. Digital software provides advices to the customer with a personalized information link to his/her needs. Ignilife grants special attention to prevention by safe living practices and healthy behaviours in accordance to the patient's risk factors. The underlying logic is that such a behaviour will reduce the demand for both cure and care, along with the number of unworked days leading to significant savings and positive returns on investment at the global level.

The digital service includes three phases. First, the evaluation phase identifies the healthy profile for the patient in a holistic approach with a dynamic and interactive questionnaire trying to define his/her risks at present and in the future. At the end of this stage, the patient receives a personal health score with a detailed report that he/she should share with his/her relatives and GP. The software programme processes the answers given by the patient through the questionnaire to suggest targets and prioritize actions to improve his/her experience with Ignilife. Second is the definition of a personalized rhythm and program taking into account all the aspects of the health profile of the customer/patient. It reviews four mains domains: clinical risks, nutrition, physical activity and emotional health. As a target, the patient can choose to lose weight, control stress, eat healthy or improve sleep, and the digital application guides him/her, day after day, with simple and small actions that trigger significant and lasting change at last. The commercial flyer argues that motivation is maintained by defining well-calibrated targets, that is, not too easy to reach but still reachable, daily implication and progressive learning. The role of small wins in the progression is underlined and the promise of easy activities to follow the program is put forward. Third, an evaluation is made with a visual and interactive scorecard to assess the progression. Each progress is rewarded to keep patient's motivation high. This leads the patient to receive gratifications like free products, or commercial services on health and welfare. . . . Ignilife provides to the patient's digital environment the possibility to directly collect data from connected objects, to store all Electronic Health Records in a unique personal database that can be shared with clearly identified persons for free. Messages alert him/her in case of deviant behaviours. Ignilife also propose to connect patients with similar conditions by a social network called Ignilife users.

Visiomed Group is one of Ignilife's competitors. It is a small enterprise that develops "BewellConnect", that is, a product that provides a personal health assistant service. It has also launched several health-oriented innovations developed on smart and connected objects. Visiomed Group's expertise in reliable and precise medical connected measurement tools has led to propose a new concept targeting patients suffering from chronic diseases (diabetes, hypertension, cardiac pathologies, asthma . . .), pregnant women, seniors, people living in remote areas with problems of access to medical resources, travellers and hypochondriacs who wish to be reassured 24 hours a day and 7 days a week. As an innovation leader the group promises to enable its clients to monitor their health in an autonomous way by empowering them to make a diagnosis, thanks to the distant support provided by medical doctors and allied professionals.

This group has a physiological approach trying to collect data through connected objects. The data is contextualized, precise, reliable and secure. It is useful to assess the severity of a series of signs and enables to guide medical interpretation. From this background, the company has launched a range of services with a choice between three levels. At the first level, BewellCheck-up collects a set of data about the patient's body including medical data (measure of temperature, blood pressure, pulse, saturation in oxygen, glycaemia, heart rhythm), localization of the pain, an assessment of the patient's risks by asking the right questions to define his/her symptoms (fever, headache), taking into account his/her profile and histories (diabetes, high blood pressure, cardiac insufficiency) and geographical situation in terms of offers of care around him/her (remote place, duration of transport to get access to a doctor) and give a first diagnosis (list the most likely causes of your ill-being or pain) with an estimation of the medical emergency degree and guide him/her in the health system. The software guides the patient with ergonomic and intuitive approach, slightly the same situation as if the patient faced a physician in emergency conditions. In a few minutes, it can review the most likely roots of the patient's problem. The service is supported by a revolutionary artificial intelligence system that supports medical decision developed with the help of a team of emergency physicians. The software allows sending a report with the patient's data, answers, histories, to his/her regular medical doctor and proposes to the patient to get in touch with a medical advising platform reachable by phone 24 hours a day and 7 days a week via MyDoc. This advising phone platform is operated by physicians and offers a full time access from several points of the app on a smartphone. This enables the patient to directly get in touch with a regulating doctor of the medical platform on the phone, who assesses the situation, recommends the patient, guides him/her to an emergency service or sends assistance to him/her (ambulance, emergency medical service). This service is fully accessible in France and from foreign countries. The medical team is based in France and answers in French. The extra service combines the two offers in one BewellCheck-up plus MyDoc called BewellConnect.

The set of services is channelled through a mobile application on a smartphone/tablet/computer with a payment that depends on both the uses and how frequently the provider is called. As an example, Visiomed proposes nine packs of services with two dimensions: the nature of the service (BewellCheck-up or MyDoc or BewellConnect the both) and the intensity of uses (free usages called "Discover", with commitment of 12 months called "Privilege", and with commitment of 24 months called "Serenity"). For an aged chronicle patient with cardiac pathology and hypertension who accepts a commitment of 24 months, he/she has to pay 31.90 € a month to access with no time limitation restricting the access to the whole digital environment (follow-up and medical advices by phone). Digital connected objects have to be added to the registration fee: a thermometer (99 €), a tensiometer (109 €) and ECG (349 €), easily amounting to 557 €. The patient can test the service before committing him/herself. Going for intensive use, that corresponds to 3 calls per month and full usage of surveillance medical, requires a monthly increase of 69.7 €, that is, 836.4 € per year.

These two examples show that digital devices take part to the emergence of a new relationship between the patient and his/her health. He/she will become the self-organizer of his/her health condition helped by medical professionals depending on the severity of his/her illness. The company highlights the potential of digitalization to redesign care in a more connected way with the patient as proposed by Porter and Olmsted Teisberg (2006, p. 167 and following) in care cycles.

4.3 Digital Innovations and Community-Based Patients Health-Care Providers

Another start-up in Monaco called IMSPro provides an interesting model coordinating by a software solution named "Askamon" the various health professionals around a group of patients. Askamon solution allows, they argue, to centralize, consult and enrich medical data for a better follow-up and rationalization of health costs. Based on community work in predefined environments it centralizes and allows exchanges of medical information between health professionals. So, every professional selects the information that he/she needs, whenever his/her status: medical doctor, physiotherapist and paramedic. This sharing of information allows to improve significantly care coordination and to optimize the coverage and the patient's follow-up. Askamon simply and exhaustively meets all users' needs, they argue. Built on intuitiveness, clarity and simplicity of uses, it is user-friendly whatever the level of the user at using computers. This is a tool induced from the ground field that evolves with daily practice. It is reachable by all electronic devices and software environment.

Firstly developed for the high-level sport world, the start-up now targets companies, health industries, insurers, health institutions and primary care centres. The company provides a personal health record (PHR) that is only used under the agreement of the patient condition, and the agreement shall be given for each caregiver. The system compiles consultations, prescriptions, pathologies, medical histories and reports on the same electronic record. It gives the opportunity to edit all administrative documents, to establish assessments of general health status of patients at any time and finally it contributes to the care organization management. In case of statutory medical follow-up, the software plans, organizes, controls and reports at any time on medical obligations. This part is especially relevant for the firm with a medical department, in the context of dangerous activities, for expatriated staff or for all medical statutory follow-up contexts. The patient has a complete access and a full management of his PHR. He/she can add information, discuss with physicians and find oriented advices on sport activity, nutrition, well-being via multimedia supports.

From the database built on a specific group, with the standardization and in the respect of the legacy, the PHR allows epidemiologic studies to evaluate treatment and therapy or prevent diseases or wounds accidentally.

It also makes it possible to interface Askamon with medical digital equipment or administrative systems. For example, the billing system of the National Health System can be reached; some medical connected devices can also carry out medical tests on the person.

The last step is a performance management tool, which is of special interest to the clients, that is, the health-care providers who would like to manage their group of patients with a same pathology on the long term, or who have to deal with a large population as the pension funds, or mutual insurance companies. The software allows relevant tools for medical prevention, used by companies to improve human resource management and hence global performance.

IMSPro would like to implement this software solution with an unlimited access 24 hours a day and 7 days a week. This could ideally be done with full access for the final user from as many digital devices as required. The data storage is also unlimited. IMSPro proposes a global solution covering all medical needs of the client company employees connecting them to all required health professionals.

We can notice, at this stage, that Askamon solution first targeted clients with strongly homogeneous beneficiaries' medical profiles, for example high-level sports organizations, and the company has now diversified its market mix with by company clients who have more disparate medical profiles, with insurance companies. At last, this case represents an interesting mix of individual and organizational approach focusing a specific community. It should be viewed as an original situation, in which political aspects are centred on the patient's interests, decision-makers define general aims, and the organization of care is completely carried out by/with health professionals. Such an experience could well be considered as a bottom-up approach laboratory. If IMSPro has clearly identified clients dealing with a defined community of care, it is not the case of all start-ups, which propose to take care of a patient community.

Other start-ups target the providers of services at home rather than the patient and his/her family carers. It is the case of DVSanté, which is a silver economy start-up in Nice. It proposes a dematerialized global platform dedicated to better meet the needs of persons suffering of loss of autonomy, who live at home (Bottero 2016). This is achieved by a group of partners having a relevant expertise in various domains related to the needs of the person. The existing institutions in charge of home care waste much time in coordination by phone. Thanks to the professional platform, DVSanté uses a user-friendly and rapid tool, which allows the care coordinators and the actors to gain in efficiency and in productivity. It is the first private platform for health-care professionals that is accessible for free. It allows in a few clicks to organize for the patient to remain at home by putting him/her in contact with the health professionals who can bring the most complete answers to his/her needs. This includes nurses, physiotherapists, speech therapists, chiropodists, health aid and helping staff at home. It also required medical equipment, leading to adapt accommodation, transport, general services, catering, assistance, leisure activities, holidays, and putting in touch with relevant specialized structures (day care hospital, care services at home, nursing home . . .). This young start-up claims to make the current system of care more fluid in organizing continuous care to the patients from hospital to home, including the intermediate structures (long-term care, convalescent homes, nursing homes . . .). This is reached thanks to an effective coordination between the various stakeholders. What is at stake is to fully cover all patients' needs at home. This is carried out by tracing health professionals' contributions to a patient real time. This saves critical time, it is argued. The business is presented as a solution intermediating patients and medical professionals: searching for and connecting allied health professionals and home service providers with a guarantee of quality, follow-ups through several tools (a quality charter, an app for home services and an interface hospital/home). Resorting to specialized partners they also offer organizational consultancy (pharmaceutical or logistics platform, operating room organization, patient flow) and app development services. According to the start-up CEO, the digital devices proposed allow to reduce the patient's hospital length of stay while guaranteeing a better communication between the hospital and home professionals, by bringing comfort and safety. Those solutions give the opportunity to the caregivers at home to become relevant intermediaries between the service providers generally unknown by the patient and their future customers. The company provides a unique digital service of intermediation and sharing of medical data within a territory. The large majority of health institutions buy this services offer as some big health institutions like teaching hospitals or cancer institutes. Not surprisingly, health professionals like the digital services designed by DVSanté because they improve coordination between themselves. This issue of coordination is indeed critical when the patient lives at home. The territorial aspect is more acute in this business, which is not completely stabilized yet. DVSanté tools are completely free of charge for health professionals, that is, nursing consultants at home, and give them the opportunity to put in contact their patients with home service providers. These providers have to give back a percentage of the revenues that they generate through the platform. Another source of revenues comes from hospitals. The software hence enables to optimize the part of the care path, which is outside the hospital, and this generates subsequent savings in term of internal organization and length of stay at the benefit of the hospital. According to DVSanté CEO (Sierra 2016), the return on investment for the hospital of the annual fees to DVSanté is around four months. He declares to prospect mutual insurance companies with an interest for covering the risk of hospitalization of their beneficiaries.

This second type of digital health innovation is striking because it was originally designed to help caregivers to deal with the needs of a patient at home. These patients may be less medically homogeneous than sport champions, and the contribution of the innovator moves step by step towards a service of intermediation of health professionals for a population on a defined territory.

4.4   Digital Innovations and Territorial Performance Management of Health-Care Delivery

IMS Health should be qualified as an "international digital company". Founded in 1954, it is the leading global information and technology services company (operating in more than 100 countries) providing more than 5,000 clients in the health-care industry with tailored solutions to measure and improve performance. It employs around 7,000 experts in data management and saves on cloud platform huge volume of information from health systems. They consider themselves as the Unique Foundation for Driving Healthcare Performance operating at the heart of what is shaping the future of health care: information and technology services. They connect their assets and expertise across all questions raised by their clients. The company collects big data in health, develops strong expertise on data mining to exploit information and identifies ways to improve their offer.

To make clear how big the business is, here are some examples. More than 500 pharmaceutical *wholesalers and distributors* report on their shipment of products to every distribution channel—including hospitals, clinics, retail and mail-order pharmacies, pharmaceutical chains, mass merchandisers and food stores. *Health plans* principally in North America send anonymous medical claims data for a record of patient care. Tens of thousands of *pharmacies* send information on the prescriptions from *US Government*, Medicare and Medicaid databases and the health records of military forces and their families. *Physicians* report on consultations worldwide on Electronic Medical Reports (EMR) that include diagnoses, patient types and therapies.

Thousands of *hospitals* report on the products they purchase, the treatment and discharge records worldwide. *Laboratory and imaging companies* report on their results like medical imaging. Data also come from a panel of *healthcare stakeholder groups*, including physicians, worldwide who regularly participate in quantitative and qualitative research studies. Thanks to a mix of automation and human intelligence IMS Health tries to collect structured and unstructured social media data related to drugs, treatments and healthcare companies, while respecting patient privacy. The company also exploits its cloud-based listening platform; customers can hence gain insights from the Web real time. The company works also with *patient anonymous* information with specific conditions or those receiving a particular treatment about their quality of life, reasons for treatment changes, structured measures of disease severity and treatment and care information. *Promotional expenditures* for individual products are assessed, with both qualitative and quantitative feedback on all the commercial activity. IMS Health has also invested in *Genomic sequence* data for the opportunities it gives to improve health, patient by patient. The company collects data on the sales of ethical *pharmaceutical products*, capturing more than 95% of the value of the global market. The company conducts qualitative research with physicians, *dentists*, pharmacists, *nurses, payers* and patients by face-to-face interviews, focus groups and questionnaires trying to understand attitudes, motivations and intentions. All these data are useful for a Global Customer Base—including government agencies, payers, providers and nearly every major pharmaceutical and biotech company worldwide—to rely on the information collected, services and technologies to guide strategic and tactical planning and drive more effective marketplace interactions. All these customers are segmented as follows: consumer health, medical device and diagnostics, pharmaceutical manufacturers, specialty/oncology, generics manufacturers, payer/provider/government and pharmacies and wholesalers.

But even if this health big brother seems to be on track, few elements show some failures and points out some avenues for improvement. The company recognizes that "available information is very fragmented and difficult to bring together in a meaningful way". What is required is to have "partnering with high-value physicians, engaging proactively with physicians and populations and acquiring clearer insights into care dynamics." This shows that information needs to be more focused on care processes or on a clearly identified health condition. Also, the company has many expectations in what is called "Real-World" Evidence (RWE) or Data (RWD) and proposes to create a specific RWE ecosystem with its customers focused on anonymous patient-level data. Moreover, the so-called Better Together by Design proposes to move "from big data by collectively leveraging our best-in-breed capabilities". This shows that the complexity of health, even if digital information is centralized in Big Data, needs to be addressed by a large, collective and engaged group of actors suggesting the value of empowering the actors.

Another fascinating experience is of HealthPartners (Isham George et al. 2013). HealthPartners is a Minnesota-based, consumer-governed, non-profit organization, founded in the 1950s. It provides health insurance through a large integrated system (from prevention to hospitals, five at least, more than 75 medical and dental clinics, and a network of contracted providers). HealthPartners' mission is to "improve the health of our members, our patients and the community." In 2010, the leaders heard a presentation from the University of Wisconsin for the Robert Wood Johnson Foundation's County Health Rankings program. The result was: "contribute to health outcomes, the model estimates that clinical care contributes 20 percent, health behaviours contribute 30 percent, social and economic factors 40 percent, and the physical environment 10 percent. In other words, the three nonclinical care factors are responsible for an estimated 80 percent of health outcomes" (Isham George et al. 2013, pp. 1446–1447). It was hence decided to implement what is called a "community business model—a type of multisectoral partnership that involves actors that are seldom accustomed to work together and not always aware of how their actions affect population health" (Isham George et al. 2013, p. 1447). To do so, the company strategy integrated aims and performance measurement system "secondary" influence on health outcomes, such as health behaviours, social and economic factors and the physical environment. To better understand how this partnership works, the example of *"yumPower School Challenge"* can help. A number of school districts and a children's media outlet, Radio Disney became partners of the challenge. The challenge of each participating school was one part of the "healthy eating" campaign. It included advertising, cooking classes and a website with expert advices and resources. The main purpose was "the promotion of the consumption of five fruits and vegetables a day for people of all ages". Schools volunteered to compete for cash prizes that could be used to promote health and well-being. The whole budget invested by HealthPartners was around $300,000 after integrating creative components of the campaign, staff time to support schools, and evaluation services. This action was tightly accompanied by HealthPartners leaders even if it was not the case of twenty others initiatives, in which HealthPartners was involved.

Even if digital devices are not the main purpose of this kind of collective partnership, we understand how digital solutions play a central role in terms of communication, evaluation and following-up for each school. Another point that deserves attention is the notion of community in that example: as HealthPartners is a Minnesota-based organization which deals with a huge objective towards the population of this territory, which is to improve health of their members, that is, patients and beyond all people living in the geographic zone.

4.5 Towards a Business Model Typology for Digital Health

A series of models have been drawn from other sectors like e-commerce or disruptive innovations in general business companies to be applied to health care. We will first review these models and what can be learnt from then. We will then propose a new typology the distinctive feature of which is that it is drawn directly from digital health cases.

4.5.1 Reviewing Existing Typologies of Health Business Models

In 2000, the first typology of business models (BM) on health digitalization was proposed inspired by e-commerce (Parente 2000). Eight years later, a new typology of BM was designed borrowing from disruptive innovation theoretical frameworks applied to health delivery (Hwang and Christensen 2008). Several recent papers also address this issue (Davey et al. 2010; Kimble 2015).

Davey (2010, p. 24) puts that a "business model performs two important functions: it creates value and it captures a portion of that value". According to Hwang and Christensen (2008, pp. 1331–1332) and Kimble (2015, pp.27–29), a business model should present four elements: (1) A *value proposition* or *offer* should provide a product or a service done more effectively, conveniently and affordably; (2) a *set of resources* that may bring together people, supplies, intellectual property, equipment, and cash; (3) a *profit or finance formula* compares prices, costs, mark-ups, margins, asset turns, and volumes necessary to profitability; (4) a *client* or a *process*, that is, the beneficiary of the offer or the process that would transform the health system on the long term.

Parente (2000, p. 94) highlights "Health e-commerce b-to-b models" based on Web sales directly to providers through online auction and services (consulting, strategy or performance measurement . . .). Several examples presented in the previous section (n° 2) seem to fall into this category. After deep analysis they tried to add (for IMS Health) or to design (for DVSanté) not only a digital business model but a basis aiming at enriching the answer brought to a series of health problems. For example, IMS Health collects information for businesses from their clients but it aims at getting a better understanding of the business model to propose to design with the client the relevant database for analysis and decision-making activities. The "b-to-c model" (Parente 2000, p. 95), which allows customers to purchase health products through Internet, also seems relevant to our cases. The author presents the case of Vivius, which gives the opportunity to build one's own health plan. Interestingly yet he noticed that this service must be self-funded by the patient or partially financed by an employer contribution. This case is in between a person-based BM aligned with health individualization principles (e.g. Ignilife) and a community-based BM targeting company employees (IMSPro-Askamon).

Hwang and Christensen (2008, pp. 1332–1333) classify BM depending on three types of disruptive innovations: solution shops, value-adding process businesses and facilitated user networks. The "solution shop" can solve unstructured problems with skills and the talent of the people employed as distinctive features. Providing unique combination of services for each customer being their target. IMS Health illustrates the solution shop, as it sells digital information and digital treatment to its clients. As we previously saw, they yet try to move to a more global hand to hand business involving more and more stakeholders in the design of the database, in collecting data and also in the meaningful way to analyse information on a given health condition. This suggests that even if the project is to build a huge data warehouse on health, the need to develop a reflection on how to use it remains critical. "Value-adding process businesses" transform resources in greater value outputs. They generally focus on process excellence providing better quality services at lower cost. It seems to be the case for IMSPro and DVSanté, as far as quality is concerned, their costs being not lower. Services provided are new and increases the fees to be paid by end-users, raising the issues of equity and accessibility to this new health process. "User networks" is probably the most distinctive BM, as it describes situations where "same people buy and sell and deliver and receive things to and from each other". Digital health is close to this type as each stakeholder must be involved in improving people's health. HealthPartners is certainly the best illustration of this type of BM.

Jason and Christensen (2008) stress two limits that we consider as a call for proposing a complementary typology of Health Digitalization BM. The first limit refers to the lack of retail market. Authors argued that a disruptive innovation needs to meet a competitive market to increase sales and they denounce the third-party payer system in health that introduces an intermediation between clients and providers. Beyond this limit lies one of the most critical issues in health, leading to identify products and clients understood as the final users. Three levels can be listed, we argue: individual, community and population. The second limit is put as follows: "In health care, most technological enablers have failed to bring about lower costs, higher quality, and greater accessibility."

4.5.2 Proposing a New Business Model Typology for Digital Health

In addition to these limits, a new typology for health digitalization is also required, we argue, because previous typologies were all built with no consideration given to the foremost health challenge: how can health digitalization address the most challenging financial issues faced by the health system? Three challenges should be tackled by health digitalization BM, we argue.

The first challenge lies at the *individual* level and relates to the need for organizing a well-coordinated care/life pathway for the patient or his/her caregiver. Beyond their social, political and economic dimensions' health issues are personal matters. Hence there is a need for giving to the patient the opportunity to be actor of his/her health coordinating in efficient ways information, behaviours, incentives and social and environmental factors to not only organize acute episodes of care but also to prevent them and decrease risks. The financial model here is the payment individualized upon each final user/client. It puts light on associated questions of equity, accessibility and affordability of health services. Should digital health be considered as medical procedures financed by the National Health Service or is it simply a choice by the patient of better welfare?

The second challenge is situated at a *community* level, that is, a group of persons with homogeneous health needs. At this level and moving from individuals to the group, the health system should gain in efficiency and effectiveness by optimizing care processes, systemizing epidemiologic studies and associated advices and developing specific preventive actions for the community with homogenous health needs. Even if health is personal matter, its social dimension is obvious because one's health impacts others and reciprocally. Digital technology offers us both to improve health and dramatically cut costs for standardized care processes through a co-responsibility of patients. This organization is very interesting to better understand how digital technologies could improve quality, efficiency, accessibility and affordability of health. In the case of IMSPro, the situation is unfortunately simplified by the fact that the payer is the employer of the beneficiaries of the digital health services. The question of the generalization of this community approach and the question of the diversity of the communities needs in a general population remain unanswered.

The third challenge is at the level of a territory *population*. The population includes several communities with different health needs. Social and non-medical health services are then required and need to be organized in an integrated way to get disruptive progresses. IMS Health clearly illustrates the challenge of information digitalization. Specifically, monopolistic positions observed in such contexts raise the issue of knowledge-sharing and information property. Preventive actions should integrate social and economic considerations, health behaviours factors and physical environment ones (County Health Rankings). This population level is completely linked to the smaller one. Health Partners and IMS Health experiences show the necessity of co-building, allowed by a contextual approach with a mutual respect of actors, to tackle these challenges.

Finally, we can summarize this by crossing the four elements of business models with the three focus levels to improve health with the help of the digital devices (see Table 4.1).

As shown by Table 4.1 most of the digital health innovations that we analysed fall either into individual or community focus types. Nevertheless, two of them are distinctive by their population focus with a business model reconciling finance and ethics.

4.6 Conclusion

Digital Health disrupts healthcare sector. By providing individualized care it contributes to raise quality of care and reduce the needs for cure. Nevertheless, the new services induced by the revolution may not be accessible to the largest number of people. We first review and characterized DH innovations depending of the level on which they focus. This leads to three types of DH innovations: individualized, community and population. We then propose a typology of business models grounded on this distinction crossed with the BM elements (offer/value, resources, finance/profit formula and clients/process). We identified one BM enabling to empower patient and to preserve access for the largest part of the population reconciling individual and general interests.

The intertwining of business models and ethical issues leads us to call for future work "(the) purpose (of which) is to nurture collective and dynamic re-ordering among actors in a conscious attempt to identify, work through and rethink the rights and responsibilities that are appropriate for supporting the intentions of those who produce and use

Table 4.1 Convergence between connected health, business models and impacts on the population

BM elements / Health levels	Offer/value proposition	Resources	Finance/profit formula	Client/process	Examples
Individual	Customized services for individuals with medical expertise, digital devices, mobile technologies and several services/advices	Medical and IT expertise and innovation IT equipment Web platform Communication devices Confidentiality Security of data	Prices adapted to the package of services Volume of sales enabling to cover costs	Patient/person	BewellConnect for patient Ignilife for individual
Community	Customized services for a group with homogenous medical needs with medical, epidemiologic and other health expertise, digital devices, mobile technologies and data management/data mining	Innovation Medical and IT expertise IT equipment Web platform Communication devices Mass storage Confidentiality Security of data Process expertise	Hand-to-hand prices based on the level and intensity of services provided Identification of a purchaser	Companies Prevention bodies Top-level sports organization… Hospitals Health Institution Regional health authority	IMSPro DVSanté
Population	Collective experiences designed to improve health at politic, strategic and operational levels coherently	All society skills and assets relevant to the objective with digital expertise	Long-term investment Co-payment Co-implication Co-responsibility	Collective process of improvement of health outcomes for the population of a territory	HealthPartners IMS Health

information to deliver care" (Garrety et al. 2014, p. 75). Isham George et al. (2013, p. 1451) state the same point in a slightly different way: "national bodies such as the Institute of Medicine have called for more robust partnerships as well as a framework to ensure that different actors work together to produce better public health processes and outcomes." Digital Health technology may support co-production experiments but the critical issue that it raises remains unchanged in an even acuter way: how can institutions provide the conditions favouring such developments to benefit to the large majority of people including the most fragile fringe. In such a search Ostrom's work on commons (1990) could be usefully applied to health care as we argued previously (Angelé-Halgand and Garrot 2014).

Bibliography

Angelé-Halgand, Nathalie, and Thierry Garrot. "Les biens communs à l'hôpital: De la T2A à la tarification au cycle de soins" *Comptabilité, Contrôle, Audit* T20, V3 (2014): 15–41.

Angelé-Halgand, Nathalie and Thierry Garrot. "Discipliner par le chiffre: L'hôpital financiarisé au risque de la réification?" *Entreprise Et Histoire* 79 (2015): 41–58.

BewellConnect (2015). BewellConnect Santé. https://www.bewell-connect.com/fr/sante/. Accessed August 20, 2016.

Bottero, L., (2016). DV Santé se rapproche de Monali. Resource document. *La Tribune Provence-Alpes-Côte d'Azur.* http://marseille.latribune.fr/innovation/2016-03-03/dv-sante-se-rapproche-de-la-bordelaise-monali.html. Accessed August 20, 2016.

County Health Rankings (2016). Our Approach. *Madison (WI): University of Wisconsin Population Health Institute.* http://www.countyhealthrankings.org/our-approach. Accessed August 26, 2016.

Davey Shirley, M. et al. "The Health of Innovation: Why Open Business Models Can Benefit the Healthcare Sector" *Irish Journal of Management* 30, 1 (2010): 21–40.

DVSanté. DVSanté. http://www.dvsante.com. Accessed August 20, 2016.

Garrety, Karin et al., "National Electronic Health Records and the Digital Disruption of Moral Orders" *Social Science & Medicine* 101 (2014): 70–77.

Hunt, J., Rt. Hon (2013). Paperless NHS News Story Gov.UK. Resource document. *Department of Health*. https://www.gov.uk/government/news/paperless-nhs-jeremy-hunt-leads-discussion. Accessed August 25, 2016.

Hwang, Jason and Clayton M. Christensen "Disruptive Innovation in Health Care Delivery: A Framework For Business-Model Innovation" *Health Affairs* 27, 5 (2008): 1329–1335.

Ignilife (2014). Prenez le contrôle de votre santé. http://ignilife.com/#_=_. Accessed August 20, 2016.

IMS Health (2016a). Imshealth Market Insight. http://www.imshealth.com/en/solution-areas/healthcare-market-insights. Accessed August 18, 2016.

IMS Health (2016b). imshealth Real-World Evidence. http://www.imshealth.com/en/solution-areas/real-world-evidence. Accessed August 18, 2016.

IMSPro. Askamon. http://www.imspro.mc/index.php?option=com_content&view=article&id=54&Itemid=62&lang=fr. Accessed August 20, 2016.

IMSPro. Nos Solutions. http://www.imspro.mc/index.php?option=com_content&view=article&id=48&Itemid=55&lang=fr. Accessed August 20, 2016.

Isham, George J. et al., "HealthPartners Adopts Community Business Model to Deepen Focus on Nonclinical Factors of Health Outcomes" *Health Affairs* 32, 8 (2013): 1446–1452.

Kimble, Chris "Business Models for E-Health: Evidence from Ten Case Studies" *Global Business & Organizational Excellence* 34, 4 (2015): 18–30.

Minvielle, Etienne et al., "Managing Customization in Health Care: A Framework Derived from the Services Sector Literature" *Health Policy* 117 (2014): 216–227.

Ostrom, Elinor. *Governing the Commons—The Evolution of Institutions for Collective Action*. Cambridge, UK: Cambridge University Press, 1990.

Parente, Stephen T "Beyond the Hype: A Taxonomy of E-Health Business Models" *Health Affairs* 19, 6 (2000): 89–102.

Porter, Michael and Elizabeth Olmsted Teisberg. *Redefining Health Care—Creating Value-Based Competition on Results*. New York: Harvard Business School Press, 2006.

Sierra, E., (2016). DV Santé: Un Service Mobile Pour fluidifier le parcours de soins !. Resource Document. *Métropole Nice Côte d'Azur*. http://www.nicecotedazur.org/developpement-economique/la-maison-de-la-métropole-nca/actualités. Accessed August 19, 2016.

Visiomed GROUP SA (2015). Nos produits. http://visiomed-lab.com/Nos-produits_585.html. Accessed August 18, 2016.

Part II

New Challenges for the Practice of Medicine

5

Formulating eHealth Utilizing an Ecological Understanding

Grant P. Cumming, Douglas McKendrick, Jamie Hogg, Tara French, Eva Kahana, David Molik and Joanne S. Luciano

G.P. Cumming (✉)
Dr Gray's Hospital, NHS Grampian, University of Highlands and Islands and University of Aberdeen, Elgin, Scotland, Aberdeen, UK
e-mail: grant.cumming@nhs.net

D. McKendrick
Dr Gray's Hospital, University of Aberdeen, NHS Grampian, Elgin, Scotland
e-mail: d.mckendrick@nhs.net

J. Hogg
Dr Gray's Hospital, Elgin, NHS Grampian, Aberdeen, UK
e-mail: jamie.hogg@nhs.net

T. French
Institute of Design Innovation, The Glasgow School of Art, Glasgow, UK
e-mail: t.french@gsa.ac.uk

E. Kahana
Elderly Care Research Center, Department of Sociology, Case Western Reserve University, Cleveland, USA
e-mail: exk@case.edu

D. Molik
Cold Spring Harbor Laboratory, New York, USA
e-mail: dmolik@cshl.edu

J.S. Luciano
School of Informatics and Computing, Indiana University, Bloomington, IN, USA
e-mail: jluciano@indiana.edu

Predictive Medicine, Inc., Belmont, MA, USA
e-mail: jluciano@predmed.com

© The Author(s) 2017
L. Menvielle et al. (eds.), *The Digitization of Healthcare*,
DOI 10.1057/978-1-349-95173-4_5

5.1   Introduction

Health care is a complex adaptive system, which requires an integrated and participatory approach to understand and improve the health of citizens (Rouse 2008). To address the complex societal challenges facing health-care delivery (Crisp 2010; WHO 2011) caused by ageing populations, globalization, and long-term/chronic conditions, a shift from the traditional reactive model to a proactive, patient-centric health-care model is advocated (Wanless 2002; WHO |World Health Statistics 2011). Furthermore in addition to the traditional biomedical model of delivering health care (principally targeting infectious diseases), psychological, social, environmental, and cultural factors are increasingly recognized to impact on human functioning in the context of disease and illness (McHattie et al. 2014). The future of health care therefore requires increasing effort directed toward improving personal choices regarding life risks (Keeney 2008) and requires the full engagement of people in their own health-care and lifestyle decisions (Wanless 2002; Crowley and Hunter 2005).

The biopsychosocial (BPS) model was theorized in 1977 as a "blueprint for research, a framework for teaching, and a design for action" for the "social, psychological, and behavioural dimensions of illness." (Engel 1977) The implications of the BPS perspective have been described (Hickey 2013). These are:

1. The individual is the *only* person who can effect the behavioral change, though they might need some help, from family, friends, colleagues, or professional helpers.
2. In those cases where professional assistance seems needed, the blueprint for effective assistance is: (a) to help the individual understand the factors/circumstances that brought about the problem in the first place, (b) to help the individual identify and define the problem in specific terms; perhaps dismantle the problem into component, (c) to encourage a sense of competence and empowerment, and (d) to develop, with the individual, specific plans for replacing sub-optimal habits with habits that are more productive.

However, some argue that the model is open to interpretation and that the BSP model "is a vision and an approach to practice rather than an empirically verifiable theory" (Epstein and Borrell-Carrio 2005). As such, an ecological understanding of health, based on the reciprocal relationship between three interrelated dimensions involving: "the naming or identification of health statuses and conditions, health/illness as forms of capacity and capability, and health/illness as it is perceived by those who have it" (DeNora 2015) provides a way in which to consider the complexities of health. An ecological understanding of health considers health as multidimensional and temporal, influenced by intrinsic and extrinsic factors (DeNora 2015). In this approach, health is in a state of flux, it is constantly changing based upon the external influences upon the individual. By adopting an ecological understanding of health, medicine can become personalized to the individuals needs based on lived experience rather than a streamlined process based on biomarkers and predictive modeling (precision medicine).

Social media has provided a new way for patients to obtain and share information that enables a deeper understanding of their medical condition and treatment options (Eysenbach and Jadad 2001; Medicine 2.0 2008). Medical researchers, doctors, government policy makers, and others, are also making use of the Web, social media applications, and the large volumes of data produced. When applied to the process of utilizing information communication technologies (ICTs) to deliver health care, an ecological model of health may provide a lens, or frame of reference, through which to design, implement, interrogate, explore, and evaluate the effects of these interventions. It also provides a framework to observe how P4 medicine (P4 Medicine Institute) (personalized, participatory, preventative, and predictive) and in particular Digital P4 Medicine (Highlands Islands Enterprises 2012) impacts on health care and its delivery.

5.2 Major Concepts

As knowledge about individual variation in genomics, genetics, proteomics, epigenetics, and drug response increases; an evolution from a "one size fits all" model to precision medicine with personalized treatment protocols is possible. The understanding of these complex relationships is being explored in the emerging fields of systems biology (P4 Medicine Institute) and Big Data analytics (Hansen et al. 2014; Shiao et al. 2015). In addition, the participation of citizens in health-related digital social networks (Denecke 2014b) means that information from these sites can be correlated with those from systems biology and insights gained for the health of that individual (Hood 2013). This digital participation of citizens in their health has contributed to the health professional–citizen relationship becoming an increasingly shared model of decision-making (Elwyn et al. 2012). Gender-specific medicine (Legato and Bilezikian 2009) and a life course approach to health (Schafer and Ferraro 2012) further tailor treatment plans to the end-user. The academic disciplines of Health Web Science (HWS) (Luciano et al. 2014) and Medicine 2.0 (Medicine 2008) with the development of Health Web Observatories (HWO) (The Web Science Trust 2016) provide an infrastructure to develop tools utilizing metadata for further personalization of medicine and to evaluate Internet provided health care within a P4 framework. Health care provided through the conduit of the Internet, that employs an effective behavioral model (Murray 2012), may have a pivotal role in changing health behaviors. However current evaluation and impact of Internet delivered health care is limited not only in cost utility and cost effectiveness (Torre-Díez et al. 2015; Bergmo 2015) but also in its scope in terms of feedback and interaction between the Health Web, health-care providers, and patients.

5.2.1 Preferable Health Outcomes

Providing health care in an increasingly patient-centered way can achieve preferred health outcomes (Hancock and Bezold 1993). These are the health outcomes, which are preferred by patients and involve a balance between medical evidence and the patients' wishes. This can be thought of as personalization of health care, which through dialogue takes the best medical evidence and information available and creates a management plan that fits with the patient's lifestyle and preferences. However, these preferable health outcomes may be a compromise on best medical evidence to accommodate the patient's wishes.

5.2.2 Gender-Specific Medicine

Gender-specific medicine is the study of how normal human biology, physiology, and diseases differ between men and women in terms of prevention, clinical signs, therapeutic approach, prognosis, and psychological and social impact (Legato and Bilezikian 2009). This field can contribute to the personalization of health care through recognizing that disease affects gender differently. Currently, the discourse on gender-specific medicine has not yet addressed transgender medicine.

5.2.3 Life Course Approach

A life course approach to health acknowledges the long-term effects of biological, behavioral, and social exposures during gestation, childhood, adolescence, and young adulthood on health and chronic disease in later life and across generations. It therefore recognizes the influence of genetics, epigenetics, gender, and lifestyle and environment on health and attempts to understand and predict health trajectories throughout the lifetime of individuals (Halfon and Hochstein 2002). Mitigating against potential health problems with early intervention including lifestyle/behavioral changes then becomes part of the P4 health ambition. The life course approach therefore allows the possibility of intervention before childhood adversity poses a health threat to successful aging (Schafer and Ferraro 2012).

5.2.4 Health Web Science and Medicine 2.0

HWS is a subdiscipline of Web Science (Luciano et al. 2013, 2014; Denecke 2015) that complements and overlaps with disciplines under the aegis of Medicine 2.0. HWS studies the role and impact of the Web on health and well-being and conversely the impact of health-related uses of the design of the Web structure and evolution that explicitly includes an alliance with nonmedical stakeholders. Medicine 2.0 or next-generation medicine enabled by emerging technologies (Medicine 2.0 2014) on the other hand emphasizes anything that uses the Internet as a conduit to deliver health care.

5.2.5 Health Web Observatory

The Web Science Trust hosted by the University of Southampton is a charitable body, which supports the global development of Web Science (Web Observatory 2016). The Trust introduced the concept of a Web Observatory 2016 as a collection of data sources and data analytic tools that enable experimentation on the Web (Hall and Tiropanis 2012). Web Observatories work by the insertion of metadata into a website and using software to associate these sites. Examples of this may be the connection of disparate data sources to find out something new, or the targeting of a community or website to change some variable and assess its impact.

An HWO is a system that is envisioned to provide an infrastructure to ask and answer questions about the Health Web, the users of the Health Web, and the way that each affects each other within the domain of health-related uses, based upon a collection of metadata, disparate data sources, and Health websites (Fig. 5.1). It will be a key tool to informing the decision-making process to reach a preferred health outcome.

An HWO requires three capabilities. First, the ICT infrastructure that provides the capability to interrogate, curate, visualize, and make sense of health-related data from disparate databases. Second, the health professionals interface that provides (a) the capability to identify individuals who function as the main connectors in a health social network (b) be able to target these individuals with relevant health information, and (c) for health professionals to be able to assess the stage of health behavior change a person is in (Prochaska and Velicer 1997). Third, the individual's interface, required to provide the confidence and trust that the individual is not being manipulated for nefarious reasons and thus to be able to research and share information according to their personal values.

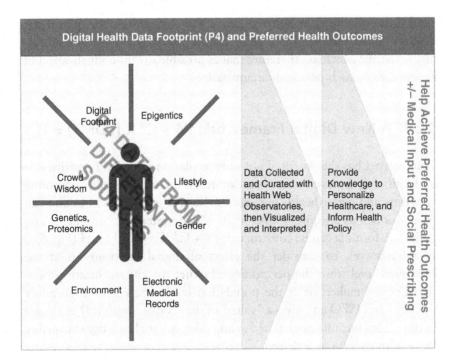

Fig. 5.1   Health Web Observatory

5.2.6 Metadata

Metadata is structured information that describes, explains, locates, or otherwise makes it easier to retrieve, use, or manage an information resource (NISO Press 2004). Metadata therefore allows navigation across data repositories to efficiently find, manage, and track information and allows the creation of associations and relationships between items and users across one or more repositories or related applications. The value of metadata lies in its ability to more efficiently classify and organize information, as well as to yield deeper insight into the actions taking place (M-Files 2013). In the HWO (Fig. 5.1), metadata will give insight into the many ways each citizen engages with the Health Web, for example, the path a citizen takes when clicking through a website, how long they stay on a page, and what content is selected in addition to capabilities described in Section 2.5. It will also address the question – does an online intervention change health policy as a result of community activism? Metadata therefore makes possible the individualization of health care to each personal circumstances.

5.2.7 A New Digital Framework: P4 + C^n X (i-DMT) = H

The Internet has the potential not only to play an important positive role in facilitating interventions that can result in more health-promoting behaviors and better health trajectories (Kahana et al. 2014) but also can be envisioned as affecting health in its wider context (environments and policy). A formula can be constructed: P4 + C^n X (i-DMT) = H (Fig. 5.2) as a framework to consider the effect of digital interventions at the individual level from the perspective of either the citizen, health professional/policy maker, or at the population level. The equation therefore describes an HWO and gives a "value" of the state of health (H) at a point in time. This formula can be used as an evaluating tool to judge the quality of a health website or activity.

Here, P4 is how personalized, predictive, participatory, and preventive the application is. If the formula is visualized as a single action this may be a measure of how interactive the application is. C^n represents the various effectors on the systems, for example, how collaboratively the intervention was designed or how interactive the application is with multiple users. i-DMT are the technology platforms through which a citizen may be exposed to health care using the Internet as a conduit and is comprised of eHealth via "D" laptop/desktop computer, M-Health (mobile health) such as tablets and smartphones, and T-Health or exposure though the television. i-DMT can be viewed as a measure of accessibility to the information.

The challenge to the HWS community is to develop tools that measure H and inform which of the other component parts of an HWO need to be changed to close the difference between current health and a preferred health outcome. From this "gap analysis" a feedback loop is provided that informs future interventions and policy. The authors are developing an ecological model incorporating digital P4 principles, which can be captured and evaluated in the formula in Fig. 5.2.

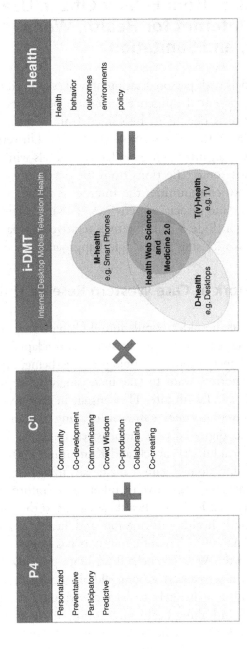

Fig. 5.2 Formulating health care

5.3   Exemplars from Elderly Citizen Use of the Internet for Health, Women's Health, and Sanitation

Web-enabled models with personalization of health care, citizen empowerment, and their potential influence on health behaviors support the argument that there is benefit to be gained from a move from more traditional medicine. The work from Case Western University emphasizes the benefits to be gained among older individuals while work from the UK will provide some reflections from the development of selected applications. In both communities the Internet is increasingly used for Health Information and associated activities. The underlying principles of the applications include a collaborative iterative approach to design within a P4 framework using an ecological approach.

5.3.1   Aging Work at Case Western Reserve University

The rapid growth of the older population globally has raised important questions about changing resources, lifestyles, and adaptations of older adults that can enhance health, psychological well-being, and longevity. Older adults of tomorrow want to take increasingly active roles in their health maintenance and health care. They engage in proactive adaptations that can serve to prevent normative stressors of aging (Kahana et al. 2014).

Research on the digital divide emphasizes underuse of computer technology by older adults (Peacock and Künemund 2007). Yet, older users of computer technology gain a major advantage by bridging the generation gap and becoming active members of an information society (Godfrey and Johnson 2009). In a health care context the Internet offers major access to both health information and health communication (Kahana and Kahana 2007). Use of computers has grown exponentially in recent years and the Web has helped facilitate proactive adaptations and initiative and assertiveness among elderly health-care consumers (Selwyn et al. 2003) and is likely to have contributed to more enlightened health beliefs in linking health-promoting life styles to avoidance of chronic illnesses, such as diabetes and cancer.

Longitudinal studies (Kahana et al. 2002; Kelley-Moore et al. 2006; Kahana et al. 2012, 2013) of successful aging in retirement communities and urban settings in the USA, afforded an opportunity to consider changing orientations and patterns of proactive behaviors of older adults. 1,000-retirement community-dwelling older adults were followed in annual face-to-face surveys and also conducted interviews with urban-dwelling elders in two large metropolitan areas. These elders were surveyed about use of the Web at different time points between 1995 and 2014. Internet use increased from 4.5% in the 1995 cohort to 40.5% in the 2008 survey. The findings indicate increasing comfort among elderly users of the Web. Indeed those who reported computer use generally did so on a daily, or at least weekly basis. It was found that older adults who use the Internet for health information and health communication are more confident in their interactions with physicians and their confidence bolsters their positive expectations regarding medical care. The elderly are not inclined to participate in Web-based support groups.

The growing reliance on cell phones has opened up many new opportunities to older adults regarding health monitoring and health-promoting activities. Smart phones offer an effective tool for promoting behavioral change, such as improving diets and increasing physical activity (Seçkin and Kahana 2015).

Older adults have traditionally been reluctant to speak up to their doctors and engage in self advocacy in obtaining health care (Kahana et al. 2014). Yet, active communication in health care and shared decision-making between patients and physicians can greatly benefit older patients (Kahana et al. 2011; Kreps and Maibach 2008). It was found that older adults who use the Internet for health information and health communication are more confident in their interactions with physicians and their confidence bolsters their positive expectations regarding medical care.

5.3.2 Nappies, Miscarriage, Toilets, and Menopause

It was found that preliminary evidence suggested that after providing information online about the use of disposable and reusable nappies that the Internet has the potential to change behaviors when (Miller et al. 2011) people's beliefs were being nudged to enable them to see advantages in the use of reusable nappies. The persuasive factor was the reduction in landfill. In the formula in Fig. 5.2 the website would not have resulted in an optimal score as it was a read only website. However the information presented had been developed with the end-user and the website has now been redeveloped to provide information for the region.

The miscarriage website was designed in collaboration with end-users and using a modified patient preference design demonstrated the potential of a web-based intervention to reduce psychological morbidity following miscarriage (Klein et al. 2012) and therefore positively impacting on health outcomes. As it is only delivered on one platform it would not produce an optimal score in the formula than if the intervention was delivered on multiple platforms. Compared with the nappy example the website is participatory and preventative. Further work is required to ascertain whether or not it needs to be delivered on other platforms and research is being undertaken to see if a questionnaire can be developed to predict psychological morbidity to improve the predictive utility of the website.

A website for rating and finding public toilets was built after showing the need for better access to toilets in an online survey (Cumming et al. 2011). This has not been a success in terms of uptake despite positive feedback. A mobile app is currently being developed, which would enable access to public toilet information when the need arises. The website capability is limited by the fact that people need to plan ahead for their toilet requirements and does not allow for the unpredictability of the need to use the facilities. Thus an app would provide additional capability and the expectation would have a value closer to optimal in Fig. 5.2. Further work is required to address this question in practice.

www.menopausematters.co.uk is a patient-tailored, physician-led website which, although partly dependent for funding on pharmaceutical sponsorship, remains independent of the industry. The site aims to educate women and health professionals and to empower and enable women to be proactive in the management of their menopause promoting evidence-based practice and recommendation. The site was created in consultation with the end-user through feedback questionnaires. Through online surveys, the website obtains "snapshots" of Internet literate women's views on all aspects of their menopause experiences and provide feedback to them and their health professionals in peer-reviewed journals and national/international conferences. Preliminary evidence has suggested the power of online storytelling to empower women to seek help for their vaginal atrophy and the information is used to educate health professionals to enquire directly about this symptom of the menopause thereby changing citizen behavior and health professional practice/policy. While www.meno pausematters.co.uk allows health professionals and women to select expertly prepared information (Web 1.0) or interact with one another (Web 2.0) via the forum, it is limited with respect to personalization. It is envisaged that www.menopausematters.co.uk will work closely with www.managemymenopause.co.uk (Cumming et al. 2016). The main aims of www.managemymenopause.co.uk are to provide more personalized health care. www.managemymenopause.co.uk utilizes a patient questionnaire and three risk prediction tools to generate a tailored advice document that provides risk advice and information on lifestyle modification and pharmacological interventions. The website will "remember" a woman and can therefore tailor the information to the woman as she ages or as the information underpinning the management of menopause changes. Virtual clinics are becoming increasingly utilized within the United Kingdom National Health Service (NHS). A novel evolution of virtual clinics using digital technology to deliver and facilitate patient engagement with health provision is NHS Grampian's No Delays (see Chapter 11). A menopause component is in the process of being designed.

5.4   Conclusions

An HWO and a new digital framework for evaluating and developing digital interventions is one of the responses to a growing consensus that current health models are unsustainable. Furthermore, medicine is also moving from a reactive to a proactive model of health care. Information and communication technologies (ICTs) utilizing the Internet are having an increasing footprint in the delivery of and personalization of health care with the convergence of social networks and precision medicine. Embracing a new digital framework within an ecological model of health, it is suggested that medicine utilizing ICTs, which is personalized, predictive, participatory, and preventive (P4), has the potential to change health behaviors and health policy. The exemplars have demonstrated elements of digital P4 medicine and the use of a pragmatic formula for evaluating the intervention. Older adults who use the Internet for health information and health communication are more confident in their interactions with health professionals and their confidence bolsters their positive expectations regarding medical care. HWO aimed at curating metadata from websites and Web data have the potential to increase the utility of social networks, social machines, documentation, and online interventions. However, the challenge to the Web Science and Medicine 2.0 communities is to develop new tools to enable the triangulation of data to understand end-user interaction with the Web and thus identify new integrated strategies for preferable health outcomes.

References

Bergmo, Trine Strand. 2015. "How to Measure Costs and Benefits of eHealth Interventions: An Overview of Methods and Frameworks," *Journal of Medical Internet Research* 17, no. 11: e254, doi: 10.2196/jmir.4521.

Crisp, Nigel. 2010. *Turning the World Upside Down: The Search for Global Health in the 21st Century.* CRC Press. http://www.crcnetbase.com/doi/book/10.1201/b13481.

Crowley, Philip, and David J. Hunter. 2005. "Putting the Public Back into Public Health," *Journal of Epidemiology and Community Health* 59, no. 4: 265–267.

Cumming, G. P., H. D. Currie, and R. Moncur. 2011. "The Effects of Urinary Incontinence and Availability of Publically Accessible Toilets: An Online Survey," *Menopause International* 17, no. 1: 14–15, doi: 10.1258/mi.2011.011004.

Cumming, G. P. et al., 2016. "The Future of Post-Reproductive Health: The Role of the Internet, the Web, Information Provision and Access," *Post Reproductive Health.* doi: 10.1177/2053369116647858.

De La Torre-Díez, Isabel et al. 2015b. "Cost-Utility and Cost-Effectiveness Studies of Telemedicine, Electronic, and Mobile Health Systems in the Literature: A Systematic Review," *Telemedicine and E-Health* 21, no. 2: 81–85, doi: 10.1089/tmj.2014.0053.

Denecke, Kerstin. 2014. "Ethical Aspects of Using Medical Social Media in Healthcare Applications," *Studies in Health Technology and Informatics* 198: 55–62, http://www.ncbi.nlm.nih.gov/pubmed/24825685.

Denecke, Kerstin. 2015. "Applications of Social Media in Healthcare," *Health Web Science.* 7–16, doi: 10.1007/978-3-319-20582-3_2.

DeNora, Tia. 2015. *Music Asylums: Wellbeing Through Music in Everyday Life.* Farnham, Surrey: Ashgate Publishing, Ltd.

Elwyn, Glyn. et al., 2012. "Shared Decision Making: A Model for Clinical Practice," *Journal of General Internal Medicine* 27, no. 10: 1361–1367.

Engel, George L. 1977. "The Need for a New Medical Model: A Challenge for Biomedicine," *Science* 196: 129–136.

Epstein, Ronald, M., and Francesc Borrell-Carrio. 2005. "The Biopsychosocial Model: Exploring Six Impossible Things," *Families, Systems, & Health* 23, no. 4: 426.

Eysenbach, Gunther, and Alejandro R. Jadad. 2001. "Evidence-Based Patient Choice and Consumer Health Informatics in the Internet Age," *Journal of Medical Internet Research* 3, no. 2: e19, doi: 10.2196/jmir.3.2.e19.

Godfrey, Mary, and Owen Johnson. 2009. "Digital Circles of Support: Meeting the Information Needs of Older People," *Computers in Human Behavior* 25, no. 3: 633–642, doi: 10.1016/j.chb.2008.08.016.

Halfon, Neil, and Miles Hochstein. 2002. "Life Course Health Development: An Integrated Framework for Developing Health, Policy, and Research," *Milbank Quarterly* 80, no. 3: 433–479, doi: 10.1111/1468-0009.00019.

Hall, Wendy, and Thanassis Tiropanis. 2012. "Web Evolution and Web Science," *Computer Networks* 56, no. 18: 3859–3865, doi: 10.1016/j.comnet.2012.10.004.

Hancock, Trevor, and Clement Bezold. 1993. "Possible Futures, Preferable Futures," *The Healthcare Forum Journal,* 37: 23–29.

Hansen, M. M. et al., 2014. "Big Data in Science and Healthcare: A Review of Recent Literature and Perspectives: Contribution of the IMIA Social Media Working Group," *Yearbook of Medical Informatics* 9, no. 1: 21.

Hickey, Phil. 2013. "Medical Model vs. Psychosocial/Behavioral Model," *Behaviorism and Mental Health.* http://behaviorismandmentalhealth.com/2013/08/01/medical-model-vs-psychosocialbehavioral-model/.

Highlands Islands Enterprises. 2012. "P4 Digital Healthcare Scoping Study," http://www.hie.co.uk/common/handlers/download-document.ashx?id=fe60f4e4-b9eb-4745-933b-bff13b6eab3c.

Hood, Leroy. 2013. "Systems Biology and p4 Medicine: Past, Present, and Future," *The Rambam Maimonides Medical Journal* 4, no. 2: e0012.

Kahana, Eva et al. 2002. "Long-Term Impact of Preventive Proactivity on Quality of Life of the Old-Old," *Psychosomatic Medicine* 64, no. 3: 382–394, doi: 10.1097/00006842-200205000-00003.

Kahana, Eva, and Boaz Kahana. 2007. "Health Care Partnership Model of Doctor-Patient Communication in Cancer Prevention and Care Among the Aged," in *Handbook of Communication and Cancer Care*, eds. O'Hair, H. Dan, Gary L. Kreps, and Lisa Daniel Sparks, New York, NY: Hampton Press, 37–54.

Kahana, Eva, Boaz Kahana, and Jeong Eun Lee. 2014. "Proactive Approaches to Successful Aging: One Clear Path Through the Forest," *Gerontology* 60, no. 5: 466–474, doi: 10.1159/000360222.

Kahana, Eva, Jessica Kelley-Moore, and Boaz Kahana. 2012. "Proactive Aging: A Longitudinal Study of Stress, Resources, Agency, and Well-Being in Late Life," *Aging & Mental Health* 16, no. 4: 438–451, doi: 10.1080/136078 63.2011.644519.

Kahana, Eva et al. 2011. "Health-Care Consumerism and Access to Health Care: Educating Elders to Improve Both Preventive and End-of-Life Care," in *Access to Care and Factors that Impact Access, Patients as Partners in Care and Changing Roles of Health Providers*, ed. Jennie Jacobs Kronenfeld, vol. 29. Bingley, UK Emerald Group Publishing Limited, 173–193. http://www.emeraldinsight.com/doi/abs/10.1108/S0275-4959%282011% 290000029010.

Kahana, E. et al. 2013. "Altruism, Helping, and Volunteering: Pathways to Well-Being in Late Life," *Journal of Aging and Health* 25, no. 1: 159–187, doi: 10.1177/0898264312469665.

Keeney, Ralph, L. 2008. "Personal Decisions are the Leading Cause of Death," *Operations Research* 56, no. 6: 1335–1347.

Kelley-Moore, J. A. et al. 2006. "When do Older Adults Become 'Disabled'? Social and Health Antecedents of Perceived Disability in a Panel Study of the Oldest Old," *Journal of Health and Social Behavior* 47, no. 2: 126–141, doi: 10.1177/002214650604700203.

Klein, S. et al. 2012. "Evaluating the Effectiveness of a Web-Based Intervention to Promote Mental Wellbeing in Women and Partners Following Miscarriage, Using a Modified Patient Preference Trial Design: An External Pilot: External Pilot of a Web-Based Intervention Post-Miscarriage," *BJOG: An International Journal of Obstetrics & Gynaecology* 119, no. 6: 762–767, doi: 10.1111/j.1471-0528.2012.03302.x.

Kreps, Gary L., and Edward W. Maibach. 2008. "Transdisciplinary Science: The Nexus Between Communication and Public Health," *Journal of Communication* 58, no. 4: 732–748, doi: 10.1111/j.1460-2466.2008.00411.x.

Legato, Marianne J., and John P. Bilezikian. 2009. *Principles of Gender-Specific Medicine*, vol. 2 London, Burlington & San Diego: Gulf Professional Publishing.

Luciano, Joanne S. et al. 2013. "The Emergent Discipline of Health Web Science," *Journal of Medical Internet Research* 15, no. 8: e166, doi: 10.2196/jmir.2499.

Luciano, Joanne S. et al. 2014. "Health Web Science," *Foundations and Trends in Web Science* 4, no. 4: 269–419, doi: 10.1561/1800000019.

McHattie, Lynn-Sayers, Grant Cumming, and Tara French. 2014. "Transforming Patient Experience: Health Web Science Meets Medicine 2.0," *Medicine 2.0* 3, no. 1.

Medicine. 2.0. 2008. "Presentations and Authors," *Medicine 2.0'08* (Toronto, Canada, September 3–4, 2008) http://www.medicine20congress.com/ocs/index.php/med/med2008/schedConf/presentations. Accessed May 20, 2016.

Medicine. 2.0. 2014. "Introductory Talk to Medicine," *Medicine 2.0'14* (Malaga, Spain, October 9–10, 2014). http://www.medicine20congress.com/ocs/index.php/med/med2014b. Accessed May 20, 2016.

M-Files. 2013. "What Is Metadata, and Why Is it Important?" http://www.mfiles.com/blog/what-is-metadata-and-why-is-it-important. Accessed May 20, 2016.

Miller, Janice, Carol Bennett, and Grant Cumming. 2011. "Potentially Changing Health Behaviour Using Nappy 'Nudges'," *British Journal of Midwifery* 19, no. 4: 246–251, doi: 10.12968/bjom.2011.19.4.246.

Murray, Elizabeth. 2012. "Web-Based Interventions for Behavior Change and Self-Management: Potential, Pitfalls, and Progress," *Medicine 2.0* 1, no. 2: e3, doi: 10.2196/med20.1741.

NISO Press. 2004. "Understanding Metadata," *National Information Standards*, 20. http://www.niso.org/publications/press/UnderstandingMetadata.pdf.

Peacock, Sylvia E., and Harald Künemund. 2007. "Senior Citizens and Internet Technology: Reasons and Correlates of Access Versus Non-Access in a European Comparative Perspective," *European Journal of Ageing* 4, no. 4: 191–200, doi: 10.1007/s10433-007-0067-z.

Prochaska, James O., and Wayne F. Velicer. 1997. "The Transtheoretical Model of Health Behavior Change," *American Journal of Health Promotion* 12, no. 1: 38–48.

Rouse, William B. 2008. "Health Care as a Complex Adaptive System: Implications for Design and Management," *(The Bridge) National Academy of Engineering* 38, no. 1: 17–25.

Schafer, M. H., and K. F. Ferraro. 2012. "Childhood Misfortune as a Threat to Successful Aging: Avoiding Disease," *The Gerontologist* 52, no. 1: 111–120, doi: 10.1093/geront/gnr071.

Seçkin, Gül and Eva Kahana. 2015. "Smart Phone Health Applications," in *Encyclopedia of Mobile Phone Behavior*, ed. Zheng Yan. Hersey, PA: IGI Global, 898–905. doi: 10.4018/978-1-4666-8239-9.ch073.

Selwyn, Neil et al. 2003. "Older Adults' Use of Information and Communications Technology in Everyday Life," *Ageing and Society* 23, no. 05: 561–582, doi: 10.1017/S0144686X03001302.

Shiao, S. P. K., Yu, C. A., Xie, C., Ho, S. (2015, February). *Big Data Analytics on Common Gene Mutations in Epigenetics Methylation Pathways: Population Health Issues for Cancer Prevention*. 2015 AACR Computational and Systems Biology of Cancer Conference, San Francisco, California. DOI: 10.13140/2.1.4214.1762.

The Web Science Trust. 2016. http://www.webscience.org. Accessed May 20, 2016.

Wanless, Derek. 2002. *Securing Our Future Health: Taking a Long-Term View*. London: HM Treasury: 16.

Web Observatory. 2016. *The Web Science Trust*. http://webscience.org/web-observatory. Accessed May 20, 2016.

WHO |World Health Statistics 2011. http://www.who.int/whosis/whostat/2011/en/. Accessed May 20, 2016.

6

Evaluation Frameworks for Health Virtual Communities

Christo El Morr and Linda Eftychiou

6.1 Introduction

Virtual communities (VCs) or online communities are groups of users of an online system communicating to achieve a goal. Many aspects of VCs have been researched for many years, among which is evaluation. VC evaluation has been the subject of many research projects (Phippen et al. 2004; Avila et al. 2011; Seffah et al. 2006) that looked particularly into *usability* (Alfano et al. 2012; Farinha and Silva 2013; Koh and Kim 2003; Zarinah and Siti 2009), *effectiveness* (Bender et al. 2013; Ellonen et al. 2013; Vasconcellos-Silva et al. 2013), and *impact* (Aujoulat et al. 2007; Cox 2007; Loane and D'Alessandro 2013).

However, the measurements used to evaluate VCs do not take into account some particularities of the Health Virtual Communities (Health VCs) such as the impact of the patient's health condition on

C. El Morr (✉) · L. Eftychiou
School of Health Policy & Management, York University,
Toronto, Canada
e-mail: elmorr@yorku.ca; linda.eftychiou@hotmail.ca

© The Author(s) 2017
L. Menvielle et al. (eds.), *The Digitization of Healthcare*,
DOI 10.1057/978-1-349-95173-4_6

software usability and the effect of the Health VC on health outcomes. In this chapter, we give an overview of existing literature related to VC evaluation, and summarize the main VC evaluation limitations and challenges, particularly the need for a framework for VC evaluation. We then look into the available frameworks to evaluate information technology and information systems and their ability to VCs, and lay out the need for a framework to evaluate Health VC.

6.2   Virtual Communities and Health Virtual Communities

VCs are a community of people meeting in a virtual location (online) to achieve a goal or purpose (Levinson and Christensen 2003). A VC is formed of a group of people socially interacting (Weissman 2000), performing specific roles within the community to accomplish an aim (e.g., the reason behind the community) (Preece 2000). VC concept started to flourish with the emergence of the web era at the beginning of 1990s. However, Rheingold coined the term "virtual community" before the web was born, while he was participating in an online community for conversation and discussion in the 1980s: the Whole Earth 'Lectronic Link (WELL) (Rheingold 2000).

An online community has explicit and implicit policies that govern members' interaction. These policies cover specific roles (e.g., such as administrator) and communication mechanisms. A computer system is the technological heart of a VC; it aims at supporting the social interaction between community members within the agreed-upon policies and roles. Members of the community may have many roles depending on the purpose of the VC and its policies (e.g., administrator, consumer of information, and producer of information).

The concept of VC has been approached from many angles by researchers working in wide variety of fields (El Morr and Kawash 2007).

Moreover, with the emergence of mobile technology, Mobile Virtual Community (MVC) emerged as a potent research and development field. Researchers in VCs investigated the infrastructure needed to sustain accessible services (Kaji et al. 2002; Sousa and Garlan 2002), the user interface requirements (Cole and Stanton 2003; Rantanen et al. 2004), wearable computing (Kortuem and Segall 2003), impact on workplace (Churchill et al. 2004), education (Cole and Stanton 2003; Schubert and Koch 2003), and applications such as gaming (Carter and Fisher 2004; Mandryk and Inkpen 2004). With the introduction of Geographic Positioning System (GPS) to mobile devices, location-based services were quick to appear as a topic of interest, especially in lifestyle applications (Brown et al. 2005; Tasch and Brakel 2004). Health-care VCs were relatively slower to emerge (Jimison et al. 1999; Patrick et al. 1999). Health VCs had their own characteristics and critical issues to solve such as trust of between members and trust of information (Abdul-Rahman and Hailes 2000). Among the first known project is the Comprehensive Health Enhancement Support System (CHESS) that targeted patients with HIV (Gustafson et al. 1999) and breast cancer (Arnold et al. 2003). Other projects addressed health-care services for cancer patients (Leimeister et al. 2003; Arnold et al. 2004, 2003), elderly (Abascal et al. 2004), primary care (Abos Mendizabal et al. 2013), pediatric (Bers et al. 2010), health promotion (Crespo 2007), emergency preparedness (Curran et al. 2009), Parkinson disease (Dorsey et al. 2016), rural health (Godden and Aaraas 2006), diabetes (Vorderstrasse et al. 2014), chronic kidney diseases (El Morr et al. 2014), and other variety of health-care-related problems.

Health VCs are divided into two categories, patient-centric communities (Temesgen et al. 2006; Cheng and Arthur 2002) that evolve around the patients' needs, and Virtual Communities of Practice (VCoP) that are geared toward communication between specific health-care professionals (e.g., nurses, doctors) (Davies et al. 2003). While both types of communities need to be evaluated each has different objectives, type of users, and environments; any evaluation framework should take into account these variations in characteristics.

6.3   Virtual Community Evaluation

6.3.1   Background on Evaluation of VC

Since the inception of VCs, researchers followed many approaches to evaluate different aspects of VCs. For instance, some researchers were interested in demonstrating the effect of VCs on collaboration, they reported that VCs increase chances of collaboration (Ansell 2007; Rooke et al. 2012), while others looked into knowledge exchange (Alexander et al. 2003; El Morr et al. 2008). Moreover, basic evaluations techniques were put in place (Kilpatrick 2001; Fletcher et al. 2002), these techniques used simple metrics, such as the number of page views and the number of hits (Fletcher et al. 2002). Furthermore, researchers looked into different aspects of VC impact such as improving adherence to VC objectives (e.g., therapeutic program) (Richardson et al. 2010), the VC impact on products and services (Sullivan et al. 2007), and usability and sociability (Preece 2000).

In health care, many studies have looked into VC impact such as strategies to enhance patient adherence to therapy (Richardson et al. 2010), enhancement of community member use of the VC (Bender et al. 2013). The types of VC the researchers looked at where of both types: peer-to-peer (Eysenbach et al. 2004) and VCoPs (Li et al. 2009; Probst and Borzillo 2008), the latter showed improvement in health-care practice among its professional members (Ranmuthugala et al. 2011).

From the social perspective, the impact of VC on users behavior has been investigated by researchers in psychology and social sciences, using a variety of techniques including ethnography (Paccagnella 1997), or what was later called e-ethnography or virtual ethnography (Hine 2000).

Despite all these efforts and progress, the use of metrics remains limited and used mainly for VC from the business perspective (e.g., customer to product relationship) (Sterne and Cutler 2000). However, we have seen lately some Internet-related measurements that go beyond the simple number of page views and number of hits to include login, time and date of login, the number of referrals a VC member makes to a resource accessed through the VC, and the number of "sharing" made inside the VC (Nonnecke et al. 2006; Wellman et al. 2002). It was a matter of time till few frameworks to evaluate VCs have emerged.

6.3.2 An Example of VC Evaluation: Evaluating a Physician VCoP

Based on a questionnaire analysis, Jones et al. (Jones et al. 2013) specify five aspects for the success of a VC, in particular the VCoP; these aspects include (1) *Access* and *Usage* (e.g., availability of Internet at home, time spent online, purpose of online activity), (2) *Confidence* using computer tools (e.g., discussion boards, Wikis, blogs), (3) perceived *Usefulness* of the online experience in relation to the purpose (e.g., keeping in touch with others, job networking, social support, resourcefulness, knowledge sharing), (4) *Barriers to use:* (e.g., privacy, time), and lastly (5) *Intention to Use* (i.e., likeliness of future use). The same authors analyzed the Probst success model (Probst and Borzillo 2008) in VCoP and found that (1) a motivating *leadership*, (2) clear *objectives*, (3) senior executive *sponsorship*, (4) *Boundary Spanning* (engaging in benchmarking), (4) the existence of a *risk-free environment*, and (5) the use of *measurements* to assess the value of a VC are all important major characteristics of a successful VCoP (Barnett et al. 2012). Most of the work in VC evaluation was based on particular study objectives, which stirred more work toward the development of a framework for VC evaluation.

6.3.3 Work Toward a VC Evaluation Framework

In an article published in 2004 (Phippen 2004), Phippen noticed the lack of techniques available to analyze the web logs and uncover rich community experiences over time, and suggested the use of advanced web analytics, adapted from the business domain, in VC evaluation. The author suggested the application of advanced business analytics to understand the complexity of VC interactions and stressed the need of an evaluative strategy that goes beyond measurements. However, the author did not propose a particular framework for VC evaluation, instead he settled for demonstrating that the advance web analytics, such as resource usage and language usage, can serve the evaluation purpose in VCs.

In 2007, Hersberger et al. suggested a framework for evaluating information exchange and VCs (Hersberger et al. 2007). The framework was based on Gusfield community theory (Gusfield 1978; McMillan 1996) and has put emphasis on the information-sharing behaviors, as well as the affective contexts in online communities. While the framework is beneficial in understanding how communities are formed or shaped, it does not look into the measurements needed to evaluate VCs. Such measurements appeared in the work of Blanchard et al. who investigated the sense of community and its impact on certain types of VCs (Blanchard et al. 2011; Chandra et al. 2013). Blanchard's work, building on McMillan and Chavis (McMillan and Chavis. 1986), and developed a clear measurement of the "sense of community" in a virtual environment, that is, the Sense of Virtual Community (SOVC). These were all important methods to VC evaluations, however none of them suggested a framework or took a holistic approach to the problem.

6.4   VC Evaluation: Perspectives on VC Evaluation Frameworks

Currently there are three frameworks that could be used to evaluate a VC, the Technology Acceptance Model (TAM) (Holden and Karsh 2010; Chuttur 2009), Reach Effectiveness Adoption Implementation Maintenance (RE-AIM) (Ridgeway et al. 2015), and Guide to Monitoring and Evaluating Health Information Products and Services (Sullivan et al. 2007).

6.4.1 The Technology Acceptance Model (TAM)

For an IT system to become successfully adopted, a user must be *motivated* to use the system. Fred Davis proposed the TAM (Davis 1986) as a framework to measure a user's motivation to adopt an IT system, using three factors: *perceived ease of use* (i.e., how easy it is to use/ navigate), *perceived usefulness* (in terms of completing tasks), *and attitude toward using* the system (Fig. 6.1). Attitude toward a system is at the root of the model, with perceived ease of use directly influencing perceived usefulness and in turn impacting one's attitude to either use or reject a system. Davis hypothesized that these in turn are influenced by the way a system is designed—that is, system characteristics (Chuttur 2009).

TAM became the basis for researchers in the IT field when developing and testing a new system; however, variability between studies made it difficult to compare TAM studies.

The model is constantly evolving, as Davis himself and other researchers have added other variables and relationships over time (Chuttur 2009). However, TAM was originally developed for IT outside of the health-care field (such as in education, finance, etc.), its concepts and measures are not always translatable in practice by health-care researchers and professionals. Since IT systems in health care are often used by clinicians, Holden and Karsh (Holden and Karsh 2010) recommend carrying out a beliefs elicitation study to grasp the prominent beliefs and reasons behind clinicians' choice to use (or not to use) an IT system. We believe that this same approach can be translatable in terms of VCs with the target population being users of the VC for developers to gain insight into the success (or failure) of VCs.

Modified TAM has been suggested to evaluate the user acceptance of technology in health care. Gagnon et al. have used a modified TAM,

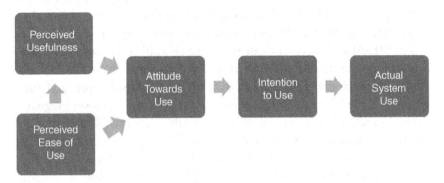

Fig. 6.1 TAM model

adapted from a telemedicine acceptance model (Chau and Hu 2002) to assess health-care professional adoption of tele-monitoring systems (Gagnon et al. 2012). The model took into consideration the individual context, the technological context, and the organizational context, and included TAM into the individual context. That modified version of TAM proved to be a good predictor of acceptance with the presence of facilitators in the organization as the most prominent predictor of adoption. Terrizi et al. included a dimension of trust and information sharing into TAM and showed statistically significant effect of the modified model to acceptance (Terrizzi et al. 2012).

TAM model has been validated and deemed reliable many times, it is a good candidate to be adapted to evaluate Health VCs; however, it is limited to the acceptance and adoption of the Health VC.

6.4.2 The RE-AIM Framework

The RE-AIM Framework developed by Glasgow et al. (Glasgow, Vogt, and Boles 1999) offers a framework to evaluate the impact of health promotion interventions: Reach, Effectiveness, Adoption, Implementation, and Maintenance. *Reach* measures the number of participants in a system as well as their representativeness; *Effectiveness* assess patient reported outcomes such as satisfaction level, perceived quality of care, and utilization; *Adoption* assess the extent to which participants actually use the intervention with ease; *Implementation* is ensuring the intervention is implemented as outlined in the planning stages; and lastly, *Maintenance* is a post-study measurement that assesses the extent to which users continue to use the intervention (Fig. 6.2).

The RE-AIM framework can therefore be applied to various health-care settings that traditionally often require frequent visits to the doctor's office. For example, Ridgeway et al. (2015) developed a prenatal care system and used RE-AIM to evaluate if the system can empower pregnant women to retain more control over their health care as well as the system sustainable adoption and implementation. RE-AIM was used in public intervention in many contexts, particularly Internet-based programs (Glasgow et al. 2007) and proved to be effective; it would be a good candidate to evaluate health VC impact.

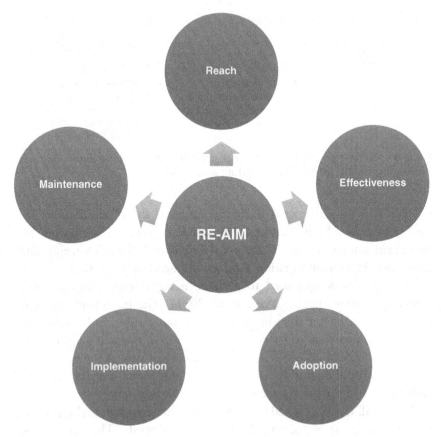

Fig. 6.2   RE-AIM model

6.4.3   The Guide to Monitoring and Evaluating Health Information Products and Services

When developing public health programs, it is important to ensure the information products and services are of high quality determined by best practices and evidence-based policies and guidelines (Sullivan et al. 2007). Due to a lack of guidelines on assessing information products and services the *Guide to Monitoring and Evaluating Health Information Products and Services* [89] was developed. The guide consists of 29 indicators that measure *reach, usefulness, use,* and *impact* of information products and

Fig. 6.3 Partial depiction of the conceptual framework for monitoring and evaluating health information product and services

services and how this can ultimately improve the dissemination and quality of public health services. The Guide suggested a framework for evaluation known as the "Conceptual Framework for Monitoring and Evaluating Health Information Product and Services" (Fig. 6.3).

The framework was used to evaluate many systems among which virtual discussion forums (Avila et al. 2011). The framework suggests that when reach and usefulness (i.e., user satisfaction and quality) of information products and services are maximized, this will help increase the use (i.e., adoption) of these same products, as well as inform discussions around public health policy and program formation, training and education, and further research (Sullivan et al. 2007).

Avila et al. (Avila et al. 2011) applied this framework to evaluate a VC that functions as a forum. Researchers developed "The Knowledge Gateway," an online platform that supports VCoPs. The platform aimed at increasing collaboration, promoting knowledge sharing, and exchange of information and in best-practices approaches among reproductive health-care professionals. The authors suggested a two-step evaluation:

- Determining the value of the discussions;
- Exploring the data in-depth via interviews.

To determine the value of the forum discussions they analyzed the *Reach, Usefulness,* and *Use. Reach* analysis encompassed the analysis of the number of registered participants and the number of participants who downloaded, shared, or forwarded resources to others.

Usefulness was investigated to understand users' satisfaction and their perception of quality. Users were asked if they felt that there was (1) the right amount of discussions, (2) if the forums met their goals, (3) if they had the right frequency of email notifications about online postings, and (4) if it was useful to have a guest expert in the online discussion in place.

Finally, *Use* analysis was based on the actual member use, or intent to use, of information available in the community, which measures if the collaboration between members was facilitated by the VC.

An in-depth exploration survey and telephone interviews were conducted to understand how the environment was informed, for instance whether evidence-based information contributed to policy-making and an increase in resources, whether the programs and practices were enhanced (e.g., adoption of evidence-based practice), and whether the collaboration and capacity building were facilitated (e.g., increase availability and access to information, surge in sharing of knowledge and experiences). However, the approach of Avila et al. was limited to online discussion forums of VCoP.

6.5 Conclusion

VCs are very important rising technologies that are increasingly used in health care. Research in VC evaluation has been focused on few aspects of a complex problem and therefore was limited in scope. TAM is a framework with proven track record and focuses on evaluating the adoption of a technology, RE-AIM targets the impact of an intervention, and the Conceptual Framework for Monitoring and Evaluating Health Information Product and Services has the advantage of being information system specific and tested in VCoP.

While the RE-AIM framework offers a complete cycle of evaluation including the implementation and maintenance of a system, we are inclined to The Framework for Monitoring and Evaluating Health Information Product and Services as it offers a pragmatic evaluation of a solution based on its direct effect measured by the four factors: reach, usefulness, use, and impact.

However, we believe that it is necessary to conduct a practical comparative study of the three above-mentioned frameworks in the Health VC context. Such study would uncover the advantages and disadvantage of each framework for Health VCs and eventually develop and propose a new framework dedicated for Health VC evaluation.

The need to an evaluation framework for Health VCs is high; such framework would take into consideration some new aspects that are specific to VCs, such as connectedness and community. These aspects can be added to the existing model. Future work is likely to give birth to a new Health VC Evaluation Framework.

From a management point of view, current practices in many countries link allocation of resources to performance indicators of the different health-care initiatives. Evidence-based resource allocation requires valid tools; therefore, managers dealing with VCs need evaluation criteria to measure Health VCs the performance as well as impact and allocate resources based on evidence. In addition to resource allocation challenges, there is a need to make the case for the effectiveness and cost effectiveness of Health VCs, especially for start-up companies. Managers and Chief Executive Officers (CEOs) of start-ups need a framework to evaluate their Health VC solutions to raise more funds and sell their products. Having a framework for Health VC evaluation will not only allow evaluation of Health VC solutions but also allow managers, health-care providers, and patients to compare solutions' performances and make decisions accordingly. Future research and development in Health VC evaluation will open new perspectives for health-care providers, patients, and vendors of eHealth solutions and might trigger innovation in the Health VC area.

References

Abascal, Julio, Myriam Arrue, Inmaculada Fajardo, Nestor Garay, and Tomás Jorge. 2004. "The use of guidelines to automatically verify Web accessibility." *Universal Access in the Information Society* 3(1): 71–79.

Abdul-Rahman, Alfarez, and Stephen Hailes. 2000. "Supporting trust in virtual communities." 33rd Hawaii International Conference on System Sciences, Maui, Hawaii, 4–7 January.

Abos Mendizabal, Galder, Roberto Nuño Solinís, and Irune Zaballa González. 2013. "HOBE+, a case study: A virtual community of practice to support innovation in primary care in Basque public health service." *BMC Family Practice* 14: 168–168. doi: 10.1186/1471-2296-14-168.

Alexander, Ardichvili, Page Vaughn, and Wentling Tim. 2003. "Motivation and barriers to participation in virtual knowledge sharing communities of practice." *Journal of Knowledge Management* 7(1): 64–77.

Alfano, Iole, Manuela Carini, and Lorella Gabriele. 2012. "Building SCIENAR, a virtual community of artists and scientists: Usability testing for the system improvement." In *Virtual communities, social networks and collaboration,* edited by A. Athina Lazakidou, 147–161. New York, NY: Springer New York.

Ansell, C. 2007. "Fostering innovation and collaboration." *Medical Device Technology* 18(1): 52.

Arnold, Y., J.M. Leimeister, and H. Krcmar. 2003. "CoPEP: A development process model for community platforms for cancer patients." The XIth European Conference on Information Systems (ECIS).

Arnold, Y., M. Daum, and H. Krcmar. 2004. "Virtual communities in health care: Roles, requirements and restrictions." Multikonferenz Wirtschaftsinformatik (MKWI), Multikonferenz Wirtschaftsinformatik (MKWI), March 9–11, 2004.

Aujoulat, I., W. d'Hoore, and A. Deccache. 2007. "Patient empowerment in theory and practice: Polysemy or cacophony?" *Patient Education and Counseling* 66(1): 13–20.

Avila, Megan, Kavitha Nallathambi, Catherine Richey, and Lisa Mwaikambo. 2011. "Six years of lessons learned in monitoring and evaluating online discussion forums." *Knowledge Management & E-Learning: An International Journal* 3: 621–643.

Barnett, Stephen, Sandra C. Jones, Sue Bennett, Don Iverson, and Andrew Bonney. 2012. "General practice training and virtual communities of practice—a review of the literature." *BMC Family Practice* 13(1): 1–12. doi: 10.1186/1471-2296-13-87.

Bender, J. L., M. C. Jimenez-Marroquin, L. E. Ferris, J. Katz, and A. R. Jadad. 2013. "Online communities for breast cancer survivors: A review and analysis of their characteristics and levels of use." *Support Care Cancer* 21: 1253–1263. doi: 10.1007/s00520-012-1655-9.

Bers, Marina U., Laura M. Beals, Clement Chau, D. Keiko Satoh, Elizabeth D. Blume, David Ray DeMaso, and Joseph Gonzalez-Heydrich. 2010.

"Use of a virtual community as a psychosocial support system in pediatric transplantation." *Pediatric Transplantation* 14(2): 261–267. doi: 10.1111/j.1399-3046.2010.01271.x.

Blanchard, Anita L., Jennifer L. Welbourne, and Marla D. Boughton. 2011. "A model of online trust." *Information, Communication & Society* 14: 76–106. doi: 10.1080/13691181003739633.

Brown, Barry, Matthew Chalmers, Marek Bell, Malcolm Hall, Ian MacColl, and Paul Rudman. 2005. "Sharing the square: Collaborative leisure in the city streets." In *ECSCW 2005: Proceedings of the ninth European conference on computer-supported cooperative work*, 18–22 September 2005, Paris, France, edited by Hans Gellersen, Kjeld Schmidt, Michel Beaudouin-Lafon, and Wendy Mackay, 427–447. Dordrecht: Springer Netherlands.

Carter, William, and Scott S. Fisher. 2004. "Mobile sound communities." *Proceedings of the 2004 ACM SIGCHI International Conference on Advances in Computer Entertainment Technology*, Singapore.

Chandra, Anita, Janice C. Blanchard, and Teague Ruder. 2013. "Rand corporation, and district of Columbia healthy communities collaborative." *District of Columbia Community Health needs assessment, Research report.* Santa Monica, CA: RAND Health.

Chau, Patrick Y. K., and Paul J. Hu. 2002. "Examining a model of information technology acceptance by individual professionals: An exploratory study." *Journal of Management Information Systems* 18(4): 191–229.

Cheng, Eric Y., and David Arthur. 2002. "Constructing a virtual behavior change support system: A mobile internet healthcare solution for problem drinkers." European Conference on Information Systems: ECIS 2002 Proceedings, paper 47.

Churchill, Elizabeth, Andreas Girgensohn, Les Nelson, and Alison Lee. 2004. "Blending digital and physical spaces for ubiquitous community participation." *Communication of the ACM* 47(2): 38–44. doi: 10.1145/966389.966413.

Chuttur, Mohammad. 2009. Overview of the technology acceptance model: Origins, developments and future directions. All Sprouts Content.

Cole, Helen, and Dana Stanton. 2003. "Designing mobile technologies to support co-present collaboration." *Personal and Ubiquitous Computing* 7(6): 365–371. doi: 10.1007/s00779-003-0249-4.

Cox, P. (2007). Financing Sustainable Healthcare in Europe: New Approaches for better outcomes. Retrieved from Luxembourg: http://www.sitra.fi/julkaisut/muut/The_Cox_Report.pdf.

Crespo, Richard. 2007. "Virtual community health promotion." *Preventing Chronic Disease* 4(3): A75–A75.

Curran, Janet A., Andrea L. Murphy, Syed Sibte Raza Abidi, Douglas Sinclair, and Patrick J. McGrath. 2009. "Bridging the gap: Knowledge seeking and sharing in a virtual community of emergency practice." *Evaluation & the Health Professions* 32(3): 312–325. doi: 10.1177/0163278709338570.

Davies, John, Alistair Duke, and York Sure. 2003. "OntoShare: A knowledge management environment for virtual communities of practice." KCAP.

Davis, Fred D. 1986. "A technology acceptance model for empirically testing new end-user information systems: Theory and results." Sloan School of Management, Massachusetts Institute of Technology.

El Morr, Christo, and Jalal Kawash. 2007. "Mobile virtual communities research: A synthesis of current trends and a look at future perspectives." *International Journal for Web Based Communities* 3: 386–403.

El Morr, C., C. Cole, and J. Perl. 2014. "A health virtual community for patients with chronic kidney disease." *Procedia Computer Science* 37: 333–339.

El Morr, Christo, Julien Subercaze, Pierre Maret, and Marcia Rioux. 2008. "A virtual knowledge community for human rights monitoring for people with disabilities." IADIS International Conference on Web Based Communities, July 24–26, 2008.

Ellonen, Hanna-Kaisa, Miia Kosonen, Anssi Tarkiainen, and Lisbeth Tonteri. 2013. "The positive outcomes of a sense of virtual community." *International Journal of Web Based Communities* 9: 465–482. doi: 10.1504/IJWBC.2013.057216.

Eysenbach, G., Powell, J., Englesakis, M., Rizo, C., & Stern, A. (2004). Health related virtual communities and electronic support groups: systematic review of the effects of online peer to peer interactions. *BMJ*, 328(7449), 1166.

Farinha, Carla, and Miguel Mira Silva. 2013. "Requirements elicitation with focus groups: Lessons learnt." The 21st European Conference on Information Systems, 2013.

Fletcher, P., A. Poon, B. Pearce, and P. Comber. 2002. *Practical Web Traffic Analysis: Standards, Privacy, Techniques, and Results*. Birmingham, UK: Glasshaus.

Gagnon, Marie Pierre, Estibalitz Orruño, José Asua, Anis Ben Abdeljelil, and José Emparanza. 2012. "Using a modified technology acceptance model to evaluate healthcare professionals' adoption of a new telemonitoring system." *Telemedicine Journal and E-Health* 18(1): 54–59. doi: 10.1089/tmj.2011.0066.

Glasgow, R. E., T. M. Vogt, and S. M. Boles. 1999. "Evaluating the public health impact of health promotion interventions: The RE-AIM framework." *American Journal of Public Health* 89(9): 1322–1327.

Glasgow, R. E., C. C. Nelson, K. A. Kearney, R. Reid, D. P. Ritzwoller, V. J. Strecher, M. P. Couper, B. Green, and K. Wildenhaus. 2007. "Reach, engagement, and retention in an Internet-based weight loss program in a multi-site randomized controlled trial." *Journal of Medical Internet Research* 9. doi: 10.2196/jmir.9.2.e11.

Godden, David J., and Ivar J. Aaraas. 2006. "Making it work 2: Using a virtual community to focus on rural health issues." *Rural and Remote Health* 6(2): 540–540.

Gusfield, J.R. 1978. *Community: A Critical Response*. New York, NY: Harper & Row.

Gustafson, David H., Robert Hawkins, Eric Boberg, Ronald E. Susanne Pingree, Frank Graziano Serlin, and C. L. Chan. 1999. "Impact of a patient-centered, computer-based health information/support system." *American Journal of Preventive Medicine* 16(1): 1–9.

Hersberger, Julia A., Adam L. Murray, and Kevin S. Rioux. 2007. "Examining information exchange and virtual communities: An emergent framework." *Online Information Review* 31(2): 135–147. doi: 10.1108/14684520710747194.

Hine, C. 2000. *Virtual Ethnography*. London, UK: SAGE Publications.

Holden, Richard J., and Ben-Tzion Karsh. 2010. "The technology acceptance model: Its past and its future in health care." *Journal of Biomedical Informatics* 43(1): 159. doi: 10.1016/j.jbi.2009.07.002.

Jimison, Holly, Linda Adler, Molly Coye, Al Mulley Jr, and Thomas R. Eng. 1999. "Health care providers and purchasers and evaluation of interactive health communication applications address reprint requests to: Mary Jo Deering, PhD, Office of Disease Prevention and Health Promotion, U.S. Department of Health and Human Services, 200 Independence Avenue, SW, Washington, DC 20201." *American Journal of Preventive Medicine* 16(1): 16–22.

Jones, Sandra C., Sue Bennett, Don Iverson, Andrew Bonney, and G. Eysenbach. 2013. "Perceptions of family physician trainees and trainers regarding the usefulness of a virtual community of practice." *Journal of Medical Internet Research* 15(5): 1–1.

Kaji, N., K. Ragab, T. Ono, and K. Mori. 2002. "Autonomous synchronization technology for achieving real time property in service oriented community system." Autonomous Decentralized System, 2002. The 2nd International Workshop on, November 6–7, 2002.

Kilpatrick, Ian. 2001. "Too many hits are bad for your web site." *Manager* 25: 17.

Koh, Joon, and Young-Gul Kim. 2003. "Sense of virtual community: A conceptual framework and empirical validation." *International Journal of Electronic Commerce* 8: 75–93.

Kortuem, Gerd, and Zary Segall. 2003. "Wearable communities: Augmenting social Networks with Wearable Computers." *IEEE Pervasive Computing* 2(1): 71–78. doi: 10.1109/mprv.2003.1186728.

Leimeister, J. M., M. Daum, and H. Krcmar. 2003. "Towards m-communities: The case of COSMOS healthcare." The 36th Annual Hawaii International Conference on System Sciences (2003).

Levinson, D., and K. Christensen. 2003. *Encyclopedia of Community: From the Village to the Virtual World.* California, USA: Sage Publications.

Li, L. C., J. M. Grimshaw, C. Nielsen, M. Judd, P. C. Coyte, and I. D. Graham. 2009. "Use of communities of practice in business and health care sectors: A systematic review." *Implementation Science* 4: 27. doi: 10.1186/1748-5908-4-27.

Loane, Susan Stewart, and Steven D'Alessandro. 2013. "Communication that changes lives: Social support within an online health community for ALS." *Communication Quarterly* 61: 236–251. doi: 10.1080/01463373.2012.7 52397.

Mandryk, Regan L., and Kori M. Inkpen. 2004. "Physiological indicators for the evaluation of co-located collaborative play." Proceedings of the 2004 ACM conference on Computer supported cooperative work, Chicago, IL, USA.

McMillan, David W. 1996. "Sense of community." *Journal of Community Psychology* 24(4): 315–325. doi: 10.1002/(SICI)1520-6629(199610) 24:4<315:: AID-JCOP2>3.0.CO;2-T.

McMillan, David W., and David M. Chavis. 1986. "Sense of community: A definition and theory." *Journal of Community Psychology* 14(1): 6–23. doi: 10.1002/1520-6629(198601)14:1<6:: AID-JCOP2290140103>3.0.CO;2-I.

Nonnecke, Blair, Dorine Andrews, and Jenny Preece. 2006. "Non-public and public online community participation: Needs, attitudes and behavior." *Electronic Commerce Research* 6(1): 7–20.

Paccagnella, Luciano. 1997. "Getting the seats of your pants dirty: Strategies for ethnographic research on virtual communities." *Journal of Computer-Mediated Communication* 3(1). http://onlinelibrary.wiley.com/ doi: 10.1111/j.1083-6101.1997.tb00065.x.

Patrick, Kevin, Thomas N. Robinson, Farrokh Alemi, and Thomas R. Eng. 1999. "Policy issues relevant to evaluation of interactive health communication applications Address reprint requests to: Mary Jo Deering, PhD, Office of Disease Prevention and Health Promotion, U.S. Department of Health and Human Services, 200 Independence Avenue, SW, Washington, DC 20201." *American Journal of Preventive Medicine* 16(1): 35–42.

Phippen, A.D. 2004. "An evaluative methodology for virtual communities using web analytics." *Campus-Wide Information Systems* 21(5): 179–184. doi: 10.1108/10650740410567518.

Phippen, A., L. Sheppard, and S. Furnell. 2004. "A practical evaluation of Web analytics." *Internet Research* 14: 284–293. doi: 10.1108/10662240410555306.

Preece, Jenny. 2000. *Online Communities: Designing Usability supporting Sociability.* USA: John Wiley & Sons Ltd.

Probst, Gilbert, and Stefano Borzillo. 2008. "Why communities of practice succeed and why they fail." *European Management Journal* 26(5): 335–347. doi: http://dx.doi.org/10.1016/j.emj.2008.05.003.

Ranmuthugala, Geetha, Jennifer J. Plumb, Frances C. Cunningham, Andrew Georgiou, Johanna I. Westbrook, and Jeffrey Braithwaite. 2011. "How and why are communities of practice established in the healthcare sector? A systematic review of the literature." *BMC Health Services Research* 11(1): 1–16. doi: 10.1186/1472-6963-11-273.

Rantanen, Matti, Antti Oulasvirta, Jan Blom, Sauli Tiitta, and M Martti. #228, ntyl, and #228. 2004. "InfoRadar: Group and public messaging in the mobile context." Proceedings of the third Nordic conference on Human-computer interaction, Tampere, Finland.

Ray, Dorsey E., Meredith A. Achey, Christopher A. Beck, Denise B. Beran, Kevin M. Biglan, Cynthia M. Boyd, Peter N. Schmidt, Richard Simone, Allison W. Willis, Nicholas B. Galifianakis, Maya Katz, Caroline M. Tanner, Kristen Dodenhoff, Nathan Ziman, Jason Aldred, Julie Carter, Joohi Jimenez-Shahed, Christine Hunter, Meredith Spindler, Zoltan Mari, John C. Morgan, Dedi McLane, Patrick Hickey, Lisa Gauger, Irene Hegeman Richard, Michael T. Bull, Nicte I. Mejia, Grace Bwala, Martha Nance, Ludy Shih, Lauren Anderson, Carlos Singer, Cindy Zadikoff, Natalia Okon, Andrew Feigin, Jean Ayan, Christina Vaughan, Rajesh Pahwa, Jessica Cooper, Sydney Webb, Rohit Dhall, Anhar Hassan, Delana Weis, Steven DeMello, Sara S. Riggare, Paul Wicks, Joseph Smith, H. Tait Keenan, Ryan Korn, Heidi Schwarz, Saloni Sharma, E. Anna Stevenson, and William Zhu. 2016. "National randomized controlled trial of virtual house calls for people with Parkinson's disease: Interest and barriers." *Telemedicine Journal and E-Health: the Official Journal of the American Telemedicine Association.* doi: 10.1089/tmj.2015.0191.

Rheingold, H. 2000. *The Virtual Community:Homesteading on the Electronic Frontier.* Cambridge, MA: MIT Press.

Richardson, C. R., L. R. Buis, A. W. Janney, D. E. Goodrich, A. Sen, M. L. Hess, K. S. Mehari, L. A. Fortlage, P. J. Resnick, B. J. Zikmund-Fisher, V. J. Strecher, and J. D. Piette. 2010. "An online community improves adherence in an internet-mediated walking program. Part 1: Results of a randomized controlled trial." *Journal of Medical Internet Research* 12: e71. doi: 10.2196/jmir.1338.

Ridgeway, Jennifer L., Annie LeBlanc, Roger W. Megan Branda, Megan A. Harms, Kate Nesbitt Morris, Bobbie S. Gostout, Lenae M. Barkey, Susan M. Sobolewski, Ellen Brodrick, Jonathan Inselman, Anne Baron, Angela Sivly, Misty Baker, Dawn Finnie, Rajeev Chaudhry, and Abimbola O. Famuyide. 2015. "Implementation of a new prenatal care model to reduce office visits and increase connectivity and continuity of care: Protocol for a mixed-methods study." *BMC Pregnancy and Childbirth* 15: 323. doi: 10.1186/s12884-015-0762-2.

Rooke, T. W., A. T. Hirsch, S. Misra, A. N. Sidawy, J. A. Beckman, L. K. Findeiss, J. Golzarian, H. L. Gornik, J. L. Halperin, M. R. Jaff, G. L. Moneta, J. W. Olin, J. C. Stanley, C. J. White, J. V. White, and R. E. Zierler. 2012. Foundation American college of cardiology, association American heart, angiography society for Cardiovascular, interventions, radiology society of interventional, medicine society for Vascular, and surgery society for vascular. "2011 ACCF/AHA focused update of the guideline for the management of patients with peripheral artery disease (updating the 2005 guideline): A report of the American college of cardiology foundation/ American heart association task force on practice guidelines: Developed in collaboration with the society for cardiovascular angiography and interventions, society of interventional radiology, society for vascular medicine, and society for vascular surgery." *Catheter Cardiovascular Intervention* 79(4): 501–531. doi: 10.1002/ccd.23373.

Schubert, P., and M. Koch. 2003. "Collaboration platforms for virtual student communities." *System Sciences* 2003. Proceedings of the 36th Annual Hawaii International Conference on, 6–9 January 2003.

Seffah, Ahmed, Mohammad Donyaee, Rex B. Kline, and Harkirat K. Padda. 2006. "Usability measurement and metrics: A consolidated model." *Software Quality Journal* 14: 159–178. doi: 10.1007/s11219-006-7600-8.

Sousa, João Pedro, and David Garlan. 2002. "Aura: An architectural framework for user mobility in ubiquitous computing environments." In *Software Architecture: System Design, Development and Maintenance*, edited by Jan Bosch, Morven Gentleman, Christine Hofmeister, and Juha Kuusela, 29–43. Boston, MA: Springer US.

Sterne, J., and M. Cutler. 2000. *E-metrics: Business Metrics for the New Economy*. Cambridge, MA: NetGenesis and Target Marketing.

Sullivan, Tara M, Molly Strachan, and Barbara K Timmons. 2007. *Guide to Monitoring and Evaluating Health Information Products and Services*, edited by Ward Rinehart. Washington, DC: Constella Futures; Cambridge, Massachusetts: Management Sciences for Health. Baltimore, Maryland: Baltimore, Maryland: Center for Communication Programs, Johns Hopkins Bloomberg School of Public Health.

Tasch, Andreas, and Oliver Brakel. 2004. "Location based community services. New services for a new type of web communities." IADIS Conference on Web Based Communities.

Temesgen, Zelalem, James E. Knappe-Langworthy, Mary M. St Marie, Becky A. Smith, and Ross A. Dierkhising. 2006. "Comprehensive health enhancement support system (CHESS) for people with HIV infection." *AIDS and Behavior* 10(1): 35–40.

Terrizzi, Sabrina, Susan Sherer, Chad Meyerhoefer, Michael Scheinberg, and Donald Levick. 2012. "Extending the technology acceptance model in healthcare: Identifying the role of trust and shared information." AMCIS 2012 Proceedings, July 29, 2012.

Vasconcellos-Silva, Paulo Roberto, Darlinton Carvalho, and Carlos Lucena. 2013. "Word frequency and content analysis approach to identify demand patterns in a virtual community of carriers of hepatitis C." *Interactive Journal of Medical Research* 2: e12. doi: 10.2196/ijmr.2384.

Vorderstrasse, Allison, Ryan J. Shaw, Jim Blascovich, and Constance M. Johnson. 2014. "A theoretical framework for a virtual diabetes self-management community intervention." *Western Journal of Nursing Research* 36(9): 1222–1237. doi: 10.1177/0193945913518993.

Weissman, David. 2000. A Social Ontology. Michigan, IN: Yale University Press.

Wellman, Barry, Jeffrey Boase, and Wenhong Chen. 2002. "The networked nature of community online and offline." *IT & Society* 1(1): 151–165.

Zarinah, M. K., and Salwah S. Siti. 2009. "A web-based requirements elicitation tool using focus group discussion in supporting computer-supported collaborative learning requirements development." *International Journal of the Computer, the Internet and Management* 17: 1–8.

7

When Medicine Is Becoming Collaborative: Social Networking Among Health-Care Professionals

Christine Thoër, Florence Millerand
and Nina Duque

7.1 Introduction

Staying informed on the newest evidence-based practices is necessary for health-care professionals (HPCs) and plays a critical role in the quality of care provided (Archambault et al. 2013). However, remaining up-to-date is becoming more and more of a challenge for HCPs as health-care knowledge changes and expands rapidly (McGowan et al. 2012). Tacit knowledge (clinical experiences, skills, and know-how) is of particular importance to enhancing the quality of medical diagnosis and decisions (Panahi 2014).

With the development of the Internet, arrays of online resources for health-care professionals looking for scientific knowledge and best practices have emerged. Among them, are specialized medical websites such as Medscape, QuantiaMD, and iMedExchange. Online information can be

C. Thoër (✉) · F. Millerand · N. Duque
Research Group Health and Media, Department of Public and Social
Communication, UQAM, Montreal, Canada
e-mail: thoer.christine@uqam.ca; millerand.florence@uqam.ca;
duque.nina@uqam.ca

© The Author(s) 2017
L. Menvielle et al. (eds.), *The Digitization of Healthcare*,
DOI 10.1057/978-1-349-95173-4_7

accessed in different ways (Labrecque et Beaupré 2013). The passive approach (push) consists in registering on various websites to receive email alerts on medical topics such as critical reviews or better practice suggestions. The second method is active (pull), the user retrieves information on demand. The third, which we focus on in this chapter, is interactive and calls for a discussion of information with colleagues using various tools such as Wikis, blogs, open social networking platforms (e.g., Twitter or Facebook), and online professional networks. Use of these resources for information sharing as a part of continuing educational activities or discussing clinical issues is growing (Georges et al. 2013). Informal communication among colleagues (oral or written) is not a new phenomenon; it is rooted in the medical culture (Kuo 1998). When looking for new medical developments or when caring for a patient with severe problems, clinicians will often turn to peers and colleagues (Haug 1997). Social media websites and web-based applications offer new potentials for supporting informal communication, allowing for the rapid dissemination of information to a broad audience (Ellison and Boyd 2013). Understanding how everyday communication practices take place online is essential.

This chapter examines the professional use of social networking websites and applications in health-care practices. We outline the reasons HCPs use social media and examine the potential impacts on professional development, collaboration, mentoring, and patient outcomes. We then identify the factors that enable an active participation in these networks as well as ways to address identified use barriers. We conclude by suggesting future research directions.

7.2 How and Why Do Health-Care Professionals Use Social Media to Communicate with Peers?

7.2.1 Professional Social Media Use Is on the Rise

Social media use by health professionals has increased in the past decade (George et al. 2013; Hamm et al. 2013; Antheunis et al. 2013). Social Media websites and applications can be used for social or professional networking (Facebook, Twitter, LinkedIn), media sharing (YouTube), content production (blogs), collaborative writing and knowledge aggregation (Wikis and Google Docs), and virtual reality and gaming environment interactions (George et al. 2013; Hamm et al. 2013; Antheunis et al. 2013). Health-care professionals can also access information and interact with peers on specialized professional online communities developed by health-care organizations, professional associations, health care and pharmaceutical companies, or as part of ongoing research projects. Such networks are commonly restricted to targeted professions (George et al. 2013; Hamm et al. 2013; Antheunis et al. 2013). Studies that evaluate the use of social media by HCPs are of variable quality. An online US survey of 4,000 connected physicians (with access to computers and mobile technology) conducted by QuantiaMD, found that more than 90% of the doctors surveyed use social media websites and web-based applications for personal purposes with Facebook topping the list of website use. Moreover, 65% of the physicians used some form of social media for professional purposes, chiefly online physician communities (28%), LinkedIn (17%), and Facebook (15%) (Modahl et al. 2011). Online media is now the preferred information source for health profession students whose rates of social media use are found to be over 90%, a fact not so surprising, as most of them have grown up in a technologically socially mediated world (Brown et al. 2014; Usher et al. 2014; Giordano et Giordano 2011; George et al. 2013). However, social media use varies widely among HCPs, between age cohorts and across practice settings (Adilman et al. 2016), but most studies have focused on physicians and nurses (Rolls et al. 2016). There are also national differences. A survey conducted in 2012 and involving 6,700 physicians in European countries, the USA, Japan, Brazil, India, China, and Russia showed that the use of social media and online physician communities for professional networking is much more developed in emerging countries, the UK, Germany, and the USA than it is in Italy or France (Cegedim Strategic Data 2012).

What motivates social media use by HCPs is also varied. A qualitative study conducted among 22 physicians around the world revealed six critical adoption factors: staying connected with colleagues, reaching out and networking with the wider community, sharing knowledge, engaging in continued medical training, benchmarking, and branding (Panahi 2014). These motivations are examined in the following sections.

7.2.2 Using Social Media to Address Information Overload

Finding and sharing medical information online regarding issues relevant to their field and staying updated on evidence-based practice guidelines has become very popular, especially among the younger physicians (Almaiman et al. 2015). Online resources act as "apomediaries" helping users seek, filter, and select relevant information (Eysenbach 2008). Following what colleagues are sharing and discussing among themselves is likewise an effective way of addressing informational overload as well as being one of HCPs most popular activities on open and restricted social networks (Antheunis 2013). Through Twitter, for instance, health-care workers can quickly find peer-reviewed information (Panahi 2014). Social media also facilitates tacit and experiential information exchange such as clinical experiences or practical tips. They enable the sharing of information through stories that are "usually carriers of profound contextual understanding, knowledge, and experience that a person shares with other people in very simple language" (Panahi 2014). As Grindrod et al. (2014) point out; social media has reintroduced the power of patient stories and anecdotes that are included in the making of collective medical knowledge.

7.2.3 Social Media Use for Professional Education

Likewise, social media tools are increasingly used for educational purposes and, especially so, by medical students (George et al. 2013). In some US pharmacy programs, students are provided access to course material on Facebook, which seems to be their preferred option (Grindrod et al. 2014). Social media also offer access to information that complements those offered in the traditional medical school curricula, and this knowledge has the benefit of being retrievable on demand (Cartledge et al. 2013). In a qualitative study on Twitter use by medical students, participants reported that the active use of Twitter provided them with access to corresponding information, enabling them to increase their learning opportunities through the sharing of articles and study techniques, while connecting, outside of the classroom, with students and instructors sharing similar interests (Chretien et al. 2015). These students were also able to reach experts they might not have been able to otherwise. However, such benefits were only observed among the active users of Twitter, which represented a minority in the study. Another qualitative study focusing on the use of collaborative writing applications such as Google Docs by medical residents cited that learning consolidation was the main advantage of using social media, but at the same time revealed that motivating residents to contribute to these platforms or applications was a challenge (Archambault et al. 2009). While feedback from users is positive, more evidence on the effectiveness of social media use for educational purposes is needed (Cartledge et al. 2013).

7.2.4 Asking for Advice from Peers Online

Seeking medical advice at the point of care is another often-mentioned objective for utilizing social networking platforms and participating in specialized online communities. Health-care professionals are progressively turning to social media to connect with peers and colleagues when they have questions regarding diseases, diagnoses, or treatment options. Social media is especially useful as it provides the opportunity to exchange texts, photos, and videos. On restricted password protected networks intended for HCPs only, these contents can be exchanged securely.

Crowdsourced social networked answers to clinical questions likewise seem effective in providing expert advice rapidly. For particular health-care specialties, such as clinicians requiring information during infectious disease outbreaks, accessing information in real-time is critical (Goff et al. 2015). In addition to using their personal computer to access information, many HCPs are now using their mobile devices. Studies conducted in emergency departments show that such devices enable HCPs to retrieve information in varying environments and times, while "fitting better" within the daily workflow (Curran and Abidi 2007). By providing exchange opportunities between organizations, social media use can also reduce the professional isolation experienced by HCPs working in rural areas (Rolls et al. 2014). It also updates HCPs on the various ways of practicing medicine around the world allowing them to benchmark the most efficient ones (Panahi 2014).

7.2.5 Collaborative Knowledge Development

Collaborative platforms offer the opportunity to develop and apply knowledge embedded in use. This practice mirrors the concept of Communities of Practice where participants organized around a common purpose engage in a process of collaboration and reflective practice (Wenger 1998). In the health-care field, collaborative platforms and web-based writing applications such as Wikis allow users to create online content that can be accessed or edited by professionals within specific health departments or by anyone wanting to contribute if the Wiki is not restricted. Such tools show potential for updating evidence-based clinical practice guidelines and optimizing clinical practice (Archambault et al. 2013). For example, they can be used at the point of care to store and update protocols within emergency departments (Archambault et al. 2013). Social media can also facilitate health-care research project collaborations as well as enable access to study results. Platforms such as Twitter expand professional and scientific audiences, contributing to the dissemination of knowledge on a global scale (Goff et al. 2015).

7.2.6 Understanding the Broader Health-Care Context and the Patient's Perspective

Social media offers HCPs and students the opportunity to discuss controversial health-care issues, health policies, or health-care reforms with other caregivers and health sector actors (including patients), developing a better understanding of the context in which they practice health care (Chretien et al. 2015).

Social media, especially health blogs, Twitter, or forums allow clinicians access to the patient's perspective, changing the way they see and do medicine (Chretien et al. 2015). Through blogs, chronic patients and family caregivers share their illnesses and everyday life experiences, including interactions with the health-care systems, giving meaning to their experiences. A patient's disease narrative is crucial to understanding and contextualizing the lived experience of being ill. This key health-care dimension can be very helpful in improving communication between HCPs and their patients, and, especially, in promoting reflective practices and empathy. It also helps clinicians better understand the way patients navigate the health-care system, enabling them to direct patients towards the best resources (Batt-Rawden et al. 2014).

7.2.7 Building a Meaningful Professional Identity

Sharing a profile on social media is, furthermore, used for "personal branding" reasons serving to establish one's professional status and credibility while developing partnership opportunities and interprofessional collaborations (Panahi 2014). Social networking platforms offer spaces where HCPs can discuss with peers about their practice experiences (Lagu et al. 2008). Blogs are especially popular. These types of online publications are easy to produce, and the information published is more inviting and accessible than those found in academic journals. Additionally, they allow HCPs to communicate their stories and to express their views and feelings in alternative manners. They can address the doubts, fears, and frustrations experienced in their daily practice (Vartabedian et al. 2011). Participation on open networking platforms such as Twitter also contributes to a professional sense of meaning and community (Chretien et al. 2015) and promotes interest and passion for patient care (Batt-Rawden et al. 2014).

Health-care professionals differ in their use of social media, but a common outcome is a noticeable change in the way they interact and learn. While the reasons HCPs use social media vary, the main benefits seem to be a widening of knowledge networks, access to expertize from colleagues and peers, and the provision of emotional support (Pereira et al. 2015). Active social media use can enhance professional practice and judgment and provide better patient care.

7.3   Barriers to Social Media Use for Health-Care Professionals

While social media use among HCPs is growing, studies have reported several barriers to their adoption. HCPs face several social media adoption challenges (Panahi 2014), and regular professional use of social media is still limited especially for microblogging platforms such as Twitter and Wikis (Chretien and Kind 2013).

7.3.1 Privacy Issues and Liability and Litigation Concerns

Privacy issues and concerns about liability and litigation are some of the main obstacles. Posting information, photos, or videos on a social networking website can be a breach of patient confidentiality and could result in legal actions taken against the HCP or his employer (Ventola 2014). This legal obstacle explains in part the lack of support given to social media use from regulating bodies and medical schools whose discourse has mainly focused on the risks and ethical issues that are associated with its practice (George et al. 2013; Grindrod et al. 2014). Anonymization of personal health information shared on the Internet is one way to minimize risks, but it can sometimes prove difficult. Information provided in a particular case, even if anonymous, could still allow for patient identification within the health-care community (Ventola 2014). Communicating through password-restricted communities might be helpful, but HCP participation in specialized online communities is still limited. Changes in the open social networking platforms that many HCPs use personally, for example, Facebook's private groups offer potential avenues for addressing these privacy issues (George et al. 2013). Another recommendation from regulating bodies is that HCPs draw a strict line between their personal and professional identities when dealing with patients and peers online by using separate social media profiles. Although the line between social and professional use is easily blurred: if I blog on my nursing practice, is it professional or personal? Some applications (such as Google+ for instance) allow users to tailor their profile information to different audiences (George et al. 2013). Users might find, nonetheless, that establishing clear personal/professional profile boundaries is not always the best thing to do. A 2015 study by Chretien et al. (2013) on Twitter use among medical students showed that participants preferred using their personal Twitter account to exchange medical and scientific information with colleagues, emphasizing the importance of being authentic as it proved useful to develop one's professional network (Chretien et al. 2013). Concerns over privacy are also an issue in the classroom as "friending" colleagues or students on Facebook could be considered a violation of age and gender boundaries (Grindrod et al. 2014).

7.3.2 Concerns with the Quality of Information on Social Medial

The scientific quality of the information resources available on social media is also of concern among HCPs as these platforms facilitate fast dissemination of information from varying sources (Panahi 2014). Sufficient participation on social media platforms improves the quality of the information offered as incorrect information is flagged, but trust and identifying whom to follow is a chief concern for many HCPs. In Panahi's (2014) study, conducted among twenty-two active social media user physicians, participants reported establishing trusted online relations first by connecting with people they knew offline, then by using peer recommended resources, through authenticity, and by relying on professional standing, and engaging in consistent communication, and lastly, by favoring non-anonymous posting and moderated websites (Panahi 2014). Reliability of information is also an issue on collaborative writing applications because of the lack of traditional authorship (Archambault et al. 2009).

7.3.3 Limited Time and Lack of Social Media Skills

Other barriers and challenges that HCPs experience when using social media include the lack of skills and self-efficacy to exploit theses online resources efficiently and to deal with information overload and anarchy (Antheunis et al. 2013; Pereira et al. 2015). Finding time to follow health-care issues and topics and post information can also be a problem and some HCPs have limited access to social media in their place of work. Finally, a lack of understanding of the benefits that social media use can provide HCPs and a feeling that professional engagement on these platforms is a waste of time limits their use, especially with older and established HCPs (George et al. 2013).

7.4 Addressing Social Media Use Barriers

To improve the potential of social media use, researchers have identified several ways to address the barriers to their use and to foster HCPs participation and engagement on these platforms.

7.4.1 Guiding Social Media Practice

There is a need to provide HCPs and medical students with directives and clear guidelines to help them develop the best possible social media practices (Househ 2013). Faculty should address e-professionalism and encourage students to reflect on their use of social media (Grindrod et al. 2014). Professional organizations and regulation bodies should also focus less on social media misuse and instead develop strategies to use these platforms effectively to communicate with patients and peers (George et al. 2013). University curricula, as well as continuing education programs, should include workshops on HCP social media strategies and provide institutional credits for participation. One way this could be done is by reaching out and partnering with non-medical disciplines such as Communication Studies (George et al. 2013).

7.4.2 Encouraging Active Social Media Users to Act as Mentors

Active professional participation on social networks is equally an issue. Compensating established HCPs leaders for sharing information and for engaging on these platforms (for example, by providing continuing education credits) would be very useful as the available time HCPs have to participate on social media is limiting. Their experience can serve as best practice examples for students and other professionals (George et al. 2013). Social media can also be used to strengthen mentoring activities especially for HCPs who subspecialize (Ventola 2014) as well as encouraging the positive use of these platforms (George et al. 2013).

7.4.3 Using Social Media Will Make You a Better Health-Care Professional

Incorporating social media use into health-care training should target enhancing HCPs' reflective practice. Patients' presence on these platforms is increasing, and this is changing the way they deal with their health issues as well as the way they interact with HCPs (Thoër 2013; Grindrod et al. 2014). HCPs should take advantage of these patient-focused networks to gain insights on patient experience and on ways to manage treatments better so that patients can easily adopt them. Social media also offers great interaction enhancing potential between patients and various professionals. Because medical knowledge is no longer within the exclusive control of medical experts on social media, it is crucial that HCPs participate on these platforms (Thoër 2013; Grindrod et al. 2014). HCPs engagement on social networks is critical to improving the quality of health information provided to the community through the Internet (Ventola 2014).

7.5 Conclusion

Social media use by health-care professionals is on the rise, but its use is still limited and varies according to specific professions and practice settings. This relatively slow appropriation of social media by HCPs can be explained in part by the fact that regulation bodies, medical training centers, and schools and health-care organizations have not encouraged their use. Moreover, these practices may be seen as contrary to the prevailing medical culture, which prioritizes individual and face-to-face communication, confidentiality, and the formal production and movement of knowledge (Brown et al. 2014; George and Green 2012). Practices are rapidly changing, and the younger generations are more apt to adopt social media. Several organizations and schools are now promoting efficient and active use of social media.

The literature suggests that there are several benefits to social media use by HCPs. Among them, they enhance the sharing of evidence-based and tacit knowledge. Accordingly, their use could facilitate and accelerate the exchange of informal information that is at the heart of HCPs practices. Also, as social media can expand connections and networks of relationships as one of their key features, an increased use by HCPs may foster the development of new contacts and partnerships between HCPs within a professional domain as well as between domains. There are, however, legitimate concerns regarding confidentiality, private/public boundaries, and the accuracy of online information. Further research will be needed to understand exactly how it is that social media use contributes to improved knowledge, skills, and quality of care outcomes as well as health-care professionals' satisfaction (Batt-Rawden et al. 2014; McGowan et al. 2012). So far, research on social media and HCPs has focused mainly on documenting uses with a marked preference on doctor-patient communication practices. Examining how and in what contexts the use of social media transforms communication practices among health-care professionals will be essential in understanding and evaluating the impacts of social media use by HCPs. It will also be necessary to document how health professionals, other than doctors, use these platforms for peer interactions. These traces will help identify successful social networking strategies and those that should be shared as well as promoted among clinicians (George et al. 2013).

As such, further research is needed to develop, implement, and evaluate the training strategies that would encourage the appropriation of social media in clinical practice, for patient communication, but also among colleagues and peers. In general, communication between HCPs occupies little space in most training programs (Galarneau, et al. 2016). The increase in social media use by patients, as well as by HCPs, offers researchers not only the opportunity to reflect on professional health communication practices but also an occasion to reconsider and rethink these practices. While professional social media use is still limited, we believe that it will become an essential tool for everyday medical practice.

References

Adilman, Rachel, et al. 2016. "ReCAP: Social Media Use Among Physicians and Trainees: Results of a National Medical Oncology Physician Survey." Journal of Oncology Practice 12 (no. 1): 79–80. doi: 10.1200/JOP.2015.006429.

Almaiman, Sarah, et al. 2015. "The Prevalence of Using Social Media Among Healthcare Professionals in Saudi Arabia: A Pilot Study." Studies in Health Technology and Informatics 213: 263–266.

Antheunis, Marjolijn L., Kiek Tates, and Theodoor E. Nieboer. 2013. "Patients' and Health Professionals' Use of Social Media in Health Care: Motives, Barriers and Expectations." Patient Education and Counseling 92 (no. 3): 426–431. doi: 10.1016/j.pec.2013.06.020.

Archambault, Patrick, et al. 2009. "Towards an Understanding of Communities of Practice: Objective Measures of Mechanisms of Action and Impact Are Needed." Journal of the Canadian Academy of Child and Adolescent Psychiatry 18 (no. 3): 196–197.

Archambault, Patrick, et al. 2013. "Wikis and Collaborative Writing Applications in Health Care: A Scoping Review." Journal of Medical Internet Research 15 (no. 10): e210. doi: 10.2196/jmir.2787.

Batt-Rawden, Samantha, et al. 2014. "The Role of Social Media in Clinical Excellence." The Clinical Teacher 11 (no. 4): 264–269. doi: 10.1111/tct.12129.

Brown, James, Christopher Ryan, and Anthony Harris. 2014. "How Doctors View and Use Social Media: A National Survey." Journal of Medical Internet Research 16 (no. 12): e267. doi: 10.2196/jmir.3589.

Cartledge, Peter, Michael Miller, and Bob Phillips. 2013. "The Use of Social-Networking Sites in Medical Education." Medical Teacher 35 (no. 10): 847–857. doi: 10.3109/0142159X.2013.804909.

Cegedim Strategic Data. 2012. "Physicians in Emerging Markets More Open to Using Social Networking Sites Compared to their European Counterparts." http://www.cegedim.fr/Communique/CSD_PhysicianProfessionalUse SocialMedia_26062012_eng.pdf.

Chretien, Katherine C., and Terry Kind. 2013. "Social Media and Clinical Care: Ethical, Professional, and Social Implications." *Circulation*, 127 (no. 13), 1413–1421. doi: 10.1161/CIRCULATIONAHA.112.128017.

Chretien, Katherine C., et al. 2015. "A Digital Ethnography of Medical Students Who Use Twitter for Professional Development." Journal of General Internal Medicine 30 (no. 11): 1673–1680. doi: 10.1007/s11606-015-3345-z.

Curran, Janet A., and Syed Sibte Raza Abidi. 2007. "Evaluation of an Online Discussion Forum for Emergency Practitioners." Health Informatics Journal 13 (no. 4): 255–266. doi: 10.1177/1460458207079834.

Ellison, Nicole B., and danah Boyd. 2013. "Sociality Through Social Network Sites." In The Oxford Handbook of Internet Studies. W. H. Dutton (Ed.), 151–172. Oxford: Oxford University Press.

Eysenbach, Gunther. 2008. "Medicine 2.0: Social Networking, Collaboration, Participation, Apomediation, and Openness." *Journal of Medical Internet Research*, 10 (no. 3): e22. doi:10.2196/jmir.1030.

George, Daniel R., and Michael J. Green. 2012. "Beyond Good and Evil: Exploring Medical Trainee Use of Social Media." Teaching and Learning in Medicine 24 (no. 2): 155–157. doi: 10.1080/10401334.2012.664972.

George, Daniel R., Liza S. Rovniak, and Jennifer L. Kraschnewski. 2013. "Dangers and Opportunities for Social Media in Medicine." Clinical Obstetrics and Gynecology 56 (no. 3): 453–462. doi: 10.1097/GRF.0b013e318297dc38.

Giordano, Carolyn, and Christine Giordano. 2011. "Health Professions Students' Use of Social Media." Journal of Allied Health 40 (no. 2): 78–81.

Goff, Debra A., Ravina Kullar, and Jason G. Newland. 2015. "Review of Twitter for Infectious Diseases Clinicians: Useful or a Waste of Time?" Clinical Infectious Diseases: An Official Publication of the Infectious Diseases Society of America 60 (no. 10): 1533–1540. doi: 10.1093/cid/civ071.

Grindrod, Kelly, et al. 2014. "Pharmacy 2.0: A Scoping Review of Social Media Use in Pharmacy." Research in Social and Administrative Pharmacy 10 (no. 1): 256–270. doi: 10.1016/j.sapharm.2013.05.004.

Hamm, Michele P., et al. 2013. "Social Media Use by Health Care Professionals and Trainees: A Scoping Review." Academic Medicine 88 (no. 9): 1376–1383. doi: 10.1097/ACM.0b013e31829eb91c.

Haug, J.D. 1997. "Physicians' Preferences for Information Sources: A Meta-Analytic Study." Bulletin of the Medical Library Association 85 (no. 3): 223–232.

Househ, Mowafa. 2013. "The Use of Social Media in Healthcare: Organizational, Clinical, and Patient Perspectives." Studies in Health Technology and Informatics 183: 244–248. doi: 10.3233/978-1-61499-203-5-244.

Kuo, David. 1998. "Curbside Consultation Practices and Attitudes Among Primary Care Physicians and Medical Subspecialists." JAMA 280 (no. 10): 905. doi: 10.1001/jama.280.10.905.

Labrecque, M., and P Beaupré. October 3–4, 2013. "L'information clinique de qualité pour les soignants: Accessible en ligne au bout des doigts!" Paper Presented at La communication au cœur de la e-santé, Montréal, UQAM.

Lagu, Tara, et al. 2008. "Content of Weblogs Written by Health Professionals." Journal of General Internal Medicine 23 (no. 10): 1642–1646. doi: 10.1007/s11606-008-0726-6.

McGowan, Brian S., et al. 2012. "Understanding the Factors That Influence the Adoption and Meaningful Use of Social Media by Physicians to Share Medical Information." Journal of Medical Internet Research 14 (no. 5): e117. doi: 10.2196/jmir.2138.

Modahl, Mary, Lea Tompsett, and Tracey Moorhead. 2011. "Doctors, Patients & Social Media." QuantiaMD and Care Continuum Alliance (Ed.). http://www.quantiamd.com/q-qcp/social_media.pdf.

Panahi, Sirious. 2014. *Social Media and Tacit Knowledge Sharing: Physicians' Perspectives and Experiences*. PhD dissertation (Queensland University of Technology).

Pereira, Ian, et al. 2015. "Thou Shalt Not Tweet Unprofessionally: An Appreciative Inquiry into the Professional Use of Social Media." Postgraduate Medical Journal 91 (no. 1080): 561–564. doi: 10.1136/postgradmedj-2015-133353.

Rolls, Kaye, et al. 2014. "Analysis of the Social Network Development of a Virtual Community for Australian Intensive Care Professionals." CIN: Computers, Informatics, Nursing 32 (no. 11): 536–544. doi: 10.1097/CIN.0000000000000104.

Rolls, Kaye, et al. 2016. "How Health Care Professionals Use Social Media to Create Virtual Communities: An Integrative Review." Journal of Medical Internet Research 18 (no. 6): e166. doi: 10.2196/jmir.5312.

Sophie, Galarneau, et al. 2016. "La communication entre médecins dans le contexte de la prestation de soins au patient." In La communication professionnelle en santé (2nd edition). Claude Richard Lussier (Ed.), 725–740. Montréal: Pearson- Erpi Médecine.

Thoër, Christine. 2013. "Internet: Un facteur de transformation de la relation médecin-patient?" Communiquer. Revue De Communication Sociale Et Publique (no. 10): 1–24. doi: 10.4000/communiquer.506.

Usher, Kim, et al. 2014. "Australian Health Professions Student Use of Social Media." Collegian (Royal College of Nursing, Australia) 21 (no. 2): 95–101.

Vartabedian, Bryan S., Emily Amos, and Jay Baruch. 2011. "Anonymous Physician Blogging." American Medical Association 13 (no. 7): 440–447.

Ventola, C.L. 2014. "Social Media and Health Care Professionals: Benefits, Risks, and Best Practices." Pharmacy and Therapeutics 39 (no. 7): 491–520.

Wenger, Etienne. 1998. Community of Practice: Learning, Meaning and Identity. Cambridge: Cambridge University Press.

8

The Design of Online Communities Devoted to Health and Better Living: Using Social Interaction Features to Foster Online Contributions

Sandrine Prom Tep, Aude Dufresne
and Sylvain Sénécal

8.1 Medicine Without Doctors

The emergence of Internet and the social Web brought transformation to all communication-related domains. In April 2006, the *PatientsLikeMe* Online Health Community (OHC) was launched in the USA, to help

S. Prom Tep (✉)
ESG UQAM Business School, Departement of Marketing, UQAM,
Montréal, Québec, Canada
e-mail: promtep.sandrine@uqam.ca

A. Dufresne
Department of Communication, University of Montréal, Montréal, Canada
e-mail: aude.dufresne@umontreal.ca

S. Sénécal
Department of marketing, and RBC Financial Group Ecommerce Chair holder,
HEC Montréal, Montréal, Québec, Canada
e-mail: sylvain.senecal@hec.ca

© The Author(s) 2017   **135**
L. Menvielle et al. (eds.), *The Digitization of Healthcare*,
DOI 10.1057/978-1-349-95173-4_8

patients with severe chronic diseases such as fibromyalgia, multiple sclerosis, and epilepsy, to share medical data and knowledge about the diseases along with treatment and lifestyle issues linked to their condition. On September 8 in 2010, Angie Merek in an article from the *Smart Money* magazine, hailed the *PatientsLikeMe* OHC as the beginning of Health 2.0 and the new wave of medicine without doctors were patients help each other (Angie 2010). By December 2010, *PatientsLikeMe* had over 40 full time employees and revenues of over $8 million (*Wall Street Journal* 2010). In the medical domain, patients can now search by themselves information on health, illness, treatment, and medication. They regularly confront and complete information they might have received from their doctor or through the health system. The position of medical professionals is thus transformed.

First, they are no longer the unique source of information for their patients, who now not only search medical information on the Web, but also try to connect to eHealth communities to get advice. As a consequence, medical professionals expect that patients are likely to be informed, and rely on this new state of affairs to adapt the interaction they need to have with them. However, these growing sources of information on the Web also raise problems in the medical system. Patients may arrive misinformed, with preconceptions, or information inappropriate for their case. Medical professionals are then put in a position of having to clarify the situation and persuade the patients about what is in fact true and recommended. While information available on the Web becomes a complement to medical service it nevertheless raises new challenges related to the quality of this information, and also for guiding the patient on applying this information to their specific case. As for the emergence of social Web in the medical and health domains, it opens up vast opportunities for interaction where OHCs of interest are developing to support and inform patients and caregivers, and also to discuss health issues, prevention, care, and post-treatment practices. Not only may this become a very important source of information but also a mean of exchanging experiences and obtaining support through experiential pragmatic advice from the community. Moreover, as the condition of a patient changes and/or the medical domain evolves, eHealth communities are useful to get explanations quickly, and to obtain personal and continuous informational and social support complementing that offered by the medical system. OHCs also offer more personalized information exchange, whereby participants may also receive empathic support from the community. These opportunities, however, raise many important challenges:

- How can the medical system interact with those eHealth communities to improve the quality of information which is made available not only to patients but also to caregivers, family members, and friends, as it is especially important and complex in the medical domain?
- How to promote a better integration of health-related Web services, eCommunities and the medical professional system, to ensure that eHealth can complement what the medical system offers in terms of informational and emotional support?
- How is it possible to ensure the quality of medical information in the OHC? Medical experts should be encouraged to participate, even though the time to do so remains limited by their practice. In that regard, the contributions they make should be highlighted among the exchanges, as they may be more valuable and less frequent.
- How much credibility do users give to the content they find in those sources of information? How can it be improved so patients believe in it and use it as guidance in dealing with their medical or health problems?
- Many eHealth services are being offered, and many OHCs are emerging, but not all of them succeed in gathering interesting and appropriate content for the community from a long-term perspective. How can the exchanges be stimulated to obtain a critical mass of content? How to ensure that the content in those OHCs remain dynamic and refreshed, so newcomers are attracted by up-to-date content and motivated to contribute by the compelling experience?
- How can the system per se encourage users to feel comfortable in sharing their experiences, points-of-view, and interrogations? And how can it foster efficient information exchange among users to support information search relevancy, highlighting solutions to problems found in the community?
- How can OHCs and social Web be better integrated in medical practice, so that medical professionals be aware of them, participate, act as moderators in those OHCs, and recommend them to their patients?

8.2 How Can the Design of an Online Community Improve Its Social Interaction Efficiency?

This research explores how the design dimensions of the social media platform interface can contribute to the success of an OHC. Its objective is to study those functional dimensions which are relevant to ensure participants' interest, involvement, and intention to contribute. Putting aside aspects covered by other studies such as content per se and semantics, content structure, volume, valence, this research focuses on social usability. In other words, how can the design of the online community (OC) platform improve its social interaction efficiency (Yi et al. 2010; Amblee and Bui 2012)? It tries to assess the impact of social interaction features built into the interface for the purpose of improving access to information and navigation through the OC content, increasing participant intention to browse, read, and contribute. The field for this research is PassportSante.net, the second most important French-speaking eHealth OC, in which various versions of the interface for accessing the same content are compared. The research measures the impact of social functionalities on the perception that users have of the system, the credibility of its content, and on their intention to contribute, thus adding their experience and points of view. The research is interdisciplinary, drawing from research in different domains: social psychology, human-computer interaction, persuasion, and electronic marketing.

8.3 Participative Online Environments

8.3.1 Social Media and Interactive Marketing

Social media are at the heart of interactive marketing nowadays as they convey the so-called voice of the consumer which is much more genuine and credible than any advertising and official marketing discourse (Hu and Sundar 2010). For this credibility motto, it is very important for brands and businesses in general to understand what is truly occurring on these new digital platforms, and in what aspects they are deemed social. People express themselves online, and these consumer-to-consumer (C2C) exchanges make up for the various forms of electronic word-of-mouth also known as eWOM (Hennig-Thurau et al. 2004). Hence, it becomes strategic for organizations to leverage this C2C communication and recognize the true value of the consumers' involvement with their brands or OCs of interest—such as health and well-being matters—through these channels, instead of focusing only on their marketing efforts return on investment (ROI) (Hoffman and Fodor 2010). Instead of counting sales generated by brand OCs, marketers should focus on members, participants, and contributors, as well as participant contributions through user-generated content and shares, etc. (Mangold and Faulds 2009). The idea behind this research is to leverage this social interaction and to optimize any social communication channel through features, which help generate more user contributions in a social media space (Kaplan and Haenlein 2010).

8.3.2 User-Generated Content (UGC)

According to Preece and Schneiderman's framework (2009), various forms of participation coexist online on a reader-to-leader continuum, as most people simply browse content and participate through views, as lurkers online, and very few, known as posters or curators, take active leading roles as content initiators. Lurkers and posters are the two extreme anchors of the creative spectrum (Nonnecke and Preece 2000). Hence, online contribution can extend from a vocal active minority to a silent passive majority in a ratio of 1 to 99, or the 1% rule from Internet culture (Hargittai and Walejko 2008). To encourage users to contribute online, a motivational perspective is needed.

8.3.3 Motivation to Contribute Online

In 2003, Schau and Gilly wrote, "We are what we post. Self-presentation in personal webspace," (2003), and showed that self-expression is the foremost driver of online personal articulations. Hennig-Thurau et al.

(2004) confirmed this theory in their search of what motivates consumers to articulate themselves on the Internet, and found that social interaction is the second utmost driver of eWOM via consumer opinion platforms. These research studies are aligned with Lazar and Preece (1998), who showed earlier that OCs must offer some technological attributes, as well as social and psychological ones, to attract Internet users.

8.3.4 Interpersonal Influence

Persuasive communication has been studied since World War II propaganda times (Hovland 1957). The general idea is to convince people of one message and favorably influence their attitude toward the subject of the message. Girandola et Joule (2008) push this theory further and show that, to ensure that the influence is fully efficient and lasting, the persuasive communication message should motivate a behavioral change accompanying the attitude change or reinforcement. Hence participating online through lurking is a good start, but to make the OC thrive and survive over time, we must influence users to contribute. Regarding effective interpersonal influence, Cialdini (2001) states that social influence principles can be used, for example, social proof (we tend to do what others do), authority and similarity heuristics (we tend to believe what experts and likewise people say), and the foot-in-the-door tactic (we accept a second offer more easily if we have already conceded once). These influence principles all operate in the human information process to bias judgment (Petty and Cacioppo 1986), through both our willingness and ability to judge information received, according to an elaboration likelihood continuum (i.e., thorough processing or mental shortcuts). The persuasion trick, therefore, lies in the appropriate use of influence principles toward a desired goal, or simply convincing people of what you want them to be convinced of. As a result, the attitude is modified (reversed or further reinforced), as well as the behavioral intention linked to it according to the decision-making Theory of Reasoned Action (TRA) from Fishbein and Ajzen (1975). So, if you want to convince OC members to participate, show them social interaction cues. Ratings for instance are traces of users evaluating existing content. User profiles are indications guiding OC members through content source credibility, supporting social inference cues which may exert the authority or similarity influence principles.

8.3.5 Technological Persuasion

According to the TAM model (Davis 1989), technology adoption relies on technological characteristics such as usefulness and ease-of-use attributes. This software productivity-oriented model has been adapted to the Web environment to consider hedonic dimensions such as enjoyment while browsing webpages (Davis et al. 1992; Moon and Kim 2001). Web adoption is Web 1.0 goal, but when it comes to social media or OCs, these Web 2.0 platform managers are the ones responsible for making the online environment a place encouraging user contributions. The interactive medium's capacity of convincing users to contribute is a required attribute of immediate and long-term success for any interactive social space. In social computing research (Dasgupta 2010), persuasive technology refers to any software system capable of influencing the users' behavior. Fogg (2003) refers to this interdisciplinary phenomenon as CAPTology/Computers as Persuasive Technology.

8.3.6 Website Sociability

Support for social interaction on a website or any virtual environment is called *social usability* (Preece 2000). A social functionality is a social interaction feature built into a software system design to effectively act upon social usability. By adding or hiding elements in the interface, the system can communicate more or less persuasively, and motivate users into one targeted direction or another (e.g., have users contribute content actively beyond lurking content only). This type of enticing design follows persuasive ergonomics, and heuristic guidelines exist for orienting conception and evaluation in that direction (Brangier et al. 2015), making social influence, and functional design strongly intertwined.

8.3.7 Social Interaction Features: Ratings and User Profiles

As mentioned earlier, increased credibility is associated with eWOM according to the similarity influence principle. People tend to believe what peer consumers/users say more than what brands wish them to believe. And this is all the more true online, since people do not know each other a priori or at least at first. For such reasons, providing user profiles as a social interaction feature can truly influence OC members according to the authority or similarity principle. User profiles inform users of the contributor's position and help others evaluate their contributions in that perspective. For instance, a user is likely to judge a piece of advice for a medical treatment more valuable if posted by a doctor or a nurse, if looking for medical expertise, but might value a patient's point of view more if in search of medical treatment feedback from patients or experience-oriented information in general. Besides user profiles, ratings also help users search for and evaluate content according to what is rated best (quality), or most often (popularity), etc. Just like we found on Amazon (Dufresne et al. 2010), users search products according to the five-star quality rating system and user profiles statistics derived from peers' comments. Hence, peers' contributions help to quickly find the most interesting items and influence attitudes toward products. Very similarly, OHC members do appreciate some content ranking of the opinions shared, to scan through information and quickly find relevant and valuable pieces amidst the tons of content aggregated in the OHC. And so, both user profiles and ratings participate in the value chain of content, as these two social interaction features support online social interaction through eWOM. They are part of the system design, just as a "share" button supports social interaction through content on Facebook for instance. Built on this literature review, the following section presents our research model.

8.4 OHC Adoption and Online Contribution

From a scientific contribution standpoint, our work has enabled us to extend Davis' classical model (Davis 1989), dealing with adoption of information systems, to the context of virtual communities and

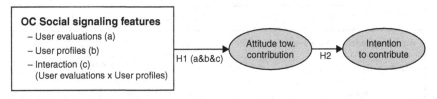

Fig. 8.1 Research model

participative sites. It does so by adding the dimension of social utility to the perception of ease of navigation and information utility, given that adoption in the form of online contributions is absolutely necessary to the survival of participative business models, from a marketing point of view. Derived from this literature review, we have conceptualized the following research framework presented in Fig. 8.1.

8.5 Influencing Online Contribution: An Experiment

To investigate how social functionalities of the interface could influence perception of users on the eHealth platform, we experimented with access to the same eHealth content using four different versions of the interface (2×2 experiment design), depending on the presence or absence of users' evaluations and users' profiles (see Figs. 8.2, 8.3 and 8.4). In this OC, user evaluations consisted of comments and ratings of comments ranging from one-to-five stars indicating increasing levels of message appreciation.

Figures 8.2 and 8.3, respectively, show the absence/presence conditions of user evaluations at the topic level and at the message level of the Nutrition section of PasseportSante.net to ensure coherence for participants browsing from the Nutrition topics to the corresponding message threads. As shown in Fig. 8.2, for limited display-space reasons, only user names were provided at the topic level in PasseportSante.net OC, and user profile detailed information manipulations were then only

Topics	Replies	Author	Views	Last Post
Fat Loss supplements ★★★★★	1	Kalupion	80	by **Loulie** Fri Sep 24, 2010 1:11 pm
Vitamins and hormonal disorders make...	4	Souhila	1206	by **Adison** Thu Sep 23, 2010 3:24 pm
Goji berries ★★★☆☆	3	Stella25	1136	by **Learflx** Thu Sep 23, 2010 11:14 am
White tea good for stress ★★☆☆☆	6	Mikesport	601	by **Simpel** Thu Sep 23, 2010 8:52 am
Do you know any decongestant herbs?	2	Mikesport	131	by **Learflx** Wed Sep 22, 2010 11:22 pm

Topics	Replies	Author	Views	Last Post
Fat Loss supplements	1	Kalupion	80	by **Loulie** Fri Sep 24, 2010 1:11 pm
Vitamins and hormonal disorders make...	4	Souhila	1206	by **Adison** Thu Sep 23, 2010 3:24 pm
Goji berries	3	Stella25	1136	by **Learflx** Thu Sep 23, 2010 11:14 am
White tea good for stress	6	Mikesport	601	by **Simpel** Thu Sep 23, 2010 8:52 am
Do you know any decongestant herbs?	2	Mikesport	131	by **Learflx** Wed Sep 22, 2010 11:22 pm

Fig. 8.2 User evaluations at the topic level with and without ratings

Username:	Message: **Goji berries**
Stella25	I have noticed that eating Goji berries help boost my immune system... Rating: ★★★☆☆

Username:	Message: **Goji berries**
Stella25	I have noticed that eating Goji berries help boost my immune system...

Fig. 8.3 User Evaluations at the message level with and without ratings

Username:	Message: **Goji berries**
Stella25 - Female - London, ON - Teacher - Member since: 2001 - Total posts: 45	I have noticed that eating Goji berries help boost my immune system... Rating: ★★★☆☆

Username:	Message: **Goji berries**
Stella25	I have noticed that eating Goji berries help boost my immune system... Rating: ★★★☆☆

Fig. 8.4 Manipulation of user profiles at the message level

performed at the message level, with the absence/presence conditions illustrated in Fig. 8.4.

As for the procedure used for the experiment, all content versions have been pretested to be considered distinct from the Internet users' perspective. OC managers recruited members directly using email invitations to participate in the study. Active posting members were deliberately excluded from the study, to avoid the risk of them recognizing the manipulated environments and guessing the research objective. The research project was presented to the OC members as a study about online user behavior in which participants had to complete an online navigation task and answer questions before and after the task. After completing the pre-experiment questionnaire, participants were given instructions asking them to browse the nutrition section of the manipulated OC website for 15 minutes. They had to select and read thoroughly at least three nutrition-related messages.

To increase involvement, they were instructed to read the messages bearing in mind that they should be able to present the OC to friends with a well-informed opinion if asked about it. And to increase realism, they were also told that they could freely choose to react or not to the messages by rating them or writing back a comment about any of the messages read, before moving on to the second questionnaire. In compliance with the Institutional Review Board (IRB) for ethics and human research, participants were informed about the procedure of the study before getting started, so that they could freely accept to participate. As incentive to participate in the study, they were entered in a draw to win an iPad. All questionnaires were filled anonymously with a unique identifier parameter linking pre- and post-task questionnaires. After completing the first short questionnaire focusing on online usage habits, knowledge of and attitude toward the Internet, and the level of interest in general health issues, participants were randomly assigned to one of the four conditions of the experiment, each offering exactly the same OC nutrition-related content. Using existing valid and reliable scientific scales, the post-experiment questionnaire measured the attitude toward online contribution and intention to contribute.

8.6   The Effect of Social Functionalities on Contributing Online

With a sample size of 404 participants well representing the Internet users' population, the two sets of hypotheses were tested through analysis of variance and simple linear regression. The positive main effect of user evaluations on attitude toward contribution (H1a) was significant, while it was not the case for user profiles (H1b). Very interestingly, the results showed the presence of a highly significant interaction between the two factors (H1c) and confirmed the well-established positive relation between attitude and intention (H2). All the ANOVA testing was conducted with a significance level of 0.05. The results are summarized further in Table 8.1. Aside from the intention to contribute increased by the presence of social functionalities, it appears that these Web features also influenced effective

Table 8.1 Hypotheses testing results summary

Hyp.	Description	Result
H1a	USER EVALUATIONS → ATTITUDE toward Contribution (ATC) (+)	S
H1b	USER PROFILES → ATC (+)	NS
H1c	USER EVALUATIONS x USER PROFILES → ATC (+)	S
H2	ATC → Intention to contribute (+)	S

contributions from participants during the experimentation (i.e., ratings along with content messages and new member accounts creation). A contribution rate of 6.9% was registered in the database at the end of the experiment and regardless of the various experimental conditions. Considering the average 1% rule acknowledged as the online contribution rate from the Internet Culture and usually reported as the norm for participative sites (Wikipedia 2016), this experiment outcome is interesting to stress, since the content to be explored during the experiment was not spontaneously chosen by the participants. As part of the research protocol, each participant was instructed to freely browse through the content of a specific theme, and they could act upon the content or not as they wished. This research experiment constraint, being stated, it is reasonable to expect that the effect of the social functionalities might be higher in more realistic conditions.

8.7 Designing OHCs to Support Social Interaction

As a conclusion, it appears from this research that social functionalities are important for the OHC efficiency of PasseportSante.net. Not only do they enable users to access relevant information more easily while researching a health problem, but they also foster the users' implication in the virtual community through sharing, and thus improving, the information available. First, we found that user evaluations were important, making it easier to access more recent and more appreciated information. Ratings appear to make navigation easier, especially for new users wishing to browse for the type of information that can be found on the system; contributions can be thus sorted on a given topic, based on evaluations made by others. By helping to discriminate the more interesting contributions, this enhanced navigation may convince more users to take the time to read and analyze content and enrich their own contribution to the debate. Users are valued for adding information and content evaluation to what others have already contributed on any topic of interest within the OHC. This should bring convergence in the debate, and filter out redundant or less relevant contributions. Second, we also found that the inclusion of profile information about the contributor is a helpful OHC design element. Since source credibility is important in convincing participants of the quality of the information, profiles can serve as a gauge of the importance of a contribution whether from the patient or the medical side. Profiles may also create a more personalized and bonding reference for users, enabling them to identify with a contributor and the information or experience they shared. As for the presence of profiles, the study finds that they are especially useful and efficient in combination with the rating feature. The research shows that the impact of user profiles as such is important but not significant; however, when user profiles are combined with rating interactive features, their dual impact is significant. At this stage, it is important to state that the user profiles used in the research were not very detailed, providing only limited information on the contributors (i.e., nickname, gender, location, work status, membership duration, and total number of posts). Nevertheless, the preliminary results suggest that user profile interactive features should be developed further to obtain stronger impact on the attitude toward contribution and the intention to contribute of OHC members. This being the case, the medical expertise of the source could be added, number of years of practice, or the role and relation of the contributor to a patient (e.g., patient, family, caretakers, etc.). A short personalized summary of the contributor's illness experience could also be useful to increase empathy and bonding among members.

Such information would be relevant, and serve to orient users in choosing contributions depending on their needs. The effect of the interaction between ratings and user profiles on the attitude toward contribution suggests that enriched profiles, when combined with ratings, would really highlight the best contributions. User profiles could then add meaningful value to the contributions. In addition to guiding the user toward the best content, they would enhance contributors' loyalty, encouraging them to return and pursue interactions on the OHC as its benefits would appear very clear to them. First time OHC users are also likely to be hooked by improved guidance to interesting and relevant content, and encouraged to explore more around their problems and other topics which may concern them. Eventually, this should also encourage more professional explorations and contributions to the OHC content, whether for giving advice, answering questions, or providing reference to reliable documentation, thus enriching even more the quality of the content in the eHealth community through feedback. As for the integration of those eHealth communities with medical practice, the participation of eHealth professionals could lead to the habit of referring patients to specific sections of the OHC, where support and suggestions may be found on strategies and practices for specific cases as a complement to traditional information sources, to offer extended support and documentation to patients and families. Also it might be interesting for them to use the e-platform to stay aware of practical strategies and reactions of the community to a given medical context. Last but not least, OHCs could be used to streamline health-care delivery. For instance, in the Netherlands, Tactive Telemedicine provides online treatment for people suffering from alcohol addiction. "It allows structured asynchronous interaction between counselor and patient, while aid workers from recognized mental health services provide treatments on a franchise basis. The goal is to replicate one-to-one cognitive behavioral therapy with a professional counselor in an online environment. Tactive delivers more than 5.500 units of treatments per year, with most ranging from 12 to 16 weeks" (Kimble 2015, p. 24). As a final word in conclusion, health care is nowadays an information-intensive activity which seems ripe for Internet initiatives. In view of this, social interaction is beneficial to both OHC members and their platform managers, and features such as ratings and user profiles play a critical role in fostering user contributions to OHCs, helping them reach the critical mass necessary for survival, by highlighting content which is relevant and meaningful both for newcomers and existing loyal members.

References

Amblee, Naveen, and Tung Bui. 2012. Harnessing the influence of social proof in online shopping: The effect of electronic word of mouth on sales of digital microproducts. *International Journal of Electronic Commerce* 16: 91–113.

Angie, Merek. 2010. "Medicine without doctors." *Smart Money*, 8 September.

Brangier, Éric, Michel C. Desmarais, Alexandra Nemery, and Sandrine Prom Tep. 2015. Évolution de l'inspection heuristique: vers une intégration des critères d'accessibilité, de praticité, d'émotion et de persuasion dans l'évaluation ergonomique. *Journal d'Interaction Personne-système* 4: 69–84.

Cialdini, Robert B. 2001. *Influence: Science and Practice*, 5the éd., Boston, MA, Pearson Education, 260 p.

Dasgupta, Subhasish. 2010. *Social computing: Concepts, methodologies, tools and applications*. Hershey: Information Science Reference.

Davis, Fred D. 1989. Perceived usefulness, perceived ease-of-use and user acceptance. *MIS Quarterly* 13: 319–340.

Davis, Fred D., Richard P. Bagozzi, and Paul R. Warshaw. 1992. Extrinsic and intrinsic motivation to use computers in the workplace. *Journal of Applied Social Psychology* 22: 1559–1816.

Dufresne, Aude, Sandrine Prom Tep, and Sénécal. Sylvain. "Physiological measures, eye tracking and task analysis to track user reactions in UGC." Paper presented at the Measuring Behavior International Conference on Methods and Techniques in Behavioral Research, North Brabant, Eindhoven, August 24–27, 2010.

Fishbein, M. et I. Ajzen 1975. *Belief, Attitude, Intention and Behavior: An Introduction to Theory and Research* Addison-Wesley Publishing Company.

Fogg, Bernard J. 2003. *Persuasive technology: Using computers to change what we think and do*. San Francisco: Morgan Kaufmann Publishers.

Girandola, F. and Joule R.V. 2008. La communication engageante. *Revue Electronique de Psychologie Sociale* 2: 41–51.

Glynn, Mangold W., and David J. Faulds. 2009. Social media: The new hybrid element of the promotion mix. *Business Horizons* 52: 357–365.

Hargittai, Eszter, and Gina Walejko. 2008. The participation divide: Content creation and sharing in the digital age. *Information, Communication and Society* 11: 389–408.

Hennig-Thurau, Thorsten, Kevin P. Gwinner, Gianfranco Walsh, and Dwayne D. Gremler. 2004. Electronic word-of-mouth via consumer opinion platforms: What motivates consumers to articulate themselves on the Internet? *Journal of Interactive Marketing* 18: 38–52.

Hoffman, Donna L., and Marek Fodor. 2010. Can you measure the ROI of your social media marketing? *MIT Sloan Management Review* 52: 41–49.

Hovland, C.I. 1957. *The order of presentation in persuasion*. New Haven: Yale University Press.

Hu, Yifeng, and Shyam S. Sundar. 2010. Effects of online health sources on credibility and behavioral intentions. *Communication Research* 37: 105–132.

Kaplan, Andreas M., and Michael Haenlein. 2010. Users of the world, unite! The challenges and opportunities of social media. *Business Horizons* 53: 59–68.

Kimble, Chris. 2015. Business models for E-health: Evidence from ten cases studies. *Global Business and Organizational Excellence* 34: 18–30.

Lazar, Jonathan, and Jennifer Preece. 1998. "Classification schema for online communities." Paper presented at Association for systems Americas Conference (AMCIS) Maryland, Baltimore.

Moon, Ji-Won, and Young-Gul Kim. 2001. Extending the TAM for a World-Wide-Web context. *Information and Management* 38: 217–230.

Nonnecke, Blair, and Jennifer Preece. 2000. "Lurker demographics: Counting the silent." Paper presented at the SIGCHI conference on human factors in computing systems, South Holland, The Hague, 1–6 April.

Petty, Richard E., and John T. Cacioppo 1986. The elaboration likelihood model of persuasion. In *Advances in experimental social psychology*, ed. Leonard Berkowitz, 123–205. San Diego: Academic Press.

Preece, Jennifer. 2000. *Online communities: Designing usability and supporting sociability*. New York: John Wiley & Sons, Inc.

Preece, Jennifer, and Ben Schneiderman. 2009. The reader to leader framework: Motivating technology mediated social participation. *AIS Transactions on Human Computer Interaction* 1: 1–21.

Schau, Hope Jensen, and Mary C. Gilly 2003. We are what we post? Self-presentation in personal webspace. *Journal of Consumer Research* 30: 385–404.

Wikipedia. "1% rule (Internet culture)." Accessed September 10, 2016. https://en.wikipedia.org/wiki/1%25_rule_(Internet_culture).html.

Yi, Cheng, Zhenhui Jiang, and Isak Benbasat. 2010. "Towards organized search and unexpected discoveries: The impacts of product tags and featured users on online product search." Paper presented at the 31st International Conference on Information Systems, Missouri, Saint Louis, 15–18 December.

Part III

E-Health and Actual Challenges

9

Mobile Health: Telemedicine's Latest Wave but This Time It's for Real

Kyle J. Rose

Advancements in mobile phone technology have enabled portable devices of all different types to become increasingly powerful. Devices are more connected to our lives today than they have ever been, including the phone itself. It now follows us everywhere, even into the most intimate environments we face in our daily routines. As the phone has stepped into its new role, a fury of new applications and software have been developed accordingly. Many of these are related to health and health care in some manner.

The purpose of this chapter is not to make the case for mobile health. mHealth has arrived whether we like it or not. Millions are already using health apps every minute. Instead, I explore how these tools are being used, by whom, and for what reasons. I have selected a case study on Mobile Health in Diabetes (INSEAD 3/2016–6204) to help guide us

K.J. Rose (✉)
Founder of Delta PM Diabetes, Board Member – International Diabetes Federation, Delta PM Diabetes, San Francisco, USA
Executive in Residence/Visiting faculty at INSEAD's Healthcare Management Department, INSEAD, Fontainebleau, France

© The Author(s) 2017
L. Menvielle et al. (eds.), *The Digitization of Healthcare*,
DOI 10.1057/978-1-349-95173-4_9

through a discussion of what I have observed. It focuses on the diabetes market as a model. Out of more than 165,000 health apps[1] in the market, diabetes is arguably the therapy field offering the strongest business proposition for mHealth.[2] Not surprisingly its prevalence has soared. According to the International Diabetes Federation, there are 415 million[3] people with diabetes in the world and 642 million people are projected to have diabetes by 2040.

By early 2016, over 1,500 different apps and software tools related to diabetes management already existed in the market. As is the case for the entire health app category (and even more for apps outside of health), there is huge range in frequency of usage and retention. Some of them are used only once by users before being deleted, while other users become entirely dependent, using them every day for years. What is driving these vastly different behaviors and how do we define what is considered success in mobile health?

9.1   A Personal Story—Chronic Disease

An important factor in this discussion is the chronic nature of certain diseases like diabetes. When an individual is diagnosed with a chronic disease, by definition, it will not go away. Sometimes that notion does not sink in right away, but over time, this becomes a reality and thus emerges a complicated relationship between an individual and their disease. Quite naturally, some periods will be more difficult to handle than others during this lengthy journey. Experiencing a roller coaster of emotions is common although what is experienced, and at what moments and frequency, remains unique from individual to individual.

Attempting to view the world through a patient's eyes can be helpful in understanding why some therapy approaches in mobile health products resonate better with the patient community than others. It seems

---

[1] IMS Institute for Healthcare Informatics, Patient Adoption of mHealth (September 2015).

[2] Research2Guidance, *Diabetes Management Solutions Industry Report* (2015/2016).

[3] International Diabetes Federation Atlas 7th Ed, International Diabetes Federation (2015).

like an obvious strategy that would be employed by any company attempting to develop a health product however so many times market research does not quite accomplish this. Instead, it rather becomes a mere check box on a long list of pre-product launch activities. This is especially true in the start-up digital world where lightning-fast progress is expected by most stakeholders involved.

The 16th of June 1996 will be a day I remember for the rest of my life. Little did I know that a trip to the opticians for an eye exam would result in the diagnosis of a chronic disease: insulin-dependent diabetes.

At that moment, I was petrified about what this would mean, especially in my daily life. I barely remembered having studied diabetes in my school's health class. How long would this "condition" last? How could I get better? Could I still do all of the things I had already planned: traveling, sports, moving to a new location to study. How would others react?

We lived in a rural part of America at the time (Idaho, USA). This contributed to my family's feeling of isolation as the nearest diabetes specialist was 150 kilometers away, and there was a three month lead time for a doctor's appointment.

I remember receiving an intimidating stack of papers and literature at the hospital upon diagnosis. This was meant to be my "education" but it didn't make much sense to me and felt overwhelming. I did what was asked of me and practiced injecting my insulin into 3 apples that week. Then I was sent home to live my new life. From then on, I would be dependent on the injection of a drug I knew very little about in order to survive, a realization I would not be able to fully comprehend until much later on. Fortunately, my family was there to support me along the way. Not everyone was so lucky, but it would still prove to be extremely difficult and test our family beyond anything we had experienced before. —I recalled in Spring of 2016.

My experience was not so atypical. Diagnosis is a scary time and it is just the beginning. Diabetes self-management involves significant psychological and behavioral challenges which are often ignored but perhaps represent the greatest challenge in day-to-day living with diabetes. Sometimes this is due to the impact of stress on daily diabetes management. Stigma associated with having diabetes and stereotypes prevalent in society today make things even worse.

People with diabetes often go through similar periods and transitions in their "diabetes life." These periods are also referred to as trigger points by some and typically include diagnosis, hospitalization, first child, and a first encounter with complications. Those are the times when people are most likely to reach out for help and search for new or better solutions. Health products, including apps, which are able to provide support at such a delicate time in a patient's life have already taken the first step in developing a long-term relationship with that person. These struggles are pain points which can persist for some time. Knowing that a tool, or therapy, is available when in need can be extremely comforting, making a person more likely to increase his/her engagement and interest levels. Add to this a communication style from the company which resonates/aligns with the real experience of someone living with the disease, and that engagement will more naturally be retained over a prolonged period of time.

9.2   Evolution of Communities and Technology

Grassroots community work has played a vital role in helping people with diabetes all around the world. Patient support groups are common in metropolitan areas and often led by a diabetes health-care professional (HCP) from a local hospital or sometimes are organized by a committed group of affected families. There are also camps for children with diabetes, their loved ones, and adults with diabetes. Both the camp and support group environments intend to bring people together who may be experiencing similar feelings and frustrations. At camp, standard camp/outdoor activities are intertwined with diabetes education offering a life-changing experience for many and a support structure they need.

Unfortunately, these groups are not everywhere and often rely on funding from charity organizations which limits their capacity. Since 1996, at the same time as the diabetes epidemic has emerged with staggering prevalence statistics, fewer physicians have specialized in the field. Combined, this is leading to patients spending increasingly less time with their doctors and often looking for support elsewhere.

The Internet has helped, and online communities/forums such as the well-known Diabetes Online Community (DOC) have provided a "virtual camp of sorts." Finding patients on line who have comparable experiences can provide potent support. Many doctors have moved from initial doubt to a supportive role with regards to these virtual communities and many are even directing patients to select sites.

However, while online peer-to-peer support offers tremendous benefits, it does not replace the need for HCPs. If a patient with diabetes spends a mere 15 minutes with their doctor every 3–4 months in the best of cases, can one reasonably expect them to manage their condition successfully with that guidance alone?

"Probably not," answers Sylvie Picard, MD Diabetologist in Dijon, France. "It takes a very long time if we want to both look at collected blood glucose data when it is available and actually speak to them. The status quo in healthcare systems is failing the patient with diabetes."

It is not surprising that telemedicine and telehealth have emerged as possible solutions to this dilemma. Although these models are not new, advances in technology means that they are both perceived and implemented in a very different way.[4] In the case of mobile health, thousands of health-related mobile apps and connected devices are launching every few months. Today's new consumer technology allows them to be readily available at the click of a button.

9.3 A Time of Change and Different Perspectives

Care teams and their patients have entered a new era of medicine which is no longer entirely one-directional. While there are substantial cultural differences around the world regarding this subject, there is a clear trend toward a more collaborative approach between doctor and patient.

---

[4] Chick, S. and Rose, K.J. Mobile Health in Diabetes: mySugr's Monster Approach. INSEAD (04/2016–6204). "Unlabeled" Section.

Many factors have contributed to this change including widespread access to medical knowledge due to online resources.

A challenge, however, is that these two roles have inherently different perspectives. From a patient perspective, diabetes requires self-management decisions/actions multiple times throughout any given day. Maintaining glycemic control is tedious and nearly impossible to get "right" all of the time, especially when many factors beyond the patient's control impact blood sugar levels such as stress, menstruation, or illness.

> Diabetes is like being expected to play the piano with one hand while juggling items with another hand, all while balancing with deftness and dexterity on a tightrope. (Marlene Less, patient with diabetes—1983)

Sometimes a person eats the exact same meal, at the exact same time with identical medicine dosages from one day to the next but experiences vastly different post-prandial blood glucose levels (post-meal). This can be incredibly frustrating. Nonstop decision-making is necessary to even attempt to balance the components of therapy, be it nutrition, drugs, or exercise.

It might seem counterintuitive, but doctors and patients do not always have the same objectives, or at least not over the same time horizon. This is especially true given the silent nature of a chronic disease such as diabetes. While HCPs have specific guidelines for their care targeting metrics like Hemoglobin A1c blood lab measurements, people with diabetes may not have any symptoms that their blood glucose is higher than it should be. It could take 10–15 years for health complications to arise due to elevated glycemic levels. Despite serious potential outcomes like kidney disease, neuropathy, heart disease, and even blindness, it is rare for people to think that far ahead and be proactive.

A challenge in developing digital health solutions is to find a way to help both patients and HCPs achieve their objectives without feeling that the product was designed for the other party.[5] This is even more the case for mobile health products since they are typically designed for specific mobile devices. For example, perhaps

---

[5] Chick, S. and Rose, K.J. Mobile Health in Diabetes: mySugr's Monster Approach. "Differing Goals and Changing Mindsets" (2016).

a physician would like to navigate results on a tablet or larger screen than what the patient is carrying around with them all day. In general, it seems that doctors tend to prefer software strictly created for HCPs, whom they feel have the most important role, that of evaluating the data to make dosage/therapy recommendations. Many want to see statistical calculations and pattern identification analysis. In fact, these preferences are often a flat-out requirement imposed by members of the medical community to adopt these tools in their hospitals and clinics.

Many patients, on the other hand, react negatively to the medical establishment. It is not that hospitals and clinics are not welcoming but rather the feeling of being examined and being a subject. Most people in general do not associate hospitals and clinics with positive thoughts. In fact, most patients with diabetes also feel the need to be defensive in what is perceived as a harsh environment filled with one judgment after another. (William Polonsky of the Behavioral Diabetes Institute refers to this psychosocial dilemma as the "Diabetes Police"). This is exacerbated by the social stigma associated with diabetes previously mentioned and frequently leads to depression.

Instead they would prefer a consumer-facing approach that is pleasant to interact with and useful in their daily routine. They seek convenient solutions that make the tedious process of diabetes self-management a little less unpleasant, and take into account practical considerations like "How will this impact me today or tomorrow?" "I will be going out to dinner (nutrition)... I need to clean up the house (physical activity)... I forgot my insulin at home (drugs) so I may miss my shot." Day-to-day diabetes therapy is relentless and the constant burden takes its toll.

Today's mHealth technology allows for interfaces which can accommodate these different objectives and perspectives. Certain HCPs have encouraged their patients to engage in these patient-facing solutions while others have resisted stating concerns about medical content, lack of regulation, and data privacy. Often younger physicians are being exposed to these tools earlier on in their careers and are more willing to accept them as part of their toolkit.

Ultimately, mobile health is contributing to a major transformation of health-care systems and HCPs who do not find a way to adopt it may be left behind over years to come. It is not clear yet how long that will take. It has been over three years since the first reimbursement of a diabetes management software/app, named WellDoc®, was accepted as part of a patient's clinical therapy. While still uncommon, an increasing number of examples are being seen. Reimbursement would clearly provide a major boost to mHealth products as it does with any medical product. That being said, it is important to remember that not all of the mHealth world is considered medical by our regulating bodies.

Beyond choices in the type of mobile operating system on which they sit (such as iOS or Android), apps in the health category contain key differences essential to understanding the way they are regulated and their overall future potential.

9.4   Making Sense of the App Stores

It is difficult to keep up with the most recent app names and versions since they change frequently from week to week. Upon examining the long list of products, we have divided them into groups based on their function and purpose. These differ from one disease state to another, however, by understanding our structured categorization in diabetes as an example, a similar framework can then be applied more broadly across mobile health product development. It is extremely difficult for any single product to cover all of the groups since the intended use varies by category. Some companies have developed products in multiple categories but a one-fits-all approach is simply unrealistic.

Logbook and Diaries: *Including Glucose Buddy, MyNetDiary, mySugr Logbook*[6]
In diabetes care, HCP's ask their patients to record daily details relevant to diabetes management. These can include carbohydrates ingested, medication dosage, exercise, weight, and even blood pressure. Once

---

[6] Chick, S. and Rose, K.J. Mobile Health in Diabetes: mySugr's Monster Approach. "The App Store a Labyrinth of Choices" Section. (2016).

collected this data helps the HCP determine recommendations for the patient. According to evidence[7,8] over 50% of the insulin-treated population, however, do not maintain a log.

This category of applications digitizes the logbook and adds other features intended to better capture this important data, such as automatic downloading of certain medical devices already being used by patients at home.

Health and Wellness/LifeStyle: *WellDoc, Omada, Withings, iHealth, Livongo, mySugr Coach*[9]
A new category of apps has emerged with the rise of the Quantified Self philosophy which covers a wide range of products. They focus on helping set goals, track progress, and providing guidance, sometimes via customized education programs. Depending on the app, data is either manually entered or automatically connected via a peripheral, often wirelessly, connected device. It can include metrics such as heart rate, breathing quality, and even your mood. This goal-oriented educational approach fits well to diabetes therapy and can be individualized for patients' diabetes-specific needs.

Fitness and Food Apps: *Fitbit, myFitnessPal, Figwee, GoMeals, Meal Memory, RunKeeper, Calorie King, Carbs and Cals, Runtastic and Bolus (Insulin) Calculators*
The next category has to do with physical activity and nutrition, both of which overlap with a much larger group of general health apps outside of diabetes. On the sports side, it started with running trackers such as the Nike+ system measuring distance during running/walking/hiking. Motivational aspects soon were incorporated to help users measure their progress and other sports were added such as cycling and swimming.

---

[7] Arnold-Wörner, Nicole, "Compliance von Diabetikern: eine Analyse" (Dissertation 4972/1, LMU München: Faculty of Medicine 2005).

[8] Wong J.C., et al. "A Minority of Patients with Type 1 Diabetes Routinely Download." Diabetes Technology and Therapeutics (2015) August.

[9] Chick, S. and Rose, K.J. Mobile Health in Diabetes: mySugr's Monster Approach. "The App Store a Labyrinth of Choices" Section (2016).

On the food side, nutritional databases, previously difficult to browse, have been incorporated into apps. They have become easier to navigate to estimate the content of meals and snacks, including macronutrients. Since insulin-treated diabetics often base medication dosages on carbohydrate intake, this is a key aspect to diabetes self-management. Connected devices in this category include wristbands, watches, pedometers, and heart-rate straps as well as food scales and utensil sensors.

Electronic Medical Records (EMR) and Connectivity Platforms: *Glooko, Diasend, Tidepool, mySugr Scanner*
Similar to the paper-based logbook example becoming digital in the first category, the entire medical record has become more digital in recent years, with the goal of keeping all records from across different specialties in one patient file. More and more medical devices can be downloaded directly to the EMR platform, sometimes requiring a connectivity platform or middleware program to upload multiple brands (And to avoid messy download stations overflowing with separate software programs and associated cables). (Fig. 9.1)

Device-Specific Software: *Abbott, Dexcom, J&J, Medtronic Carelink, Roche, Sanofi*
The last category is made up of all of these individual programs for specific devices such as blood glucose monitors and insulin delivery systems. These devices are often used as part of daily therapy by people with diabetes and the associated data management software allows device data to be downloaded and analyzed (but typically each is restricted to one specific brand of device making it difficult to merge data from different sources).

One major differentiating factor among all health apps has to do with regulatory and data privacy considerations.[10] A small minority of the 1,500 diabetes apps have received clearance from regulatory authorities. Receiving a CE mark and/or FDA approval indicates that the company has followed strict quality guidelines and helps to

---

[10] Chick, S. and Rose, K.J. Mobile Health in Diabetes: mySugr's Monster Approach. "The App Store a Labyrinth of Choices" Section. 2016

Fig. 9.1 Diabetes Device Download Station

ensure the products perform the claimed functions. In some cases, this is mandatory, but simpler products deemed less risky by the authorities are not regulated in the same manner. Although more rigid regulations are anticipated in the future, as of early 2016, only guidelines on apps had been created by the FDA. These formal guidance documents, however, made it clear that apps could be considered regulated medical devices themselves, depending on their function.

Data privacy laws are geography-dependent. In the USA, for example, the Health Insurance Portability and Accountability Act (HIPAA) sets the standard for protecting sensitive patient data. Any company that deals with protected health information (PHI) must follow the required physical, network, and process security measures.

9.5   mySugr as an Example

My experience at Viennese-based start-up mySugr has allowed me deep insights into developments at one of the most prolific digital health companies in diabetes. With over 850,000 users in November 2016, they have achieved traction where many have not.

The initial mySugr application used a Tamagotchi-style avatar called the "diabetes monster."[11] Using gamification elements, mySugr rewarded users with points for logging data, participating in behavioral drive challenges, and generally making an effort to manage their diabetes. Each point earned brought them a step closer to "taming their diabetes monster" and beating their diabetes for the day. This quirky companion reacted to users' entries, offering words of support in a diabetes-friendly manner, treading an emotional line between laughter and tears.

Illustrating diabetes as a monster was controversial for some but resonated with many users, and not only young people, as had been predicted. People in their 50s were using it too. mySugr gained its first 1,000 users largely via word-of-mouth in the patient community, online and otherwise. Organic growth soared as users began writing touching personal reviews online, in community chat forums such as TuDiabetes, patient advocate blogs, and the App Store itself. Initially, some attributed the popularity to the fad for gaming apps like Candy Crush and Angry Birds, but soon the team at mySugr saw that their user base was connected to the product in a more profound manner. Diabetes was a very personal thing, and mySugr accompanied them through the ups and the downs. mySugr's employee base was also largely made up of people with diabetes.

Despite being medically regulated (with class I and class IIb regulated products), mySugr committed to creating a beautiful user experience with a sleek design and frequent iterations and updates.[12] Lead Designer and Co-Founder, Gerald Stangl, explained why:

---

[11] Chick, S. and Rose, K.J. Mobile Health in Diabetes: mySugr's Monster Approach. "mySugr: The Beginning" Section (2016).

[12] Chick, S. and Rose, K.J. Mobile Health in Diabetes: mySugr's Monster Approach. "The Secret Sauce and Logic Behind" Section.

Why can't a medical product deliver a similar consumer experience as Apple, Facebook, or Google? Users associate negative thoughts with hospitals and doctors, thus we intentionally distance ourselves.

Consumer giants like Apple seemed to have taken notice, having featured mySugr as one of a handful of patient-focused health apps in its 2015 "Transforming Healthcare" iBook publication.

Thanks to a combination of design, technology, and medical expertise, mySugr had developed a deep relationship with users, so much so that during quarterly feedback sessions, users frequently said they felt a sense of ownership and were part of developing the products. Every mySugr communication and touch-point went through a "diabetes sensitivity evaluation" in hope of adding a personal touch prior to implementation.

One example was in the customer service team, entirely made up of people with diabetes, who often added personal comments to their customer service responses, using their own experience to show compassion, support, and encouragement to fellow diabetics. When meeting with major Silicon Valley companies who had taken an interest in diabetes, mySugr management had been surprised to learn that this type of approach did not seem to be a priority for them. After all, it seemed to be a big part of gaining loyal users and if user growth continued at the same rate, they would soon have over 1 million users.

9.6   Mobile Health: Successes and Challenges Ahead

As the digital landscape in health care evolves, the market has become increasingly crowded as illustrated by the myriad of offerings related to diabetes.[13]

---

[13] Chick, S. and Rose, K.J. Mobile Health in Diabetes: mySugr's Monster Approach. "Mobile Health: Success and Challenges Ahead."

Few apps have been able to gain traction, and for those that have, it is not always clear what has helped.

mySugr management identified the following areas to focus on:

- Communication: connecting with patients and understanding their needs.
- Practical: tools must be useful in day-to-day therapy or risk becoming an added burden.
- Flexible: being able to adapt and react to users.
- Stickiness: the "cool factor" should not be underestimated; it gets the word out and keeps bringing people back.
- Cost: with skyrocketing health-care costs, payers more than ever want to invest in solutions that cut costs, in particular for the chronic disease population.

Avoiding a one-size-fits-all solution, mySugr has focused on people with diabetes and only people with diabetes, of which they have a deep understanding. Another example, Omada Health, has concentrated on the pre-diabetes population with educational programs. Different digital tools clearly work better for different phases of disease progression as patients' needs change.

There are several challenges and obstacles to the success of mHealth, but it is difficult to determine which is which. (How many could be merely "perceived" obstacles simply because people had been doing things the same way for so long?) One challenge is the reluctance of HCPs to adopt new technology. Not surprisingly this is changing with the new generation of doctors and as technology became more pervasive, they see an opportunity to engage with patients that otherwise lose interest in their own chronic disease management.

A second challenge has to do with the interoperability of devices. Manufacturers have not been interested in allowing their users to be able to share data openly with other ecosystems. Few standards exist and those that do exist are still not widespread, making data transfer more difficult. As the lines dividing consumer and medical device categories have become increasingly blurred, this needs to be addressed, but who will drive that change – regulators, industry, payers, or patients?

A third challenge is access. This is actually one of the obstacles that telemedicine is trying to solve, reaching people in rural areas far from doctors and hospitals.[14] Patient access solutions require expensive technology, but as smartphones have started to reach the lowest socioeconomic classes, this is becoming less of an issue.

Another is the scalability of the model. Again, this should favor telemedicine initiatives, but it is not yet clear what level of interaction between HCPs and patients is ideal in a telemedicine setting, nor in what form. Moreover, are patients similar enough to create massive scale? There have been several examples of Silicon Valley and Big Data announcing partnerships with the pharmaceutical/medical device industry in recent years. What types of collaborations are necessary to facilitate mHealth for the masses? Is big pharma the right partner or would patient associations, payers, or governments perhaps have better insights? Finally, how close are we to the tipping point in telemedicine via mobile health that will allow companies like mySugr to help millions tame their disease monsters, diabetes or otherwise?

These are just a few of the questions whose answers will help define the new shape of our health-care systems. mHealth has already began disrupting health care. The role of the HCP has historically evolved in alignment with the emergence of new medicines, equipment, and technology. Mobile health is the latest example and should be adapted to in a similar manner. It just happens to have grown very quickly via a direct to consumer channel, leaving certain influential health stakeholders such as physicians and regulators racing to catch up.

References

Arnold-Wörner, Nicole. *Compliance von Diabetikern: Eine Analyse von Einflussfaktoren anhand einer bevölkerungsbasierten Studie.* Dissertation 4972/1. LMU München: Faculty of Medicine, 2005.

---

[14] Petrut, Cristina, et al. *IDF Europe Position on Mobile Applications in Diabetes.* International Diabetes Federation Europe (2017).

Chick, S., and K.J. Rose. *Mobile Health in Diabetes: MySugr's Monster Approach*. INSEAD 04/2016–6204. Fontainebleau: France, 2016, https://cases.insead.edu/publishing/case?code=34846.

IMS Institute for Healthcare Informatics. *Patient Adoption of mHealth: Use, Evidence and Remaining Barriers to Mainstream Acceptance*, September 2015.

International Diabetes Federation. *IDF Diabetes Atlas*, 7th edn. Brussels, Belgium: International Diabetes Federation, 2015.

Petrut, Cristina, Rose, K.J., et al. *IDF Europe Position on Mobile Applications in Diabetes*. International Diabetes Federation Europe: Brussels, February 2017.

Johnson, Scott K. *Author of Scott's Diabetes Blog*. In-person Interview. San Diego, CA, USA, March 2016.

Limbourg, Andrea. Co-founder of #frdoc tweetchat. In-person Interview. Paris, December 2015.

Research2Guidance. *Diabetes Management Solutions Industry Report*, Research2Guidance: Berlin 2015/2016.

Wong, J.C, A.B. Neinstein, M. Spindler, and S. Adi. "A Minority of Patients with Type 1 Diabetes Routinely Download and Retrospectively Review Device Data." *Diabetes Technology and Therapeutics*. August 1, 2015, 17(8): 555–562. doi: 10.1089/dia.2014.0413. Epub July 2, 2015.

10

Social Media Strategies in Health Care

Françoise L. Simon, Loick Menvielle,
Matthieu Salvadore and François Meurgey

F.L. Simon (✉)
Mount Sinai School of Medicine and Columbia University,
New York, USA
e-mail: fls4@cumc.columbia.edu

L. Menvielle
Department of Marketing and Strategy, EDHEC Business School,
BP3116, 393- 400
Promenade des Anglais, France
e-mail: loick.menvielle@edhec.edu

M. Salvadore
Department of Marketing, Sorbonne University, Paris, France
e-mail: Mathieu.Salvadore@univ-paris1.fr

F. Meurgey
ASIT Biotech, Brussels, Belgium

Oukelos Sprl, Brussels, Belgium
e-mail: francois.meurgey@biotech.be; fmeurgey@oukelos.com

© The Author(s) 2017
L. Menvielle et al. (eds.), *The Digitization of Healthcare*,
DOI 10.1057/978-1-349-95173-4_10

10.1 Introduction

In recent years, the health-care sector has experienced radical changes regarding the empowerment of patients in relation to their diseases or those of their loved ones. The Internet has been a true catalyst by offering more outlets for consumers to express their deepest personal health-related concerns. The first patient groups, particularly for diseases such as AIDS and cancer, laid the foundations for a participatory and collaborative approach, between patients but also with the various stakeholders, such as health-care professionals or biopharmaceutical companies.

Many of these changes would not have been possible without Information and Communication Technologies (ICT), making these tools a weapon of choice to express and convey messages that some practitioners may have been tempted to ignore. As an illustration, the community of acor.org patients (Association of Cancer Online Resources) is one of the largest groups in the world (130 communities of patients with different types of cancers). This type of social media enables patients, their loved ones, and also caregivers to share and exchange information on the disease. These virtual forums offer new places to share experiences and exchange information, fostering anew among the various stakeholders a dialogue that was sometimes too limited, to the benefit of the patient. Limited to a marginal audience until a few years ago, social media is now increasingly inserting themselves in our daily lives and is also beginning to dominate the medical world.

10.2 Social Media: From One World to Another

Mentioning social media is not a new phenomenon, either to describe traditional consumer uses or to illustrate the business strategies of large organizations wanting to attract new customers, to strengthen commercial relationships or to reinforce brand loyalty. The Internet has become a communication medium accessed by more than 46% of the world population, nearly 3.4 billion users. The number of active users of social networks is around 2.2 billion led by Facebook with close to 1.5 billion users. As technologies and practices evolve, major trends appear to be turning more and more to mobile media strategies. Other social media, such as video sharing websites, have also dramatically modified the behavior of individuals. YouTube has become a major vehicle for the dissemination of content and messages, on the strength of its 1 billion monthly active users and 4 billion video views per day, 25% of which on mobile devices.[1]

These examples of the pervasiveness of social media in our environment have largely conquered the commercial sphere from mass market to luxury goods, as well as politics and culture. Health has recently become the subject of greater interest from players and investors in the field, who see there a growing potential in line with behavioral changes in society. In the USA alone, of 87% of adults using the Internet, 72% of them sought medical information through this channel.[2] Nearly a quarter of Internet users have accessed information on specialized websites such as HealthGrades,[3] RateMDs[4], or Vitals[5] to guide their choice of doctor. The principle remains the same: practitioners, regardless of their area of expertise, are evaluated by their patients. These new kinds of platforms allow users to access multiple resources: medical information, specialized blogs, or discussion forums dedicated to various pathologies. The work of Gao et al. (2012) demonstrated that the rating of doctors was not subject to negative overvaluation from disgruntled patients but reflected objective assessments of practitioners' skills. Researchers have demonstrated a positive correlation between physician evaluations on the Internet platform and their professional skills such as experience, advice, and education.

10.3 Patient to Patient Versus Patient to Provider

The development of these types of platforms and more generally of medical social networks is powerfully forging a new relationship to health. The necessary demand for interaction, speed, and immediacy of response

---

[1] https://www.statista.com/topics/1164/social-networks/

[2] http://www.pewinternet.org/data-trend/internet-use/latest-stats/

[3] http://www.healthgrades.com/

[4] https://www.ratemds.com

[5] http://www.vitals.com/

required by patients or their families inevitably has redefined medicine in favor of a participatory approach (Guistini 2006). Some medical social networks can be dedicated solely to providers, whereas other larger networks can also involve patients, their families, and caregivers.

As an example, PatientsLikeMe.com—one of the largest communities of patients in the world—was founded based on information-sharing to enable patients to better understand their disease and to improve their own condition (Simon and Meurgey 2014). Based on the principle of open resources, this type of platform has enabled patients and scientists to connect easily (Schwamm 2014). These platforms provide an opportunity for patient dialogue, enabling them to establish a social connection often broken by the disease or to guide them in their course of care. For practitioners, these sites provide the opportunity to obtain additional opinions on various pathologies (via opinions of colleagues both for widespread conditions and orphan diseases). Multimedia communities have now emerged by posting numerous medical videos online (Burke et al. 2009), using YouTube as a teaching tool for transmitting information to future practitioners. This turns out to be a meaningful resource that contributes to the improvement of the learning process.

In a more comprehensive evaluation, Silber (2009) believes that these social media help patients make choices or confront dilemmas. The information asymmetry and the power held by practitioners are declining, changing the traditional balance of power between doctor and patient. The multiplicity of platforms, especially those dedicated to patients, allows them to break the isolation associated with the disease. These communities induce a proactive approach on the part of the patient leading to interaction with other disease sufferers. Community spirit and guidance on this type of interface lead to a true sharing of experience, enabling patients to approach the disease from a different perspective (Frost and Massagli 2008). In addition to the sites mentioned previously, the recurrent use of patient groups on Facebook maintains links between patients while Twitter or specialized blogs are also important vectors of medical communication.

To illustrate the use of social networks by specialized medical sites, the following table provides a selected overview of the main patient or practitioner sites in the USA. The use of social networks is now an essential tool employed by the various players in the field of medical communication. Some American institutions have largely benefited from these social media and can be considered as references in the field. The Mayo Clinic[6] is exemplary in the field of media usage such as Facebook, but also Twitter and YouTube to disseminate messages. Since 2008, Kaiser Permanente[7] has developed a number of services (Internet, mobile, video tools...) for its 3.4 million members and 8,000 practitioners. These widely available resources enable users to monitor their condition, collect data or for other purposes around the patient journey (Table 10.1).

10.4 Toward Regulation of Social Media and Digital Tools

The growth of social networks in the medical sphere but also the development of connected medical devices have led regulatory bodies to study the phenomenon and start issuing guidance on how to protect individuals against the risks associated with the spread of inaccurate information. The Food and Drug Administration (FDA) has addressed three major areas through new regulations designed to adapt to a changing market and its players. The main guidelines concern marketing posts on social networks and medical advertising,[8] the balance of risks and benefits associated with information that is broadcast on these domains[9] and finally the type of corrective actions that companies faced with disinformation issues can take.[10]

---

[6] https://www.facebook.com/MayoClinic; https://twitter.com/mayoclinic; https://www.youtube.com/user/mayoclinic; https://plus.google.com/+MayoClinic; http://www.pinterest.com/mayoclinic/; http://instagram.com/mayoclinic; https://www.flickr.com/photos/mayoclinic/

[7] http://healthy.kaiserpermanente.org/

[8] http://www.fda.gov/downloads/Drugs/GuidanceComplianceRegulatoryInformation/Guidances/UCM381352.pdf

[9] http://www.fda.gov/downloads/Drugs/GuidanceComplianceRegulatoryInformation/Guidances/UCM401087.pdf

[10] http://www.fda.gov/downloads/Drugs/GuidanceComplianceRegulatoryInformation/Guidances/UCM401079.pdf

Table 10.1 Major medical platforms according to intended target

Intended target	Features	Example of Internet sites	Associated social networks					
			Facebook	Twitter	Google+	YouTube	LinkedIn	Others
Patients	Physician evaluation, search for competencies and advice from other health-care users	http://www.healthgrades.com/	X	X	X	X	X	X
		https://www.ratemds.com/	X	X	X			
		http://www.vitals.com/	X	X			X	X
		http://www.drscore.com/	X	X				
		http://www.ratemymd.ca/	X	X	X			X
		http://www.doctor.com/	X	X	X			
Health-care providers (HCPs)	Sites exclusively dedicated to physicians/ health-care providers. Exchange of medical opinions and diagnoses	http://www.sermo.com/	X	X		X	X	
		http://www.doccheck.com/	X	X	X	X		X
		https://secure.quantiamd.com/	X	X		X	X	
		http://www.medscape.com/	X	X	X	X	X	

Patients (mainly) but open to all						
Sharing site on the disease among patients and caregivers, but open to HCPs.	http://www.patientslikeme.com/	X	X		X	X
	https://www.rareconnect.org/	X	X		X	
Characteristics vary by pathology.	http://www.carecloud.com/	X	X	X	X	
	http://www.acor.org/	X	X			
Exchanges on innovation in the medical field (new treatments)	http://www.mdjunction.com/			X	X	X
	http://www.healingwell.com/	X	X		X	
	http://www.askapatient.com/	X	X	X		
	http://www.healthetreatment.com/	X	X			
	https://www.healthtap.com	X	X	X	X	X

The case of TIROSINT™ (levothyroxine sodium capsules from Institut Biochimique SA or IBSA) is one of the most significant steps taken by the FDA[11] to end false, partial, and misleading information spread about the drug via social networks, namely Facebook. Social media but also blogs and other digital interfaces are now the subject of heightened attention in order to guard against abuses. The existing guidance for the pharmaceutical industry mostly governs the topic of off-label usage. Similarly, posts on social media should include very clearly the approved product label when providing information on a drug. Post hoc surveys should not include advertising claims and cannot be considered as sufficient evidence.

In Europe, a similar vigilance is now being implemented to avoid any abuses. Thus, measures to promote ethical behavior and good conduct by researchers are integrated into the RESPECT program under the auspices of the European Commission. The International Federation of Pharmaceutical Manufacturers and Associations (IFPMA) has adopted the principle of self-regulation by companies. The low investment in digital marketing by the European players can justify this type of approach for now, but this will need to change quickly because the digital world knows no borders, and because of the increasing power of patient advocacy.

10.5 Social Content Risk Assessment

Although many of these measures have been put in place to guarantee and preserve the integrity of individuals, companies can also suffer the consequences of misinformation directed against them via social media. Thus, some players in the pharmaceutical industry have adopted a strategy to avoid direct exposure of branded products and to limit communications to unbranded disease awareness. This is the case of J & J on YouTube, opting for corporate and general content related to cancer, AIDS, autism, or even diabetes. AstraZeneca elected a similar approach on Twitter,

---

[11] http://www.fda.gov/downloads/drugs/guidancecomplianceregulatoryinformation/enforcementactivitiesbyfda/warninglettersandnoticeofviolationletterstopharmaceuticalcompanies/ucm388800.pdf

coming into contact with patients via #RXSave and enhancing corporate programs developed by the firm such as AZ & Me.

To preserve or enhance the corporate brand equity, several strategic directions can be identified on how to leverage social networks. This requires first for the company to determine its level of visibility on these networks, leading to more or less significant consequences depending on the specificity of information. Avoiding direct product information lowers the risk of significant damage for the company, in case of adverse effects. By contrast, if products are clearly identified, the company risks substantial damage to its brand. The visibility level will also drive more or less measurable benefits for the company (disease awareness, company image, brand equity, etc.). The following graph shows a stepwise approach, with benefits and disadvantages depending on the specificity of information (Fig. 10.1).

In general, pharmaceutical companies face the highest challenges in using social media. Multiple regulations are significant barriers and may explain the delay in adopting this type of strategy. However, digital tools have many advantages for the industry. They enable easy collection of information, a kind of "crowdsourcing" to assess what is happening about a product or

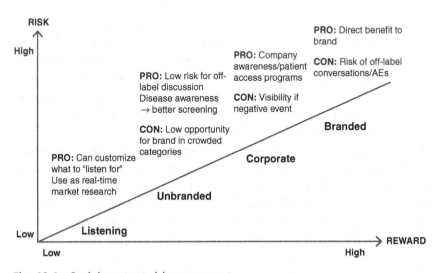

Fig. 10.1 Social content risk assessment

Source: F. Simon and K. Risch, "Social Media Strategies in Healthcare" (2014)

service and to identify consumers' unmet needs. For the health industry, these virtual spaces also allow the application of pharmacovigilance methods. The use of medical information monitoring via social media accelerates the transmission of information back to pharmaceutical companies to improve their processes. In the case of rare diseases, for example, social media contribute to the acceleration of knowledge and better understanding of all issues related to a given pathology, whereas "traditional" methods of transmission of medical information tend to be slower.

The skillful use of social media also allows stakeholders to create a quasi-customized content that optimizes their relationship with patients. These tools also provide an opportunity to test new initiatives and to measure directly target responses. One of the major advances related to these means of communication is the collaborative approach (Schleyer et al. 2008). By mobilizing Internet users in these sharing sites, this actively contributes to the enhancement of information through close integration with other social media (Eysenbach 2007, 2008b). For health-care stakeholders, these spaces also contribute to the sharing of scientific information among researchers. The social network Facebook, for example, can thus be diverted from its initial use to optimize collaboration among scientists (Titus et al. 2008).

In the past few years, Sanofi has initiated a new strategy to enhance its ability to innovate by bringing together new co-creators and stakeholders. This approach relies on crowdsourcing techniques incorporating the principles of co-creation and co-participation, showing the company's capacity to innovate through different means and putting the user experience on center stage. This new method of concept creation enables manufacturers to implement prototypes in a very short time. Starting in 2011, Sanofi has launched various open innovation challenges around the treatment of diabetes. One of the results is an original mobile application (Ginger.io) that collects data to understand the relationship between health status and individual behavior. This data set is then analyzed at the macro level to identify the links between certain behaviors and stages of the disease (Simon et al. 2014).

Other similar initiatives have been undertaken by Sanofi, using crowdsourcing methods to encourage regular feedback from patients. They become active players in the creation of health-care products and services.

In this regard, the community "Diabetes Mine" has contributed to producing an application module for blood glucose monitoring. Apple users can download the iBGStar app co-developed by Sanofi and Apple, and may then buy a device they can insert into their iPhone or iPod to measure their blood sugar levels, allowing them to save this information or communicate it remotely. These new approaches to innovation change the role of the patients, who then take an active role in these new products and services (Wright et al. 2009), becoming actual co-developers with companies (often start-ups) and researchers (Gunther 2007, 2008a).

10.6 Medical Social Media Are Changing the Relationship to Health

The democratization of the acquisition of medical knowledge made possible by the Internet has generated different behaviors (IMS 2014). For Dedding et al. (2011), this approach is helping change multiple relationships in health care. In some cases, the use of new media complicates the links between practitioners and patients. The development of this participatory medicine generates a redistribution of tasks and responsibilities between patients and physicians, and induces a new balance of power in health (IMS 2013).

A study by PricewaterhouseCoopers (2012) highlights the effects generated by social media, changing the nature of interactions between individuals and organizations. Four factors contribute to these changes: User-generated content, community and group effects, and the rapid dissemination of open, two-way information. According to the study, 42% of Americans have used social media to consult medical information regarding treatment or for advice on practitioners. Trust is a fundamental component and varies depending on the target of the information. Sixty-one percent of respondents in this study are likely to give a modicum of trust to health-care providers, 41% would be willing to share information with them. However, concerning the pharmaceutical industry, the overall confidence level is found to be lower: 37% of respondents have confidence in information from industry players, and only 28% would be likely to share information with them. The age of users of these social media influences their level of commitment: 80% of respondents in the 18–24 age group are likely to share medical information and 90% of them would be willing to contribute to social networks. By contrast, 45% of 45–64-year-olds would share the same type of information and 56% would consider contributing.

The sharing of information therefore depends on the level of trust by consumers regarding health-care players. Among all respondents, 47% are willing to share information with doctors. Men (51% of them) are more likely to communicate on social networks with doctors they do not know versus 43% of women. Exchange between patients is endorsed to a smaller extent whereas the nursing and hospital sector enjoys a high level of trust. In contrast, sharing with the private and commercial sector, including pharmaceutical companies, generates less enthusiasm overall, and even less among women.

Social media are changing modes of communication between doctors and patients. Providers must adapt to a new way of communicating, from a flow with one transmitter to multiple receivers to a dialogue open to all and where the recipients themselves become sources of information. The rapid spread of information is also a new factor to which actors from the health sphere must adapt. Consumer involvement with regard to medical social media is built gradually over time and is part of a long-term relationship approach that requires significant top-level commitment and investment by health-care players.

Medical social media have also changed the way consumers view their health, especially in the way they manage a disease or join groups of patients to share their experience. This approach often allows patients to reconnect with the outside world. In many cases, the disease is causing a social breakdown. Social media can help break patients' isolation and positively affect their psychological state. Beyond this positive effect, social media also have an effect on the health literacy of patients. They provide additional information and help open a dialogue among patients themselves or their family, caregivers, or health-care providers in general. Because of these new exchanges and the accompanying enrichment of knowledge, the level of patient expectations has also risen and generates a need for more sophisticated communications.

In this respect, the experience of the Mayo Clinic is emblematic in many ways, as the hospital demonstrates best practices regarding the use of social networks and new media. Seven media are used to feed informational flows to patients and third parties: Twitter, Facebook, Google+, YouTube, Pinterest, Instagram, LinkedIn, and Flickr (Table 10.2).

YouTube is the most popular in terms of number of hits per video and offers rich content based on conditions, treatments, and patient experiences. This way of communicating via the testimonies of patients treated within the institution, positively influences their perception toward the hospital. These videos help lower patients' initial fears and encourage engagement with the Mayo Clinic brand. Other videos fostering the transparency of medical knowledge contribute to establish the legitimacy of the brand through its pedagogical values. All of these techniques reinforce a positive perception toward the brand—which was already broadly favorable, in the case of the Mayo Clinic. The use of social media therefore contributes to increased brand awareness, but also helps shape the brand's meaning and value for patients.

In the past decade, health professionals and especially providers and hospitals were among the first to invest in social media. Their use of digital communication has been more comprehensive than that of the pharmaceutical industry. The Mayo Clinic is one of the best examples of the deployment of an integrated, multichannel strategy, which was able to link efficiently researchers, providers, and patient advocates through digital health. In addition to their positive effects on the brand equity of the institution, these media establish a new way to communicate with patients by being closer to their concerns, recognizing their unmet needs and speaking their language. As noted earlier, the trust granted by patients to their physicians and medical institutions appears to be generally much higher than their confidence in the pharmaceutical industry, which makes their engagement on social media much easier.

The proper use of social media cannot simply consist of feeding a flow of information on these channels, but should also help stimulate debate, generate new ideas and facilitate crowdsourcing for players in the field. Beyond these immediate achievements, the ultimate goal is to support a new model of personalized medicine and a new way of defining the doctor–patient relationship. Patients are becoming better educated and

Table 10.2 Social media used by the Mayo Clinic

	Subscribers	Consultations/Tweets	Comments
Twitter	831,121	17,323 Tweets (in 2014) vs 32,271 Tweets (in 2016)	783 photos and videos (in 2014) vs 5,429 (in 2016), and 823,300 subscriptions (in 2014) vs 1 320,790 subscriptions (in 2016)
Facebook	533,116 likes (in 2014) vs 891,512 likes (in 2016)	N.A	Several other pages are linked: Mayo Clinic Diet, Health System, Heathy Living, Proceedings, Transplantation etc...
Google+	297,189 (in 2014) vs 603,020 (in 2016)	3,483,558 visits	
Pinterest	12,622 (in 2014) vs 24,120 (in 2016)	N.A.	21 boards (in 2014) vs 29 boards (in 2016) including from 2 to 113 pins (in 2014) vs from 16 to 126 pins (in 2016), from general health issues to oncology or cardiology (to cite but a few examples)
LinkedIn	48,168 (in 2014) vs 88,549 (in 2016)	N.A.	Networking and links to other social networks
YouTube	20,779 (in 2014) vs 44,457 (in 2016)	From 686,726 views to fewer than 100 views (in 2014) vs 1,619,965 (in 2016) 30 playlists including from 7 to 183 videos. Arrayed around pathologies, treatment or patient experience.	Top consultation: 1 video: 686,736 views in 2014 vs 1,619,965 in 2016 7 videos between 300,000 and 400,000 views vs 17 videos in 2016 9 videos entre 100,000 and 200,000 views vs 17 videos in 2016

Table 10.2 (continued)

	Subscribers	Consultations/Tweets	Comments
Instagram	1,627 (in 2014) vs 23,502 (in 2016)	N.A.	15 posts but activity on Instagram has only started mid-July 2014 vs 154 posts in 2016
Flickr	N.A.	N.A.	91 albums (in 2014) vs 120 albums

Source: Adapted from Mayo Clinic social media—survey in August 2014 and in August 2016.

have greater autonomy to make informed decisions, but the use of these new technologies also has mixed consequences. In the majority of cases, the increased knowledge of non-professionals improves their relationship with practitioners and understanding of the disease. However, for some very proactive, wellness-oriented patient, segments, these relationships can be disturbed by multiple information sources (CMA 2013).

10.7 Limitations and Future Research

The limitations of this study are linked to the fact that many initiatives in this emerging field are small, fragmented, and subject to significant barriers; these include consumer privacy concerns, the lack of technology integration between hospital systems, physician offices, and patient mobile apps, as well as country-specific and fast-changing regulation.

In addition, although several existing databases can track some metrics for health-care social media, there is not sufficient evidence to link them to marketing effectiveness and return on investment for manufacturers and service providers.

The objective of this chapter was to identify opportunities and challenges for firms and major stakeholders. The development of a new personalized medicine model will support the increasing worldwide use of digital health, including telemedicine and social media. Future research directions may reflect the progress of technology integration from hospital systems to mobile devices, and the standardization of regulation across major markets.

10.8 Conclusion

Broader access to information, greater transparency, the dissemination of medical knowledge, and new media resources have profoundly transformed health-care behavior. Through social media, the health sector is facing radical changes in the way it communicates or connects with patients, but it still lags behind other business sectors such as consumer goods. Not only extensive regulation but also the harm that some health-care players may suffer from an inappropriate use of social media lead them to exercise caution, especially in the case of biopharmaceutical companies.

Hospitals and medical institutions have so far taken the best advantage of digital media. The trust level they enjoy is more favorable than that of the pharmaceutical industry and supports their wide use of new channels. These allow a personalized dialogue with patients and change the dynamics of medical relationships. In particular, they reinforce the overall brand image of these institutions by bringing them closer to their customers and giving patients a voice to be heard and respected.

For health-care players, this new approach provides the opportunity to take patient requests and their unmet needs more seriously. Social media are therefore helping challenge established principles of medical innovation, and enabling biopharmaceutical companies to leverage this potential crowdsourcing, paving the way for a true co-creation process, from research and development to disease awareness, product diffusion and service optimization.

References

Adam, Wright, W., Bates David, Blackford Middleton, Tonya Hongsermeier, Kashyap Vipul, M. Thomas Sean, and F. Sittig Dean. "Creating and sharing clinical decision support content with Web 2.0: Issues and examples," *The Journal of Biomedical Informatics*, 42(2) (2009): 334–346.

Burke Sloane, C., Shonna Snyder, and C. Rager Robin. "Assessment of faculty usage of youtube as a teaching resource," *Internet Journal of Allied Health Sciences and Practive*, 7 (2009): 1.

Christine, Dedding, Van Doorn Roeasja, Winkler Lex, and Ria Reis. "How will e-health affect patient participation in the clinic? A review of e-health studies and the current evidence for changes in the relationship between medical professionals and patients," *Social Science and Medicine*, 72 (2011): 49–53. Pubmed.

CMA.ca. *Internet use by* patients *seeking health information.* [Online] Available from: http://www.cma.ca/advocacy/internet-patients. Accessed November 8, 2013.

Dean, Guistini. "How Web 2.0 is changing medicine," *BMJ*, 333(7582) (December 23, 2006): 1283–1284.

Denise, Silber. "Médecine 2.0: les enjeux de la médecine participative," *La Presse Médicale*, 38(10) (2009): 1456–1462.

Eysenbach, Gunther. "From intermediation to disintermediation and apomediation: New models for consumers to access and assess the credibility of health information in the age of Web2.0," *Studies in Health Technology and Informatics*, 129(1) (2007): 162–166.

Eysenbach, Gunther. "Medicine 2.0: Social networking, collaboration, participation, apomediation, and openness," *Journal Medical Internet Research*, 10(3) (2008a): e22.

Eysenbach, Gunther. "Credibility of health information and digital media: new perspectives and implications for youth," In Metzger MJ and Flanagin AJ editors. *Digital media, youth, and credibility*. The John D and Catherine T MacArthur Foundation Series on Digital Media and Learning. Cambridge, MA: MIT Press, 2008b.

Frost, Jeana H., and Michael P. Massagli. "Social uses of personal health information within Patients Like Me, an online patient community: What can happen when patients have access to one another's data," *Journal Medical Internet Research*, 10(3) (2008): e15.

Gao, G. Guodong, J.S. McCullough, Ritu Agarwal, and Ashish K. Jha. "A changing landscape of physician quality reporting: Analysis of patients' online ratings of their physicians over a 5-year period," *Journal Medical Internet Research*, 14(1) (2012): e38.

IMS, "Patient apps for improved healthcare, from novelty to mainstream," October 2013, Report 65 pages, 2013.

IMS, "Engaging patients through social media, is healthcare ready for empowered and digitally demanding patients?" January 2014, Report, 47 pages, 2014.

PriceWaterhouse, "Social media 'likes' healthcare: From marketing to social business." Report 38 pages, April 2012

Schwamm Lee, H. "Telehealth: Seven strategies to successfully implement disruptive technology and transform health care," *Health Affairs*, February, 33(2) (2014): 200–206.

Simon, Françoise, and François Meurgey, "New strategies for digital health," Proceedings, 13th International Marketing Trends Conference, Venice, January 22–26, 2014

Simon F., Risch K., Wainwright R, and Ypkoi N, "Social Media Strategies in Healthcare, presentation at Columbia University," July 19, 2014.

Titus, Schleyer, Spallek Heiko, S. Butler Brian, Subramanian Sushmita, Weiss Daniel, and Louisa M. Poythress, "Facebook for scientists: Requirements and services for optimizing how scientific collaborations are established," *Journal Medical Internet Research*, 10(3) (2008): e24.

11

Trust and Provenance in Communication to eHealth Consumers

Grant P. Cumming, Tara French, Jamie Hogg,
Douglas McKendrick, Heidi Gilstad, David Molik
and Joanne S. Luciano

G.P. Cumming (✉)
Dr Gray's Hospital, NHS Grampian, University of Highlands and Islands and
University of Aberdeen, Elgin, Scotland, Aberdeen, UK
e-mail: grant.cumming@nhs.net

T. French
Institute of Design Innovation, The Glasgow School of Art, Glasgow, UK
e-mail: t.french@gsa.ac.uk

J. Hogg
Dr Gray's Hospital, Elgin, NHS Grampian, Aberdeen, UK
e-mail: jamie.hogg@nhs.net

D. McKendrick
Dr Gray's Hospital, Elgin, NHS Grampian and, University of Aberdeen,
Aberdeen, UK
e-mail: d.mckendrick@nhs.net

© The Author(s) 2017   **189**
L. Menvielle et al. (eds.), *The Digitization of Healthcare*,
DOI 10.1057/978-1-349-95173-4_11

11.1 Introduction

The Internet is used as a conduit for health information with searches for health information ranking highly in Europe (Higgins et al. 2011) and America (Fox 2011). This information can complement information provided by the health professional, provide the end user with information to ask new questions of their health provider, empower them to own their health and can influence whether or not the end user will attend a health professional consultation (Moreland et al. 2015).

The Internet can also be used for other health-related purposes including telemedicine, eHealth (the transfer of health resources and health care by electronic means) and mobile health (M-Health): the use of wireless technology to deliver health services and information using mobile communication devices such as tablet computers, smart phones and other monitoring devices (De La Torre-Díez et al. 2015). Monitoring devices are becoming increasingly ubiquitous with both external (including environmental and wearables) and internal devices making it possible to access data about ones environments on the Internet, anytime, anyplace, on any device and on any network (CERP-IoT 2009), thereby realising Kevin Ashton's vision of the Internet of things (IoT) (Ashton 2009). A recent

H. Gilstad
Health Informatics Research Group, Department of Neuromedicine and Movement Science, NTNU Norwegian University of Science and Technology, School of Medicine, NTNU, Norway
e-mail: heidi.gilstad@ntnt.no

D. Molik
Cold Spring Harbor Laboratory, New York, USA
e-mail: dmolik@cshl.edu

J.S. Luciano
School of Informatics and Computing Indiana University, Bloomington, IN, USA
Predictive Medicine, Inc., Belmont, MA, USA
e-mail: jluciano@indiana.edu; jluciano@predmed.com

Pew report expects the IoT to be thriving by 2025 (Anderson and Rainie 2014) with Cisco predicting that there will be 50 billion connected devices by 2020 (Evans 2011).

There are four categories of medical devices that meet the IoT criteria which are wearable external medical devices, internally embedded medical devices, stationary medical devices and consumer products for health monitoring (Glasser 2015). The latter devices have given rise to the quantified self-movement (the incorporation of technology) to collect personal daily life data using wearable sensors (Swan 2013). These movements are gaining momentum and further pushing adoption and development, so much so, that more invasive monitoring for personal use includes vaginal sensors used to track ovulation (Wooder 2016). The term "early adopters" can now even be extended to the unborn with the recent availability of wearable sensor products which continually monitor the foetus and provide pregnancy data to both health-care professionals and parents (Wooder 2016).

Anything that has a sensor has the potential to communicate with anything else that has a sensor. Furthermore, algorithms and analytics that are monitoring the stream of data from these sensors can then in turn orchestrate further activity of these sensors. Companies are now employing health-care specialists to make sure that the data these devices collect are used in a meaningful way by health-care professionals and individuals (New Scientist 2016). The IoT can therefore be visualised as a digital ecosystem, whereby technology is no longer a fixed architecture carrying out fixed functions. "Technology can now be seen as a system—a metabolism of things—executing things which can sense their environment and reconfigure actions to execute appropriately" (Arthur 2009).

Interrogating the Internet for health information and combining this information with that from the IoT, together with health professional patient information systems, and the emerging field of systems biology means that we are entering a new era of medicine in which each person can be "near fully defined at the individual level, instead of how we presently practice medicine which is at a population level" (Topol 2012).

Handling the quantity of "Big Data" generated from the IoT through curation, visualisation and interpretation of data are therefore fertile areas for innovation (Luciano et al. 2013, 2014). The data from the Internet has the potential to turn prediction into an equation (Tucker 2014), and qualitative predictive models of human behaviour can be written. However caution must be highlighted—the data is so big that everything can be significant and the scientific method no longer works. False correlations are commonplace and new ways to test the causality of connections are urgently required—correlations do not necessarily mean causation and to over fit is human (Pentland 2012).

11.1.1 Personalising Health Care

The future of medicine is increasingly being mediated through predictive, participatory, preventative and personalised (P4) modes (see Chapter 5). However, personalisation of health care may be a compromise on best medical evidence and advice to accommodate the patient's wishes to give a preferred health outcome (Hancock and Bezold 1993) from the patient's perspective. The evidence and options influencing a patient's decision-making are increasingly being influenced by information and communication technologies (ICTs) utilising the World Wide Web and the Internet. As online health information becomes more ubiquitous (i.e. available from specialised health websites, forums, health-related apps, general health websites) and accessible from different platforms it is becoming increasingly difficult for the end user to aggregate, evaluate the credibility and reliability and make sense of the information.

11.1.2 eHealth Literacy

A fundamental problem is how to turn data into wisdom for the citizen, that is, how does the citizen make sense of information? Health literacy involves the ability to read, understand, evaluate and use health information to make appropriate decisions about health and health care. Making sense of health data is an emerging field of consumer health informatics/health literacy (Abaidoo and Larweh 2014).

The notion of eHealth literacy is a new concept for creating, evaluating and understanding online health resources for the public (Kushniruk 2015) and its definition and scope is evolving (Norman 2011; Quaglio et al. 2016) as there are many demands to be covered (Chan and Kaufman 2011). eHealth literacy has been defined as "the ability of individuals to seek, find, understand, and appraise health information from electronic resources and apply such knowledge to address or solve a health problem" (Stellefson et al. 2011). In the Lily model, and the accompanying assessing tool, the eHealth Literacy Scale (eHEALS), six fundamental literacies that are required to be an eHealth literate: (1) traditional literacy and numeracy, (2) media literacy, (3) information literacy, (4) computer literacy, (5) science literacy and (6) health literacy (Norman and Skinner 2006). The model however lacks a focus on socio-contextual aspects in the analytic framework and the assessment tool (Norman 2011; Gilstad 2014).

11.2 Major Concepts

The possibility of understanding complex relationships in precision medicine are being explored in the emerging fields of systems biology (Cumming 2014; P4 Medicine Institute 2016) and Big Data analytics (Shiao et al. 2015).

11.2.1 Data Mining

Data mining is the process of using artificial intelligence, machine learning and statistics to extract information (patterns and knowledge) from data sets.

11.2.2 Big Data

Big data is data which is too large to process by traditional means. Traditional generally means that the data is either too large or changes too often for a single desktop computer to handle, necessitating solutions such as distributed storage or distributed computing.

11.2.3 Broad Data

This distinction between Big data and Broad data is important. Analysis and conclusions from Big data on a subject may come from one source only, whereas analysis and conclusions from Broad data on a subject come from many data sources (Hendler 2013; Tiropanis et al. 2013). This enables triangulation and increases the veracity of the conclusions.

11.2.4 Governance, Provenance and Trust of Internet-Based Health Care

Content on the Internet is unregulated; anyone can publish anything on the Internet. There is accurate medical information on the Internet along with dangerous information (NNLM 2016). The Internet therefore is a powerful tool that has the potential to do harm if the information is incorrect, ambiguous or negatively impacts on an end users need to seek health professional advice. There is an increasing body of literature on the quality and content of health-related websites using matrices that assess quality, readability, information coverage and provenance of information (i.e. where data came from and its history) (Buneman et al. 2000), including authorship, updating of information and competing interests with commercial sponsorship. A number of kitemarking sites are available aiming to give assurance/reassurance regarding the reliability and quality of information on health-related websites. For example, the HON code of conduct (Health On the Net Foundation 2016) offers a multi-stakeholder consensus on standards to protect citizens from misleading health information.

However, kitemarking may not be cost effective. It has been argued that to establish and run a comprehensive kitemarking system for patient information in the UK, it would involve tens if not hundreds of people including subject experts, information professionals, designers, etc. It would probably cost many millions of pounds and involve untold bureaucracy (Delamothe 2000).

11.3 Exploring How Personalisation Might Occur

11.3.1 Health Information Sites

In this new era of medicine, many types of data are being collected, from many sources (IoT), on multiple timescales, and is of varying quality. "This Big and Broad Data needs to be validated to make sure that it is true and certain, 'true' in the sense that data findings accurately reflect the situation and 'certain' in the sense that the data are supported by evidence" (Guion 2002). The methods that are used to establish validity, analyse data from multiple perspectives using multiple methods. This is called triangulation of data. As data volume continues to increase, triangulation of health data will need to be automated to support the decision-making processes in medicine.

Information asymmetry deals with the study of decisions in transactions where one party has more or better information than the other. This creates an imbalance of power in transactions which can sometimes cause the transactions to go awry. For example, in pharmaceutical clinical trials, not all the information is available to the public and in industry, information asymmetry makes it possible for organisations to present themselves as environmentally responsible, when in fact they are not ("greenwashing").

The I-Choose project (Sayogo et al. 2016; Jarman and Luna-Reyes 2016, Luciano et al. 2016) aimed to address this information asymmetry using an information technology infrastructure to enable consumers to purchase coffee based on the consumer's individual values and preferences. The price of coffee varies considerably, as do consumer preferences. Some want the lowest price, while others are willing to pay a premium for coffee that is certified as having been produced to fair trade standards. However, when we purchase coffee, we do not know the provenance. We do not know if it was grown in a way that exploited children, or farm workers, or damaged some distant ecology, or even used unhealthy pesticides. Different fair trade organisations have different criteria, and some may call themselves with a name that implies fair trade, when they are far from it. Thus, consumers have to make purchasing decision with only limited and incomplete information, thereby affecting their ability to choose among various products based on their personal preferences. We suggest that the same is true for decision-making in health care.

The I-Choose project developed a set of questions that were indications of transparency and preference, such as was there an inspection of the coffee farm by an independent third party? Or did the inspection include an assessment of the use of pesticides, or children under the age of 15? and was the date and inspector's name recorded and the report signed? Personal preferences, such as the use of child labour or pesticides, are achieved by assigning weights to questions.

In the medical domain, the principles and design of the ICT infrastructure remain the same, however, the questions need to be adapted.

11.3.2 No Delays

A novel way of using digital technology to deliver and facilitate patient engagement with health provision is NHS Grampian's No Delays concept which uses video on demand to provide personalised patient postcards (Digital Life Sciences 2016). No Delays aims to transform outpatient services by helping people to take responsibility for their own care, provide care as close to home as possible and reduce the need for attendance at hospital clinics or unscheduled admission to hospital.

The No Delays platform is not a static website but a dynamic resource that allows clinicians to work interactively with patients to improve understanding of their condition and/or treatment. No Delays allows health-care teams to digitise elements of their local care pathway by creating interactive packages of digital content that can be personalised by health-care professionals and prescribed to patients according to their needs. The interaction is based on trust and choice. The face-to-face consultation establishes the context of the digital interaction. Patients and their families are receptive to new knowledge and information if they see it as immediately relevant to them. The clinical team create video-on-demand packages which encompass all the knowledge that they know, from their experience in clinic, are applicable to common presentations of illness. The module can be sent when the context is right.

NHS Services are free at the point of access and the development of alternative Internet-based services that succeed will depend on people choosing them over face-to-face encounters. The alternative must be trusted, come from a trusted source and comprehensive enough to provide the equivalent value. The Internet is not in itself a trusted source and the role of the NHS clinical team is pivotal in the design of the resources.

11.4 Discussion

11.4.1 Build It and They Will (*Not*) Come

Too many eHealth projects have come under the assumption of build it and they will come—and they did not (Greenhalgh et al. 2010). Implementing the UK's Delivering Assisted Living Lifestyles at Scale (DALLAS) programme and the lessons learned from it provide a useful framework in which to implement digital health-care tools and services at scale (Devlin et al. 2016). Engagement with the target audience utilising co-productive, co-creative, collaborative principles with an agile iterative methodology across multi-platforms is key to ensuring uptake of digital health-care tools (McHattie et al. 2014). As such there is an increasing recognition of the role of Design in shaping the future of health care (French et al. 2016). In particular, approaches that employ Participatory Design can lead to sustainable solutions for health-care delivery by involving end users of products and services at an early stage of the design process, leading to enhanced results in terms of efficiency and usability (Bowen 2010).

11.4.2 Evaluation

There is a great need for evaluating digital health interventions. Data will tell us how many people have downloaded a certain app (e.g. to stop smoking) but we do not know how many have actually stopped smoking or whether or not an intervention has had a negative effect on the citizen. In a review of cost utility and cost effectiveness of Internet health provision, the authors concluded that due to methodological flaws economic evaluations are limited due to disparate estimation methods, lack of randomised controlled trials, lack of long-term evaluation studies, small sample sizes and absence of quality data and appropriate measures. Similar conclusions were reached in a Norwegian review (Bergmo 2015), which observed that despite a limited number of large-scale services and sparse evidence eHealth is cost-effective, interest in eHealth continues to grow.

11.5 Conclusion

The future of medicine is shifting to a patient-centric model enabled by ICTs. One aspect of this model involves an increasing need to triangulate data from multiple sources. These data sources will be of variable quality and new ways of weighting the data sources will be required to enable informed decision-making. Implicit in this approach is eHealth literacy and engagement with the technology. The exemplar of I-Choose may provide a framework for personal health-related searches with the end user providing the weighting of the criteria that matters to them. The information from this health-related search and if necessary, subsequent dialogue with the health professional results in the preferred health management/treatment for that citizen. No Delays on the other hand is all about the health professional engaging the citizen at the right time and providing them with medically correct information using ICT. More research is needed to evolve the tools to enable the interrogation of disparate data source, to curate, visualise and make sense of the data and also to assess the impact of ICT on health care and its delivery. The cost effectiveness of these interventions also need to be addressed.

References

Abaidoo, Benjamin, and Benjamin Teye Larweh. 2014. "Consumer Health Informatics: The Application of ICT in Improving Patient-Provider Partnership for a Better Health Care," *Online Journal of Public Health Informatics* 6: 2, doi: 10.5210/ojphi.v6i2.4903.

Anderson, Janna, and Lee Rainie. 2014. "The Internet of Things Will Thrive by 2025," *Pew Research Internet Project*: 14.

Arthur, W. Brian. 2009. *The Nature of Technology: What It Is and How It Evolves*. New York: Free Press.

Ashton, Kevin. 2009. "That 'Internet of Things' Thing," *RFiD Journal* 22, no. 7: 97–114

Bergmo T. S. 2015. "How to Measure Costs and Benefits of eHealth Interventions: An Overview of Methods and Frameworks," *Journal of Medical Internet Research* 17, no. 11:e254. doi: 10.2196/jmir.4521.

Bowen, S. 2010. "Critical theory and participatory design," *Proceedings of CHI*. https://www.cl.cam.ac.uk/events/experiencingcriticaltheory/Bowen-ParticipatoryDesign.pdf

Buneman, Peter, Sanjeev Khanna, and Wang-Chiew Tan. 2000. "Data Provenance: Some Basic Issues," *FST TCS 2000: Foundations of Software Technology and Theoretical Computer Science*, ed. Sanjiv Kapoor and Sanjiva Prasad, Vol. 1974 (Berlin, Heidelberg: Springer Berlin Heidelberg), 87–93. http://link.springer.com/10.1007/3-540-44450-5_6

Chan, Connie V., and David R. Kaufman. 2011. "A Framework for Characterizing eHealth Literacy Demands and Barriers," *Journal of Medical Internet Research* 13, no. 4: e94, doi: 10.2196/jmir.1750.

Cluster of European Research Projects on the Internet of Things (CERP-IoT). 2009. "Internet of Things, Strategic Research Roadmap," *European Commission*. http://www.internet-of-things-research.eu/pdf/IoT_Cluster_Strategic_Research_Agenda_2009.pdf. Accessed August 28, 2016.

Cumming, Grant P. 2014 "Connecting & Collaborating—Healthcare for the 21st Century," (Proceedings of the Second European Workshop on Practical Aspects of Health Informatics [PAHI], Trondheim, Norway, May 19–20, 2014), http://ceur-ws.org/Vol-1251/abstract1.pdf. Accessed August 28, 2016.

De La Torre-Díez, Isabel et al. 2015. "Cost-Utility and Cost-Effectiveness Studies of Telemedicine, Electronic, and Mobile Health Systems in the Literature: A Systematic Review," *Telemedicine and E-Health* 21, no. 2: 81–85, doi: 10.1089/tmj.2014.0053.

Delamothe, Tony. 2000. "Quality of Websites: Kitemarking the West Wind," *BMJ* 321, no. 7265: 843–844, doi: 10.1136/bmj.321.7265.843.

Devlin AM, et al. 2016. "Delivering digital health and well-being at scale: lessons learned during the implementation of the dallas program in the United Kingdom," *Journal of the American Medical Informatics Association* 23, no. 1: 48–59, doi:10.1093/jamia/ocv097.

Evans, Dave. 2011. "CISCO White Paper," *The Internet of Things: How the Next Evolution of the Internet Is Changing Everything*. https://www.cisco.com/c/dam/en_us/about/ac79/docs/innov/IoT_IBSG_0411FINAL.pdf. Accessed August 28, 2016.

Fox, Susannah. 2011. *The Social Life of Health Information*. Washington, DC: Pew Internet & American Life Project. http://www.pewinternet.org/files/old-media//Files/Reports/2011/PIP_Social_Life_of_Health_Info.pdf

French, T., Teal, G., and Raman, S. 2016. "Experience Labs: co-creating health and care innovations using design tools and artefacts," In: Lloyd, P., Bohemia, E., eds. *Proceedings of DRS2016: Design + Research + Society - Future-Focused Thinking*, Brighton, UK, 7: 2965–2979.

Gilstad, Heidi. 2014. "Toward a Comprehensive Model of eHealth Literacy," Paper for Practical Aspects of health Informatics (PAHI), CEUR Workshop Proceedings 2014, 63–72.

Glasser, John. 2015. "How The Internet of Things Will Affect Health Care," *Hospitals & Health Networks*. http://www.hhnmag.com/articles/3438-how-the-internet-of-things-will-affect-health-care. Accessed May 21, 2016.

Greenhalgh T, and Russell J. 2010. "Why Do Evaluations of eHealth Programs Fail? An Alternative Set of Guiding Principles," *PLoS Med* 7, no. 11: e1000360. doi:10.1371/journal.pmed.1000360.

Guion, Lisa Ann. 2002. *Triangulation: Establishing the Validity of Qualitative Studies*. Gainesville, FL: University of Florida Cooperative Extension Service, Institute of Food and Agricultural Sciences, EDIS.

Hancock, Trevor, and Clement Bezold. 1993. "Possible Futures, Preferable Futures," *The Healthcare Forum Journal* 37: 23–29.

Health On the Net Foundation. 2016. https://www.healthonnet.org/. Accessed May 21, 2016.

Hendler, Jim. 2013. "Broad Data: Exploring the Emerging Web of Data," *Big Data* 1, no. 1: 18–20, doi: 10.1089/big.2013.1506.

Higgins, O. et al. 2011. *A Literature Review on Health Information Seeking Behaviour on the Web: A Health Consumer and Health Professional Perspective*. Stockholm, Sweden: European Centre for Disease Control.

Jarman, H. and L. F. Luna-Reyes (Eds.) 2016. *Private Data and Public Value: Governance, Green Consumption, and Sustainable Supply Chains*. Public Administration and Information Technology (PAIT) Series, Springer.

Kushniruk, Andre W. 2015. "Editorial: eHealth Literacy: Emergence of a New Concept for Creating, Evaluating and Understanding Online Health Resources for the Public," *Knowledge Management & E-Learning* 7, no. 4: 518–521.

Luciano, Joanne S. et al. 2013. "The Emergent Discipline of Health Web Science," *Journal of Medical Internet Research* 15, no. 8: e166, doi: 10.2196/jmir.2499.

Luciano, Joanne S. et al. 2014. "Health Web Science," *Foundations and Trends in Web Science* 4, no. 4: 269–419, doi: 10.1561/1800000019.

Luciano, Joanne S. et al. 2016. "Using Ontologies to Develop and Test a Certification and Inspection Data Infrastructure Building Block," *Private Data and Public Value*, ed. Holly Jarman and Luis F. Luna-Reyes (Cham: Springer International Publishing), 89–107. http://link.springer.com/10.1007/978-3-319-27823-0_5

McHattie LS, Cumming G, and French T. 2014. "Transforming Patient Experience: Health Web Science Meets Medicine 2.0," *Medicine* 2.0. 3, no. 1: e2. doi: 10.2196/med20.3128.

Moreland, Julia, Tara L. French, and Grant P. Cumming. 2015. "The Prevalence of Online Health Information Seeking Among Patients in Scotland: A Cross-Sectional Exploratory Study," *JMIR Research Protocols* 4, no. 3:e85, doi: 10.2196/resprot.4010.

National Network of Libraries of Medicine. 2016. http://nnlm.gov/. Accessed May 21, 2016.

New Scientist. 2016. "The Algorithms That Make Sense of Your Health Data," https://www.newscientist.com/article/dn28338-happily-healthy/. Accessed May 21, 2016.

Norman, Cameron. 2011. "eHealth Literacy 2.0: Problems and Opportunities With an Evolving Concept," *Journal of Medical Internet Research* 13, no. 4: e125, doi: 10.2196/jmir.2035.

Norman, Cameron D., and Harvey A. Skinner. 2006. "eHealth Literacy: Essential Skills for Consumer Health in a Networked World," *Journal of Medical Internet Research* 8, no. 2: e9, doi: 10.2196/jmir.8.2.e9.

P4Medicine, 2016. *P4 Medicine Institute.* http://p4mi.org/p4medicine. Accessed May 20, 2016.

Pamela, Shiao, S. et al. 2015. "Big Data Analytics on Common Gene Mutations in Epigenetics Methylation Pathways: Population Health Issues for Cancer Prevention," presented at the 2015 AACR Computational and Systems Biology of Cancer Conference, San Francisco, California, February 8–11, 2015, doi: 10.13140/2.1.4214.1762

Pentland, A. 2012. "Big Data's Biggest Obstacles," *Harvard Business Review Blog.* https://hbr.org/2012/10/big-datas-biggest-obstacles. Accessed May 21, 2016.

Quaglio, Gianluca et al. 2016. "Accelerating the Health Literacy Agenda in Europe," *Health Promotion International,* daw028, doi: 10.1093/heapro/daw028

Sayogo, Djoko S. et al. 2016. "Ontological Modeling of Certification and Inspection Process to Support Smart Disclosure of Product Information," *International Journal of Public Administration in the Digital Age* 3, no. 2: 86–108, doi: 10.4018/IJPADA.2016040106.

Shiao, S. P. K., Yu, C. A., Xie, C., Ho, S. (2015, February). *Big Data Analytics on Common Gene Mutations in Epigenetics Methylation Pathways: Population Health Issues for Cancer Prevention.* 2015 AACR Computational and Systems Biology of Cancer Conference, San Francisco, California. DOI: 10.13140/2.1.4214.1762.

Stellefson, Michael et al. 2011. "eHealth Literacy Among College Students: A Systematic Review with Implications for eHealth Education," *Journal of Medical Internet Research* 13, no. 4: e102, doi: 10.2196/jmir.1703.

Swan, Melanie. 2013. "The Quantified Self: Fundamental Disruption in Big Data Science and Biological Discovery," *Big Data* 1, no. 2: 85–99, doi: 10.1089/big.2012.0002.

Tiropanis, Thanassis et al. 2013. "The Web Science Observatory," *IEEE Intelligent Systems* 28, no, 2: 100–104.

Topol, Eric J. 2012. *The Creative Destruction of Medicine: How the Digital Revolution Will Create Better Health Care.* New york: Basic Books.

Tucker, Patrick. 2014. *The Naked Future: What Happens in a World That Anticipates Your Every Move?* New york: Penguin.

Wooder, Stella. 2016. "Connected Women: How Medical Devices Are Set to Revolutionise Women's Healthcare," *Team Consulting Ltd.* https://www.teamconsulting.com/insights/connected-women-how-medical-devices-are-set-to-revolutionise-womens-healthcare/. Accessed May 21, 2016.

12

Current Perspectives on e-Mental-Health Self-Help Treatments: Exploring the "Black Box" of Public Views, Perceptions, and Attitudes Toward the Digitalization of Mental Health Care

Jennifer Apolinário-Hagen

12.1 e-Mental Health Self-Help Treatments: Insights into the Digitalization of Mental Health Care

Over the past decade, the Internet has profoundly changed everyday interactions and relationships in private and public areas, including the access to health information and innovations in mental health care. Considering both the increasing usage of the Internet as informal mental health counselor and persisting barriers for help-seeking individuals in traditional face-to-face settings, Internet-based self-help treatments for mental health problems have been suggested as suitable instruments to

J. Apolinário-Hagen (✉)
Department of Health Psychology, Institute for Psychology, University of Hagen (FernUniversität in Hagen), Universitätsstr. 33, Hagen, Germany
e-mail: Jennifer.Apolinario-Hagen@fernuni-hagen.de

© The Author(s) 2017
L. Menvielle et al. (eds.), *The Digitization of Healthcare,*
DOI 10.1057/978-1-349-95173-4_12

increase the public access to professional help. However, commonly cited benefits of Web-delivered electronic mental health (i.e., e-mental health) programs or mobile mental health applications (i.e., m-health apps) have been repeatedly challenged by the facticity of health-care systems. Drawing on the growing evidence based on the effectiveness of online treatments for prevalent mental disorders like depression contrasting with their lethargic implementation into health care, looking into the "black box" of prospective service users (i.e., involved mental aspects) may help in identifying psychological barriers such as acceptability issues. Hence, this chapter aims to illustrate current perspectives and new challenges surrounding "human factors" within digitalization of mental health care.

12.1.1 Defining the Subject of e-Mental Health and m-Mental Health Treatments and Its Relevance to Mental Health Care

Generally, e-mental health and m-mental health involve the utilization of technology for the Web-delivered supply of psychological services in health promotion, prevention, self-help, psycho-education, monitoring, counseling, psychotherapy, aftercare, and rehabilitation (Van Der Krieke et al. 2014; Lal and Adair 2014; Musiat et al. 2014). Actually, the diversity in content and provision modes of e-mental health interventions is also reflected by the application of various and partially inconsistent definitions or program labels (Oh et al. 2005; Wells et al. 2007; Lin et al. 2013; for example, see Fig. 12.1).

In view of the ubiquitous discrepancy between the demand for and supply with effective mental health services for common mental problems, the implementation of online self-help treatments into primary care is considered as a viable problem-solving strategy (Mayo-Wilson and Montgomery 2013; Musiat and Tarrier 2014).

Considering the increasing financial pressure and scarce capacities of health care, particularly in underserved rural areas, widely cited advantages of online treatments (see Table 12.1) involve the cost-effective and convenient access to therapies, independently from time and region of

Fig. 12.1 Terminology for diverse and equal e-therapy types and delivery modes

Table 12.1 Roadmap for e-mental health services

New simple solutions for old complex issues? Hopes and concerns of patients and health professionals	
Potential benefits and hopes	New challenges and concerns
• Expanding the access to evidence-based mental health interventions, e.g., by closing treatment gaps in rural areas[1–3] • Bridging time for patients waiting for conventional treatments[1,2] • Supplying treatments at lower costs[1–4] • New options for "consumer engagement" and participation[1] • Overcoming the stigma of mental illness with low-threshold, anonymous services[4]	• Deterioration of health care by replacing conventional psychotherapy units with online self-help treatment services[1,5] • Poor therapeutic interactions and relationships, unfamiliarity with the technology[1,5,6] • Usage of inappropriate, ineffective, or harmful online self-help services[1] • New and old barriers for underprivileged patients, e.g., demands on writing skills[1,5,7] • Confidentiality and data security issues[8–10]

References: [1]Lal and Adair 2014; [2]Musiat and Tarrier 2014; [3]Hage et al. 2013; [4]Klein and Cook 2010; [5]Apolinário-Hagen and Tasseit 2015; [6]Wangberg et al. 2007; [7]Conn 2010; [8]Bennett et al. 2010; [9]Gulliver et al. 2015; [10]Wells et al. 2007.

residence (Hage et al. 2013; Lal and Adair 2014; Musiat and Tarrier 2014; Moock 2014; Hedman et al. 2012). In addition, opportunities for anonymously reachable online services may comfort the access for some target groups by overcoming obstacles such as self-stigma (Klein and Cook 2010).

Table 12.2 Examples for iCBT programs varying in their delivery modes (degree of guidance)

Main delivery mode	Common features	Online program examples
Unguided iCBT self-help → e-/m-Mental health	Structured iCBT without therapist support as adjunctive treatment (e.g., via apps) or combined with online communities (peer-to-peer)	→ **"MoodGYM"**[1] → **"Deprexis"**[2]
(Therapist-) Guided iCBT → e-/m-Mental health	Structured iCBT with tailored support by an online-therapist or online-coach, usually via text messaging (e.g., chat or e-mail)	→ **"GET.ON"**[3] → **"Happy @ Work→"**[4]
Videoconferencing psychotherapy (VCP) → Video-based therapy	Web-and video-based one-to-one psychotherapy using Web-cam and video-chat software, optionally including instant messaging	Provided individually by licensed psychotherapists via online platforms (with similar conditions to face-to-face therapy)

References: [1]Twomey et al. 2014; [2]Krieger et al. 2014; [3]Ebert et al. 2014; [4]Geraedts et al. 2013. The usual iCBT program-duration is at least eight weeks. For further information on programs: see websites of National Health Services.

In general, delivery modes of psychological services (see Table 12.2) correspond with acceptability concepts for e-mental health usage (Peñate and Fumero 2016). The delivery modes range from fully automated apps, guided structured self-learn modules to videoconferencing psychotherapy (VCP). For instance, VCP is less conveniently accessible than m-health apps, but more flexible in terms of therapeutic strategies and treatable psychiatric conditions (Backhaus et al. 2012; Moock 2014). The vast majority of e-mental health programs is based on principles of cognitive behavior therapy (CBT), usually termed as computerized (cCBT) or Internet-based CBT (iCBT). In contrast to iCBT, for other approaches like positive psychology (e.g., Trompetter et al. 2016), psychodynamic psychotherapy (e.g., Johansson et al. 2013), or informal online self-help formats, respectively, peer-to-peer communities (e.g., Ali et al. 2015), there are merely preliminary results on their efficacy and feasibility available.

Among iCBT approaches, the solidest evidence base from randomized controlled trials (RCTs) has been established for therapist-guided iCBT programs for the treatment of mild to moderate depression and some anxiety disorders, with effect sizes comparable to face-to-face CBT (Arnberg et al. 2014; Olthuis et al. 2016). However, overestimation effects due to selection bias (Sucala et al. 2012), relatively high dropout rates and non-adherence in several iCBT trials are challenging (Donker et al. 2013; Karyotaki et al. 2015), especially in terms of trials with primary care patients (Deen et al. 2013) and unguided online treatments (Twomey et al. 2014).

In contrast to promising study findings on the effectiveness and acceptability of several online mental health treatments, the rarely available data on the actual uptake and adherence to iCBT outside of trials turned out being mostly unconvincing (Fleming et al. 2016). Drawing this research-practice mismatch, understanding perceptions, hopes, and worries (see Table 12.1) that may be relevant for help-seeking persons' individual decisions for engaging with a specific e-mental health service appears to be essential to improve implementation (Musiat et al. 2014).

12.2 Bringing Light into the Black Box: Exploring Expectations, Perceptions, and Attitudes Toward e-Mental Health Interventions

Attitudes reflect the sum of affective, positive or negative appraisals to a psychological object on attributive dimensions such as "harmful-beneficial" (see Ajzen 2001, p. 28). Research findings suggest that perceptions and general views on self-help can play a crucial role in shaping attitudes toward self-help, which are associated with individual experiences with mental disorders, self-help, and searching for help in primary care, and with perceived control, helplessness, engagement, and stigma associated with traditional face-to-face treatments (Khan et al. 2007). Equivalently, personal experiences, preferences, and personality facets may be particularly important for online self-help as well (Klein and Cook 2010). Regarding the clinical relevance, in a trial Boettcher et al. (2013) found out that the expectation toward online self-help predicted therapeutic outcomes and adherence. If these feature are as same important for help-seeking contexts and views outside of trials, is subject of the next section.

12.2.1 Insights into the Black Box of Users' Perceptions and Attitudes Toward e-Mental Health

As a reference to iCBT, whose basic principles stem from behaviorism, the term "black box" (see Fig 12.2) includes invisible inner human domains like intentions, which can be indirectly observed in actual behavior. The "C" in CBT reflects the cognitive component that has been added to behavioral therapy, respecting the insight of the "black box."

Applied to the uptake of e-mental health, attitudes and perceptions could be predictors of acceptability that can be support developers to provide persuasive and meaningful, respectively user-centered e-mental health services, whose effectiveness is not restricted to clinical trials.

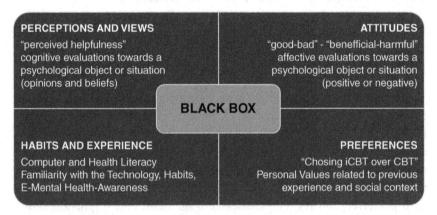

Fig. 12.2 Considerations on the "black of box" of e-mental health users

12.2.1.1 Technology Acceptance Meets e-Mental Health: "To Use or Not to Use?" Is the Question

As a framework for predicting intentions to use and actual usage behavior, the "Unified Theory of Acceptance and Use of Technology" (UTAUT; Venkatesh et al. 2003) has been applied to e-mental health, besides several other contexts. Considering the efficacious dissemination of e-mental health interventions, "theory base," "human support," "application fields," and "technical implementation" were identified as vital features (Lin and Baumeister 2015). Of the determinants of the UTAUT (Venkatesh et al. 2003), the determinant "performance expectancy," which includes perceived usefulness, relative advantage, extrinsic motivation, and outcome expectations, appears to cover key aspects for individual decisions in help-seeking contexts. Accordingly, several non-clinical surveys using community samples have employed "perceived helpfulness" as indicator for the acceptability of e-mental health services.

For instance, Oh et al. (2009) showed that perceived helpfulness of e-mental health services was positively associated with improved acceptability and intention to use online self-help treatments among young Australians. In another Australian study (see Klein and Cook 2010), over three-thirds of the 218 respondents of the online survey indicated a preference for face-to-face mental health services to e-mental health services in case of mental problems. In addition, those respondents who reported preferring e-mental health treatments ("e-preferers") scored significantly higher on "self-stigma" and perceived helpfulness of Internet-based programs without therapist assistance in comparison to "non e-preferers" (see Klein and Cook 2010).

Concerning associations between provision mode and perceptions on e- and m-mental health services, an online survey with 490 persons from the English general population by Musiat et al. (2014) revealed an overall lower acceptability of m-mental health apps compared to e-mental health programs, self-help books, and face-to-face treatments. Musiat et al. (2014) further showed that participants with a history of mental health problems reported the lowest likelihood of using m-health apps in case of mental health problems. Overall, participants perceived traditional face-to-face treatments as significantly more helpful than online self-help treatments. However, previous use of health information websites was associated with improved views on online self-help. The findings both on preference to traditional services and positive associations with Internet usage are in line with another survey by Eichenberg et al. (2013), who used a representative, large sample (*n* = 2.411) of the German general population. Overall, a preference to traditional services was also confirmed in several other surveys (e.g., Casey et al. 2013; Choi et al. 2015). There is evidence that most persons are unaware of e-mental health options or use the Internet especially for health information (see Eichenberg et al. 2013), especially regarding elderly patients with good socioeconomic background (see Crabb et al. 2012). The aforementioned studies used self-developed questionnaires, but there are also studies using qualitative and mixed methods for subpopulations in community samples. For instance, Mar et al. (2014), who investigated preferences of young Canadians ("Generation Y") by using interviews, identified that participants were open to the idea of online self-help and that they preferred features like interactivity and support via an online community. Another example is a mixed-methods study using focus groups and an online survey (see Ellis et al. 2013) that revealed a preference of young Australians males for self-help to professional help as well as important features for the development of services for this target group.

To conclude, the presented findings suggest different degrees in acceptability depending on the surveyed target group, with improved acceptability rating among young and well-educated persons. Within survey using general population samples, a mostly low acceptability and willingness of future using e-mental health in comparison to traditional face-to-face therapies were found. Conversely, these studies were conducted years ago and thus it remains unclear if the ongoing dissemination of online programs has raised e-awareness and acceptability in the meantime or if assessments on e-mental health were affected by other factors. For instance, concerns about data security can be an obstacle to engage with online self-help services, especially among well-educated populations (see Bennett et al. 2010; Gulliver et al. 2015).

12.2.2 Improving Acceptability and Attitudes Toward e-Mental Health Treatments

Recent research findings indicated that psycho-educational information could result in improved acceptability and attitudes toward e-mental health. For example, in an RCT conducted with an online Australian population sample (n = 217), Casey et al. (2013) explored the impact of brief educational video and text-based information on attitudes toward e-mental health. While the text-based information significantly informed the willingness of future using in comparison to the video condition (two and a half minutes long) and the control condition, neither the text nor the video-intervention had an impact on the perceived helpfulness of e-mental health in comparison to the control group. In contrast to this, another RCT by Ebert et al. (2015) showed that a psycho-educational video on online psychotherapy (seven minutes long) provided to depressive primary care patients in Germany (n = 128) resulted in significant improvements regarding acceptability toward online therapy in comparison to the control condition (Ebert et al. 2015). Because both studies were comprised of different small samples and this research field is still at an early stage, these findings should be considered with caution.

Another next rationale step might be to educate and raise e-awareness among service users, but also among health professionals, especially regarding potentially biased views of therapists. In line with these considerations, Gun et al. (2011) showed that the surveyed 1.104 Australian professionals and 648 laypersons assessed online treatments programs as acceptable, especially when they have previously used such interventions. Moreover, concerns among health professionals should be addressed adequately as well. For instance, Wells et al. (2007) showed that the health professionals in their survey were concerned about confidentiality of client information. Another study (see Wangberg et al. 2007) revealed that attitudes toward online therapies among Norwegian psychologists were overall neutral, whereas psychodynamic-orientated therapists tended to rather express negative attitudes, including concerns about poor therapeutic relationships. Moreover, results of a qualitative study (see Bengtsson et al. 2015) suggested that behavioral therapists viewed face-to-face CBT as a stronger experience than iCBT, especially with respect to the therapeutic working alliance, despite their generally positive views on online therapies. In accordance with this, Gun et al. (2011) recommended that program developers should make use of strategies for informing knowledge on e-mental health treatments and involving both therapists and patients in creating best-practice guidelines for a successful implementation of online interventions.

According to best-practice projects, involving key stakeholder can indeed increase commitment, trust, and positive attitudes toward e-health programs among relevant target groups (Van Gemert-Pijnen et al. 2011). For example, the person-based approach (PBA) can be applied to enhance acceptability and feasibility of digital health intervention by gaining a depth understanding of user needs, beliefs, attitudes, and their psychosocial context. For this purpose, the PBA combines both theory-grounded and evidence-based approaches to digital intervention development, including the usage of qualitative research and mixed methods to go beyond the mere assessment of acceptability, ease of use or usability, or satisfaction with e-mental health programs (Yardley et al. 2015). To conclude, there are several opportunities, but also many challenges to enhance the impact of e-mental health. By understanding the publics' and users' "black box," chances as well as challenges can be best addressed to improve the uptake and usefulness of e-mental health interventions in health care.

12.3 Discussion: Chances, Side Effects, and Challenges for the Digitalization of Mental Health Care

Appealing possibilities of overcoming regional, temporal, or psychological barriers (e.g., stigma of mental illness) via using the Internet to supply effective treatments seem plausible at first sight, though; wishful thinking of providers and researchers solely has yet been shown to be insufficient to considerably affect actual uptake of online self-help treatments in mental health care. Regarding public views on the innovation "e-mental health," there should be several to-dos on the agenda of health professionals and researchers to not stay behind the expectations on improving the access to professional support for help-seeking individuals with mental problems through the Internet.

12.3.1 Current Perspectives and Limitations: Public Views on e-Mental Health

Concerning the diversity of proposed benefits of seeking help online (see Table 12.1), besides efficacy trials, interestingly few of these suggestions were tested in surveys. For instance, only few studies have investigated if online services are able to improve mental health-related help-seeking behavior among young individuals (Kauer et al. 2014). Although the Internet is increasingly used as "mental health advisor," outside of clinical trials, the willingness of using online self-help treatments was reported as relatively low by most respondents in general population samples (see Eichenberg et al. 2013). In addition, the potential of reducing self-stigma in general populations through e-mental health has been rarely investigated. Moreover, study findings appear inconsistent. For instance, while Klein and Cook (2010) showed that "e-preferers" scored significantly higher on "self-stigma" than "non e-preferer," results from another study by Crisp and Griffith (2014) indicated that survey respondents who were interested in participating in an e-mental health intervention reported a lower perceived stigma than those who were not willing to participate.

Furthermore, in surveys investigating perceptions of different e-mental health services, the majority of participants from general populations reported a clear preference of using traditional face-to-face-therapy to e-mental health treatments in case of mental problems (e.g., Crabb et al. 2012; Casey et al. 2013; Choi et al. 2015). In addition, study findings in community samples also suggested an overall lower perceived helpfulness of online self-help treatments in comparison to conventional face-to-face therapies (e.g., Musiat et al. 2014). On the other hand, increasing awareness of e-mental health treatments by offering information may help to improve the readiness of future using e-mental health (Gun et al. 2011; Casey et al. 2013; Ebert et al. 2015). However, research data on acceptability and attitudes toward e-mental health outside of clinical trials is currently still limited. Additionally, some studies examining the likelihood of future usage of e-mental health in community samples did not use explicit measures on attitudes nor had their scope on acceptability issues (e.g., Crisp & Griffiths 2014; Younes et al. 2015). As a methodological limitation, most studies in the general population used self-developed surveys or grounded the rationales of their surveys solely on other research findings (e.g., Casey et al. 2013) or proposed or benefits of e-mental health (see Lal and Adair 2014), without giving a reference to theoretical framework like the UTAUT (see Venkatesh et al. 2003). In addition, the availability and awareness of e-mental health services differs broadly across national health-care systems (Moock 2014). Hence, the illustrated findings are whether neither definitive nor exhaustive, but instead cover research fields relevant to current debates.

12.3.2 Future Directions and Implications for Practice and Research

Due to the limited amount of large-scale high-quality studies, further research is required for conclusive recommendations. Currently, scoping reviews (e.g., Lal and Adair 2014) can though serve as a good starting point for health professionals to keep up with the newest developments to support their clients with a fundament for informed decisions. However, it remains yet unclear how the digitalization of mental health care will affect relationships and interactions in health care, including interpersonal contacts between professionals and help-seeking individuals. For instance, there is evidence that the therapeutic relationship might have a less relevant impact on the outcomes of online treatments than it has in traditional face-to-face therapies

(Andersson et al. 2012). Nonetheless, health professionals should be aware of the potential impact of health information websites on health behavior (Eichenberg et al. 2013).

Overall, applying participatory, collaborative, and PBAs from best practice e-health projects can enhance the quality of e-mental health research and implementation (see Van Gemert-Pijnen et al. 2011). For instance, PBAs using mixed methods can contribute to a deeper understanding of user perspectives, including mechanisms involved in the dissemination and implementation of successful e-mental health programs (Yardley et al. 2015).

In conclusion, the evidence base on the users "black box," including public views, perceptions, preferences, acceptability, and attitudes toward e-mental health self-help treatment services, remains fragmentary, but there are several promising approaches and concepts available and further efforts on the way to change this deficiency. Participatory approaches can offer the foundation for feasible and meaningful innovations in mental health care. Involving users a key stakeholder and increasing e-mental health literacy among both users and providers are likely to provide the best guidance on the question "to use or not to use" e-mental health self-help treatments and to improve the uptake of innovations within the process of digitalization of mental health care (Table 12.3).

Table 12.3 Roadmap for e-mental health services

Roadmap: *Investigating the black box of key holders toward e-mental health services*
• **Exploring psychological barriers for the acceptability of e-mental health:** Large-scale high-quality RCTs and studies using mixed-methods are strategies for a better understanding of psychological factors that are essential for a successful implementation and dissemination of e-mental health services.
• **Creating awareness and support shared decision-making:** Comprehensive, evidence-based information for different stakeholder groups can help the knowledge transfer and improve the impact of e-mental health services.
• **From conceptual patchwork to holistic framework:** Guidance for making digital interventions meaningful can be provided via the application and further validation of technology acceptance models, collaborative, participatory, or person-based approaches.

Bibliography

Ajzen, I. "Nature and operation of attitudes." *Annual Review of Psychology* 52 (2001): 27–58.

Ali, K., L. Farrer, A. Gulliver, and K. M. Griffiths. "Online peer-to-peer support for young people with mental health problems: A systematic review." JMIR Mental Health 2, no. 2 (2015): e19. doi: 10.2196/mental.4418.

Andersson, G., B. Paxling, P. Roch-Norlund, G. Ostman, A. Norgren, J. Almlov, L. Goren et al. "Internet-based psychodynamic versus cognitive behavioral guided self-help for generalized anxiety disorder: A randomized controlled trial." *Psychotherapy and Psychosomatics* 81, no. 6 (2012): 344–355. doi: 10.1159/000339371.

Apolinario-Hagen, J. A., and S. Tasseit "Access to psychotherapy in the era of Web 2.0—new media, old inequalities? /Zugang zur psychotherapie in der Ära des Web 2.0—Neue Medien, Alte Ungleichheiten?" *International Journal of Health Professions* 2, no. 2 (2015). doi: 10.1515/ijhp-2015-0010.

Arnberg, F. K., S. J. Linton, M. Hultcrantz, E. Heintz, and U. Jonsson "Internet-delivered psychological treatments for mood and anxiety disorders: A systematic review of their efficacy, safety, and cost-effectiveness." *PloS One* 9, no. 5 (2014): e98118. doi: 10.1371/journal.pone.0098118.

Backhaus, A., Z. Agha, M. L. Maglione, A. Repp, B. Ross, D. Zuest, N. M. Rice-Thorp, J. Lohr, and S. R. Thorp "Videoconferencing psychotherapy: A systematic review." *Psychological Services* 9, no. 2 (2012): 111–131. doi: 10.1037/a0027924.

Bengtsson, J., S. Nordin, and P. Calbring "Therapists' experiences of conducting cognitive behavioural therapy online vis-à-vis face-to face." *Cognitive Behavior Therapy* 44, no. 6 (2015): 470–479.

Bennett, K., A. J. Bennett, and K. M. Griffiths "Security considerations for e-mental health interventions." *Journal of Medical Internet Research* 12, no. 5 (2010): e61. doi: 10.2196/jmir.1468.

Boettcher, J., B. Renneberg, and T. Berger "Patient expectations in internet-based self-help for social anxiety." *Cognitive Behaviour Therapy* 42, no. 3 (2013): 203–214.

Casey, L. M., A. Joy, and B. A. Clough "The impact of information on attitudes toward e-mental health services." *Cyberpsychology, Behavior and Social Networking* 16, no. 8 (2013): 593–598. doi: 10.1089/cyber.2012.0515.

Choi, I., L. Sharpe, S. Li et al. "Acceptability of psychological treatment to Chinese- and Caucasian-Australians: Internet treatment reduces barriers but face-to-face care is preferred." *Social Psychiatry Psychiatr Epidemiol* 50, no. 1 (2015): 77–87. doi: 10.1007/s00127-014-0921-1.

Conn, V. S. "Internet-based interventions to change health behaviors." *Western Journal of Nursing Research* 32, no. 1 (2010): 3–4. doi: 10.1177/0193945909348464.

Crabb, R. M., S. Rafie, and K. R. Weingardt "Health-related Internet use in older primary care patients." *Gerontology* 58, no. 2 (2012): 164–170. doi: 10.1159/000329340.

Crisp, D. A., and K. M. Griffiths "Participating in online mental health interventions: Who is most likely to sign up and why?" Depression Research and Treatment 2014 (2014): 790457. doi: 10.1155/2014/790457.

Deen, T. L., J. C. Fortney, and G. Schroeder "Patient acceptance of and initiation and engagement in telepsychotherapy in primary care." *Psychiatric Services* 64, no. 4 (2013): 380–384.

Donker, T., P. J. Batterham, L. Warmerdam et al. "Predictors and moderators of response to Internet-delivered Interpersonal psychotherapy and cognitive behavior therapy for depression." *Journal of Affective Disorder* 151, no. 1 (2013): 343–351. doi: 10.1016/j.jad.2013.06.020.

Ebert, D. D., D. Lehr, H. Baumeister, L. Boss, H. Riper, P. Cuijpers, J. A. Reins, C. Buntrock, and M. Berking "GET.ON mood enhancer: Efficacy of Internet-based guided self-help compared to psychoeducation for depression: An investigator-blinded randomised controlled trial." *Trials* 15 (2014): 39. doi: 10.1186/1745-6215-15-39.

Ebert, D. D., M. Berking, P. D. Cuijpers, D. Lehr, M. Pörtner, and H. Baumeister "Increasing the acceptance of internet-based mental health interventions in primary care patients with depressive symptoms: A randomized controlled trial." *Journal of Affective Disorders* 176 (2015): 9–17.

Eichenberg, Christiane, Carolin Wolters, and Elmar Brähler "The internet as a mental health advisor in Germany—Results of a national survey." *PloS One* 8, no. 11 (2013): e79206. doi: 10.1371/journal.pone.0079206.

Ellis, L. A., P. Collin, P. J. Hurley et al. "Young men's attitudes and behaviour in relation to mental health and technology: Implications for the development of online mental health services." *BMC Psychiatry* 13 (2013): 119. doi: 10.1186/1471-244X-13-119.

Fleming, T. M., D. de Beurs, Y. Khazaal, A. Gaggioli, G. Riva, C. Botella, ... H. Riper "Maximizing the Impact of e-Therapy and Serious Gaming" *Time for a Paradigm Shift. Frontiers in Psychiatry* 7, no. 65 (2016). doi: 10.3389/fpsyt.2016.00065.

Geraedts, Anna S., Annet M. Kleiboer, Noortje M. Wiezer, Willem Van Mechelen, and Pim Cuijpers "Web-based guided self-help for employees with depressive symptoms (Happy@Work): Design of a randomized controlled trial." *BMC Psychiatry* 13 (2013): 61. 10.1186/1471-244X-13-61.

Gulliver, A., K. Bennett, A. Bennett, L. M. Farrer, J. Reynolds, and K. M. Griffiths "Privacy issues in the development of a virtual mental health clinic for university students: A qualitative study." *JMIR Mental Health* 2, no. 1 (2015): e9. doi: 10.2196/mental.4294.

Gun, S. Y., N. Titov, and G. Andrews "Acceptability of Internet treatment of anxiety and depression."*Australian and New Zealand Journal of Psychiatry* 19, no. 3 (2011): 259–264. doi: 10.3109/10398562.2011.562295.

Hage, E., J. P. Roo, M. A. Van Offenbeek, and A. Boonstra "Implementation factors and their effect on e-Health service adoption in rural communities: A systematic literature review." *BMC Health Services Research* 13 (2013): 19. doi: 10.1186/1472-6963-13-19.

Hedman, E., B. Ljotsson, and N. Lindefors "Cognitive behavior therapy via the Internet: A systematic review of applications, clinical efficacy and cost-effectiveness." *Expert Review of Pharmacoeconomics & Outcomes Research* 12, no. 6 (2012): 745–764. doi: 10.1586/erp.12.67.

Johansson, R., A. Nyblom, P. Carlbring, P. Cuijpers, and G. Andersson "Choosing between Internet-based psychodynamic versus cognitive behavioral therapy for depression: A pilot preference study." *BMC Psychiatry* 13 (2013): 268. doi: 10.1186/1471-244X-13-268.

Karyotaki, E., A. Kleiboer, F. Smit et al. "Predictors of treatment dropout in self-guided web-based interventions for depression: An 'individual patient data' meta-analysis." *Psychological Medicine* 45, no. 13 (2015): 2717–2726. doi: 10.1017/S0033291715000665.

Kauer, S. D., C. Mangan, and L. Sanci "Do online mental health services improve help-seeking for young people? A systematic review." *Journal of Medical Internet Research* 16, no. 3 (2014): e66. doi: 10.2196/jmir.3103.

Khan, N., P. Bower, and A. Rogers "Guided self-help in primary care mental health—Meta-synthesis of qualitative studies of patient experience." *British Journal of Psychiatry* 191, no. 3 (2007): 206–211.

Klein, B., and S. Cook "Preferences for e-mental health services amongst an online Australian sample." *E-Journal of Applied Psychology* 6, no. 1 (2010): 27–38. 10.7790/ejap.v6i1.184.

Krieger, T., B. Meyer, K. Sude, A. Urech, A. Maercker, and T. Berger "Evaluating an e-mental health program ('deprexis') as adjunctive treatment tool in psychotherapy for depression: Design of a pragmatic randomized controlled trial." *BMC Psychiatry* 14 (2014): 285. doi: 10.1186/s12888-014-0285-9.

Lal, S., and C. E. Adair "E-mental health: A rapid review of the literature." *Psychiatric Services* (Washington, D.C.) 65, no. 1 (2014): 24–32. 10.1176/appi.ps.201300009.

Lin, J., D. D. Ebert, D. Lehr et al. "Kognitiv-behaviorale Behandlungsansätze: State of the Art und Einsatzmöglichkeiten in der Rehabilitation." *Rehabilitation* 52 (2013): 155–163.

Lin, J., and H. Baumeister "Internet- und Mobilebasierte Interventionen in der Psychotherapie." *Public Health Forum* 23 (2015): 176–179.

Mar, M. Y., E. K. Neilson, I. Torchalla et al. "Exploring e-mental health preferences of generation Y." *Journal of Technology in Human Services* 32, no. 4 (2014): 312–327. 10.1080/15228835.2014.943457.

Mayo-Wilson, E., and P. Montgomery "Media-delivered cognitive behavioural therapy and behavioural therapy (self-help) for anxiety disorders in adults." *The Cochrane Database of Systematic Reviews* 9 (2013): CD005330. 10.1002/14651858.CD005330.pub4.

Moock, J. "Support from the internet for individuals with mental disorders: Advantages and disadvantages of e-mental health service delivery." *Frontiers in Public Health* 2 (2014): 65. doi: 10.3389/fpubh.2014.00065.

Musiat, P., and N. Tarrier "Collateral outcomes in e-mental health: A systematic review of the evidence for added benefits of computerized cognitive behavior therapy interventions for mental health." *Psychological Medicine* 44, no. 15 (2014): 3137–3150. doi: 10.1017/S0033291714000245.

Musiat, P., P. Goldstone, and N. Tarrier "Understanding the acceptability of e-mental health–attitudes and expectations towards computerised self-help treatments for mental health problems." *BMC Psychiatry* 14 (2014): 109. doi: 10.1186/1471-244X-14-109.

Oh, E., A. F. Jorm, and A. Wright "Perceived helpfulness of websites for mental health information: A national survey of young Australians." *Social Psychiatry and Psychiatric Epidemiology* 44 (2009): 293–299. doi: 10.1007/s00127-008-0443.

Oh, H., C. Rizo, M. Enkin et al. "What is eHealth (3): A systematic review of published definitions." *Journal of Medical Internet Research* 7, no. 1 (2005): e1. doi: 10.2196/jmir.7.1.e1.

Olthuis, J. V., M. C. Watt, K. Bailey, J. A. Hayden, and S. H. Stewart "Therapist-supported Internet cognitive behavioural therapy for anxiety disorders in adults." *The Cochrane Database of Systematic Reviews* 3 (2016): CD011565. doi: 10.1002/14651858.CD011565.pub2.

Peñate, W., and A. Fumero "A meta-review of Internet computer-based psychological treatments for anxiety disorders." *Journal of Telemedicine and Telecare* 22, no. 1 (2016): 3–11.

Sucala, M., J. B. Schnur, M. J. Constantino et al. "The therapeutic relationship in e-therapy for mental health–a systematic review." *Journal of Medical Internet Research* 14, no. 4 (2012): e110. doi: 10.2196/jmir.2084.

Trompetter, H. R., E. T. Bohlmeijer, S. M. Lamers, and K. M. Schreurs "Positive psychological wellbeing is required for online self-help acceptance and commitment therapy for chronic pain to be effective." *Frontiers in Psychology* 7 (2016): 353. doi: 10.3389/fpsyg.2016.00353.

Twomey, C., G. O'Reilly, M. Byrne, M. Bury, A. White, S. Kissane, A. McMahon, and N. Clancy "A randomized controlled trial of the computerized CBT programme, MoodGYM, for public mental health service users waiting for interventions." *British Journal of Clinical Psychology* 53, no. 4 (2014): 433–450.

Van Der Krieke, Lian, Lex Wunderink, Ando C. Emerencia, Peter De Jonge, and Sjoerd Sytema "E-mental health self-management for psychotic disorders: State of the art and future perspectives." *Psychiatric Services (Washington, D. C.)* 65, no. 1 (2014): 33–49. doi: 10.1176/appi.ps.201300050.

Van Gemert-Pijnen, J. E., N. Nijland, M. van Limburg, H. C. Ossebaard, S. M. Kelders, G. Eysenbach, and E. R. Seydel "A holistic framework to improve the uptake and impact of eHealth technologies." *Journal of Medical Internet Research* 13, no. 4 (2011): e111. doi: 10.2196/jmir.1672.

Venkatesh, V, M. G. Morris, G. B. Davis et al. "User acceptance of information technology: Toward a unified view." *MIS Quarterly* 27, no. 3 (2003): 425–478.

Wells, Melissa, Kimberly J. Mitchell, David Finkelhor, and Kathryn A. Becker-Blease. "Online mental health treatment: concerns and considerations." *Cyberpsychology & Behavior* 10, no. 3 (2007): 453–59. doi:10.1089/cpb.2006.9933.

Wangberg, S. C., D. Gammon, and K. Spitznogle "In the eyes of the beholder: Exploring psychologists' attitudes and use of e-therapy in Norway." *Cyberpsychology & Behavior* 10, no. 3 (2007): 418–423.

Yardley, L., L. Morrison, K. Bradbury, and I. Muller "The person-based approach to intervention development: Application to digital health-related behavior change interventions." *Journal of Medical Internet Research* 17, no. 1 (2015): e30. doi: 10.2196/jmir.4055.

Younes, N., A. Chollet, E. Menard, and M. Melchior "E-mental health care among young adults and help-seeking behaviors: A transversal study in a community sample." *Journal of Medical Internet Research* 17, no. 5 (2015): e123. doi: 10.2196/jmir.4254.

13

Patient Communities: A New Paradigm for Medicine

Anne-Françoise Audrain-Pontevia,
William Menvielle and Loick Menvielle

A.-F. Audrain-Pontevia (✉)
Department of Marketing, École des Sciences de la Gestion,
Université du Québec à Montréal, 320, rue Sainte-Catherine Est,
Montréal, H2X 1L7 Québec, Canada
e-mail: audrain_pontevia.anne_francoise@uqam.ca

W. Menvielle
Department of Marketing, École des Sciences de la Gestion,
Université du Québec à Trois-Rivières, 3351 boulevard
des Forges, Trois-Rivières, G9A 5H7 Québec, Canada
e-mail: William.Menvielle@uqtr.ca

L. Menvielle
Department of Marketing and Strategy, EDHEC Business School,
BP3116, 393- 400 Promenade des Anglais, France
e-mail: loick.menvielle@edhec.edu

© The Author(s) 2017
L. Menvielle et al. (eds.), *The Digitization of Healthcare*,
DOI 10.1057/978-1-349-95173-4_13

13.1 Introduction

For proof that the "digitalization of health" is very real, one only has to consider that, when it comes to health, people today turn reflexively to the Internet. In fact, one out of every 20 Google searches globally deals with health concerns, and that figure has increased steadily by 15% every year since 2011 (Bell et al. 2016).

In 2014, 69% of the population of France looked up health information on the Internet, a number that has been increasing since 2010 (Richard 2016). In the USA in 2011, almost three quarters of the population did the same. More than 70% of patients use the Internet when experiencing various symptoms, and a similar proportion of physicians turns to information and communication technologies (ICT) to determine a diagnosis (Bell et al. 2016).

The researching and exchange of medical information online is done using different tools, such as blogs, websites (e.g., Wikipedia), social media sites and virtual patient communities or OHCs. With the latter, users may find an abundant source of useful information supplied and "analyzed" by other OHC members with whom it is possible to create relationships (Kannan et al. 2000).

By allowing access to medical information, the Web creates a new paradigm among medical patients, researchers, and even health professionals in a collaborative knowledge process (Kreps and Neuhauser 2010). People—whether they are more or less educated, sick (or not)—can read, write, and share this medical information, using it as much or as little as they wish, passing it along from OHC leaders to followers. Does this mean the physician is being forgotten? Not necessarily.

This new behavior by Internet customers deserves further study, including how it affects relationships with physicians. As noted by Johnston et al. (2013), social media associated with Web 2.0 technologies are fundamentally changing the way individuals manage their health care. At the other end of the spectrum, physicians also use the Web and its tools, which alter how they do their jobs and changes their relationships with patients (Murray et al. 2003).

The goal of this chapter is to present the results of research measuring the link between the usage frequency of OHCs, also known as virtual health communities (VHCs), and how this affects the quality of the patient–physician relationship, and users' confidence in and attitudes toward this relationship. This link is something that needs to be investigated further according to Demiris (2006) and Eysenbach (2003).

13.2 Literature Review and Conceptual Framework

13.2.1 Virtual Health Communities

A VHC is an Internet platform that brings together individuals who share a social contract that enables them to network with each other. Together, they exchange information, offer moral support, discuss possible treatment therapies, and consult with experts (Demiris 2006). VHCs bring together patients with different pathologies (Kreps and Neuhauser 2010) with the goal of enabling them to share their experiences, medical and treatment information, and information about the possible side effects of medication. The literature shows that VHC sites offer several advantages. Firstly, they offer moral support for patients (Akrich and Méadel 2009; Thoër 2013). Secondly, they help restore a sometimes-distorted social link with the disease (Sillence et al. 2007). And thirdly, they provide patients with easier access to medical information (Erdem and Harrison-Walker 2006). This has the effect of reducing the asymmetry of information and, at the same time, increasing patients' questioning of the power traditionally held by the physician.

Patients' participation in VHCs helps them to be involved more effectively in medical decisions (Street et al. 2009). This directly and indirectly changes the relationship with the health professional (Thompson 2007). It also alters the impact of the psychosocial factors that influence patients' confidence in the relationship, the quality of the relationship, and patients' attitude toward health staff.

13.2.2 Virtual Communities: The Idea of Confidence

Trust is an essential variable in relationship marketing and is particularly important in the context of the patient–physician relationship (Erdem and Harrison-Walker 2006). In this case, a trusted relationship can be defined as a reliable and integrated connection between the health-care provider and the recipient.

Confidence also plays a major role in maintaining a long-term relationship between the two (i.e., service provider and consumer). It also positively influences satisfaction and cooperation, thereby reducing uncertainty and the propensity to withdraw (Morgan and Hunt 1994). Information technology enables the reinforcement of the patient's confidence in his/her physician (Andreassen et al. 2006). In effect, individuals who frequently search for health information on the Internet tend to have more confidence in their physician. This may be explained by the fact that patients who surf the Web acquire medical knowledge, so they may be better able to discuss certain topics with their physician (Andreassen et al. 2006; Sofres 2013).

This positive link is also verified by patients: For a large proportion of patients with chronic conditions, the medical information they obtain on the Internet enables them to better understand their illness, and allows them to confirm their physician's advice (de Boer et al. 2007). For these authors, patients with chronic health conditions who use VHCs have a higher degree of confidence in their physician. And, compared with other patient groups, they trust their physicians more and have a higher level of commitment toward them.

Given the above, the following hypotheses were posited:

- Hypothesis 1 (H1): For individuals in general, participation in a VHC affects their confidence in their physician.
- Hypothesis 2 (H2): For individuals who are sick, participation in a VHC affects their confidence in their physician.

13.2.3 Virtual Communities: The Quality of the Relationship for Physicians

The concept of a patient–physician relationship is a key concept in health care (Ridd et al. 2009). The democratization of the Internet and improved access to health information increases users' knowledge, places the focus on the patient rather than the disease, and improves the relationship between the two stakeholders (Kaba and Sooriakumaran 2007). A study undertaken with women who had breast cancer shows that surfing the Internet in search of credible, high-quality health information positively affected their relationship with their physician (Shaw et al. 2007). With regard to people with chronic illnesses, Internet surfing contributes to an enriched relationship with their physician. Therefore, the information collected is shared, discussed, and dealt with differently by the physician and the patient (Anderson et al. 2003), and it forces health professionals to review their practices. As McMullan (2006) states, the incursion of digital information and the development of VHCs compete to redefine the patient–physician relationship, forcing the adoption of a patient-centric vision: patient self-education leads to a more collaborative, rather than paternalistic, dynamic.

In light of these studies, it is proposed that the following hypotheses on the quality of the patient–physician relationship in a VHC context be tested:

- Hypothesis 3 (H3): Participation in a VHC affects how individuals in general perceive the quality of their relationship with their physician.
- Hypothesis 4 (H4): Participation in a VHC affects how individuals who are chronically ill perceive the quality of their relationship with their physician.

13.2.4 Virtual Communities: Attitude Toward Physicians

Frequent use of VHCs allows patients to increase their sense of control over their disease by providing them with knowledge and self-awareness (Wald et al. 2007). Certain studies have shown that the disclosure of personal information in VHCs generates more empathetic and friendly relationships between the person being treated and the caregiver (Dedding et al. 2011). By helping to encourage VHCs and the exchange of information, patients are better informed, making their relationships with health-care professionals more harmonious. This, in turn, facilitates the exchange of information and improves the effectiveness of meetings (Broom 2005; Dedding et al. 2011).

This leads to the following hypotheses:

- Hypothesis 5 (H5): Participation in a VHC affects the attitude of individuals toward their physician.
- Hypothesis 6 (H6): Participation in a VHC affects the attitude of patients with chronic conditions toward their physician.

13.3 Research Methodology

13.3.1 Survey Sample

An online survey was developed to test these six research hypotheses. In 2015, a total of 245 French citizens were contacted in through online communities using an online questionnaire. Of these, 213 provided usable data. Nearly 28% of respondents indicated they suffered from a chronic illness.

Fifty-four percent of respondents were women, which is consistent with the results of Ybarra and Suman (2006), who found that women are significantly more likely than men to use the Internet as a source of health information. The average age of the respondents was 34 years old, ranging in age from 18 to 62 years. Data was collected anonymously.

13.3.2 Measurement

Drawing on marketing and sociological literature, standard research measurement scales were adapted to make it possible to assess the trust that VHC-participating patients have in their physician, their perception of the quality of the relationship with their physician, and their attitude toward their physician.

Each construct was composed of several items measured on seven-point Likert-type scales (1 = strongly disagree and 7 = strongly agree). The data was factor-analyzed to assess the dimensionality and consistency of the scales. The reliability of each scale was assessed using Cronbach's alpha coefficient.

13.3.3 Method

To test the first set of hypotheses (H1, H3, and H5), t-tests were run for each of the following constructs:

a. the patient's perceived trust toward their physician;
b. the patient's perceived relationship with their physician; and
c. the patient's attitude toward their physician. This final construct was divided into two groups:

- members who do not interact with VHCs, or who claim to interact poorly with VHCs; and
- members who say they interact frequently with VHCs.

Patients who interacted daily or weekly with a VHC were considered high-frequency participants (m_{97}), whereas those who connected once a month or less were considered low-frequency participants (m_{116}).

Similarly, to test the second set of hypotheses (H2, H4, and H6), the means were compared for each of the three abovementioned constructs for high-frequency users (m_{cd37}) with chronic conditions versus low-frequency users (m_{cd23}) with chronic conditions, respectively.

13.4 Results

13.4.1 T-Test Results

13.4.1.1 Results for H1, H3, and H5

The t-test results indicate that frequent participation in VHCs does not significantly impact the patient's trust toward their physician; thus, H1 is not supported. In terms of the perceived quality of the relationship, the data shows that being a frequent user modifies the patient's perceived quality of the relationship toward their physician ($t = -2.310$; $p < 0.05$). Similarly, for frequent users, the data reveals a significant difference regarding attitudes toward their physician compared with less-frequent users ($t = 2.440$; $p < 0.05$). Therefore, H3 and H5 are supported by the data here.

13.4.1.2 Results for H2, H4, and H6

Let us now consider patients with a chronic condition. Regarding trust toward their physician, there was no significant difference found (at $p < 0.05$) between high- and low-frequency VHC users; thus, H2 is not supported.

The data indicates that a difference exists between high- and low-frequency users regarding their perception of the quality of their relationship with their physician. Specifically, the data shows that those who participate frequently in a VHC perceive their relationship with their physician to be of better quality than do other VHC members ($t = -1.892$; $p < 0.05$); H4 is supported by the data.

Similarly, the data underlines that members who frequently use a VHC have a better attitude toward their physician than less-frequent users ($t = 2.528$; $p < 0.05$); thus, H6 is supported here.

13.5 Discussion

The research objectives were to study the effects of participation in VHCs by the individuals in a physician–patient relationship. In the end, four of the six hypotheses were validated.

Firstly, looking at the impact that participation in VHCs has on members' trust in their physicians, the data reveals that being a frequent Internet user, whether sick or healthy, does not affect the level of trust. In France, the physician seems to be the primary and most credible source for health information, and these results are consistent with other studies. This low level of confidence in the Internet (compared with confidence in one's physician) could be explained by the heterogeneity of the quality of health information available online, a valid reality for many developed countries (Beck et al. 2014).

Secondly, the relationship between the frequent use of virtual communities and the quality of the user's relationship with respect to his/her physician was studied. A significant link was found between participation in these communities and the quality of the user's relationship with his/her physician, both for individuals in general, and for those with chronic conditions. These results confirm previous studies arguing in favor of the efficiency and benefit of looking for health information on the Internet, and the positive effect this has on the physician–patient relationship. (Thoër 2012).

Thirdly, the results show a significant correlation between patients' attitude toward their physician and the time spent by patients in VHCs, both for individuals in general and for those with chronic conditions. Again, the hypothesis agrees with the results of the study, suggesting that the time spent surfing the "health" Internet creates new forms of relationships between physicians and patients (Dedding et al. 2011) while improving the efficacy of meetings (Broom 2005) and the quality of care (McGeady et al. 2008).

On a managerial level, this study sheds new light on the variables affecting the patient–physician relationship. It also points to actions that physicians could take to improve their relationships with patients. It suggests that doctors should seek to build more pedagogical or educational communication with their patients—either by answering their specific questions, or by guiding them to sources of safe, credible information on the Internet.

While this study does highlight the contribution of VHCs toward strengthening the relationship between physician and patient, it also has its limitations. The first is the lack of a representative sample, since only the

Web was used to identify respondents (either sick or healthy). The second limitation is the low external validity of results. It would therefore be appropriate to conduct further research using a more representative sample of the French population. It would also be interesting to test these hypotheses with populations in other countries with different health systems (e.g., countries where it is easier or harder to access a doctor). This study also suggests future research possibilities. For example, it is recommended that additional variables be added, such as type of disease (i.e., chronic or acute) and their severity. To enhance the explanatory power of this model, other variables to assess the patient–physician relationship could be added, such as the level of involvement in VHCs (Akrich and Méadel 2009), motivation to participate in VHCs (Demiris 2006), or perceptions about the validity of information found on VHC websites.

References

Anderson, James G., Michelle R. Rainey, and Gunther Eysenbach, "The Impact of Cyberhealthcare on the Physician–Patient Relationship," *Journal of Medical Systems* 27, no. 1 (2003): 67–84, doi:10.1023/a:1021061229743.

Andreassen, H. K., "Patients Who Use E-Mediated Communication With Their Doctor: New Constructions of Trust in the Patient-Doctor Relationship," *Qualitative Health Research* 16, no. 2 (February 1, 2006): 238–248, doi:10.1177/1049732305284667.

Akrich, Madeleine, and Cécile Méadel, "Les échanges entre patients sur l'Internet," *La Presse Médicale* 38, no. 10 (2009): 1484–1490.

Altan Erdem, S., and L. Jean Harrison-Walker, "The Role of the Internet in Physician–Patient Relationships: The Issue of Trust," *Business Horizons* 49, no. 5 (September 2006): 387–393, doi:10.1016/j.bushor.2006.01.003.

Beck, François et al., "Use of the Internet as a Health Information Resource Among French Young Adults: Results From a Nationally Representative Survey," *Journal of Medical Internet Research* 16, no. 5 (May 13, 2014): e128, doi:10.2196/jmir.2934.

Bell, David, Brian Fox, and Ryan Olohan, *Pharma 3D: Rewriting the Script for Marketing in the Digital Age* (The Wharton School, Google, and McKinsey & Company Inc, 2016), 75, accessed on October 4, 2016, http://www.pharma3d.com/#chapter-856435.

Broom, A., "Virtually He@lthy: The Impact of Internet Use on Disease Experience and the DoctorPatient Relationship," *Qualitative Health Research* 15, no. 3 (March 1, 2005): 325–345, doi:10.1177/1049732304272916.

De Boer, Maaike J., Gerbrig J. Versteegen, and Marten Van Wijhe, "Patients' Use of the Internet for Pain-Related Medical Information," *Patient Education and Counseling* 68, no. 1 (September 2007): 86–97, doi:10.1016/j.pec.2007.05.012.

Dedding, Christine et al., "How Will E-Health Affect Patient Participation in the Clinic? A Review of E-Health Studies and the Current Evidence for Changes in the Relationship between Medical Professionals and Patients," *Social Science & Medicine* 72, no. 1 (January 2011): 49–53, doi:10.1016/j.socscimed.2010.10.017.

Demiris, George, "The Diffusion of Virtual Communities in Health Care: Concepts and Challenges," *Patient Education and Counseling* 62, no. 2 (August 2006): 178–188, doi:10.1016/j.pec.2005.10.003.

Eysenbach, Gunther, "The Impact of the Internet on Cancer Outcomes," *CA: A Cancer Journal for Clinicians* 53, no. 6 (November 1, 2003): 356–371, doi:10.3322/canjclin.53.6.356.

Johnston, Allen C., James L Worrell, Paul M. Di Gangi, and Molly Wasko, "Online Health Communities: An Assessment of the Influence of Participation on Patient Empowerment Outcomes," *Information Technology and People* 26, no. 2 (2013): 213–235.

Kaba, R., and P. Sooriakumaran, "The Evolution of the Doctor-Patient Relationship," *International Journal of Surgery* 5, no. 1 (February 2007): 57–65, doi:10.1016/j.ijsu.2006.01.005.

Kannan, P. K., Ai-Mei Chang, and Andrew B. Whinston, "Electronic Communities in e-Business: Their Role and Issues," *Information Systems Frontiers* 1, no. 4 (2000), 415–426.

Kreps, Gary L., and Linda Neuhauser, "New Directions in eHealth Communication: Opportunities and Challenges," *Patient Education and Counseling* 78, no. 3 (March 2010): 329–336, doi:10.1016/j.pec.2010.01.013.

McGeady, David, Jaakko Kujala, and Karita Ilvonen, "The Impact of Patient–Physician Web Messaging on Healthcare Service Provision," *International Journal of Medical Informatics* 77, no. 1 (January 2008): 17–23, doi:10.1016/j.ijmedinf.2006.11.004.

McMullan, Miriam, "Patients Using the Internet to Obtain Health Information: How This Affects the Patient–Health Professional Relationship," *Patient*

Education and Counseling 63, no. 1–2 (October 2006): 24–28, doi:10.1016/j. pec.2005.10.006.

Morgan, Robert M., and Shelby D. Hunt, "The Commitment-Trust Theory of Relationship Marketing," *Journal of Marketing* 58, no. 3 (July 1994): 20, doi:10.2307/1252308.

Murray, Elizabeth et al., "The Impact of Health Information on the Internet on the Physician-Patient Relationship: Patient Perceptions," *Archives of Internal Medicine* 163, no. 14 (July 28, 2003): 1727, doi:10.1001/ archinte.163.14.1727.

Richard, Jean-Baptiste, "Baromètre santé Inpes 2014: Quelle utilisation d'Internet dans la recherche d'informations santé ?" 10èmes Journées de la prévention et de la santé publique, Paris, June 9–11, 2015, accessed October 4, 2016, http://inpes.santepubliquefrance.fr/jp/cr/pdf/2015/Richard.pdf.

Ridd, Matthew et al., "The Patient–Doctor Relationship: A Synthesis of the Qualitative Literature on Patients' Perspectives," *British Journal of General Practice* 59, no. 561 (April 1, 2009): 116–133, doi: 10.3399/bjgp09X420248.

Sillence, Elizabeth et al., "How Do Patients Evaluate and Make Use of Online Health Information?," *Social Science & Medicine* 64, no. 9 (May 2007): 1853–1862, doi:10.1016/j.socscimed.2007.01.012.

Shaw, B. et al., "Doctor–Patient Relationship as Motivation and Outcome: Examining Uses of an Interactive Cancer Communication System," *International Journal of Medical Informatics* 76, no. 4 (April 2007): 274–282, doi:10.1016/j.ijmedinf.2005.12.002.

Street, Richard L. et al., "How Does Communication Heal? Pathways Linking Clinician–Patient Communication to Health Outcomes," *Patient Education and Counseling* 74, no. 3 (March 2009): 295–301, doi:10.1016/j.pec.2008.11.015.

Thoër, Christine, "Les espaces d'échange en ligne consacrés à la santé: De nouvelles médiations de l'information santé," in *Internet et santé: Acteurs, usages, et appropriations*, edited by Joseph Josy Lévy and Christine Thoër (Québec: Presses Universitaires du Québec 2012), 57–92.

Thoër, Christine, "Internet: Un facteur de transformation de la relation médecin-patient?," *Revue Internationale Communication Sociale Et Publique*, no. 10 (2013): 1–24

Thompson, Andrew G.H., "The Meaning of Patient Involvement and Participation in Health Care Consultations: A Taxonomy," *Social Science & Medicine* 64, no. 6 (March 2007): 1297–1310, doi:10.1016/j. socscimed.2006.11.002.

Wald, Hedy S., Catherine E. Dube, and David C. Anthony, "Untangling the Web—The Impact of Internet Use on Health Care and the Physician–Patient Relationship," *Patient Education and Counseling* 68, no. 3 (November 2007): 218–224, doi:10.1016/j.pec.2007.05.016.

Ybarra, Michele L., and Michael Suman, "Help Seeking Behavior and the Internet: A National Survey," *International Journal of Medical Informatics* 75, no. 1 (January 2006): 29–41, doi:10.1016/j.ijmedinf.2005.07.029.

Part IV

From M-Health to New Perspectives at the Digital Age

14

Big Data and Privacy Fundamentals: Toward a "Digital Skin"

David Manset

We may be witnessing the advent of the era of Big Data, but new regulations, including the European Union's General Data Protection Regulation (GDPR) (European Commission 2012) and EU–US Privacy Shield (European Commission 2016a) will, in the near future, greatly impact the way sensitive data can be accessed, shared, and processed.[1]

This societal evolution will require health-care information systems to make a giant leap toward empowering the "data subject"—you, me,

---

[1] According to the European Commission, the GDPR will enable people to better control their personal data while modernizing and unifying rules to create a "digital single market" that will "make Europe fit for the digital age" (see: http://europa.eu/rapid/press-release_IP-15-6321_en. htm, accessed October 3, 2016).

The EU–US Privacy Shield is a framework designed to "protect the fundamental rights of anyone in the EU whose personal data is transferred to the United States." It also "(brings) legal clarity for businesses relying on transatlantic data transfers" (see: http://europa.eu/rapid/press-release_IP-16-2461_en.htm, accessed October 3, 2016).

D. Manset (✉)
be-studys, be-almerys, 336 Rue Saint Honore, Paris, France
e-mail: david.manset@almerys.com

© The Author(s) 2017
L. Menvielle et al. (eds.), *The Digitization of Healthcare*,
DOI 10.1057/978-1-349-95173-4_14

everyone—when it comes to building and sharing an acceptable "quantified self."

This chapter explores the lessons learned in 20 international studies regarding the processing of medical data and the associated legal and technical implications. It concludes with a possible response to the (big) data-protection dilemma in terms of the fundamental principles at stake, and the potential technological paradigms that could support the development of a fair(er) digital economy.

14.1 Introducing the Big Data Dilemma

Our society is undergoing a digital transformation. The health-care and insurance sectors, which serve as foundational pillars for most national systems of government, are moving from silo-based, complex and slow-changing monopolistic and information systems to decoupled, rapidly growing and heterogeneous data landscapes.

Facilitated access to health-care information systems, the reduced cost of genome sequencing, and the unprecedented volume of connected devices now flooding the market are among the many signs of an emerging ubiquitous and interconnected society powered by Big Data.

This globalization is leading us inexorably toward the question of our "quantified self" (Picard and Wolf 2015). In other words: How much personal data should be shared with "society"? What are the associated risks and benefits? What is the actual value of our data, and who owns it? What will this mean for concerned individuals, organizations, and information systems? These are questions that must be pondered with care and scrutinized in terms of good practices and applicable laws (Leonard Kish and Eric Topol 2015).

In the next section, we explore Europe's legal framework, the issues associated with the use of sensitive data and the applicable technologies and new paradigms, and conclude with a look at a set of basic but foundational principles and technologies that enable digital trust.

14.2 Europe's Legal Framework

The legal framework of data protection in Europe builds on a complex and historical regulatory background inscribed in a corpus of bodies, laws, and charters. This is what the following privacy compass (Fig. 14.1) illustrates. It features a 360-degree outlook, together with some of the proposed scientific and technological approaches described in this chapter.

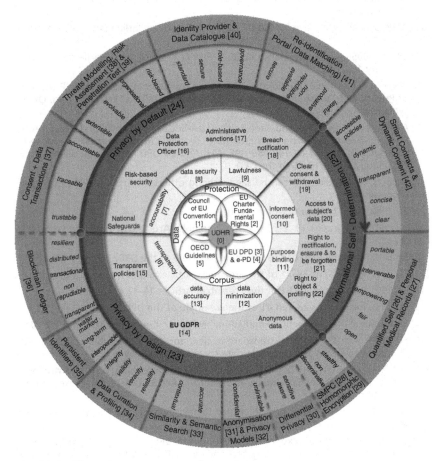

Fig. 14.1 The privacy compass references

(Continued)

Fig. 14.1 (continued)

DPD = Data Protection Directive; e-PD = e-Privacy Directive; EU = European Union; GDPR = General Data Protection Regulation; OECD = Organisation for Economic Co-operation and Development; UDHR = Universal Declaration of Human Rights.

[0] Lauterpacht, Hersch. "Universal Declaration of Human Rights, the." Brit. YB Int'l L. 25 (1948): 354.

[1] "Convention for the Protection of Individuals with Regard to Automatic Processing of Personal Data." *Treaty Office*. Council of Europe, Web. March 28, 2016.

[2] "Abstract of EU: Charter Of Fundamental Rights Of The European Union." *International Legal Materials* 40.2 (2001): 1–265. European Commission. Web. March 28, 2016.

[3] "31995L0046—Directive 95/46/EC." *EUR-Lex*. European Parliament. Web. February 15, 2016.

[4] "32002L0058—Directive 2002/58/EC." *EUR-Lex*. European Parliament. Web. February 15, 2016.

[5] "Recommendation of the Council Concerning Guidelines Governing the Protection of Privacy and Transborder Flows of Personal Data (2013)." (n.d.): n. pag. OECD. Web. March 28, 2016.

[6] Ali Gholami, Anna-Sara Lind, Jane Reichel, Jan-Eric Litton, Ake Edlund, Erwin Laure, Privacy Threat Modeling for Emerging BiobankClouds, *Journal of Procedia Computer Science* 37 (2014): 489–496, 493. And EU DPD, Paragraphs 38–40 of the Preamble, Articles 10–15 of the DPD.

[7] Aspects of the principle can be seen, among others, in Art. 17 DPD (Security of processing).

[8] EU DPD. Art. 17 (Security of processing).

[9] EU DPD. Paragraphs 18, 23, 28 of the Preamble, Article 6 of the Data Protection Directive.

[10] EU DPD. Paragraph 30 of the Preamble, Article 7 of the DPD.

[11] EU DPD. Paragraphs 28–31 of the Preamble, Articles 6 and 7 of the DPD.

[12] EU DPD. Paragraphs 59–61 of the Preamble, Articles 16–17 of the DPD.

[13] EU DPD. Paragraphs 28 and 41 of the Preamble of the DPD.

[14] "EU General Data Protection Regulation." European Council, Web. March 28, 2016.

[15] EU GDPR, Art. 11 ("concise, transparent, clear and easily accessible policies"), Art. 15 ("right to access and to obtain data for the data subject").

[16] Art. 5(1) point (f); Art. 22 ("Responsibility and accountability of the controller"); Art. 33 ("Data protection impact assessment"); Art. 35 ("Designation of the data protection officer").

[17] Art. 5(1) point (a) GDPR principles "lawfulness, fairness and transparency," and Art. 6 GDPR "lawfulness of processing."

[18] Cornelia Graf, Peter Wolkerstorfer, Arjan Geven, and Manfred Tscheligi. A pattern collection for privacy enhancing technology. In The 2nd Int. Conf. on Pervasive Patterns and Applications (PATTERNS 2010), Lisbon, Portugal, November 21–26, 2010.

[19] EU GDPR, Art. 13a ("standardised information policies"), Art. 4(8) definition of the "data subject's consent," and Art. 7 "conditions for consent."

[20] EU GDPR, Art. 14 ("information to the data subject").

[21] EU GDPR, Art. 12 (for defining the conditions for exercising data subject rights).

[22] EU GDPR, Article 4(3aa) on data profiling definition and Article 14(1) on profiling-based decision.

[23] Cavoukian, Ann. *Operationalizing Privacy by Design: A Guide to Implementing Strong Privacy Practices.* N.p.: n.p., n.d. Information and Privacy Commissioner, 2012. Web. March 28, 2016. And "7 Foundational Principles—Privacy By Design." Privacy By Design. N.p., n.d. Web. November 11, 2015.

[24] Cavoukian, Ann. *Operationalizing Privacy by Design: A Guide to Implementing Strong Privacy Practices.* N.p.: n.p., n.d. Information and Privacy Commissioner, 2012. Web. March 28, 2016. And "7 Foundational Principles—Privacy By Design." Privacy By Design. N.p., n.d. Web. November 11, 2015

[25] Empowerment: American community psychology, social scientist Julian Rappaport (1981) and Volkszählungsurteil, BVerfGE Bd. 65, S. 1ff. and Some Federal States (Länder) have, in their own Constitutions, made data protection a seperate, independent right: see, e.g., Art. 33 of the Constitution of Berlin.

[26] Wolf, Gary. "The Quantified Self." Antephase RSS. N.p., n.d. Web. November 11, 2015.

[27] "You Should Get to Know You—UnPatients." UnPatients. N.p., n.d. Web. November 11, 2015.

[28] Goldreich, Oded. "Secure multi-party computation." Manuscript. Preliminary version (1998) and Lindell, Yehuda, and Benny Pinkas. "Secure multiparty computation for privacy-preserving data mining." *Journal of Privacy and Confidentiality* 1.1 (2009): 5.

[29] Gentry, Craig. A fully homomorphic encryption scheme. Diss. Stanford University, 2009.

[30] F. Eigner, A. Kate, M. Maffei, F. Pampaloni, and I. Pryvalov, Achieving Optimal Utility for Distributed Differential Privacy Using Secure Multiparty Computation, in: P. Laud and L. Kamm (eds.), *Applications of Secure Multiparty Computation*, IOS Press, 2015, p. 82.

[31] Garfinkel, Simon. De-Identification of Personally Identifiable Information. Rep. no. 8053. N.p.: U.S. Department of Commerce NISTIR, April 2015. Print

[32] Sweeney, Latanya. "k-anonymity: A Model for Protecting Privacy." *International Journal of Uncertainty, Fuzziness and Knowledge-Based Systems* 10.05 (2002): 557–570 and Emam, Khaled El, and Fida Kamal Dankar. "Protecting Privacy Using K-Anonymity." *Journal of the American Medical Informatics Association: JAMIA. American Medical Informatics Association*, n.d. Web. November 11, 2015. And Machanavajjhala, Ashwin et al. "l-diversity: Privacy beyond k-anonymity." ACM Transactions on Knowledge Discovery from Data (TKDD) 1.1 (2007): 3. And Li, Ninghui, Tiancheng Li, and Suresh Venkatasubramanian. "t-closeness: Privacy beyond k-anonymity and l-diversity." Data Engineering, 2007. ICDE 2007. IEEE 23rd International Conference on. IEEE, 2007.

(Continued)

Fig. 14.1 (continued)

[33] Tsymbal, Alexey et al. "The neighborhood graph for clinical case retrieval and decision support within health-e-child casereasoner." FGWM 09 (2009): 49. and

Gobeill, Julien et al. "Managing the data deluge: data-driven GO category assignment improves while complexity of functional annotation increases." Database 2013 (2013): bat041.

Müller, Henning, and HES SO. "Text-based (image) retrieval." (2010).

[34] Omiros Metaxas, Harry Dimitropoulos, Yannis Ioannidis, "AITION: A scalable KDD platform for Big Data Healthcare", in Proc. of the IEEE Int'l Conference on Biomedical & Health Informatics, Valencia, Spain, June 2014. <http://emb.citen gine.com/event/bhi-2014/paper-details?pdID=177>

[35] Kahn, Robert E. "Overview of the Digital Object Architecture." *VLSI Electronics Microstructure Science VLSI and Computer Architecture* (1989): 165–95. CNRI. Web. March 28, 2016.

[36] Nakamoto, Satoshi. "Peer-to-Peer Directory System." *Legitimate Applications of Peer-to-Peer Networks* (2008): 109–22. Web. March 28, 2016. And "Ethereum Project." *Ethereum Project.* N.p., n.d. Web. March 28, 2016. And "What Is the Hyperledger Project?" Linux Foundation, n.d. Web. March 28, 2016.

[37] Watanabe, Hiroki et al. "Blockchain contract: A complete consensus using blockchain." *2015 IEEE 4th Global Conference on Consumer Electronics (GCCE).* IEEE, 2015.

[38] Benitez, Kathleen, and Bradley Malin. "Evaluating re-identification risks with respect to the HIPAA privacy rule." *Journal of the American Medical Informatics Association* 17.2 (2010): 169–177.

[39] Wang, Linzhang, Eric Wong, and Dianxiang Xu. "A Threat Model Driven Approach for Security Testing." *Proceedings of the Third International Workshop on Software Engineering for Secure Systems.* IEEE Computer Society, 2007.

[40] Berlanga, Rafael et al. "Medical Data Integration and the Semantic Annotation of Medical Protocols." *Computer-Based Medical Systems, 2008. CBMS'08. 21st IEEE International Symposium on.* IEEE, 2008.

[41] Christen, Peter. *Data Matching: Concepts and Techniques for Record Linkage, Entity Resolution, and Duplicate Detection.* Springer Science & Business Media, 2012.

[42] J. Kaye et al., Dynamic Consent, cit., p. 3.

The core of this foundational corpus can be found in the Universal Declaration of Human Rights, which protects an individual from "arbitrary interference with his privacy, family, home or correspondence" and "attacks upon his honour and reputation" (Article 12) (UN General Assembly 1948).

Additionally, the Council of Europe's Convention for the Protection of Individuals with Regard to Automatic Processing of

Personal Data (Council of Europe 1981) recognizes privacy (i.e., respecting an individual's "private and family life, his home and his correspondence" [Article 8]) as a fundamental human right. The European Charter of Fundamental Rights also defines the "respect for private and family life" (Article 7) and adds the "protection of personal data" (Article 8) (European Union 2000). These foundational texts, together with the Organisation for Economic Co-operation and Development (OECD) Guidelines on the Protection of Privacy and Transborder Flows of Personal Data (OECD 2002), constitute a solid "data protection corpus" on which the European directives noticeably build.

Rightly emphasized by the European Union, addressing privacy and regulatory obligations is not only a fundamental issue for the strengthening of individuals' trust in the digital world, it is also an essential element in the functioning of our democratic societies. In the USA, the Health Insurance Portability and Accountability Act (HIPAA 2016) has formalized a privacy rule. The European Commission did something similar with its Data Protection Directive (DPD) 95/46/EC (European Commission 1995) and E-Privacy Directive 2002/58/EC (EPD) (European Commission 2012).

More specifically, the DPD defines health data as a special category of data to which a higher level of data protection applies. Ali Gholami (Ali Gholami et al. 2014) identified a set of key principles from the DPD:

1. Lawfulness—all sensitive data processing must be conducted within the regulatory framework of the present directive
2. Informed consent (of the sample or data subject)—constitutes the main source of legitimacy for the processing of sensitive data
3. Purpose binding—ensures that personal data processing is performed according to predetermined purposes
4. Data minimization—restricts the extra or unnecessary disclosure of information to third parties, such as the platform itself in its role as the "processor"
5. Data accuracy—describes the necessity to keep data accurate and updated by the "controller"

6. Transparency—entitles the data subjects to have information about the processing of their data
7. Data security—proposes the implementation of technical measures to provide legitimate access and organizational safeguards
8. Accountability—mandates internal and external auditing, and control for various assurance reasons

Also important is that the DPD directive enables member states to reuse data for which consent to release had previously been received. According to Article 6(b), "further processing of data for historical, statistical or scientific purposes shall not be considered as incompatible, provided that Member States provide appropriate safeguards" (European Union 1995). In medical research, safeguards usually consist of an assessment by an ethical review board, which may substitute for the consent of the subject after the risks and benefits of the proposed research have been assessed. Nevertheless, the DPD gives no clear definition about what "identifying information" actually is; thus, it left decades of space for the development of a plethora of privacy-enhancing technologies (Borking 2005) with different degrees of efficacy.

Twenty years later, the more binding GDPR (European Commission 2012) was finally promulgated in April 2016 at the European level. Over the next two years, it will become directly applicable to all member states and will not require national implementing legislation. Compared with the DPD and EPD, the GDPR, by setting out a number of ad hoc provisions, devotes more attention to the matter of health data and scientific research.

Generally speaking, such legislation emphasizes "privacy by design" and "privacy by default" approaches, thereby ensuring that confidentiality is at the very heart of the design, development, and maintenance of information systems. In other words, confidentiality is no longer considered a static and immutable property; rather, it becomes an evolving condition over time and with associated risks.

More importantly, the GDPR introduces new rights for the data subject to access, erase, or modify his/her data, or even to be digitally "forgotten" altogether, with administrative and legal sanctions applying if these rights are violated. This important change was most certainly inspired by the world's first data protection law, the Data Protection Act Datenschutzgesetz [Data Protection Act] 1970, which was adopted by the State of Hesse, Germany, in October 1970.

Indeed, the most important factor in the subsequent development of privacy laws was the so-called census judgment by the German Federal Constitutional Court, which dealt with the question of informational self-determination. That judgment was based on the idea of *das allgemeine persönlichkeitsrecht* (general personality rights), which are enshrined in paragraph 2(1) of that country's constitution.

By recognizing the individual's natural rights over his/her personal data, the concept of informational self-determination makes a definitive step toward empowering the data subject (Rappaport 1981).

It is the author's belief that the combination of privacy by design, privacy by default, and the fundamental concept of informational self-determination establishes an unprecedented and powerful framework in Europe for the individual's empowerment in terms of the future collection of his/her data, and the processing of sensitive data. This framework has been further extended to the USA, thanks to the EU–US Privacy Shield adopted on July 12, 2016 (European Commission 2016a), thereby enabling Europeans to extend their rights across the Atlantic.

14.3 Digital Trust, Networks, and Technologies

Anticipating the complex needs of the GDPR regarding the protection of sensitive data and other privacy matters, a premiere network of hospitals and research centers was developed in the 2000s under the EU's Fifth Framework Programme's (FP5) MammoGrid project (Warren et al. 2007). Utilizing so-called grid computing (Foster et al. 2001), this network made it possible to share sensitive medical data across renowned European centers that were pioneering breast cancer research. In doing so, some progress was achieved regarding the anonymizing of medical information (such as DICOM[2] file headers and images and diagnostic reports), as well as the secure sharing, indexing, cataloguing, and curating of data. This is what the outer layer of the privacy compass (Fig. 14.1) reports on.

The Health-e-Child[3] project builds on this idea and is even more ambitious in scope (Skaburskas et al. 2008). It focuses on the development of a distributed platform interconnecting several more centers and addressing three major pathologies in pediatrics.

This has resulted in an interesting strategy that allows for the sourcing and preparation of sensitive data from "the inside," with proper anonymization applied on site under the strict supervision of data managers. These managers have the power to manage quality and to quarantine or even stop the sharing of data at any time. The verified data is then uploaded to a demilitarized zone (isolated) server[4] storing federated (non-centralized) content from the other connected centers. By connecting to their routing systems (e.g., proprietary radiology information systems [RIS], pharmacy information systems [PIS], and picture archiving and communication systems [PACS] databases), this architecture also makes it possible to penetrate local information systems more deeply.

Today, a number of EU Seventh Framework Programme (FP7) projects further exploit and extend this initial network, with a total set of 15 centers feeding dedicated scientific data catalogues. These projects are:

• The Model-Driven European Paediatric Digital Repository (European Commission 2016b)

---

[2] Digital Imaging and Communications in Medicine (DICOM) is the standard for handling, storing, printing and transmitting medical imaging information.

[3] Health-e-Child is a European Commission project "aimed at developing a platform to integrate information from traditional and emerging sources to support personalized and preventative medicine as well as large-scale, data-based biomedical research and training" (see: http://cordis.europa.eu/project/rcn/105287_en.html).

[4] In computing, a demilitarized zone is a sub-network that separates an internal local area network (LAN) from other untrusted networks (such as the Internet).

- neuGRID, a web portal aimed at helping neuroscientists (Redolfi et al. 2009)
- N4U (neuGRID for you) (Frisoni et al. 2011)
- CARDIOPROOF (see: www.cardioproof.eu/about/overview-on-the-project)

Just as VISA developed a network of institutions accepting and supporting their credit cards, the intent of these projects is to further extend the initial network and keep feeding research platforms by providing access to more data. In the next three years, the author, in collaboration with concerned project partners, will therefore propagate this legacy network to give life to MyHealthMyData, which is a sustainable blockchain-enabled transactional platform. (A blockchain is a distributed database that maintains a growing list of records called blocks.) MyHealthMyData will serve to "top up" this privacy-preserving information system with full transparency and traceability over time and distance.

14.4 How a Blockchain Could Help

A blockchain is the technology behind Bitcoin (Nakamoto 2008). It is a cryptographic protocol that makes it possible to run a distributed, public, and trustable "ledger" where digital-object transactions are signed with the identities of the issuer and recipient, verified by a community of peers and stored as incremental blocks in a shared database. The major benefit of the blockchain is that it brings digital trust to a potentially untrustable network.

Now, think of this ledger enabling (anonymous) consents and data transactions deployed at a European scale. It would be browsable anytime, anywhere, and by anyone, yet contain no sensitive information. Imagine a place where individuals, research groups, pharmaceutical companies, and health-care professionals could easily search for and mobilize large volumes of data on demand, while ensuring clear patient consent and privacy at all times—regardless of data complexity, data-protection laws, or the patient's geographic location.

This is the author's objective: To create this type of solid techno-logical backbone, supporting the resilience of information systems, and acting as an operational GDPR-compliant infrastructure where data transactions are informed and controlled by informational self-determination and privacy-by-design or privacy-by-default principles. Such a foundational base will open new avenues to innovative (smart) contracts (Watanabe et al. 2015) that incentivize data mobilization under strict regulatory control, while facilitating dynamic consent collection and data preparation.

Besides the advances the blockchain will bring to the development of a transparent, traceable, distributed, and trustable "ledger of consent" and its associated data transactions, it could also lead to experimentation with a novel type of social business model involving the use of specific protocols for exchanging value.

In effect, the result would be a new health-dedicated virtual currency that assigns economic value to different types of health-care transactions. Such state-of-the-art transitional money systems could "be used as crutches to re-educate atrophied collective behaviour patterns" (Lietaer 2001). The intent would be to investigate the potential use of shared economies and open-value accounting in health care (Bauwens et Stiegler 2015).

14.5 Conclusion

Although it is a fantastic opportunity to learn about ourselves, this wealth of suddenly accessible personal and sensitive data is a challenge for societies, which need to come up with advanced governance models that supplement their aggregate demand (AD) equation analyses with applicable ethical, legal, societal, and economical guidelines.

Comparable to the effect that Leonardo da Vinci's famous drawing of the Vitruvian Man had on our understanding of the proportions of a man's body (Vitruvius 1983), we are at the beginning of a new form of consciousness, a new source of knowledge that will provide humanity with an unprecedented chance to improve, learn, and grow.

However, right now, as individuals, we are "digitally naked," which is why we need to develop a digital skin—armor to protect us from outside attacks.

There is no doubt the Internet has greatly affected us all. Systemically enshrining the principles of privacy by design, privacy by default, and informational self-determination—using privacy-preserving technologies and the blockchain—may, in the longer term, better protect data subjects (i.e., you and me). And it may also direct society's information systems toward a fairer digital economy where "value" means more than money.

References

Borking, John, "The Use and Value of Privacy-Enhancing Technologies," *The Glass Consumer: Life in a Surveillance Society* (June 14, 2005): 69–96, doi:10.1332/policypress/9781861347350.003.0004.

Council of Europe "*Convention for the Protection of Individuals with Regard to Automatic Processing of Personal Data,*" 108, Council of Europe, 1981.

Datenschutzgesetz [Data Protection Act] October 7, 1970, HESSISCHES GESETZ-UND VERORDNUNGSBLATT I.

European Commission "Proposal for a Regulation of the European Parliament and of the Council on the Protection of Individuals with Regard to the Processing of Personal Data and on the Free Movement of Such Data (General Data Protection Regulation)," COM (2012) 11 final, 2012/0011 (COD), Brussels, January 25, 2012.

European Commission "The EU-U.S. Privacy Shield," July 12, 2016a, accessed on October 3, 2016a, http://ec.europa.eu/justice/data-protection/interna tional-transfers/eu-us-privacy-shield/index_en.htm.

European Commission "Model-Driven European Paediatric Digital Repository," accessed October 3, 2016b, http://cordis.europa.eu/project/rcn/108228_en. html.

European Union "Directive 95/46/EC of the European Parliament and of the Council of 24 October 1995 on the Protection of Individuals with Regard to the Processing of Personal Data and on the Free Movement of Such Data," Official, *Journal of the EC* 23, no. 6, (1995) European Parliament, Official Journal, OJ L 281 of (November 23, 1995).

European Union "Charter of Fundamental Rights of the European Union," (December 18, 2000), C 364/1 European Communities, Official Journal, 2000/C 364/01.

Foster, Ian, Carl Kesselman, and Steven Tuecke, "The Anatomy of the Grid: Enabling Scalable Virtual Organizations," *International Journal of High Performance Computing Applications* 15, no. 3 (2001): 200–222, doi:/ 10.1109/ccgrid.2001.923162.

Frisoni, Giovanni B. et al., "Virtual Imaging Laboratories for Marker Discovery in Neurodegenerative Diseases," *Nature Reviews Neurology* 7, no. 8 (July 5, 2011): 429–438, doi:10.1038/nrneurol.2011.99.

Gholami, Ali et al., "Privacy Threat Modeling for Emerging BiobankClouds," *Procedia Computer Science* 37 (2014): 489–496, doi:10.1016/j. procs.2014.08.073.

Kish, Leonard J., and Eric J. Topol, "Unpatients—Why Patients Should Own Their Medical Data," *Nature Biotechnology* 33, no. 9 (September 8, 2015): 921–924, doi:10.1038/nbt.3340.

Lietaer, Bernard, "The Future of Money: Towards New Wealth, Work and a Wiser World," *European Business Review* 13, no. 2 (April 2001), doi:10.1108/ ebr.2001.05413bab.008.

Michel Bauwens (with Jean Lievens), Sauver Le Monde. Vers Une économie Post-capitaliste Avec Le Peer-to-Peer, Paris, Éditions Les Liens qui libèrent, 2015, 268 p.

Nakamoto, Satoshi, "Bitcoin: A Peer-to-Peer Electronic Cash System," 2008, accessed on October 3, 2016, http://www.cryptovest.co.uk/resources/ Bitcoin%20paper%20Original.pdf.

OECD (2002), *OECD Guidelines on the Protection of Privacy and Transborder Flows of Personal Data*. Paris: OECD Publishing, doi: http://dx.doi.org/10.1787/9789264196391-en

Picard, Rosalind, and Gary Wolf, "Guest Editorial Sensor Informatics and Quantified Self," *IEEE Journal of Biomedical and Health Informatics* 19, no. 5 (September, 2015): 1531–1531, doi:10.1109/ JBHI.2015.2462372.

Rappaport, Julian, "In Praise of Paradox: A Social Policy of Empowerment over Prevention," *American Journal of Community Psychology* 9, no. 1 (1981): 1–25.

Redolfi, Alberto et al., "Grid Infrastructures for Computational Neuroscience: The neuGRID example," *Future Neurology* 4, no. 6 (2009): 703–722.

Skaburskas, Konstantin et al., "Health-e-Child: A Grid Platform for European Paediatrics," *Journal of Physics: Conference Series* 119, no. 8, 082011 (IOP Publishing, 2008), doi:10.1088/1742-6596/119/8/082011.

UN General Assembly, Universal Declaration of Human Rights, 10 December 1948, 217 A (III), accessed on February 24, 2017, http://www.refworld.org/docid/3ae6b3712c.html

United States *"Health Insurance Portability and Accountability Act (HIPAA),"* Washington, DC, U.S: Dept. of Labor, accessed on October 3, 2016, http://purl.fdlp.gov/GPO/gpo10291.

Vitruvius, Marcus Pollio, "De architectura," 2 volumes, translated by F. Granger, Loeb Classical Library," (1983).

Warren, R. et al., "MammoGrid—A Prototype Distributed Mammographic Database for Europe," *Clinical Radiology* 62, no. 11 (November 2007): 1044–1051, doi:10.1016/j.crad.2006.09.032.

Watanabe, Hiroki et al., "Blockchain Contract: A Complete Consensus Using Blockchain," *In 2015 IEEE 4th Global Conference on Consumer Electronics (GCCE)* (October 2015): 577–578, doi:10.1109/gcce.2015.7398721.

15

Mobile Mental Health Virtual Communities: Challenges and Opportunities

Linda Eftychiou and Christo El Morr

15.1 Introduction

Virtual communities (VCs), known as online communities, have evolved through the years (Rheingold 2000, Nonnecke et al. 2006, Preece 2000) with tangible presence in health research lately (Demiris 2005, 2006, Demiris et al. 2008, El Morr 2014, El Morr et al. 2014a, 2014b). In 2015, a study from the Canadian Mental Health Association showed that roughly one out of every five Canadians (at some point in their lives) will be diagnosed with a mental disorder, usually in the form of an anxiety disorder or depression (Canadian Mental Health Association 2016). Unfortunately, the statistic for young adults encountering a mental illness is rapidly increasing, as 31% of college students in the USA (American College Health Association 2009) and the numbers are similar in Europe (World Health Organization 2014). The total

L. Eftychiou (✉) · C. El Morr
School of Health Policy and Management, York University, Toronto, ON, Canada
e-mail: linda.eftychiou@hotmail.ca; elmorr@yorku.ca

© The Author(s) 2017
L. Menvielle et al. (eds.), *The Digitization of Healthcare*,
DOI 10.1057/978-1-349-95173-4_15

economic cost of mental health in Canada amounts to more than \$14 Billion per year (Stephens and Joubert 2001).

Young adults are used to having technology at their fingertips, whether they use their desktop computer, laptop, smartphone, iPad, and/or iWatch. The need for technology-based therapy and psycho-education to treat depression, anxiety, and other mental illnesses is in high demand as populations face many barriers when dealing with mental health. Some of these barriers are related to accessibility, lack of financial and professional resources, and social stigma (Perlick et al. 2010). Thus, technology-based programs open the door for alternative solutions to traditional therapy targeting those who would not otherwise have the ability to receive, or even seek out treatment.

On the other hand, in recent years, we have seen a rapid growth in technology, especially in regard to the integration of the Internet and mobile devices in daily lives. The Internet and mobile devices are most prominently used for communication and information sharing, and as such, it is slowly starting to make its way into the health-care system. The prominent role of technology in healthcare has the ability to improve quality of care for individual patients, as well as for population health as a whole. More specifically, the use of mobile technologies such as smartphones, tablets, personal computers, mobile applications (here-inafter Apps), and wireless networks, can allow the delivery of health care in a way that can reach a vast majority of the population. This creative new way of delivering health services and obtaining health information is known as mHealth (Kumar et al. 2013). This chapter overviews the domain of mHealth in relation to mental health and VCs and provides a perspective of current opportunities and challenges.

15.1.1 Background

In recent years, we have seen a rapid growth in technology, especially in regard to the integration of the Internet and use of mobile devices in our daily lives. The Internet and mobile devices are most prominently used for com-munication and information sharing, and as such, it is slowly starting to make its way into the health-care system for the same reasons. The prominent role of technology in health care has the ability to improve quality of care for individual patients, as well as population health as a whole. More specifically, the use of mobile technologies such as smartphones, tablets, personal computers, mobile Apps, and wireless networks, can be used to deliver health care in a way a wide range of the population offering new location-based services. This creative new way of delivering health services and obtaining health information is known as mHealth (Kumar et al. 2013).

Traditionally, health care has been delivered from health-care providers in their office, hospital room, or clinic, where typically the doctor is the "know all" source of information, and the patient simply adheres to their advice. However, a shift to a more patient-centered approach in the medical world empowered patients giving them the ability to be active participants in managing their own health and well-being. One of the ways a patient can feel in control of their health is through the use of mobile technologies to keep track of their health problems, as well as the use of the Internet as a source of knowledge. This is especially the case for patients with health issues that need monitoring on a daily basis. As such, the integration of mHealth as a part of the health-care delivery can be especially beneficial in areas such as chronic disease management, such as chronic kidney diseases, chronic heart diseases, and mental health, where patients need a continuum of care rather than a simple "cure." Some of the most common mental health problems include experiences of stress, anxiety, and depression. This chapter seeks to explore the opportunities and challenges that come into fruition when utilizing mHealth to improve access and delivery of effective mental health-care services. As well as the use of "big data" collected by smartphone mental health Apps.

15.2 mHealth and Virtual Communities Opportunities

15.2.1 Treatment Accessibility

mHealth in relation to mental health is increasingly being used by clinicians and patients due to its potential benefits in treatment accessibility, cost-effectiveness, and compliance and adherence to treatment options.

The evolvement of smartphone technology has subsequently allowed for the development of various mHealth Apps that are innovating the ways in which mental health services can be delivered and accessed. The most common features of mental health Apps are the ability to document symptoms via written posts, audio, or video recording, as well as to give automatic feedback to guide users on how to cope with these symptoms (Marzano et al. 2015). It is becoming increasingly important to be able to deliver effective mental health services outside the point of care, because individuals with mental health issues may often have problems that arise between scheduled visits. As such, web-assisted therapy can offer a solution to remote support and treatment for patients with mood and anxiety disorders outside of clinical sessions (Cuijpers et al. 2009; Litz et al. 2007; Price et al. 2014). Moreover, despite persistent effort in today's society to reduce stigma around being diagnosed with a mental illness and subsequently seeking professional help, it still very much exists. As such, mobile Apps have the ability to combat issues of access that stem from lack of availability of doctors, and fear of discrimination by family, friends, and broader society. It also allows for longitudinal health plans as clinicians are able to track and monitor their patients' symptoms in real-time, giving them better insight for treatment options (Luxton et al. 2011). By being able to collect such data outside the typical scheduled doctor's visit, a patient's treatment plan can be constructed to fit individual needs and symptoms that are felt on a daily basis. As such, patients are then even able to receive treatment through the mHealth Apps using features such as teleconferencing with the physician, receiving advice based on moods self-assessment, and even mindfulness meditation techniques. Moreover, this also has the potential of overcoming structural barriers involving distance whereby a patient whom may live in a rural area far from their practitioner specializing in mental health is now able to complete treatment at home. Televideo is a potent solution in rural areas as many smartphones today have the capabilities of video calling (Price et al. 2014).

Through mobile Apps, the patient is able to access audio instructions that are similar to what s/he would have received in a face-to-face session with a clinician; these audio instructions can help guide them through a situation. Thus, the App acts as a "virtual coach" through real-time audio and visual instruction and is essentially training the patient to deal with what they are going through at that moment (Luxton et al. 2011). Moreover, such interactions through a mHealth device and application may be especially beneficial to individuals with anxiety, who otherwise may have difficulty expressing their true feelings in a face-to-face session with a professional. For example, one App known as *Headspace* is described as a "gym membership for the mind" whereby members can partake in mindfulness meditation practices that can effectively help treat stress, anxiety, addiction, and even relationship issues.

mHealth Apps are not meant to take over the role of health-care professionals, instead they are meant to work in conjunction with normal clinical visits, extending the services and treatment availability to outside the point of care. By engaging patients in their own treatment through new technologies such as mHealth Apps, patients are able to track, monitor, and manage their mental health just like a diabetes patient monitors their blood sugar and nutrition. By doing so, the goal of mHealth for mental health is to reduce the symptoms and incidence of problems like stress, anxiety, and/or depression and prevent more serious life-threatening situations.

15.2.2 Cost-Effectiveness

One of the main factors that comes up during health IT discussions is that of cost. That is, how much will an application cost, not only the patient but the manufacturers, and the distributors (i.e., doctors, governments etc.). In the case of mHealth Apps, while the argument can be made that it is costly to build an efficient and effective App and subsequently make it available for use, it actually turns out to be cost-effective due to the vast majority and accessibility of mobile devices and the Internet. As such, this means that patients will be spending less time in the clinic (thus reducing the costs associated with this), but still receiving the same quality of care (Luxton et al. 2011). Through mobile Apps, mental health services can be delivered and accessed by patients at the comfort of their own homes. This reduces costs that are incurred by patients when it comes to traveling time (especially for those who live in rural areas), and taking the time from work or school. Price et al. (2014) stresses the benefits of mHealth for those that are financially incapable of making frequent visits to a clinic, as well as for those who are physically incapable, or find it hard, to commute. While mHealth Apps do come at a price, it has the benefit of saving a patient time and money. In 2014, 55% of Canadian owned a smart phone (Sundaram et al. 2014), and the figures are similar elsewhere such as in France, UK, or Europe in general (Statista.com2015). In today's digital world, large parts of the population in developed countries have access to the devices that can support such mobile mental health Apps; therefore, making treatment accessible and cost-efficient. This digitalization of health care could be part of normal treatment plans and maybe even covered by health-care plans. In Ontario, the costs for obtaining treatment for mental health from general practitioners and/or psychiatrists are covered by the provincial plan OHIP (Ontario Health Insurance Plan). However, the wait times to access a psychologist for non-urgent mental health issues are long, which makes the case for mHealth as support tool while waiting for a doctor. Besides, some people might choose to seek out private therapy to which mHealth services are not covered by OHIP (CAMH 2003). However, in both cases, mHealth has the potential of saving costs for the patients, as well as the public and private health sectors. Moreover, through mHealth, patients are able to detect and manage their symptoms and therefore become more involved in their own health care and knowledgeable about mental health (Buckingham et al. 2015).

15.2.3 mHealth Apps and Virtual Communities

One of the highest demographic groups that are reluctant to seek assistance for mental health problems are adolescents and young adults, especially those of Indigenous or ethnic minority groups (Rickwood et al. 2007). As such, mHealth can be used as a means of reaching out to such patient groups, especially that it is the generation that is most inclined to use technology. Many existing Apps have the potential to treat patients on a day-to-day basis; BetterHelp is an example of a mHealth App that is accessible via a desktop/laptop/tablet Web browser too. BetterHelp is an online counseling platform that matches users with experienced counselors to help people deal with life's challenges such as stress, anxiety, depression, relationships, career issues, and more (Better Help 2016). Such App can be highly effective and a convenient way to help people with mild to moderate mental health disorders. The App however is no way meant to substitute traditional face-to-face therapy, as these health-care providers are not able to diagnose or prescribe medications; instead, the App provides support with similar benefits to traditional therapy at a much lower cost and at your convenience. Mobile Apps, such as BetterHelp, can also help alleviate the stigma associated with receiving mental health care and as such it can improve the likelihood that vulnerable people, who may have not sought treatment in-person, attempt to do so via the App (Price et al. 2014). As such, an App has the potential of not only managing mild mental health problems and life's challenges but it can also be used as a preventative tool for more serious mental health disorders and associated risk factors such as self-harm, harm to others, or suicide.

VCs can add new dimensions to Apps. VCs, or online communities, are formed of a group of people with certain roles meeting together online to achieve predefined goals using a computer system. VCs could be used in the health domain (El Morr 2010), and are able to connect health professionals together forming what is known as Virtual Communities of Practice (VCoP) (Wenger 1998) as well as health professionals and patients (El Morr et al. 2014a). The possibility is open to include with the patient other people who are in the patient's circle of care such as family members (e.g., the case of people with dementia). Health VCs can be fixed if used on desktops or laptops only, or mobile if they are deployed over smart phones with certain added capacities such as the location-based services (El Morr 2007; Kawash et al. 2007). Mobile Health VCs (MHVCs) add the community dimension to mHealth, which means that the professionals as well as the patients are not only in a one-to-one interaction but rather in a community. The community dimension encourages social interaction (McKay 2006) and it has been used to communicate achievements and challenges between members (e.g., fitness Apps). In the case of mental health MHVCs, the community aspect may encourage sociability and an experience of belonging (Blanchard and Markus 2002; Blanchard and Markus 2004) and connectedness (Welbourne et al. 2013).

15.2.4 The Importance of Big Data in the Future of Mental Health Services

When it comes to improving the delivery and access of mental health care, one of the most prominent avenues for doing so is through the collection of high-quality health data that has been accumulated over a long period of time (Torous et al. 2015). Such large amounts of high quality and complex data sets are what are termed as big data. Torous, Staples, and Onnela (Torous et al. 2015) state that data collected from smartphone Apps meet the big data criteria which are velocity, volume, and variety.

As mentioned earlier, while traditionally a clinician gathers the most information on a patient during an office visit and then the patient leaves, with smartphone Apps data can be entered by the patient anytime and anywhere. For example, the most advantageous aspect of high-velocity data can be seen in patients who are at risk of suicide, as the data can be used to monitor the behaviors of such patients and therefore detect who may be displaying certain at-risk behaviors (Selby et al. 2013). Next, the data collected is of high volume and can be separated into two types: "active data" when the patient is involved in the generation of data (e.g., surveys, audio sample, journal entries), and "passive data" which refers to data generated by GPS, or communication logs from phone calls and text messages (Torous et al. 2015). The variety of data from smartphones proves to be complex and as such the analytical and statistical tools used to make sense of the data are complex. An example of the statistical methods used is decision trees that enables the researchers to divide data into classes, which in turn enables them to observe patterns and trends (Torous et al. 2015). While there might have been some worries expressed around overreliance of clinicians on smartphone Apps, the reality is that smartphone Apps are meant to enhance, not to replace, clinician evaluation and capabilities.

The use of big data through smartphone Apps has the potential to help combating the global health crisis in mental health (Fig. 15.1). This is especially true in developing countries where the burden of mental health is much higher than other parts of the world, and where we are seeing an accelerated growth rate in the use of mobile technologies (Farrington et al. 2014).

Fig. 15.1 Opportunities of mHealth and virtual communities

15.3 mHealth and Virtual Communities Challenges

Despite the potential of mHealth App, there are several challenges related to their use, these include usability and adoption, data security and privacy, quality standards and patient safety.

15.3.1 Usability and Adoption

Usability is a key component during the development of any application whether it is dedicated for health or not. The way a user is able to navigate and ultimately use an application will determine if the technology will be adopted (Price et al. 2014). If an application is challenging to use, it will be perceived as not useful to their needs (Chiu and Eysenbach 2010).

Besides, there may be reluctance in clinicians to integrate these new technologies in their medical practices (Adibi 2015). There is a clear link between adoption and usability, that is, if a mental health App is usable (i.e., easy to learn, carries out its preferred function, and has high satisfaction rates), then more people will be willing to adopt it (Archer 2009).

A way to improve usability is to provide feedback from users (i.e., patients and clinicians) during the design and testing stages. As with any technology, whether it be an electronic health record or an mHealth App, updates and improvements are inevitable as they need to evolve to fit the needs of users. Lastly, while there is wariness from some groups of people in using technologies, there has been research that shows that mental health patients hold a strong interest in using their phones to monitor health, and that smartphone ownership is close to national averages in this group (Torous et al. 2014a, 2014b). As such, an increase in adoption may be seen in younger populations when compared to the elderly population that are still set on traditional means of health.

15.3.2 Privacy and Security Issues

With the emergence and reliance of mobile devices and Apps, one of the main concerns of users is that of privacy and security, especially when patients are in a VC and need to trust each other (Abdul-Rahman and Hailes 2000; Ali Shaikh and Omer 2005; Blanchard et al. 2011). When it comes to using a mHealth App, a patient has to trust that her/his health information will be kept safe from unauthorized personnel and from the general public. With the potential of Apps being having security flaws, patients may be reluctant to use mHealth Apps, especially when it comes to giving out personal information about one's health condition, especially mental health. This risk is further heightened as one of the most common security issues is the possibility of losing one's device either by theft or misplacement (Price et al. 2014). However, all smart phones, tablets, or PCs have the option of setting a unique password that only the owner knows. Some manufacturers have used fingerprint recognition software as a means of being able to unlock your phone. Another precaution that can be taken is to require a password to access or make changes to the personal information (Price et al. 2014).

Mental health conditions unfortunately carry a stigma in today's society, therefore many fear that if their personal health information is leaked they may be targets of judgment by family, friends, employers, and greater society. As such it is not only important for patients to choose the right applications wisely but also producers of these applications should be subjected to the same ethical and evidence-based guidelines that manufacturers of medical devices and or pharmaceuticals are subjected to. It is also important for the software provider to identify and locate security flaws and weaknesses, and address it accordingly to prevent exploiting user's information. The privacy and security of patients are in the hands of the health-care providers whom must ensure that the application being used is compliant to governmental privacy standards if personal health information is being stored or exchanged (Luxton et al. 2011).

15.3.3 Quality Standards

Health-related Apps that exist today are abundant and can be used to manage and track various disorders, not just mental health. However, it is possible that mHealth Apps can result in inaccurate information that at the end does not contribute positively to evidence-based medicine, or to overall health improvements for individuals (Kumar et al. 2013). For example, there are health Apps available to measure blood pressure wirelessly, nevertheless research showed that their readings are inaccurate (Singal 2015). Thus, it is important for patients who use mHealth Apps to choose applications that are supported by evidence-based research (Luxton et al. 2011) and officially recognized as beneficial and not harmful, with clear side-effects, if any. Overall, unlike standard medical devices such as a heart monitor or blood sugar monitor, mHealth applications are essentially always evolving as they need to meet the needs of the targeted population, maintain interoperability with other existing health care applications (Archer 2009) while trying to protect patient privacy.

15.3.4 Patient Safety

As noted by Gruessner (Gruessner 2015), the mHealth field is able to engage a wider range of patients with mHealth tools to track their fitness, nutrition plans, symptoms, feelings, and treatment protocols. As such, the use of such applications brings forth the question of patient safety since, more often than not, these Apps require users to enter sensitive information. This is true for mental health Apps, where essentially a user has to enter personal health information such as symptoms and diagnoses. Therefore, it is vital to ensure that patient safety is not jeopardized by "leak," or collection of information by unauthorized individuals (Gruessner 2015). For instance, some mental health patients may become more reliant on their health applications; therefore, in instances where technology fails (e.g., application crashing, or battery failures), the patients may be put at higher risk of being unable to cope (Luxton et al. 2011). As noted earlier on, the application is not meant to take over the role of the clinician, as such, clinicians should be ensuring that the services and treatment provided by the health applications are indeed working, and if not to provide alternative forms of care (Reynolds et al. 2015).

For mobile mental health apps to be successfully integrated for use in the everyday lives of patients and even the health-care professionals, it is important to note some project management aspects that should be taken into consideration. Improving the quality and effectiveness of a mobile App requires a user-centered design; such user-centeredness should be obtained through usability testing of mHealth apps and VCs involving target audiences (e.g., patients, doctors).

Just as the use of mobile phones, tablets, laptops, and PC's have increased over the years in our social lives, the same can be projected for the future of health care. Slowly but surely mHealth apps would be the norm and integrated into the treatment plans and options for people with mental health problems. Health-care professionals and caregivers can use apps and VCs to better understand and keep track of their patient's symptoms and progress over time through big data analytics. From a managerial point of view, it is important to explore whether mobile mental health apps can actually help early detect mental health issues, or if such apps can potentially be used as a preventative tool by promoting positive mental health practices.

Furthermore, managers need to think on innovative ways to integrate successful mental health apps into treatment plans that are accessible to

Fig. 15.2 Challenges of mHealth and virtual communities

all. In Canada, this could mean having such applications covered by provincial or national health-care plans; as the highest prevalence of mental illness is found among socially and economically disadvantaged groups where cost is an issue (WHO and the Calouste Gulbenkian Foundation 2014) (Fig. 15.2).

15.4 Conclusion

In conclusion, it is clear that the use of mobile technologies is inevitable in today's technologically advanced society in which people are always on the go. The use of mHealth applications have proven to be beneficial for people with mental health disorders for reasons such as its flexibility, being source of motivation, its ability to help manage and treat disorders, and the potential to reach a wider range of patients (i.e., younger generations) that may have been hesitant in obtaining treatment in the first place. As such, mHealth Apps have the vast potential of reducing mental health disorders when they are used adequately, to their fullest potential, and in conjunction with clinical care.

However, barriers still remain in regard to privacy and security, quality, and patient safety. Due to the fact that mHealth Apps are coming into fruition only recently, more studies are needed to compare their effectiveness for patients with different mental health disorders, and different age groups. By doing so, evidence-based guidelines need to be created to which mental health App manufacturers would be subjected to. Also, clinicians or health instances, such as hospitals, could educate their patients not only on the appropriate use of mHealth Apps but also on how to choose the App that will best fit their personal health needs. Furthermore, big data is especially beneficial in the clinical world of mental health as it offers rich, high-volume, real-time data that is not only beneficial to individual patients, but to population health on a local and global scales as well. mHealth and the resulting "big data" is the future, as public health officials find ways to integrate and analyze such data into evidence-based medicine.

References

Abdul-Rahman, Alfarez, and Stephen Hailes. 2000. "Supporting trust in virtual communities." 33rd Hawaii International Conference on System Sciences, Maui, Hawaii, January 4–7.

Adibi, S. 2015. *Mobile health: A technology road map*. Bern: Springer International Publishing.

Ali Shaikh, Ali, and Rana Omer. 2005. "Formalising trust for online communities." Fourth International Joint Conference on Autonomous Agents and Multiagent Systems, The Netherlands.

American College Health Association. 2009. "Reference group executive summary." American College Health Association Accessed February 04. http://www.acha-ncha.org/docs/ACHA-NCHA_reference_group_executivesummary_fall2008.pdf.

Archer, Norm. 2009. "Mobile e-Health: Making the case." *Handbook of Research on Advances in Health Informatics and Electronic Healthcare Applications: Global Adoption and Impact of Information Communication Technologies: Global Adoption and Impact of Information Communication Technologies*, edited by K. Khoumbati, Y. K. Dwivedi, Aradhana Srivastava, and Banita Lal, Hershey, PA: IGI Global.

Better Help. 2016. "Who we are." Betterhelp.com Accessed May 6. https:// www.betterhelp.com/about/#.

Blanchard, A. L., and M. L. Markus. 2002. "Sense of virtual community – maintaining the experience of belonging." Proceedings of the 35th Annual Hawaii International Conference on System Sciences, January 7–10.

Blanchard, Anita L., and M. Lynne Markus. 2004. "The experienced 'Sense' of a virtual community: Characteristics and processes." SIGMIS Database 35: 64–79. doi: 10.1145/968464.968470.

Blanchard, Anita L., Jennifer L. Welbourne, and Marla D. Boughton. 2011. "A model of online trust." *Information, Communication & Society* 14: 76–106. doi:10.1080/13691181003739633.

Buckingham, C. D., A. Adams, L. Vail, A. Kumar, A. Ahmed, A. Whelan, and E. Karasouli. 2015. "Integrating service user and practitioner expertise within a web-based system for collaborative mental-health risk and safety management." *Patient Educ Couns* 98 (10): 1189–1196. doi: 10.1016/j. pec.2015.08.018.

CAMH. 2003. *Challenges and choices: Finding mental health services in Ontario.* Toronto, Canada: Centre for Addiction and Mental Health.

Canadian Mental Health Association. 2016. "Mental Illness in Canada: Statistics on the prevalence of mental disorders and related suicides in Canada." Canadian Mental Health Association Accessed February 04. https://alberta.cmha.ca/mental_health/statistics/.

Chiu, Teresa ML, and Gunther Eysenbach. 2010. "Stages of use: Consideration, initiation, utilization, and outcomes of an internet-mediated intervention." *BMC Medical Informatics and Decision Making* 10 (1): 1–11. doi:10.1186/ 1472-6947-10-73.

Cuijpers, P., I. M. Marks, A. Van Straten, K. Cavanagh, L. Gega, and G. Andersson. 2009. "Computer-aided psychotherapy for anxiety disorders: A meta-analytic review." *Cognitive Behavioral Therapy* 38 (2): 66–82. doi:10.1080/16506070802694776.

Demiris, George. 2005. "Virtual communities in health care." *Intelligent Paradigms for Healthcare Enterprises* 121–137: 4

Demiris, George. 2006. "The diffusion of virtual communities in health care: Concepts and challenges." *Patient Education and Counseling* 62 (2): 178–188. doi:10.1016/j.pec.2005.10.003.

Demiris, George, Lawrence B. Afrin, Karen L. Stuart Speedie, Manu Sondhi Courtney, Vivian Vimarlund, Christian Lovis, William Goossen, and

Cecil Lynch. 2008. "Patient-centered applications: Use of information technology to promote disease management and Wellness. A white paper by the AMIA knowledge in motion working group." *Journal of the American Medical Informatics Association: JAMIA* 15: 8–13. doi:10.1197/jamia.M2492.

El Morr, Christo. 2007. "Mobile virtual communities in healthcare: Self-managed care on the move." 3rd IASTED International Conference on Telehealth, Telehealth 2007, startdate 20070530-enddate 20070601, 2007.

El Morr, Christo. 2010. "Health care virtual communities: Challenges and Opportunities." *The Human Centred Approach to Bionanotechnology in Telemedicine: Ethical Considerations*, edited by G.J. Morais da Costa, M.A. da Silva Nuno, S.A. da Silva Nuno 278–298, Hershey, PA: Medical Information Science Reference, doi:10.4018/978-1-61520-670-4.ch013.

El Morr, Christo. 2014. *Research perspectives on the role of informatics in health policy management*. Hershey, PA: Medical Information Science Reference.

El Morr, C., C. Cole, and J. Perl. 2014a. "A health virtual community for patients with chronic kidney disease." *Procedia Computer Science* 37: 333–339

El Morr, Shadi Saleh Christo, Walid Ammar, Nabil Natafgi, and Karen Kazandjian. 2014b. "A health virtual community model: A bottom up approach." eTELEMED 2014, The Sixth International Conference on eHealth, Telemedicine, and Social Medicine.

Farrington, C., A. Aristidou, and K. Ruggeri. 2014. "mHealth and global mental health: Still waiting for the mH2 wedding?." *Global Health* 10: 17. doi: 10.1186/1744-8603-10-17.

Gruessner, Vera. 2015. "FDA's focus on patient safety with mobile health applications." mHealthIntelligence.com, Last Modified August 26, 2015 Accessed May 6. http://mhealthintelligence.com/news/fdas-focus-on-patient-safety-with-mobile-health-applications.

Kawash, Jalal, Christo El Morr, and Mazen Itani. 2007. "A novel collaboration model for mobile virtual communities." *International Journal for Web Based Communities* 3: 1

Kumar, S., W. J. Nilsen, A. Abernethy, A. Atienza, K. Patrick, M. Pavel, W. T. Riley, A. Shar, B. Spring, D. Spruijt-Metz, D. Hedeker, V. Honavar, R. Kravitz, R. C. Lefebvre, D. C. Mohr, S. A. Murphy, C. Quinn, V. Shusterman, and D. Swendeman. 2013. "Mobile health technology evaluation: The mHealth evidence workshop." *American Journal of Preventive Medicine* 45 (2): 228–236. doi:10.1016/j.amepre.2013.03.017.

Litz, B. T., C. C. Engel, R. A. Bryant, and A. Papa. 2007. "A randomized, controlled proof-of-concept trial of an Internet-based, therapist-assisted self-management treatment for posttraumatic stress disorder." *The American Journal of Psychiatry* 164 (11): 1676–1683. doi:10.1176/appi. ajp.2007.06122057.

Luxton, David D., Russell A. McCann, Nigel E. Bush, Matthew C. Mishkind, and Greg M. Reger. 2011. "mHealth for mental health: Integrating smartphone technology in behavioral healthcare." *Professional Psychology: Research and Practice* 42 (6): 505–512. doi:10.1037/a0024485.

Marzano, Lisa, Andy Bardill, Bob Fields, Kate Herd, David Veale, Nick Grey, and Paul Moran. 2015. "The application of mHealth to mental health: Opportunities and challenges." *The Lancet Psychiatry* 2 (10): 942–948. doi:10.1016/S2215-0366(15)00268-0.

McKay, Dana. 2006. "Making the social mobile: Mobile access to online patient communities." Computer Human Interaction (CHI)—Workshop on Mobile Social Software, 2006.

Nonnecke, Blair, Dorine Andrews, and Jenny Preece. 2006. "Non-public and public online community participation: Needs, attitudes and behavior." Electronic Commerce Research 6 (1): 7–20.

Perlick, D. A., Y. Hofstein, and L. A. Michael. 2010. "Barriers to Mental Health Service Use in Young Adulthood." *Young Adult Mental Health*, edited by J.E Grant and M.N. Potenza, New York: Oxford University Press.

Preece, Jenny. 2000. *Online communities: Designing usability supporting sociability*. USA: John Wiley & Sons Ltd.

Price, M., E. K. Yuen, E. M. Goetter, J. D. Herbert, E. M. Forman, R. Acierno, and K. J. Ruggiero. 2014. "mHealth: A mechanism to deliver more accessible, more effective mental health care." *Clinical Psychology & Psychotherapy* 21 (5): 427–436. doi:10.1002/cpp.1855.

Reynolds, Julia, Kathleen M Griffiths, John A Cunningham, Kylie Bennett, and Anthony Bennett. 2015. "Clinical practice models for the use of e-mental health resources in primary health care by health professionals and peer workers: A conceptual framework." *JMIR Mental Health* 2 (1): e6. doi:10.2196/mental.4200.

Rheingold, H. 2000. *The virtual community: Homesteading on the electronic frontier*. Cambridge: MIT Press.

Rickwood, D. J., F. P. Deane, and C. J. Wilson. 2007. "When and how do young people seek professional help for mental health problems?." *The Medical Journal of Australia* 187 (7 Suppl): S35–39.

Selby, E. A., S. Yen, and A. Spirito. 2013. "Time varying prediction of thoughts of death and suicidal ideation in adolescents: Weekly ratings over 6-month follow-up." *Journal of Clinical Child & Adolescent Psychology* 42 (4): 481–495. doi:10.1080/15374416.2012.736356.

Singal, Jesse. 2015. "Please don't use shady blood-pressure phone apps." New York Mag, Last Modified March 2, 2015 Accessed May 6. http://nymag.com/scienceofus/2015/03/please-dont-use-shady-blood-pressure-phone-apps.html.

Statista.com. 2015. "Smartphone user penetration as percentage of total population in Western Europe from 2011 to 2018." Accessed May 6. http://www.statista.com/statistics/203722/smartphone-penetration-per-capita-in-western-europe-since-2000/.

Stephens, T., and N. Joubert. 2001. "The economic burden of mental health problems in Canada." *Chronic Diseases in Canada* 22 (1): 18–23.

Sundaram, Prabhakar, Jesse Wolfersberger, and Matthew Jenkins. 2014. "Acting on the evolution of the Canadian smartphone user March 2014." catalyst.ca Accessed May 6. http://catalyst.ca/wp-content/uploads/Catalyst_Canadian-Smartphone.pdf.

Torous, John, Steven Richard Chan, Shih Yee-Marie Tan, Jacob Behrens, Ian Mathew, Erich J Conrad, Ladson Hinton, Peter Yellowlees, and Matcheri Keshavan. 2014a. "Patient smartphone ownership and interest in mobile apps to monitor symptoms of mental health conditions: A survey in four geographically distinct psychiatric clinics." *JMIR Mental Health* 1 (1): e5. doi:10.2196/mental.4004.

Torous, John, Rohn Friedman, and Matcheri Keshavan. 2014b. "Smartphone ownership and interest in mobile applications to monitor symptoms of mental health conditions." *JMIR mHealth uHealth* 2 (1): e2. doi:10.2196/mhealth.2994.

Torous, J., P. Staples, and J. P. Onnela. 2015. "Realizing the potential of mobile mental health: New methods for new data in psychiatry." *Current Psychiatry Reports* 17 (8): 602. doi:10.1007/s11920-015-0602-0.

Welbourne, Jennifer L., Anita L. Blanchard, and Marla B. Wadsworth. 2013. "Motivations in virtual health communities and their relationship to community, connectedness and stress." *Computers in Human Behavior* 29: 129–139. doi:10.1016/j.chb.2012.07.024.

Wenger, E. 1998. "Communities of practice: Learning as a social system." *The Systems Thinker* 9 (5): 2–3.

WHO and the Calouste Gulbenkian Foundation. 2014. *Social determinants of mental health*. Geneva: WHO.

World Health Organization. 2014. "Prevalence of mental disorders." *World Health Organization*. http://www.euro.who.int/en/health-topics/noncom municable-diseases/mental-health/data-and-statistics.

16

M-Health and Smartphone Technologies and Their Impact on Patient Care and Empowerment

Melvyn W.B. Zhang and Roger C.M. Ho

16.1 Introduction

Technology has advanced rapidly over the past decade and it has transformed the lifestyle of most individuals. Healthcare organizations have experienced significant changes after the introduction and integration of technology in various health-care processes. The World Health Organization in its recent statement has clearly highlighted the potential of eHealth and how it has transformed health-care organizations in their daily work. eHealth is defined as the process in which health-care resources and health care are being communicated and transferred by

M.W.B. Zhang (✉)
National Healthcare Group, National Addiction Management Service,
Institute of Mental Health, Buangkok View, Singapore
e-mail: melvynzhangweibin@gmail.com

R.C.M. Ho
Department of Psychological Medicine, National University of Singapore, Lower
Kent Ridge Rd, Singapore
e-mail: roger_ho@nuhs.edu.sg

© The Author(s) 2017   **277**
L. Menvielle et al. (eds.), *The Digitization of Healthcare*,
DOI 10.1057/978-1-349-95173-4_16

the electronic and digital medium. Looking back at the past decade, there have been major advances in both Web-based as well as Internet-based technologies, along with the introduction of smartphones as well as bio-sensor devices. This has led to the development of sophisticated electronic medical records (EMR) systems, as well as various other platforms to triage and help in the management of patient's condition. In addition, such advances have also created a revolution in the way clinicians acquire evidence-based knowledge and information, as they no longer need to turn to traditional modalities of communication, but they could instantly look up pertinent information using just the Internet. Smartphones and their accompanying applications are perhaps the latest advancements in technology.

16.2 Smartphone Technology for Health-Care Professionals

mHealth refers to mobile health and it refers largely to the usage of mobile devices in the practice of medicine (World Health Organization). Over the past few years, numerous studies have been published demonstrating the increased adoption of smartphone and smartphone-related applications by health-care professionals (Garritty and Eman 2006). Smartphones represent a new modality of technology that offers more than the conventional modalities of mobile technology. Smartphones are equipped with immense computing capabilities that allow individuals to access the Internet at their convenience. A smartphone application is a computer program that is specially designed to run on smartphones and tablet computers, usually serving a specific purpose. In fact, the health-care system itself is inherently mobile in nature, encompassing consultations and treatment at a wide variety of locations, including clinics, inpatient wards, outpatient specialist services, emergency departments, operating theatres, intensive care units, and even laboratories. To complete their day-to-day tasks, health-care professionals must be mobile while simultaneously communicating effectively and collaborating with colleagues across disciplines (Abu 2012). Hence, it is not surprising that the smartphone adoption rates have increased among health-care professionals, who realize the invaluable additions these tools can provide to their daily practices.

Previous systematic reviews have examined 23 surveys on the use of personal digital assistants (PDAs) by health-care professionals across several countries. The key findings include that younger clinicians are more likely to use this technology and family doctors and general practitioners most commonly utilized that PDAs. In particular, large practice- and hospital-based clinicians are more likely to use mobile technology (Abu et al. 2012). Thus, conventional technological modalities are currently being replaced by smartphones, which combine the basic functions of a pager, a cell phone, and a PDA with even more sophisticated capabilities. This major revolution in the medical industry may have begun in 2007 with the release of Apple's iPhone. Since then, the smartphone market has advanced rapidly (Karl 2012). Another pivotal change was the launch of the Apple Application Store in July 2008 (Karl 2012), which enabled users to download smartphone-based applications to add additional capabilities to their smartphones. A recent survey performed by Manhattan Research in 2009 (Abu et al. 2012) showed that approximately 64% of the clinicians in the USA have used smartphones, compared with 30% in 2001. Other research statistics reflect the tremendous increase in the number of smartphone applications being downloaded, from 300 million in 2009 to over 5 billion in 2010 (Mobile Future 2010). Based on the latest statistics released, it showed that as compared to 2013, almost twice the percentage of consumers have at least a health- or fitness-related application in their smartphone (PWC 2015).

With these technological advances, clinicians are no longer confined to using individual workstations or computers on wheels (Abu et al. 2012) when accessing hospital information systems, electronic health and medical records, laboratory results, and/or the latest evidence-based information to help them with clinical management. With the increased adoption of smartphones, clinicians have easier and better access to patient information, which should improve clinical care (Abu et al. 2012). Additionally, new software applications are increasingly tailored to the needs of clinicians, particularly resources for evidence-based information. In addition to clinicians, patients can benefit from this technology to monitor their own conditions. Previous studies have demonstrated the efficacy of smartphone use in disease prevention and self-monitoring as well as in the management of chronic diseases (Marshall 2008). Previous studies (Abu et al. 2012) have examined differences in the utilization of health-care applications among health-care professionals. Despite the variety of applications used, those for the diagnosis of diseases and medical calculations are the most commonly used by practicing health professionals and in studies in medicine and nursing. In this chapter, we provide an overview of mHealth and smartphone technology and how it has affected how health-care professionals practice. We provide an overview of medical applications that have been developed for patient care and explained how they have empowered patients in terms of self-management of their own conditions. We also provide an overview of psychiatric applications that have been developed and explain how they have managed to empower patients in terms of their own care. We then discuss how we could tap onto mHealth and smartphone technology, and how it could be effectively used to empower patients and transform patient care using selected examples based on our recent work. We conclude the chapter with a discussion of the limitations of mHealth.

16.3 Overview of Medical Applications and Their Impact on Patient Care and Empowerment

mHealth- and smartphone-based technologies have been successfully been deployed for usage in medical care in several aspects, such as in terms of chronic disease management, as well as patient's monitoring. There are smartphone-based applications that are potentially useful for patients who are undergoing rehabilitation as well. Some of the existing smartphone-based applications could also aid in medical diagnosis and have also been approved by the US Food and Drug Administration. In addition, smartphones and their applications have also been effective in reaching out to those who are in need of medical care in developing countries. We proceed to explore more with regard to these existing applications and explain how they have managed to successfully empower patients in their own medical care.

With regard to the utilization of medical applications for the management of chronic diseases, Ozdalga (2012) has identified an application, named as Diabeo for chronic disease self-management (Charpentier 2011). This particular application collates not only information regarding self-measured blood sugars levels but also carbohydrate counts as well as the levels of physical activity. Hence, in essence, the application facilitates and empowers individuals to take control and be aware of their chronic disease health status. Researchers have studied the application over a 6-month period in France, and a cumulative total of 180 patients have since completed the evaluation of the application. It is of significance that individuals who used such an application tended to have a lower HBA1c as compared to those individuals who have no access to the application. In addition, smartphone applications have been used as patient monitoring tools, to empower caregivers with information about their loved ones. iWander is an android-based application that has been designed to help monitor the movement of geriatric patients with Alzheimer's dementia using the Global Positioning sensors within the smartphone.

One of the core advantages of the utilization of technology is the provision of accessible care, in spite of the physical locality of the patient. Technology serves to mitigate the geographical barriers and distance. Worringham (2007) has previously described how they have utilized just a Bluetooth device with a single-lead electrocardiography (EEG) and how this has enabled patients, who have just recently suffered from a coronary artery event or having just recently underwent an angioplasty, to continue with their rehabilitation program in the comfort of their home settings. This particular form of innovation empowers patient to continue to participate in their rehabilitation program, for sustained clinical outcomes after their recent discharge from a major operation. mHealth and smartphone have also been used to improve patient's care and to reduce health-care costs incurred for certain investigations. Bsoul (2011) demonstrated the utility of the smartphone in assisting clinicians with medical diagnosis. The diagnosis of sleep apnea is now made possible remotely simply be using a smartphone coupled to a single-lead EEG. Other researchers

(Oresko 2010; Huang 2012) have highlighted how the smartphone could be used as an ECG recording device or even a Doppler device to measure blood flow.

mHealth has made health-care provision accessible for individuals in developing countries as well. mHealth and its accompanying smartphone applications have helped health-care workers in rural areas of Thailand in their treatment of malaria (Meankaew 2010). Health-care workers in Kenya have also benefitted from mHealth as it has allowed them to collate data and other information which they have obtained during home visitations.

In 2013, the World Health Organization has identified several conditions that are deemed to be prevalent globally. These conditions include iron deficiency anemia, hearing loss, migraine, poor vision, asthma, diabetes mellitus, osteoarthritis, as well as depressive disorder. The World Health Organization has identified that to date; there are several commercial applications that have been developed to cater for these highly prevalent conditions (Perez 2013).

16.4   Overview of Psychiatry Applications and Their Impact on Patient Care and Empowerment

As we are domain-experts in the field of psychiatry, it will be helpful for us to determine whether mHealth is capable of outreaching to this target population, in terms of meeting their clinical needs as well as patient empowerment. As there are no objective clinical signs in psychiatry, reaching out to this population would also be more challenging. We provide an overview of some of the applications that have been commercially developed in psychiatry and how they have helped in terms of patient care and empowerment. We then highlight some of the limitations and explain how we have managed to overcome these limitations, with the objective of producing more evidence-based applications for patient care and empowerment in psychiatry.

The conventional text-messaging service has been evaluated to be useful for patients with schizophrenia (Granholm 2011). In a previous pilot study, participants received text messages daily. If they responded, they will be given advice regarding the management of their symptoms via their mobile devices. Eighty-six percent of the participants responded and among those who have responded, they reported a reduction in the sense of self-distress. In addition, they also reported that they find themselves more compliant with their prescribed medications. Aside to text messaging, there has been further evaluation of smartphone-based applications to empower individuals in dealing with their psychotic symptoms. Palmer-Claus (2012) examined the effectiveness of self-reporting psychotic symptoms using a smartphone-based software application and found that five items scored by participants on their smartphone correlated well with validated toolkits. Thus, this implies that patients when empowered can self-monitor their own symptoms. In addition, the implementation of such a technology has also enabled patients to identify specific relapse triggers as well. The identification of psychosocial triggers is pertinent as they are factors that might trigger a relapse and might also result in poor compliance and response to the standard medications prescribed. Further studies have looked into the feasibility and the effectiveness of integrating a smartphone-based self-reported questionnaire into the daily lives of individuals living with schizophrenia. Clearly, patients feel empowered and it has a benefit for clinicians as well, as clinicians are able to better their understanding of the daily symptoms experienced by their patients.

Aside to psychosis, there have been studies demonstrating the efficacy and potential of smartphone technology for individuals who are suffering from bipolar disorder. Smartphones and wearable devices could be used for recognizing the depressive and manic states of patients and thus empowering individuals to identify their changes in state. The pilot study has demonstrated that the recognition accuracy is as high as 76% (Grunerbl 2014). Faurholt (2014) piloted daily electronic monitoring smartphone software called MONARCA on 17 patients for duration of 3 months. In that 3-month period, patients were required to complete both the Hamilton Depressive Rating Scale as well as the Young Mania Rating Scale once every 2 weeks. The results gathered show that patients felt empowered and were receptive toward such an intervention. In addition, their self-monitored depressive scores correlated with the objective measures such as their levels of physical and social activity, thus indicative of the severity and improvements in their core depressive symptoms. Similarly for depressive disorders and anxiety-related disorders, trials have demonstrated their efficacy in screening individuals with symptoms, as well as helping in the reduction of underlying anxiety symptoms through an increase in coping skills via techniques taught in the smartphone applications.

16.5 How to Harness the Potential of mHealth in Empowering Patients

One of the concerns about the current developments in mHealth and smartphone applications are issues relating to confidentiality and privacy issues, as well as limitations with regard to the existing evidence base of these applications on the application store. Zhang et al. (2015) have previously proposed several strategies to mitigate these concerns, which include that of: (a) Encouraging more peer review of health care-related applications, (b) utilization of a systematic self-certification model to rate existing applications to determine their information quality and evidence base, and (c) enabling and empowering psychiatrist and health-care professionals to be content developers of smartphone applications. Zhang et al. (2014a, 2014b) have highlighted how this could be done using cost-effective methodologies such as online application builders as well as cloud-based blogging sites to create responsive Web-based applications.

We wish to elaborate more about how we have made use of these techniques in the creation of theory-driven applications and how they have empowered our patients. We discuss this in the form of case studies and describe the respective innovations that we have created.

Case Study 1: Increasing mental health awareness among the general population/Empowering public with mental health knowledge—The Royal College of Psychiatrists (UK) Mental Health Application

Zhang and Ho (2015) have previously described how psychiatrists could be involved in the creation of evidence-based smartphone applications at the individual level, making use of the methodologies described previously by Zhang et al. (2014a, 2014b). The Royal College of Psychiatrists Mental Health application is one such example. The application contains and provides an online handheld version of the key facts information for patients. In addition, the application also has integrated video podcasts and animations to help the general public in understanding common mental health-related disorders such as depression and anxiety disorders. The application also features audio podcast of the experiences of individuals who have had experience of the various disorders. The smartphone application is an initiative of the Royal College of Psychiatrists' Patient Education and Engagement Board and its main aim is to empower the general public with readily accessible mental health information, readily on the go. Of course, the secondary aim is to help to dispel the stigma with regard to mental health disorders among the general population. It has been reported that the application was launched during the 2014 college congress and that there were approximately 346 unique downloads of the application.

Case Study 2: Empowering Individuals at risk of addictive disorders with information to seek help

Zhang et al. (2016) in their recent article have highlighted the challenges in psychiatry, in particular in addiction psychiatry. Based on the Singapore Mental Health Study, the duration of untreated addiction disorders, such as that of alcohol abuse is as much as 13 years. With the changing trends overseas, it is expected that there are more at-risk individuals who might not be seeking help early. Zhang et al. (2016) mentioned that these factors include that of the normalization of general public's perspective toward common drugs of abuse, especially so after the legalization of Cannabis overseas as well as the usage of drugs like ketamine as a rapid antidepressant. Stigma and the failure of the primary physician to pick up substance-related abuse might be a causative factor accounting for the long duration of untreated illness.

mHealth and smartphone technologies thus could help to play an integral role in the empowerment of individuals about how best to seek help once they recognize that they have a particular disorder. Zhang (2016) has addressed the limitations of the methodologies proposed previously with regard to the usage of Web-based application builders and have advocated for the usage of cross-platform techniques in the programming of new applications. Zhang et al. (2016) have advocated and highlighted that there remains a need for evidence-based psycho-educational drug applications that could empower the public with core knowledge about drugs. Of importance, Zhang et al. (2016) has recommended that the conceptualized application should mimic how prior mass media interventions have helped in terms of the dissemination of health-related information. Hence, in their conceptualized application, "Say No to Drugs" smartphone application, they have included relevant videos, aside from information to better empower patients and the general public in the acquisition of core knowledge about the harmful effects of common drugs.

As reviewed previously, most of the current smartphone applications seemed to be more focused on being an adjunctive tool for patients who are in the recovery process. Aside to the provision of psycho-education materials, one of the key interventions in addiction psychiatry pertains to the concept of harm minimization. Given the inherent effectiveness of harm minimization for a variety of addictive disorders, such a theory could be used to conceptualize and develop applications that could help at-risk individuals. Zhang et al. (2016) have described how they made use of this theory in the field of alcohol addiction as well as gambling addiction, using new cross-platform application development strategies. Their conceptualization of the alcohol tracker application serves to address the limitations raised in previous content analysis of alcohol related applications. Of note, the most recent content analysis of alcohol-related applications have highlighted that they lack evidence base and their methodology of tracking alcohol consumption could be counter-intuitive, in that it encourages individuals to challenge their limits. Their conceptualized alcohol tracker application encourages individuals to log down the absolute number of drinks they have had and this will be tracked across the span of one week. According to the National Institute of Clinical Excellence (NICE) UK guidelines, in the event that they exceed their recommended units per week, they will be prompted with a notification immediately. Aside to the provision of tracking tools to empower individuals to track their own condition, their conceptualized application also has information about alcohol abuse and dependence and its related medical complications. More importantly, they have empowered individuals through the integration of a national helpline for them to seek help for their problem. In a sample cohort of 100 Canadians, the authors have further demonstrated that both the notification as well as the information within the application has been deemed to be useful. Clearly, the theory underlying their conceptualization is that of harm minimization, through the usage of live notifications as well as provision of resources for individuals to seek help.

Zhang et al. (2016) have also described how they have successfully applied the concept of harm minimization for problem gambling in Singapore. They have managed to do so by harnessing the potential of the global positioning sensors within the smartphone device. Based on the author's conceptualization, on the surface, the application just seemed to be providing psycho-educational information to individuals, ranging from the signs and symptoms of gambling to that of how best to seek help. However, in reality, the global positioning sensor is being harnessed upon to continuously track the locality of the patient. Hence, once the at-risk gambler is within the proximity of a gambling locality, they will be prompted with a notification. The notification feature will enable the at-risk gambler to seek help by contacting his loved ones via a telephone call or via email. Hence, not only are the individuals being empowered to deal with their underlying condition, their network of loved ones are also being empowered to assist them in making a change in their lives.

Case Study 3: Empowering individuals with psychiatric disorders to better understand their treatment regiment

Healthcare professionals routinely refer to clinical practice guidelines to guide them in their management of various medical and psychiatric conditions. However, one of the major limitations with these guidelines is that they are not kept updated and relevant with the emerging changes in the research literature and evidence base. In addition, the traditional guidelines routinely serve only to empower the clinicians with making evidence-based changes in terms of their management of the patients. With the rapid advancement in technology, patients to date are more cognizant of the latest updates in medical information and would want to be better informed about their treatment plans. Zhang et al. (2016) described an innovation that serves to mitigate the above issues. The authors describe how they have implemented an innovative server feature that facilitate the rapid updating of guidelines so that clinicians could make use of latest evidence based guidelines in the treatment of various psychiatric disorders. Patients, on the other hand, are empowered to know more about their treatment plans, as they could have access to simplified version of these clinical guidelines as well. Hence, they are empowered to know what stage of the treatment plan they are currently in at the moment. In addition, patients could also use the application to take validated questionnaires, such as the GAD-7 and the PHQ-9 and their scores would be tracked chronologically across time. Hence, this would enable patients to track the severity of their depressive symptoms across time as well.

16.6 Conclusion

Despite the inherent benefits of mHealth for patient empowerment as previously described, it is also essential for health-care professional to recognize the inherent limitations of mHealth technology. It is easier to harness and tap onto mHealth technologies in developed countries, but even in developed countries, it is important to bear in mind that there might be disadvantaged individuals who might not be able to have access to a smartphone and hence, would not have access to the smartphone applications. Such an innovation would be difficult to implement in a low to middle income country and hence limits the effectiveness of mHealth-based interventions. In addition, clinicians and health-care professionals need to recognize the constant need to keep their smartphone applications updated with the latest evidence. Also, alongside the limitations highlighted previously, clinicians and health-care workers need to be critical and more cognizant that most of the current health-care applications are not developed in conjunction with a medical specialist and hence, their evidence base might be lacking. Keeping this in mind, clinicians need to be careful when they are recommending health-care applications to their patients.

Given these limitations, not only should health-care professionals be more actively involved in the conceptualization of health care-related mHealth interventions, but at the managerial level, there ought to be more supervision as well as project management.

References

Abu, S.M.M, Y. Illhoi, and S. Lincoln. A systematic review of healthcare applications for smartphones. *BMC Med Inform Decis Mak* 2012, 12: 67.

Bsoul, M, H. Minn, and L. Tamil. Apnea Medassist: Nonnecke. Real-time sleep apnea monitor using single-lead EEG. *IEEE Trans Inf Technol Biomed* 2011 May, 15(3): 416–427.

Charpentier, G, P.Y. Benhamou, D. Dardari, A. Clergeot, S. Franc, P. Schaepelnck-Belicar, B. Catargi, V. Melki, L. Chailous, A. Farret, J.L. Bosson, and A. Perfomis. The Diabeo software enabling individualized Insulin dose adjustments combined with telemedicine support improves HbA1c in poorly controlled type 1 diabetic patients: A 6 month, randomized, open-label, parallel-group, multicenter trial (TeleDiab 1 Study). *Diabetes Care* 2011, 34: 533–539

Faurholt-Jepsen, M., M. Frost, M. Vinberg, E.M. Christensen, J.E. Bardram, and L.V. Kessing. Smartphone data as objective measures of bipolar disorder symptoms. *Psychiatry Res* 2014 June 30, 217(1–2): 124–127.

Garritty, C, and K. El Emam. Who's using PDAs? Estimates of PDA use by health care providers: A systematic review of surveys. *J Med Internet Res May* 12, 2006, 8(2): e7.

Granholm, E., D. Ben-Zeev, P.C. Link, K.R. Bradshw, and J.L. Holden. Mobile assessment and treatment for Schizophrenia: A pilot trial of an interactive text-messaging intervention for medication adherence, socialization and auditory hallucinations. *Schizophr Bull* 2011, 38(3): 414–425

Grunerbl, A., et al. Smart-phone based recognition of states and state changes in bipolar disorder patients. *IEEE J Biomed Health Inform* July 25, 2014 [Epub ahead of print].

Huang, C.C., P.Y. Lee, P.Y. Chen, and T.Y. Liu. Design and implementation of a smartphone-based portable ultrasound pulsed-wave Doppler device for blood flow measurement. *IEEE Trans Ultrason Ferroelectr Freq Control* January 2012, 59(1): 182–189.

Karl, F.B.P., W. Heather, and W. Kim. Smartphone and medical related App use among medical students and junior doctors in the United Kingdom (UK): A regional Survey. *BMC Med Inform Decis Mak* 2012, 12: 121

Marhsall, A., O. Medvedev, and A. Antonov. Use of smartphone for improved self-management of pulmonary rehabilitation. *Int J Telemed Appl.* 2008, 753064, doi: 10.1155/2008/753064.

Martínez-Pérez B., I. de la Torre-Díez, and M. López-Coronado. Mobile health applications for the most prevalent conditions by the World Health Organization: review and analysis. *J Med Internet Res* June 14, 2013, 15(6): e120. doi: 10.2196/jmir.2600.

Meankaew, P., J. Kaewkungwal, A. Kharmsiriwathara, P. Khunthong, P. Singhasivanon, and W. Satimai. Application of mobile-technology for disease and treatment monitoring of malaria in the "Better Border Healthcare Programme." *Malar J* 2010, 9: 237.

Mobile Future. 2010. Social media, apps, and Data growth headline 2010 mobile trends. Assessed April 23, 2016. http://www.mobilefuture.org/content/pages/mobile_year_in_review_2010?/yearendvideo

Oresko, J.J., H. Duschl, and A.C. Cheng. A wearable smartphone-based platform for real-time cardiovascular disease detection via electrocardiogram processing. *IEEE Trans Inf Technol Biomed* May 2010, 14(3): 734–740.

Ozdalga, E., A. Ozdalga, and N. Ahuja. The smartphone in medicine: A review of current and potential use among physicians and students. *J Med Internet Res* 2012, 14(5): e128

Palmier-Claus, et al. The feasibility and validity of ambulatory self-report of psychotic symptoms using a smartphone software application. *BMC Psychiatry* 2012, 12: 172.

PWC. Issue 3: Care in the palm of your hand. Assessed June 28, 2016. http://www.pwc.com/us/en/health-industries/top-health-industry-issues/care-in-palm-of-hand.html

Worringham, C., A. Rojeck, and I. Stewart. Development and feasibility of a smartphone, ECG and GPS system for remotely monitoring exercise in cardiac rehabilitation. *PLoS One* 2011, 6(2): e14669.

Zhang, M.W., and R.C. Ho. Enabling Psychiatrists to Explore the Full Potential of E-Health. *Front Psychiatry* December 15, 2015, 6: 177. doi: 10.3389/fpsyt.2015.00177. eCollection 2015. Review. No abstract available.

Zhang, M.W., and R.C. Ho. Tapping onto the potential of smartphone applications for psycho-education and early intervention in addictions. *Front Psychiatry* March 17, 2016, 7: 40. doi: 10.3389/fpsyt.2016.00040. eCollection 2016. Review.

Zhang, M.W., R.C. Ho, and R. Mcintyre. The 'WikiGuidelines' smartphone application: Bridging the gaps in availability of evidence-based smartphone mental health applications. *Technol Health Care* January 26, 2016. Epub ahead of print.

Zhang, M, E. Cheow, Csh Ho, B.Y. Ng, R. Ho, and C.C. Cheok. Application of low-cost methodologies for mobile phone app development. *JMIR Mhealth Uhealth* 2014a, 2(4): e55. 10.2196/mhealth.3549.

Zhang, M.W., T. Tsang, E. Cheow, CSh Ho, N.B. Yeong, and R.C. Ho. Enabling psychiatrists to be mobile phone app developers: Insights into app development methodologies. *JMIR Mhealth Uhealth* 2014b, 2(4): e53. doi: 10.2196/mhealth.3425.

17

Promoting Physical Exercise Through Embodied Trainers: A Systematic Literature Review

Sergio Gago-Masague, Thomas M. Chen
and Guann-Pyng Li

17.1 Introduction

The increasing proliferation of affordable computational technologies and its subsequent prevalence within households have incited the development and use of digital health and wellness applications, such as Web and mobile health (mHealth). Technology such as game consoles, computers, mobiles, and wearable devices are becoming popular devices at home and an inexpensive solution to host appli-

S. Gago-Masague (✉) · G.-P. Li
California Institute for Telecommunications and Information Technology,
University of California, Irvine, CA, USA
e-mail: sgagomas@calit2.uci.edu; gpli@calit2.uci.edu

T.M. Chen
Computer Engineering, Purdue University, West Lafayette, IN, USA
e-mail: thomas99k@gmail.com

L. Menvielle et al. (eds.), *The Digitization of Healthcare*,
DOI 10.1057/978-1-349-95173-4_17

cations that promote health. Meanwhile, the world population is growing older, bringing a greater demand for strategies to promote healthy lifestyles. Wellness programs, remote health and self-care in the home setting are becoming increasingly important in long-term care to support rehabilitation and the elderly population. Physical training for rehabilitation is of particular importance for covering motor skills and preventing secondary conditions, such as frailty, cognitive disorders, and depression (Brown et al. 2000; Baum et al. 2003; Dawe and Moore-Orr 1995).

17.2 When Medicine Is Getting Assisted by Virtual Agents

17.2.1 Exercise Adherence

Persuasive health applications may empower users' motivation and determination to make changes in their habits to achieve a better quality of life. The lack of motivation and guidance are considered main barriers for people to overcome when trying to exercise regularly. The negative correlation between long-term sustained exercise and motivation is even more remarkable for individuals with mobility impairments who may have a particular need to exercise for rehabilitation (Kinne et al. 1999). Motivation appears to be especially relevant when training at home. Training at home can be more tedious and can trigger greater loneliness. Trainees require not only assistance but also a positive atmosphere to encourage and motivate them (Maclean et al. 2000).

Not having a personal trainer when performing physical training at home may lead to a lack of interest or even to injuries. Despite these obstacles, training at home provides several significant benefits such as saving time and travel costs while also being unhindered by weather, transport schedules, and other variables (Wijnand IJsselsteijn et al. 2006b).

17.2.2 Embodied Trainers

The term "embodied conversational agent" or just "embodied agent" refers to a form of graphical user interface, which includes humanoid features such as body and face representation. Embodied agents can also deliver verbal and nonverbal communication to improve user-application interaction (Cassell 2000). Embodied agents are also commonly referred to as "virtual humans," "virtual agents," or just "agents" through the literature. Embodied agents designed to assist in physical training are also referred to as "Embodied Trainers" (ETs), "virtual coaches," or a combination of both terms. For consistency, the present study will use the term ETs to refer to embodied agents for physical training.

One might think that using an ET may provide trainees with additional advantages when compared with other training interfaces such as improved communication and guidance similar to the one a personal trainer would provide. An ET aims to be an effective tool for self-training by using the advantages of both training modalities: a personal trainer and a computational system for training. Conversation is characteristic of interaction between humans. A human trainer can provide features of face-to-face interaction, including verbal and nonverbal communication as a natural component of human dialogue. Hence, real trainers can provide high sense of presence, that is, trainers' presence is perceived by trainees, and use locomotion, gaze, and gestures to focus the trainees' attention. All these aspects can increase learning environments' ability to engage and motivate individuals. Previous studies in cognitive training have demonstrated that sense of presence and body gestures can also be transmitted by an embodied agent (Lester et al. 1997).

ETs might offer additional advantages. For instance, human trainers by themselves are limited. Firstly, a human cannot hold the same level of attention and concentration over an extended period. Secondly, a personal trainer is not able to observe all relevant physiological and concurrently biomechanical variables characterizing a movement, neither at the same time nor the same level of precision. Additionally, ETs are not affected by emotional or physiological variables, such as "having a bad day" or being tired. An ET can always show happiness and be ready to assist users.

There are also no limitations on the schedule or amount of times an ET can help or repeat an explanation or exercise; ETs will not become frustrated for those reasons unless accordingly programmed to behave like that.

17.3 Research Questions and Goals

ETs may provide two important features when added to conventional or virtual physical training systems: (1) Providing an animated biped model as an interface to represent exercises to be mimicked by the trainee and (2) delivering verbal and nonverbal communication (e.g., intonation, mood, and facial expression) to improve communication, enjoyment and build a social bond that may drive the trainee's attitude towards a particular goal, for instance, training harder or for longer periods. Consequently, the purpose of the present study is to identify and review scientifically documented ETs that were proposed as a persuasive technology to promote physical training by providing trainees with (1) guidance and (2) motivation and/or enjoyment. The present work identifies and categorizes documented training systems involving ETs based on the training task. This study also recognizes specific features or strategies with positive effects on trainees' guidance or motivation. Moreover, technical limitations and future opportunities are presented for discussion.

17.4 Methods

A methodical and systematic literature review has been conducted to identify digital systems featuring an ET. Over the course of one academic year, the authors searched several online databases including Google Scholar, SpringerLink, Pubmed, IEEE Xplore, Wiley Online Library, and ScienceDirect. Regarding definitions, the topic of this study was focused specifically on embodied agents designed to promote physical exercise. Additionally, a focus on humanoid agents was also integrated. The search methodology is illustrated in (Fig. 17.1). The initial population of potential papers was selected by searching via key

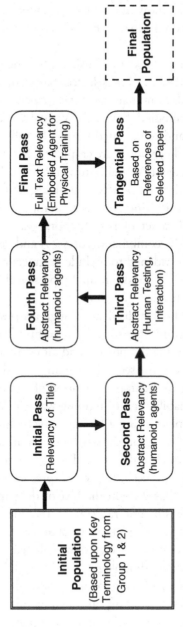

Fig. 17.1 Methodology for the present literature review of ETs

terminology. Key terminology for the various stages of the search was determined to be the following: Virtual Trainer, Embodied Trainer, Virtual Coach, Embodied Coach; Embodied Agent, Virtual Human, Virtual Agent, Agent.

The initial population was sourced using a holistic and comprehensive searching algorithm. Papers were selected based on their inclusion of keywords in a series of combinations. First, papers with titles including "Virtual Trainer," "Embodied Trainer," "Virtual Coach," or "Embodied Coach" were selected and represented Group 1. Following the formation of Group 1, two sets of keywords were employed. Set A represents primary key terms {Embodied Agent, Virtual Human, Virtual Agent, Agent} while Set B represents secondary terms {Exercise, Exercising, Training, Fitness, Physical}. Title searches utilizing every permutation of A+B created Group 2 of selected papers. If a set of permutations was too specific to yield results, Set A replaced the combination of Set A and Set B for Group 2 or search parameters were widened to include abstracts/metadata. Together, the combination of Group 1 and Group 2 represent the initial population of papers sourced for this literature review.

The population was further distilled through a series of relevant evaluations. Papers with irrelevant titles were removed first. This first pass utilized database tools to streamline the process and allow a greater population of papers to be surveyed. On the second screening, based on the abstract, all research not pertaining to the implementation of embodied agents for the purpose of physical rehabilitation or training was eliminated. On the third pass, all papers not implementing a human subject utilizing an embodied agent were discarded. On the fourth pass, based on the abstract, all research on embodied agents which did not hold at least one humanoid feature (e.g., inflection, emotion, speech, or facial expression) was dismissed. On the fifth and final pass, based upon the text of the paper, research results that were found to be still not relevant to training for motor/physical function through embodied agents were eliminated. Any papers which were found in multiple sources were counted based on their first occurrence through the search methodology.

Finally, the references of each paper in the final population were analyzed in an attempt to identify any extraneous yet relevant papers which the methodology missed. Those relevant papers found in resulting paper references were nevertheless included in the literature review to provide a more comprehensive and holistic analysis.

17.5 Results

17.5.1 Papers and Projects Selected

All literature reviewed and included were written in English and published between 1998 and 2013. In summary, 173 papers were found to satisfy the criteria based on the abstracts during the second pass of the review. Of these, 21 papers were shortlisted based on the full text's relevance to the topic. A review of the references within each of the shortlisted pieces of literature provided six additional papers relevant to the present study topic. Therefore, a total of 27 papers were selected resulting in 20 unique projects identified that involved ETs in promoting specific training tasks (Bickmore et al. 2009; Albaina et al. 2009; Watson et al. 2012; Ellis et al. 2013; Klaassen et al. 2013; Buttussi et al. 2006; Buttussi and Chittaro 2008; Davis and Bobick 1998; Ruttkay and Zwiers 2006; Ruttkay and Welbergen 2008; Reidsma et al. 2011; Eike Dehling et al. 2011; IJsselsteijn et al. 2004a; Ijsselsteijn et al. 2004b; Vermeulen 2005; IJsselsteijn et al. 2006a; Eyck et al. 2006; Laar et al. 2010; Senden 2012; Chua et al. 2003; De Morais and Wickström 2011; Pronost et al. 2008; Babu et al. 2005; Jung et al. 2011; Fasola and Mataric 2011; Dancu et al. 2012; Matthews et al. 2012).

The distribution of resulting papers by database and search stage is presented in Table 17.1.

17.5.2 Categories and Assessment

To compare how researchers approached different solutions to achieve the same goal, the 20 projects identified from the 27 papers selected in this study have been classified into five categories based on the following training goals: (1) Outdoor exercise, (2) indoor aerobics, (3) cycling, (4) martial arts, and a category of indoor

Table 17.1 Papers including Embodied trainers. Database distribution

Stage	Search strategy	Google Scholar	IEEE Xplore	SpringerLink	PubMed	ScienceDirect	Wiley Library	Total
Initial population	Key terminology	36,690	3,066	1,663	29,562	5,056	121	76,158
First pass	Title relevance	376	128	121	86	166	7	884
Second pass	Abstract Humanoid features	28	12	83	17	28	5	173
Third pass	Abstract Human interaction	21	9	8	13	24	5	80
Fourth pass	Abstract Physical activity	21	7	7	8	9	2	54
Final pass	Full text relevancy	14	5	2	0	0	0	21
	Tangential Pass (references): +6:							**27**

exercise for (5) physical rehabilitation. It is important to note that many of the papers selected did not report a formal evaluation of the implemented ET. Instead, the authors presented the technology and, in some cases, a non-conclusive preliminary test of feasibility. Based on the research questions, the following sections provide a full list of projects, references and an overview of the technology involved. However, the assessments of the results were considered only for those experiments that formally evaluated the effectiveness of ETs by comparing them with other training systems.

17.5.3 Outdoor Exercise

Table 17.2 shows an overview of six training systems which promote outdoor exercise. Five of them promoted walking, and one system was developed to assist in general outdoor exercise.

The training systems identified for outdoor fitness were designed to promote walking activities (Bickmore et al. 2009; Albaina et al. 2009; Watson et al. 2012; Ellis et al. 2013; Klaassen et al. 2013) and fitness activities (Buttussi and Chittaro 2008; Buttussi et al. 2006). Regarding technology, all systems included accelerometer-based sensors such as pedometers to track trainees' activities. All the animated ETs included in this category featured facial expression and text-based communication to set walking goals, encourage users, and provide them with feedback based on performance. Most applications automatically collected data from the tracking sensor systems. Applications that were implemented on smartphones, which are shown in Fig. 17.2, featured verbal communication by the ET and provided activity-based feedback in real time (Klaassen et al. 2013; Buttussi et al. 2006; Buttussi and Chittaro 2008). Additionally, Buttussi et al. (2006) and Buttussi and Chittaro (2008) featured GPS-based navigation to provide trainees with guidance on an outdoor fitness trail. Regarding assessment of this category of ETs, three formal evaluations were conducted and their results are discussed in Sect. 17.7 of this chapter (Watson et al. 2012; Klaassen et al. 2013; Buttussi et al. 2006).

Table 17.2 Embodied training systems for outdoor exercise

Ref.	Target population	Main devices	Tracking system	ET type	Coaching strategy	ET's interaction
Bickmore et al. (2009)	General	PDA	Integrated accelerometer	2D humanoid female	Set goals, provide progress update afterward	Facial expression, text
Albaina et al. (2009)	Elderly	Touchscreen photo-frame	Pedometer	2D animated flower with facial expression		Facial expression, text, charts
Watson et al. (2012)	People with overweight	Computer, display		2D humanoid female		
Ellis et al. (2013)	People with Parkinson disease					
Klaassen et al. (2013)	General	Smartphone	3d accelerometer-		Set goals, provide real-time progress update	Verbal, non-verbal, text
Buttussi and Chittaro (2008) and Buttussi et al. (2006)	General		integrated GPS	3D humanoid female	Introduce exercises, show trial location, provide feedback	Verbal, nonverbal

Fig. 17.2 Text-based and ET interfaces to promote walking (left) (Klaassen et al. 2013) and the MOPET system for outdoor fitness (right) (Buttussi et al. 2006; Buttussi and Chittaro 2008)

17.5.4 Indoor Aerobics

Previous ETs promoting indoor aerobics featured body-tracking systems and verbal and nonverbal communication. The nonverbal communication consisted of reproducing the training tasks and encouraging users to follow the tempo, providing feedback based on the correctness of movements.

Table 17.3 presents a summary of the selected ETs in this category.

Davis and Bobick developed a training platform at the MIT Media Lab in 1998 that has been considered the first platform including an ET (Davis and Bobick 1998). They used a TV as a display to provide aerobic sessions that could be personalized by the user based on the type of exercise, duration, music, and character for the ET. The ET was a recording of a human trainer. The system consisted of video clips, MIDI music, pre-recorded speeches, and a novel computer vision algorithm, which was built with video cameras, projectors, and infrared light emitters to locate trainees' silhouette. More recent work was implemented in the Human Media Interaction Lab at the University of Twente to develop a very compressive ET supporting indoor aerobics. In 2006 and 2008, Ruttkay et al. presented a talking ET able to analyze trainees' movements, adjust the exercises in real time and generate feedback

Table 17.3 Embodied Training systems for indoor aerobics

Ref	Target population	Main devices	Tracking system	ET type	Coaching strategy	ET's interaction
Davis and Bobick (1998)	General	Computer, display, audio synthesizer	IR computer vision system	Prerecorded videos of human trainers	Introducing exercises and reporting user's performance	Verbal, nonverbal
Ruttkay and Zwiers (2006) and Ruttkay and Herwin (2008)		Computer, display	Camera and color clothes	3D humanoid female	Introducing and representing exercises, leading tempo, reporting gestures and tempo deviations in real time	Verbal, nonverbal
Reidsma et al. (2011) and Dehling et al. (2011)			Nintendo Wii remote, pulse meter			

Fig. 17.3 Sample animations of ETs for indoor fitness presented in (Ruttkay and Herwin 2008) (left) and (Reidsma et al. 2011) (right)

(Ruttkay and Zwiers 2006; Ruttkay and Herwin 2008). More work on this training system was presented in 2011 by the same group, where the motion tracking system was improved by using a *Wii remote*^{TM} and a pulse meter (Reidsma et al. 2011; Dehling et al. 2011). These three-dimensional animated ETs, shown in (Fig. 17.3.), were able to co-perform exercises at the same time that trainees did as a mechanism for providing improved guidance. However, a comparison to measure the effectiveness of the ET with other training systems was not performed in this training category.

17.5.5 Cycling Platforms

Several ETs have been found in the cycling category. However, they can be classified in three unique projects. Regarding the technology used, all of them included verbal and nonverbal communication. They also included pulse meters and speed sensors to assess training performance and effort.

Table 17.4 shows an overview of the features of the three projects selected in this category.

The Human-Technology Interaction Group at the Eindhoven University of Technology developed several versions of a training system between 2006 and 2008 consisting of a stationary bike placed in front of a projection displaying a virtual racetrack and an ET (IJsselsteijn et al. 2004a; Ijsselsteijn et al. 2004b; IJsselsteijn et al. 2006a; Eyck et al. 2006; Vermeulen 2005) as shown in (Fig. 17.4) (left). Speed and handlebar

Table 17.4 Embodied training systems for cycling

Ref	Training Activity	Main devices	Tracking system	ET type	Coaching strategy	ET's interaction
IJsselsteijn et al. (2004a), IJsselsteijn et al. (2004b), IJsselsteijn et al. (2006a), Eyck et al. (2006) and Vermeulen (2005)	Indoor cycling	Static bike, computer, projected screen	Speed, handlebar angle, pulse meter	2D humanoid female	Adjusting effort based on trainees' heart rate	Verbal, non-verbal, text
Laar et al. (2010)	Indoor cycling	Static bike, computer, display	Speed, handlebar angle, pulse meter, spirometer, EGG			
Senden (2012)	Outdoor cycling	Smartphone	Pulsemeter, speed sensor	Customizable cartoon	Adjusting effort based on speed, heart rate, calories, distance run, time	

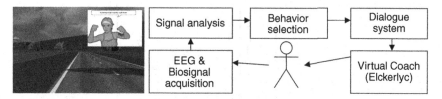

Fig. 17.4 (Left) High immersion condition presented in (IJsselsteijn et al. 2006a), and (right) modules of the ET implemented by (Laar et al. 2010)

angle were tracked to generate the navigation control in the virtual racetrack. The Human Media Interaction Lab at the University of Twente introduced a more sophisticated cycling platform in 2010 that included sensors to monitor trainees' respiration and brain activity (Laar et al. 2010). They also used the Elckerlyc platform (Van et al. 2010), which is a framework that generates verbal and nonverbal communication for embodied avatars based on a set of inputs such as trainees' performance and bio-signals as shown in (Fig. 17.4) (right). Senden developed an Android mobile application for outdoor cycling including the Elckerlyc system as well (Senden 2012). Comparison of the effectiveness of adding an ET was condcuted by Ijsselsteijn et al. (Ijsselsteijn et al. 2004b; IJsselsteijn et al. 2006a) with positive effects using the ET, as presented in Sect. 17.7.

17.5.6 Martial Arts Training

Three systems to support martial arts training have been identified in the present review. The training goals were Tai Chi and Kung Fu. All training systems used sensors to track trainees' body positions. The ETs implemented represented a 3D humanoid male in all three studies. Table 17.5 shows a summary of the most relevant features in this category.

The training task for users in the Tai Chi group was to mimic the ET's movements. Both systems used cameras to track users. The system implemented by P. Chua et al. in 2003 tracked the user's body using reflective clothes to create a trainee's representation in a virtual

Table 17.5 Embodied training systems for martial arts

Ref	Training activity	Main devices	Tracking system	ET type	Coaching strategy	ET's interaction
Chua et al. (2003)	Tai Chi	Wireless head-mounted display	Cameras, IR, reflective clothes	3D humanoid male	Visual representation of trainee's body to compare with the ET	Verbal and nonverbal
De Morais and Nicholas (2011)		Computer, display	Wristband sensors, camera		Users had to reach de maximum score	Score displayed
Pronost et al. (2008)	Kung Fu	Computer, projector	Optical system tracking trainee's glasses		A supervisor asked the ET to virtual attack trainees	None reported

environment (Chua et al. 2003). Users saw the virtual environment through a wireless head-mounted display. The environment also included a talking ET co-performing the exercises with the user. In contrast, the Tai Chi Trainer developed by Morais et al. in 2011 was displayed on a desktop computer and used wristbands with inertial sensors to track user's movement (De Morais and Nicholas 2011). Feedback based on the movements tracked was shown as a score. Lastly, the Kung Fu training system developed by Pronost et al. in 2008 consisted of a projection on a wall (Pronost et al. 2008). Trainees, who had to wear special glasses to see the screening as a 3D environment, could move along the wall during the training. The system tracked the user's glasses and responded to a supervisor's command, who was outside the scene and could ask the ET to kick virtually or punch the trainee's position. According to the authors, a real-time interaction was achieved by creating a database for the ET and simplifying the number of movements tracked and performed. No conclusive experiments comparing the ET system with a non-ET system have been reported in this category.

17.5.7 Rehabilitation at Home

A set of five previous studies has been identified in the rehabilitation category. Five targeted upper limb exercises and one of them focused on the physical therapy of the knee. Regarding technology, the ETs in this category included verbal communication, facial expression, and body movement to introduce and represent exercises (Table 17.6).

The first ET for rehabilitation presented was implemented by Babu et al. (2005). This system was designed to provide feedback in the physiotherapy field by tracking joint skeletal positions in the arm using a camera tracking a set of color markers. The ET was able to introduce the bicep curl exercise and evaluate the trainee's exercise for 30 s and, eventually, provided feedback, which consisted in the ET verbally reporting and reproducing what the user did incorrectly. Jung et al. used a bi-manual mobile manipulator in 2011 as a robot to assist in the training of the upper extremities (Jung et al. 2011). The robot included a display as a head where an ET was displayed.

Table 17.6 Embodied training systems for rehabilitation at home

Ref	Training task	Main devices	Tracking system	ET Type	Coaching strategy	ET's interaction
Babu et al. (2005)	Bicep curl	Computer, display	Camera and color markers	3D humanoid female	Feedback virtually reproducing users' error	Verbal, nonverbal
Jung et al. (2011)	Seated arm exercises (wheelchair exercises)	Robot—Bi-manual mobile manipulator	None reported	3D humanoid male, physical robot	Select hand and arm position for the exercises	
Fasola and Mataric (2011)		A physical anthropomorphic robot with expressive eyebrows and mouth. A computer displaying a virtual version of the same robot	Microsoft Kinect, Nintendo Wii remote		Introduce exercises, provide real-time feedback on trainees' gestures	
Dancu (2012)	Hand rotation	Computer, display	Microsoft Kinect sensor	3D character (Orc)	Introduce and represent exercises, report feedback	
Matthews et al. (2012)	Knee exercises		Wireless tri-axial accelerometer	3D humanoid female	Introduce exercises and provide guidance	

Fig. 17.5 (Left) Physical robot and its ET representation (Fasola and Mataric 2011), and (right) motor learning environment proposed for hand rotation (Dancu 2012)

The robot was programmed with a set of desirable hands positions and selected the level of difficulty based on the trainee's performance. Fasola and Mataric implemented a similar system in 2011 to compare the effectiveness of a physical robot with a virtual representation of the same robot (ET) (Fasola and Mataric 2011). Figure 17.5 (left) shows both training systems, which had similar characteristics, including verbal communication and expressive eyebrows and mouth. The training task was seated arm exercises (wheelchair exercises). A Microsoft Kinect system was used to track trainees' movement to provide them with real-time corrections based on arm gestures. A similar tracking system was implemented by Dancu in 2012 to develop a training framework based on the theory stating that observing external feedback is more beneficial in motor learning than focusing on one's body movement (Dancu 2012). In this case, the ET provided real-time feedback by co-performing the exercise in a virtual environment where the trainee's body was also represented as a second embodied character. Fig. 17.5 (right) shows both the ET and the trainee represented in the display. Lastly, Matthews et al. implemented another ET in the same year to deliver physical therapy for Osteoarthritis of the knee (Matthews et al. 2012). The training system consisted of a computer and a wireless tri-axial accelerometer for tracking trainees' knee movements. Regarding assessment, two of the experiments presented provided interesting results on the efficiency of adding an ET to a training system, as presented in the Discussion section.

17.5.8 ETs' Goals and Features

The projects identified focused on implementing and, in some cases, evaluating the effectiveness of particular features supporting a specific training task, instead of implementing a generic coach for training. Namely, the ETs identified aimed to (1) introduce a particular exercise, (2) represent and/or co-perform exercises with trainees, (3) provide correction when needed, (4) adjust appearance or conversation style as an empathy technique, and (5) provide encouragement. For these goals, presented training systems included features such as verbal communication, facial animation, body animation, and feedback algorithms. Table 17.7 lists the goals, features identified, and examples.

It is important to note that ETs integrated technology to evaluate users' performance and physical state. For instance, motion-tracking systems such as cameras and attached accelerometers were commonly used to collect data on trainees' performance. Gathering information based on physiological measures was also implemented to provide trainees with feedback (i.e., biofeedback). The most used physiological sensor was the pulse meter, but a spirometer to measure trainees' breath and an electro-encephalogram to monitor trainees' brain activity have also been tested (IJsselsteijn et al. 2006a; Buttussi et al. 2006; Laar et al. 2010). Moreover, the collection of these measures allowed training systems to adapt intensity for trainees to maintain an optimum level of effort. However, technology to track users' performance or physical state, despite being convenient tools for improving coaching strategies, is not only useful for ETs. Other training platforms could integrate and benefit from them as well. Hence, monitoring technology is not part of the scope of the present study.

17.6 Discussion

The overall results of this review showed that the use of ETs to promote physical exercise has been poorly tested. When trying to identify previous research in the field of virtual trainers, many systems involving just virtual environments to promote physical training were found. However, the

Table 17.7 Embodied training features and technology

Research question	ETs' goals	ETs' features used	ETs' examples
Can training systems including an ET improve guidance?	Introduce exercises in a near-natural high-level language	Verbal communication facial and body animation	Ruttkay and Herwin (2008), Reidsma et al. (2011), Buttussi and Chittaro (2008), Buttussi et al. (2006), Davis and Bobick (1998), Dehling et al. (2011), Babu et al. (2005), Jung et al. (2011), Fasola and Mataric (2011), Dancu (2012), Matthews et al. (2012)
	Represent/co-perform exercises with trainees	Body animation	Buttussi and Chittaro (2008), Buttussi et al. (2006), Davis and Bobick (1998), Ruttkay and Herwin (2008), Ruttkay and Zwiers (2006), Reidsma et al. (2011), Dehling et al. (2011), Chua et al. (2003), De Morais and Nicholas (2011), Babu et al. (2005), Jung et al. (2011), Fasola and Mataric (2011), Dancu (2012)
	Provide correction when needed	Verbal communication facial and body animation	Davis and Bobick (1998), Ruttkay and Herwin (2008), Ruttkay and Zwiers (2006), Reidsma et al. (2011), Dehling et al. (2011), IJsselsteijn et al. (2004a), IJsselsteijn et al. (2004b), Vermeulen (2005), IJsselsteijn et al. (2006a), Eyck et al. (2006), Laar et al. (2010), Senden (2012), Babu et al. (2005), Jung et al. (2011), Fasola and Mataric (2011)
Can ETs provide trainees with additional motivation and enjoyment?	Adjust appearance and conversation style		Davis and Bobick (1998), Dehling et al. (2011), Reidsma et al. (2011)
	Provide encouragement	Verbal communication facial animation	Davis and Bobick (1998), Ruttkay and Herwin (2008), Ruttkay and Zwiers (2006), Dehling et al. (2011), Reidsma et al. (2011), IJsselsteijn et al. (2004a), IJsselsteijn et al. (2004b), IJsselsteijn et al. (2006a), Senden (2012)

majority of those systems did not include an ET and were discarded. Also, many ET initially identified belonged to the field of cognitive skills training such as tutoring. Among the 20 ETs identified and presented in the results section, five did not include any evaluation at all and nine did not compare the effectiveness of the ET with other training systems, which did not contribute to the assessment of the advantages of using an ET. Only six studies conducted evaluations of the effectiveness of the features that are unique of ETs and the results were not conclusive (Watson et al. 2012; Klaassen et al. 2013; Buttussi et al. 2006; IJsselsteijn et al. 2004a; Fasola and Mataric 2011; Dancu 2012).

17.6.1 Effectiveness of ETs

Based on the research questions of this study, this section discusses the results of previously conducted studies with ETs that focused on the efficacy of the particular features of an ET, mainly (1) guidance and (2) motivation or enjoyment.

1. Regarding guidance, this chapter has already discussed how ETs provide a biped model that can introduce and represent exercises to be better understood and mimicked by trainees. For some basic training activities such as walking and cycling, this biped representation may not be extremely beneficial. However, for other training tasks, such as physical rehabilitation, where complex gestures or movements need to be performed, an ET introducing and representing the exercises may be remarkably advantageous for trainees. Dancu assessed an ET for hand rotation in the rehabilitation category showing that trainees using the ET were able to understand the movement faster and achieved twice the accuracy of trainees following just a virtual marker (Dancu 2012). However, the evaluation presented by Fasola and Mataric showed that a physical robot resulted in an even higher usability than its virtual representation, that is, an ET (Fasola and Mataric 2011). These results may indicate that a physical robot is a better companion than an ET or virtual robot to assist in physical rehabilitation. Nevertheless, it would be interesting to compare which option would represent a more cost-effective solution given that the

cost of a physical robot for rehabilitation therapy at home may be prohibitive for most families. As guidance effectiveness, Reidsma et al. also demonstrated that trainees of indoor aerobics were able to coordinate their movements with the ET even if they were not told to do so (Reidsma et al. 2011).

2. Regarding enjoyment, motivation, engagement, and empathy, they are often reflected in physical changes in trainees, such as effort and attention. Therefore, it is expected that individuals who are engaged will train longer or with higher intensity than those who are less engaged. In the case of physical training for rehabilitation, it would be expected that engaged or motivated patients would learn motor skills faster than those individuals who are less engaged. Two comparative experiments demonstrated that individuals using ETs exercised for longer periods than individuals without an ET when performing tasks such as cycling and hand rotation (IJsselsteijn et al. 2004a; Dancu 2012). Additionally, the engagement was also subjectively measured by surveying participants after interventions. Three comparative studies demonstrated that participants felt more motivated and comfortable with receiving feedback from an ET when walking and cycling (IJsselsteijn et al. 2004a; Buttussi et al. 2006; Watson et al. 2012). However, participants in a particular study for walking (Klaassen et al. 2013) reported preferring the "glance-ability" of a text and chart layout over an ET. Also, participants training in a rehabilitation category (Fasola and Mataric 2011) reported feeling more attracted to a physical robot than an ET. Again, these mixed results may indicate that a physical robot can communicate a sense of presence more efficiently than an ET. The results also suggest that a talking ET might be a better interface when combined with text or chart-based information, which may communicate a message faster than using just verbal communication.

17.6.2 Weak Points and Opportunities

The poor quality of virtual human's appearance seems to impact users' perceptions and immersion negatively, and these features may play a fundamental role regarding subjects' motivation (Ruttkay and Herwin 2008;

Reidsma et al. 2011; Bickmore et al. 2009). One of the difficulties creating the human-like appearance and realistic speech has been the lack of fast running computational platforms to execute the training systems. The goal of developing virtual trainers is not only to achieve a very high-quality render or speech but also a real-time interaction. Additionally, wearable sensors and wires could interfere with users' comfort during training, thus affecting the usability of the training system and thus the ET's usability. Nowadays, the inexpensive access to connected high-performance technology such as smartphones, tablets, laptops, and sensors like GPS, accelerometers, and compasses may present an opportunity to overcome some of the limitations reported in previous studies. The recent proliferation of algorithms for predictive analytics and speech recognition may open new possibilities for improving ETs' interactions in home training systems. Even virtual and augmented reality may open new paths to provide more immersive environments to interact with ETs.

Previous studies on virtual trainers provided new ideas to support individuals for supporting their physical training tasks. Some of them have shown the importance of trainees' motivation as a trigger to enjoy and persist in physical training. However, most of the literature identified in this study was just descriptive about the technology or limited to feasibility tests with a few participants. Due to the potential of this technology for providing new affordable tools on self-care and home rehabilitation, conducting more research to assess the use of ETs to support physical training seems to be required. Developing and testing health applications such as ETs can be time consuming and expensive. However, the availability of enhanced programming languages and open-source libraries are facilitating developers to reduce the implementing time and cost and improve the quality of new applications. Moreover, once an application is ready, it is relatively inexpensive to deploy it if it targets popular platforms that people already own, such as computers or mobile devices.

Few previous projects incorporated the ability to keep past training tracks and user information. Users reported this feature as very convenient and useful for motivation in long-term training (Albaina et al. 2009; Ruttkay and Zwiers 2006). Keeping track of data from past training sessions allows not only detailed performance reports but also allows retrieval and monitoring of data by other agents involved, such as trainers, caregivers, or health-care providers.

Planning the type, frequency and amount of feedback to provide may be a major feature for engaging trainees. When adding an ET, one also has to determine how the feedback is going to be communicated. Previous experiments with embodied agents in the tutoring field demonstrated that speech techniques and mood can have an impact on trainees' motivation as well (Wang et al. 2005; Paleari et al. 2005). However, only two of the identified ETs in this study tested politeness and mood techniques for enhancing trainees' motivation with positive effects in (Dehling et al. 2011) and almost neutral effects in (Matthews et al. 2012).

17.6.3 Limitations

Although the methodology has been designed to identify all research relevant to the field of study, some may be missing due to selected search phrases. To include possible missed papers, which contributes to increasing the validity of the findings, an exhaustive study of references in the final population of papers selected was conducted as well. Additionally, the present review was also limited due to the selection of the databases. Although these databases are the main sources to host digital health applications and related work, some relevant papers may have been missed.

17.7 Conclusions

To identify digital systems featuring ETs, a methodical and systematic literature review has been conducted resulting in 27 scientific papers and 20 different projects that presented an ET to support users in several categories of physical training such as walking, running, and cycling. Results on motivation and enjoyment, when subjectively measured by surveying participants, revealed that most patients felt engaged by the ET. However, only two experiments assessed the level of engagement as physical changes in trainees, such as effort and attention, with positive results (IJsselsteijn et al. 2004a; Dancu 2012). ETs with specific features to represent body movements have been proposed in other categories such as indoor aerobics, practicing martial arts, or training for physical rehabilitation. All projects in these categories aimed to provide improved guidance, enjoyment, or engagement by including an ET. Although varied results have been reported, outcomes suggested that ETs may be an effective interface to guide users through exercises that involved complex body movements and gestures.

It is important to note that ETs act as interfaces between users and training systems. Therefore, the effectiveness of an ET strongly depends on the efficacy of the training system for with that ET was implemented. Further evaluation of ETs should be conducted by comparison using the same training system. Most previous studies of ETs evaluated the effectiveness of the training system as a whole, including the ETs, which lead to non-conclusive results about the advantages of including an ET as an improved interface. Moreover, future work can improve some weak points collected in this review that negatively affected the usability of ETs, such as appearance and speech of the ET and feedback accuracy of the training system. Despite these limitations, most of the previous work suggested that ETs may provide helpful assistance and contribute to raising trainees' motivation, which encourages further assessment of this technology to promote wellness, self-care, and rehabilitation in the home settings.

Acknowledgments This work was sponsored by the Balsells Engineering Program and the Biorobotics Lab at the University of California at Irvine. The authors would like to thank the researchers of the projects selected in the present review for their help providing additional materials to complete and improve the present work. Special thanks to the Relational Agents Group at The Northeastern University, The Human-Technology Interaction Group at the Eindhoven University of Technology, and The Human Media Interaction Lab at the University of Twente.

References

Albaina, Inaki Merino, Thomas Visser, Charles APG Van Der Mast, and Martijn H Vastenburg. 2009. Flowie: A Persuasive Virtual Coach to Motivate Elderly Individuals to Walk. *International ICST Conference on Pervasive Computing Technologies for Healthcare* 1–7.

Babu, S, Catherine Zanbaka, J Jackson, and TO Chung. 2005. Virtual Human Physiotherapist Framework for Personalized Training and Rehabilitation. *Short Paper: Graphics Interface* 2: 9–11. Victoria, British Columbia, Canada.

Baum, Elizabeth E, David Jarjoura, Ann E Polen, David Faur, and Gregory Rutecki. 2003. Effectiveness of a Group Exercise Program in a Long-Term Care Facility: A Randomized Pilot Trial. *Journal of the American Medical Directors Association* 4: 74–80.

Bickmore, Timothy W, Daniel Mauer, and Thomas Brown. 2009. Context Awareness in a Handheld Exercise Agent. *Pervasive and Mobile Computing* 5: 226–235.

Brown, Marybeth, David R Sinacore, Ali A Ehsani, Ellen F Binder, John O Holloszy, and Wendy M Kohrt. 2000. Low-Intensity Exercise as a Modifier of Physical Frailty in Older Adults. *Archives of Physical Medicine and Rehabilitation* 8: 960–965.

Buttussi, Fabio, and Luca Chittaro. 2008. MOPET: A Context-Aware and User-Adaptive Wearable System for Fitness Training. *Artificial Intelligence in Medicine* 42: 153–163.

Buttussi, Fabio, Luca Chittaro, and Daniele Nadalutti. 2006. Bringing Mobile Guides and Fitness Activities Together: A Solution Based on an Embodied Virtual Trainer. *Work Espoo* Finl: 29–36.

Cassell, Justine. 2000. Embodied Conversational Interface Agents. *Communications of the ACM* 43: 70–78.

Chua, PT, R Crivella, B Daly, N Hu, and R Schaaf. 2003. Tai Chi: Training for Physical Task in Virtual Environments. *Proceedings of the IEEE Virtual Reality* 2003: 1–8.

Dancu, A, A C M Special Interest Group on Computer-Human Interaction, and I T University of Copenhagen. 2012. Motor Learning in a Mixed Reality Environment. *7th Nordic Conference on Human-Computer Interaction: Making Sense Through Design*, 811–812.

Davis, James W, and Aaron F Bobick. 1998. Virtual PAT: A Virtual Personal Aerobics Trainer. *Workshop on Perceptual User Interfaces—PUI '98*, 13–18.

Dawe, D, and R Moore-Orr. 1995. Low-Intensity, Range-of-Motion Exercise: Invaluable Nursing Care for Elderly Patients. *Journal of Advanced Nursing* 2: 675–681.

De Morais, Wagner O, and Wickström Nicholas. 2011. A Serious Computer Game to Assist Tai Chi Training for the Elderly. *2011 IEEE 1st International Conference on Serious Games and Applications for Health, SeGAH 2011.*

Dehling, Eike, Dennis Reidsma, Job Zwiers, and Herwin Welbergen. 2011. *The Reactive Virtual Trainer*. Enschede: University of Twente.

Ellis, Terry, Nancy K Latham, Tamara R DeAngelis, Cathi A Thomas, Marie Saint-Hilaire, and Timothy W Bickmore. 2013. Feasibility of a Virtual Exercise Coach to Promote Walking in Community-Dwelling Persons with Parkinson Disease. *American Journal of Physical Medicine & Rehabilitation /Association of Academic Physiatrists* 92: 472–481.

Eyck, Anke, Kelvin Geerlings, Dina Karimova, Bernt Meerbeek, Lu Wang, Wijnand Usselsteijn, Yvonne De Kort, Michiel Roersma, and Joyce Westerink. 2006. Effect of a Virtual Coach on Athletes' Motivation. *Lecture Notes in Computer Science* 3962 LNCS: 158–161.

Fasola, Juan, and M Mataric. 2011. Comparing Physical and Virtual Embodiment in a Socially Assistive Robot Exercise Coach for the Elderly. *center for Robotics and Embedded Systems*. http://cres.usc.edu/Research/files/Fasola_11_003.pdf

IJsselsteijn, WA, Yaw De Kort, R Bonants, J Westerink, and M De Jager. 2004a. Virtual Cycling: Effects of Immersion and a Virtual Coach on Motivation and Presence in a Home Fitness Application. *Proceedings Virtual Reality Design and Evaluation Workshop*, January 2004: 22–23.

IJsselsteijn, Wijnand, Yvonne De Kort, Joyce Westerink, Marko De Jager, and Ronald Bonants. 2004b. Fun and Sports: Enhancing the Home Fitness Experience. *Proceedings of the 3rd International Conference on Entertainment Computing (ICEC2004)* 3166 (January): 46–56.

IJsselsteijn, WA, Yaw De Kort, J Westerink, M De Jager, and R Bonants. 2006a. Virtual Fitness: Stimulating Exercise Behavior through Media Technology. *Presence: Teleoperators and Virtual Environments* 15: 688–698.

IJsselsteijn, Wijnand, Yvonne De Kort, Cees Midden, Berry Eggen, and Elise Van Den Hoven. 2006b. Persuasive Technology for Human Well-Being: Setting the Scene. *Persuasive Technology* 3962 (Chapter 1): 1–5.

Jung, Hee-Tae, Jennifer Baird, Yu-Kyong Choe, and Roderic A Grupen. 2011. Upper-Limb Exercises for Stroke Patients through the Direct Engagement of an Embodied Agent. *Proceedings of the 6th International Conference on Human-Robot Interaction—HRI '11*, March. New York, NY: ACM Press: 157.

Kinne, S, D L Patrick, and E J Maher. 1999. Correlates of Exercise Maintenance among People with Mobility Impairments. *Disability and Rehabilitation* 21: 15–22.

Klaassen, Randy, Rieks op Den Akker, and Harm op Den Akker. 2013. Feedback Presentation for Mobile Personalised Digital Physical Activity Coaching Platforms. May. *ACM.*

Laar, Bram van de, Anton Nijholt, and Job Zwiers. 2010. *Monitoring User's Brain Activity for a Virtual Coach.* August. Springer Verlag.

Lester, James C., Sharolyn A Converse, Susan E Kahler, S Todd Barlow, Brian A Stone, and Ravinder S Bhogal. 1997. The Persona Effect: Affective Impact of Animated Pedagogical Agents. *Proceedings of the SIGCHI Conference on Human Factors in Computing Systems,* 359–366.

Maclean, N, P Pound, C Wolfe, and A Rudd. 2000. Qualitative Analysis of Stroke Patients' Motivation for Rehabilitation. *BMJ* 321 (7268): 1051–1054.

Matthews, Judith T, J M Gustavo, Elizabeth A Almeida, Reid Simmons Schlenk, Portia Taylor, and Renato Ramos Da Silva. 2012. Usability of a Virtual Coach System for Therapeutic Exercise for Osteoarthritis of the Knee. *IROS 2012 Workshop on Motivational Aspects of Robotics in Physical Therapy.*

Paleari, M, C Lisetti, and M Lethonen. 2005. Virtual Agent for Learning Environment Reacting and Interacting Emotionally. *Eurecom.Fr,* 3–5.

Pronost, Nicolas, Li Qilei, Weidong Geng, Franck Multon, Richard Kulpa, and Georges Dumont. 2008. Interactive Animation of Virtual Characters: Application to Virtual Kung-Fu Fighting. *Proceedings of the 2008 International Conference on Cyberworlds,* 276–283.

Reidsma, D, E Dehling, and H Welbergen. 2011. Leading and Following with a Virtual Trainer. *4th International Workshop on Whole Body Interaction in Games and Entertainment,* 4.

Ruttkay, Zsófia, and Job Zwiers. 2006. Towards a Reactive Virtual Trainer. *Intelligent Virtual Agents,* 292–303.

Ruttkay, Zsófia, and Van Welbergen Herwin. 2008. Elbows Higer! Performing, Observing and Correcting Exercises by a Virtual Trainer. *Intelligent Virtual Agents,* 409–416.

Senden, Jeroen. 2012. A Virtual Coach on a Mobile Device Giving Flexible Feedback.

Van, Herwin Welbergen, Dennis Reidsma, and Job Zwiers. 2010. A Demonstration of Continuous Interaction with Elckerlyc. *MOG 2010: 3rd Workshop on Multimodal Output Generation* WP 10–02: 51–57.

Vermeulen, J. 2005. Characteristics of a Virtual Fitness Coach and Their Impact on Motivation. Univeristy of Twente, Master's Thesis.

Wang, Ning, W Lewis Johnson, Paola Rizzo, Erin Shaw, Richard E Mayer, Marina Rey, P Aldo Moro, and Santa Barbara. 2005. Experimental Evaluation of Polite Interaction Tactics for Pedagogical Agents. *10th International Conference on Intelligent User Interfaces*, 12–19.

Watson, Alice, Timothy Bickmore, Abby Cange, Ambar Kulshreshtha, and Joseph Kvedar. 2012. An Internet-Based Virtual Coach to Promote Physical Activity Adherence in Overweight Adults: Randomized Controlled Trial. *Journal of Medical Internet Research*, 14.

18

Assessing the Opportunities for Virtual, Augmented, and Diminished Reality in the Healthcare Sector

Silvia Cacho-Elizondo, José-Domingo Lázaro Álvarez and Victor-Ernesto Garcia

18.1 Introduction

On Wednesday, January 21, 2015, during a presentation of their Windows 10 operating system, Microsoft shocked the world by unveiling their *HoloLens* glasses and their *Windows Holographic* system. These devices are capable of providing a holistic augmented reality (AR) experience using holograms, opening a window to creativity through the *HoloStudio* (an App that lets users create holograms). Microsoft

S. Cacho-Elizondo (✉)
IPADE Business School, Mexico City, Mexico
e-mail: s.cacho@ipade.mx

J.-D. Lázaro Álvarez
Universidad Panamericana, Guadalajara, Mexico
e-mail: jlazaro@up.edu.mx

V.-E. Garcia
YBVR Inc., Sunnyvale, USA
e-mail: betitogar@gmail.com

© The Author(s) 2017   **323**
L. Menvielle et al. (eds.), *The Digitization of Healthcare*,
DOI 10.1057/978-1-349-95173-4_18

explained that this technological innovation could spark a profound evolution in industries like construction, general repair, video games, and especially medicine.

As of the writing of this chapter, *HoloLens* is still under development (a *Development Kit*, in technical language), and thus still presents deficiencies in terms of autonomy and process potential, as well as in its field of vision. However, its applications in the health-care sector have not gone unnoticed by institutions like Case Western Reserve University or the Cleveland Clinic (both in Ohio), both of which have already confirmed its disruptive potential through experimentation.

Microsoft's commitment to implementing this type of innovation in the health-care sector is not a novelty, but rather a tendency that is generating great expectations in the academic and business worlds. Many organizations are now experimenting with these technologies in diverse fields like distraction therapy, exposure therapy, surgical training, disaster training, education for professionals and patients, telemedicine, personalized prosthetics, pain relief, and many more.

Microsoft's efforts are part of a greater revolution affecting various industries. Not surprisingly, virtual reality (VR), AR, and diminished reality (DR) are now a central focus for technology companies because of their potential to transform the way people interact with their environment, machines, and with each other. This transformation is taking place in different industries, and the health-care industry is no exception. We are on the verge of an era in which the rapid growth and exposure of VR, AR, and DR can support a giant leap in the wellbeing of mankind.

Andrews and colleagues (2013) stated that, as countries move towards the development of electronic health services (*e-health services*), advances in information and communication technologies (ICTs) will be maximized with governments and private health organizations working towards integrating these technologies into their delivery of health-care programs.

Therefore, it will be necessary to look at new dimensions to the delivery of different approaches to health and lifestyle interventions.

18.2 Genesis and Historical Evolution of Virtual Realities

Even though the term Virtual Reality was coined much later, one of the earliest efforts in this area comes from the 1960s, with the work of photography director Morton Heilig, when he developed the first motorcycle simulator called *Sensorama*. This simulator allowed users to experience a complete sensory immersion with images, sounds, smells, and vibrations (1962). Conceptually, Ivan Sutherland, a computer scientist, is also regarded as a pioneer in this field with his work: "*The Ultimate Display*" (1965). Sutherland suggested that:

A display connected to a digital computer gives us a chance to gain familiarity with concepts not realizable in the physical world. It is a looking glass into a mathematical wonderland[1]

Sutherland and David C. Evans, founder of the Department of Computational Sciences at the University of Utah, created the VR system called the *Head Mounted Display* (1966). Even today, the term is used to denominate the visualization pieces of AR and VR devices.

Despite all these technological efforts, the slow-developing digital ecosystem had always stunted progress, that is, digital imaging was simply too far away to enable relevant results.

Several other attempts were made over the years, taking advantage of the rapidly progressing availability of computing power. Some notable examples are:

Video Place (1975), created by the artist Myron Krueger.
Data Glove (1977), designed by Dan Sandin, Richard Sayre and Thomas Defanti, members of the *Electronic Visualization Laboratory* team at the University of Illinois.
First Position Sensors, like the *Polhemus* (1979), based on magnetic field technology.

---

[1] The Ultimate Display, 1965.

It was not until the 1980's that the binomial concept *"Virtual Reality"* began to enter the popular lexicon, when computer scientists Jaron Lanier and Thomas G. Zimmerman founded *VPL Research*. This lab is regarded as the first company dedicated to commercially producing VR peripherals. Among these peripherals, we could find primitive versions of gloves and helmets that garnered the attention of popular media in 1985.

At the beginning of the 1990s, the gaming industry would place its attention on the potential of this technology with the arrival of *W. Industries' Virtuality Arcades* (1991); and later on, with the *Virtual Boy* console produced by Nintendo (1995).

It was at this time that Tom Caudell, a *Boeing Aviation* researcher, came up with the term *"Augmented Reality"* to categorize improvements that the company was making to its production processes. For these enhancements, the company used software to display the wiring plans for finished pieces. Months after this concept came into use, Steven Feiner, Blair MacIntyre, and Doree Seligmann developed the first prototype called Karma (1994).

The growing interest in both technologies preceded an intense surge at the beginning of the twenty-first century, which saw the launch of a multitude of devices, like:

ARQuake: The first open-air game with mobile AR devices, developed under the guidance of Bruce H. Thomas, a Computer Science Professor at the University of South Australia, (2000).

Second Life: Another development in the virtual world pioneered by the company Linden Lab (2003). Google purchased the *Earthview* application that combined satellite images, maps, land, and 3D buildings. This application would be used as the basis for programs like *Google Earth* and *Google Street View* (2004).

Wii: The successful video console, with which Nintendo sought a different kind of interaction between the user and the video game (2005).

Kinect **for Xbox 360**: A concept through which Microsoft made the traditional physical contact with video games unnecessary, developing an interface that recognizes gestures, voice, objects, and images (2010).

Other key developments sparked the revived interest in AR/VR in 2012:

1) ***Oculus Rift (VR)***: Developed by Palmer Luckey and eventually acquired by Facebook in 2014, the Oculus Rift demonstrated that the technical barrier that had previously frustrated creators had finally been overcome. Multiple companies have followed in their footstep and created a thriving ecosystem (e.g., HTC, Sony, Samsung).

2) ***Google Glass (AR)***: AR glasses that have produced perhaps the biggest industry milestone to date—the first surgical operation (a Percutaneous Endoscopic Gastrostomy) carried out by American surgeon Rafael Grossmann using this Google device (2013). Although this product did not have all the expected commercial success, Microsoft followed through shortly after by announcing its Hololens headset and Magic Leap, which are still under development in 2016. These programs were launched and funded at an extremely high valuation point, adding an equally vibrant expectation for AR capabilities.

Pokemon Go is the most recent crucial development on AR. This game, launched in 2016 in Australia, New Zealand, and the USA (July 6, 2016), instantly became a massive worldwide sensation.

The idea of Pokemon Go originated from an April Fools' prank in 2014. It combines the use of AR technology with the GPS and camera functions of various smart devices. The characters appear in AR super-imposed on the device's map, allowing players to capture them. There is an exploration element by having "Poké Stops" and "Gyms" tied to real-world locations.

The company amassed more than 100 million downloads in just a few weeks. Nintendo's share price rose by an initial 10% by July 14 and it peaked at 50% on July 22, 2016. Nintendo gained ¥1.8 trillion ($17.6 billion) in market capitalization since launch of the game.

The sudden success of Pokémon Go illustrates the potential for AR to become a game-changing technology, with its ability to attract mass interest and engagement across sectors.

18.3 Building a Conceptual Framework

In this section of the chapter, we present a conceptual framework based on a literature review of articles, case studies, blogs, and books related to VR, AR, and DR as well as health-care literature. We have also conducted several deep interviews with experts and executives in Mexico, Spain, and the USA who are already applying these technologies (notably, Spain's *New Horizons VR* CEO Edgar Martin-Blas).

Unfortunately, there is still a lack of a structured framework to guide marketers and academics in this new field and its impact on health care. Our goal is to contribute with a conceptual framework to clarify constructs, adoption barriers, and challenges to be assessed in future research projects.

18.3.1 Virtual Reality

VR is a technology that allows for the creation of a new dimension in which it is possible to interact with any other person or object. A computer generates the environment in which the user is immersed, having the perception of physically being in this virtual world through provision of real-time simulations and interactions using distinct auditory, visual, tactile, and olfactory sensory channels (Burdea 1993).

Two types of VR can be distinguished:

a) **Immersive Virtual Reality (IVR)**: Digital, 3D, stereoscopic, interactive environment that the user enters via sophisticated hardware. The VR device is usually attached to the user's body, giving the sensation to be in a real environment in which to explore and interact with virtual objects. In entertainment contexts, this convergence has been used under the concept of *Immersive Media* (Rose 2015).

b) **Non-immersive Virtual Reality (NIVR):** This is a synthetic environment featuring computer-generated images with the ability to create 3D virtual spaces. The novelty is found in the possibility of adding interactive objectives, videos, sounds, and even links to other virtual worlds. This is similar to what is offered by immersive VR, but here the area is limited to a screen, which provides an experience of limited immersion.

More than a few industries have shown great interest in VR. Some examples include for instance the use for commercial transactions, travel simulations, virtual meetings, and entertainment applications (Grimsdale 1995).

18.3.2 Augmented Reality

This reality is enabled by a technology that introduces virtual elements into the real world, effectively "*augmenting*" the number and type of elements that a user can see without occluding the real world underneath.

It is a combination of physical and intangible space, giving users the ability to create beings, images, objects, or texts through the computer.

In AR, users can superimpose virtual elements onto the real world by providing additional relevant information to the environment they are actually seeing.

AR has already proven useful in various industries, such as entertainment, engineering, military defense, and of course, medicine and health care (Azuma et al. 2001; Bimber and Raskar 2004).

There are considerable conceptual differences between VR and AR, even if technically they share common elements. The most critical difference is the degree of immersion experienced by the user. VR surrounds the user completely in a virtual world, while AR maintains users in the "*real world*."

18.3.3 Diminished Reality

At the beginning of the twenty-first century, Steve Mann (Head of the University of Toronto's Department of Electrical and Computer Engineering), coined the term diminished reality (2001) to describe a technique for manipulating the existing limits between objects as a way to provide relief for those with visual impairment.

Jan Herling and Wolfgang Broll took up this line of research at the *Ilmenau Technical University* in Germany and turned their focus to identifying and selecting objects to eliminate them.

At its core, DR uses the same techniques as AR, and shares plenty of technical means. The main difference is the objective: where AR efforts are geared towards adding and overlaying elements, DR aims to subtract or eliminate real objects (Azuma 1997). For these reasons, we will consider DR to be one subset of approaches within AR.

There are abundant applications for this technology, some examples of which are listed below:

Surgery Aids: Eliminate the scalpel out of the surgeon's hands so he or she can clearly see the area on which the operation is being performed.
Hearing Aids: Reduce noise to make music sound clearer—for example, eliminating specific instruments or crowd noise during a concert.
Real-Time Object Extraction: This could include touch-screen video cameras that remove objects during filming.
Lost Objects Aid: Making an individual's car more easily spotted in a parking garage by visually eliminating or de-emphasizing all other cars.
Surveillance Aid: Security cameras that remove the images of people not under suspicion.
Flight Aid: Airplanes with clear floors allowing pilots to better see the runway.
Star Gazing: Applications allowing users to gaze at the stars or 360° landscapes as if walls and ceilings did not exist.
Distractor Removal: Glasses that eliminate distracting advertisements and images.
Hindrance Removal: The ability to watch a concert or theater production without your view being disturbed by a tall person or someone with big hair sitting in front of you (Ford 2009).

18.4 At the Edge of Technological Convergence

AR and VR share many common elements, although they are conceptually distinct. The need for 3D graphics' capabilities and interaction patterns, made possible by both approaches, can overlap or even be identical.

AR capabilities are meant to highlight or overlay reality, but the border between doing that and abstracting the user to engage in a digital-only environment can borrow elements from VR experiences.

Furthermore, some VR devices are being equipped with font-looking cameras, which enable "pass-through" modes to display and enrich elements from the real world, and thus, borrow elements of AR experiences. It shows that in reality there is a continuum between what can be done with VR paradigms and what can be done with AR paradigms. This well-known phenomenon is denominated "*Mixed Reality*" (Milgram et al. 1994).

The simplified model shown in Fig. 18.1, though not recent, is still relevant because it synthesizes the union of these technologies in achieving the submergence of the user into an alternate media. The user is able to perceive and interact with the digital world and some of those interactions can potentially affect the real world. However, new technologies that address adjacent aspects of the user experience have emerged. Herein, we propose an update to this framework, considering the following issues:

Firstly, AR and VR provide the continuum between operating in the real world and in a fully digital world. We could map this as the Physical versus the Digital axis.

Secondly, the impact of these actions impact has expanded: whereas before it was mostly constrained to the inner user experience sphere, nowadays this could be expanded and have a larger effect on the user's environment.

Finally, there are other technologies or devices changing the digital ecosystem like:

Wearable Tech now allows for two-sided communication with the user's most internal sphere, including the measurement of vital signs, something quite beneficial in the health-care environment.
Internet of Things (IoT) devices can enable bi-directional communication with objects in the real world.

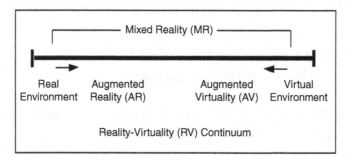

Fig. 18.1 Simplified representation of the AR/VR continuum
Source: Milgram et al. (1994)

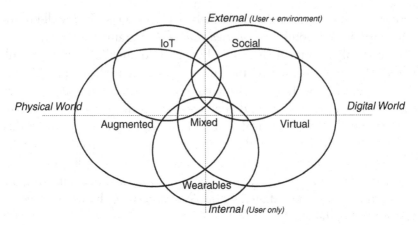

Fig. 18.2 Macro-concept of immersive media

Social Media helps bridge the gap between the personal digital experience by entering in contact with circles of people and sharing those experiences with broader audiences without having to leave the digital space.

Each of these elements expands into the original continuum. The growing capability to combine these techniques is what allows for the development of alternate worlds. Nowadays, these worlds are highly appealing for both consumers and companies because they can provide increasingly immersive experiences.

Our proposed new framework seeks to combine these latest developments and help identify the types of interactions that can be combined to achieve this new level of immersion and interactivity (Fig. 18.2)

18.5 The Impact of VR/AR/DR in the Healthcare Sector

AR and VR are technologies with which significant experimentation is occurring, health care being no exception. In the current dynamics of Digital Evolution, AR and VR represent the next natural step to continued exploration, where a new set of potential differentiators could naturally emerge.

The pharma and health-care sectors are the perfect environments in which innovative marketers today can implement recommendations made by studies such as Pharma3D (www.pharma3d.com, a joint effort between McKinsey & Company, Wharton, and Google).

The Pharma3D study states:

Finding ways to solve a problem, delight, inspire, or empathize with patients' right in the flow of what they are doing
(instead of interrupting to push a message to them).

Herein, a list of some of the most important advantages of applying these technologies in the health-care industry:

- Considerable improvements to diverse treatments and therapies
- Greater certainty in diagnoses, lowering the rate of error
- Increased safety and wellbeing of the patient through 24/7 access to more and better information
- Improved quality of training for future medical professionals
- Vital and actionable information in case of emergencies in a more realistic way
- Rise of tech entrepreneurs and startups that encourage development of a more efficient and effective medical ecosystem

18.6 Exploring the Impact of VR/AG/DR on Health Care

We have identified some potential applications for VR, AR, and DR in the field of health care and medicine. Following our analysis, we have clustered them into four categories, attending to the stage in which they can be relevant to the health-care lifecycle:

i. **Education and Prevention**
ii. **Diagnosis**
iii. **Treatment and Procedures**
iv. **Emergency**

For some of these categories, we provide concrete examples of companies and institutions working towards enabling use cases.

18.6.1 Education and Prevention

These are applications intended to provide information, track habits and otherwise act before an actual medical condition is detected.

Medical education with holographic modeled organs and body systems, and even simulated hospital environments with guided virtual instruction. Doctors and nurses can inform patients about their upcoming surgery, or provide detailed instructions prior to discharge through holographic modeling of organs, medical devices, and procedures.

Furthermore, Pharmaceutical companies can provide more innovative information about their medications.

> ***3D Simulations for Training Surgeons***: Stanford University is working on a training project for surgeons, for which they have developed simulations of 3D bodies from scans of actual people. Similar efforts have been done in a tissue-specific basis (Audette et al. 2006).
>
> ***Living Heart***: This project being developed by the Life Sciences Company of Dassault Industries, is a 3D, VR simulation of the human heart that allows those in the medical field to explore the organ in similar detail to simulations now used in the aeronautical industry.
>
> ***Flatland***: An effort to map renal physiology into a virtual environment to facilitate learning of complex renal processes (Alverson et al. 2006).

18.6.2 Diagnosis

Use cases that help patients and health-care professionals obtain and process data elements. For example, VR and AR could help patients better describe their symptoms and help nurses to locate veins more easily.

According to a study by Johns Hopkins University (USA), up to 40,500 patients die each year in intensive care units in the USA because of misdiagnosis (2012). This problem has given rise to the proliferation of Apps—*Babylon* being an example—that are capable of making diagnoses by analyzing hundreds of millions of combinations of symptoms in real time.

The Cary Ecosystems Institute in New York indicates that it has also successfully used a similar machine to predict the propagation of illnesses in rodents with 90% accuracy (2015). This technique could become a potent tool in the fight against illnesses, as rodents transmit more than 60 such diseases, and the majority of infectious illnesses that affect more than 1 billion people each year.

18.6.3 Treatment and Procedures

These are applications intended to be a direct or indirect aid in actual medical procedures. For example a startup called *Psious* offers *psychological treatments* using VR. Other illustrations of this are listed below:

Prosthetic Appendages can be adjusted more precisely by using holographic processing.

Telemedicine is becoming more personalized, allowing health-care professionals to indicate the most effective individual therapy.

Google Glass could help surgeons in the *operating room*. They can also help mothers deal with sensitivity surrounding breastfeeding.

Deep teaches patients to breathe deeply to reach a state of relaxation and relieve anxiety.

Virtual Reality Glasses for treating phobias: Some psychiatrists in the USA are already using these glasses to help patients overcome fear of flying and claustrophobia.

Pain Control is a game being developed at the University of Washington that can be used to relieve pain.

Augmented Reality Solutions have been proposed for Parkinson Disease Rehabilitation (Garcia et al. 2014).

Motor Rehabilitation using an affordable device combination of VR headsets and a Nintendo Wii gaming console (Tsekleves et al. 2014).

18.6.4 Emergencies

In non-planned cases, where response time becomes critical, AR can save lives by showing first responders all defibrillators or other emergency equipment in the immediate vicinity.

Recreating simulated environments could allow doctors and nurses to safely train for disaster response.

18.7 Challenges and Barriers in the Adoption of VR, AR, and DR

Although promising, it is clear that there are still challenges to overcome in bringing these technologies to significant degrees of adoption.

Some of these challenges are linked to the feasibility of using these technologies in a reliable way. Other adoption obstacles are related to the capability of generating engaging experiences in a cost-effective way. Finally, others barriers are related to its ability to out-perform existing approaches.

Let us further analyze some of these constraints:

18.7.1 Device Precision

A proper enablement of object tracking and object rendering in health-care use cases requires a significantly larger degree of precision than other end-user purposes in non–health-care fields. This affects mainly the AR type of use cases and must pay attention to the following elements:

> *Sensor Quality:* Cameras, temperature, and pressure sensors, among others, form part of several AR solutions today, but the degree to which they can be implemented beyond casual use (e.g., cameras for "selfies") and in health-impacting procedures is unclear.
>
> The challenge is to identify the necessary minimum thresholds of quality that devices must meet in order to be applied to health-care use cases with a degree of confidence.

Sensor Type and Interoperability: Depending on the use case, a new array of sensors geared specifically toward health-care applications might need to be developed. The extent to which these sensors can operate with AR/VR solutions in the market will determine the reach and practical feasibility of the use cases that they enable.

18.7.2 Reliability

Casual health-care use cases (e.g., weight control, periodic reminders) should be easily extrapolated from today's digital environments (e.g., Mobile Apps) into AR/VR and not impose strict reliability and uptime constraints to the platforms supporting them.

However, as already discussed in previous sections of this chapter, the potential of AR/VR is much larger, and it can even reach stages as critical as operating rooms, where the need for extremely reliable and mission critical solutions are mandatory.

This poses a challenge to AR and VR as emerging technologies, as they remain in rather immature stages of development—only one or two generations of products are being shipped and the underlying tools are undergoing continuous and significant changes.

In addition, cases of service disruption—that could be seen as minor nuisances in the original entertainment and gaming context where these technologies emerged—would be simply unacceptable in critical health-care applications.

For all these reasons, medical teams and health-care organizations seeking to make the most out of these technologies must make conscious and careful efforts to guarantee the reliability of the solutions to build trust.

18.7.3 Usability and Comfort

This is a challenge in general for AR/VR technologies. It can be even stronger in health-care applications depending on the use case. The device must not be cumbersome, painful, or otherwise uncomfortable to wear for long periods.

In the VR case, the main hurdle to overcome is device weight, where currently many devices can weigh up to 600 g. Another vital point is the Quality of Experience in VR, and specifically the need for the experience to be nausea-less and avoid special disorientation.

For the AR case, the main hindrance is in the Field of View (FOV), which is around 40–50°, significantly less than the human FOV.

Difficulty among health-care professionals and patients in commanding hardware controls and tasks, and the need for specific training is an issue shared by both AR and VR.

In this nascent industry, many *User Interfaces* (UI) and *User Experiences* (UX) elements still need to be optimized, with most of the experiences taking inherited elements from previous platforms (e.g., PC, Smartphone).

Nevertheless, this new medium can greatly benefit from new UI/UX paradigms supported by novel user input interfaces such as: *Gaze-tracking, advanced haptic,* and specifically, *hand gestures.*

18.7.4 Content Availability and Quality

The skillset needed to produce AR/VR content is unique: 3D, video, interaction design, mobile, etc. This combination of technical and non-technical skills is proving difficult to acquire and makes it difficult to grow the amount of available content.

Adding to this equation is the additional requirement of deep field knowledge for medical and health-care applications. This creates scarcity of downloadable medical content on VR and AR platforms.

There are several paths to solving this restriction, which we present as three non-exclusive options:

a) *Association with Specialized Players*: Let early niche companies be the source and filter of talent and let them have a stronger role in the experience lifecycle.
b) *Organic Growth*: Develop the talent in-house with existing resources.
c) *Partnership with Universities*: Identify the skills gap to try to develop targeted programs aimed at developing such skills.

18.8 Strategic Market Opportunities

We have analyzed the marketing opportunities of VR, AR, and DM from three key perspectives:

18.8.1 Key Actors and Benefits

VR, AR, and DR technology has attracted attention from big tech players like Facebook, Google, Apple, Microsoft, Sony, HTC, Samsung, Intel, Xiaomi, and Amazon, which have announced a number short and medium term projects. In the future, several of these companies may have a clash of interest in their quest to grow this new ecosystem.

More specifically, according to Goldman Sachs, VR and AR will generate hardware sales in the amount of US$80 billion (€71 million) in 2025, a sum currently being generated by personal computer sales. Gartner estimates that by 2020, around 40 million pairs of VR glasses will have been sold around the world.

Thus, it is clear that the market potential is present, and this already seems like a promising picture from the overall market perspective, with casual health-care applications being the first to benefit from the increased footprint of this kind of device.

More advanced applications are likely to become niche segments since elevated costs could complicate access to this technology. Clear medical and financial benefits resulting from the use of these technologies must be acknowledged to break the investment barrier, incentivizing institutions to be proactive in its adoption.

18.8.2 Links with Other Emergent Technologies

The possibility of combining VR, AR, and DR with other emergent technologies—cloud services, Internet of things, or artificial intelligence— presents other interesting opportunities for the medical industry.

Today, there is an increasing number of health devices connected to the network, which allows them to be more easily controlled wirelessly and remotely. This helps in integrating crucial information about patients in real time, regardless of their physical location.

The portable technology (*wearable*) market is growing considerably, yet is still in its initial expansion phase. This market, however, is expected to show compound growth (CAGR) of 24.5% over the next 5 years (SUPEKAR 2016).

In addition, the rapid growth of Internet of things platforms allows for the storage, centralization, analysis, crossing, and accessibility of a tremendous quantity of data useful in maintaining control over a patient's clinical evolution.

An example of the potential offered by these new technologies—specifically in the field of artificial intelligence—is IBM's *Watson* computer, which is now being used by oncologists at the Sloan-Kettering Memorial Cancer Center in New York (USA).

This IBM software accesses 600,000 medical questionnaires, 1.5 million medical histories and clinical reports, and 2 million pages of text from medical journals to help doctors develop personalized treatment plans for the symptoms, genetics, and individual history of each patient.

Furthermore, a machine named *Eve* installed at the University of Manchester utilizes artificial intelligence and two robotic arms to manipulate laboratory equipment and accelerate the process of discovering medications that manage drug-resistant malaria and other diseases.

18.8.3 Industry Implementation and Engagement

A digital engagement capability and exploration towards using AR and VR can certainly be challenging from the cultural perspective for most health care and pharmaceutical organizations.

In the Pharma3D report (McKinsey & Company et al. 2016), the authors propose a *three-step methodology* to help companies in the industry deal successfully with this type of challenge and transformation.

This methodology can be summarized as follows:

Discover how to effectively engage with patients and providers at the moments that matter most;

Design customer experiences that align content, messages, and media to build a mutually beneficial relationship; and
Deliver those experiences consistently, superbly, and efficiently.

Thinking in 3D represents a big change for pharma and health-care companies, but it is well worth it. Pharma3D research found that companies with advanced digital capabilities see increased revenues.

18.9 Conclusions

The use of portable (*wearable*) technology that incorporates VR, AR, and DR will considerably enrich our daily lives. So much so that acts like reading a product's instructions and language barriers will cease to exist, or will at the very least be marginalized.

Medical education will receive a tremendous boost, and these technologies will surely revolutionize marketing of new medicines by taking sensory experiences to a new level.

The potential of AR and VR is increasingly clear. As stated by Westwood and colleagues (2006) in "*Medicine Meets Virtual Reality*":

> Practitioners are empowered by better imaging methods, more precise robotic tools, greater realism in training simulators, and more powerful intelligence networks. The remarkable accomplishments of the IT industry and the Internet are trickling steadily into health care. The Medicine Meets Virtual Reality series can readily see the progress of the past fourteen years: more effective health care at a lower overall cost, driven by cheaper and better computers. (Westwood et al. 2006)

There are still great challenges for the proliferation of these innovations in the health-care field. The greatest obstacles are to do with education, cultural change, and acceptance, while technical difficulties and barriers related to cost are temporary (Grossmann and Ahmed 2015).

Our prediction is that innovations in altered realities will be quickly adopted in the health-care sector, as they have the potential to cause serious disruption in all medical categories. However, large-scale implementation will require strong investment on the part of individuals and institutions. This implies the risk of creating a gap in access to this technology among social segments.

As already stated, we are on the verge of widespread diffusion of revolutionary technologies capable of analyzing information, personalizing treatments, and predicting diseases before they strike with high degrees of accuracy.

The exponential grow of technological innovation in the health-care sectors will undoubtedly spark debate about patient safety and privacy, and must be regulated adequately for all interested parties. This debate will intensify as adoption patterns explode. Moreover, the benefits of an open sharing model must be carefully assessed against the potential threats derived from mismanaging this information.

Nevertheless, from the point of view of health-care corporations and health-care professionals, this technological revolution implies a full transformation to do things better for patients and creating more value for all the stakeholders involved. We greatly encourage professionals in the industry to participate actively to accelerate the growing penetration path of these technologies.

References

Alverson, D. C., S. M. Saiki Jr., T. P. Caudell, T. Goldsmith, S. Stevens, L. Saland, K. Colleran, J. Brandt, L. Danielson, L. Cerilli, A. Harris, M. C. Gregory, R. Stewart, J. Norenberg, G. Shuster, Holten J. Panaoitis 3rd, V. M. Vergera, A Sherstyuk, K. Kihmm, J. Lui, and K. L. Wang. (2006). Reification of Abstract Concepts to improve Comprehension using Interactive Virtual Environments and a Knowledge-based Design: A Renal Physiology Model. *Medicine Meets Virtual Reality*, 14. *Accelerating Change in Healthcare*. Next Medical Toolkit, Amsterdam: IOS Press.

Andrews, L., S. Cacho-Elizondo, J. Drennan, and V. Tossan. (2013). Consumer Acceptance of an SMS-assisted Smoking Cessation Intervention: A Multicountry Study. *Health Marketing Quarterly*, Taylor & Francis Group, 30, 47–62.

Audette, M. A., H. Delingette, A. Fuchs, and K. Chinzei. (2006). A Opologically Faithful, Tissue-Guided, Spatially Varying Meshing Strategy for the Computation of Patient-Specific Head Models for Endoscopic Pituitary Surgery Simulation. *Medicine Meets Virtual Reality 14: Accelerating Change in Healthcare*. Next Medical Toolkit. IOS Press.

Azuma, R. (1997). A Survey of Augmented Reality. *Presence: Teleoperators and Virtual Environments*, 6, 4, 355–385.

Azuma, R., Y. Baillot, and R. Behringer. (2001). Recent Advances in Augmented Reality. *IEEE Computer Graphics and Applications*, 21, 34–47.

Bimber, O., and R. Raskar. (2004). Modern Approaches to Augmented Reality. *25th Annual Conference of the European Association for Computer Graphics, Interacting with Virtual Worlds*, 8. doi: 10.2312/egt.20041037.

Burdea, G. C. (1993). Virtual Reality Systems and Applications. *Electro'93 International Conference*. NJ Edison.

Ford, P. (2009). Diminished Reality. *Paul Ford Blog*. www.paulford.com/diminished-reality/. Accessed July 11, 2016.

Garcia, A., N. Andre, D. Bell Boucher, A. Roberts-South, M. Jog, and M. Katchabaw. (2014). Immersive Augmented Reality for Parkinson Disease Rehabilitation. *Virtual, Augmented Reality and Serious Games for Healthcare*, 1. doi: 10.1007/978-3-642-54816-1_22.

Grimsdale, C. (1995). Foreword. *Virtual Reality Systems*. J. Vince (ed). Cambridge, ACM Press.

Grossmann, R., and S. Ahmed (2015). AR/VR & Visioning the Future Of Medical Education. *Exponential Medicine Conference*. www.exponential.singularityu.org/medicine/arvr-visioning-the-future-of-medical-education-rafael-grossmann-shafi-ahmed/. Accessed July 12, 2016

Mckinsey & Company, Wharton and Google (2016). Pharma 3D. Rewriting the Script for Marketing in the Digital Age. www.pharma3d.com/. Accessed September 9, 2016.

Milgram P., H. Takemura, A. Utsumi, and F. Kishino. (1994). Augmented Reality: A class of displays on the reality-virtuality continuum. *Telemanipulator and Telepresence Technologies*. SPIE, Vol. 2351.

Rose, F. (2015). The Power of Immersive Media. *Strategy+Business* 78, Spring.

Supekar, S. (2016). Wearable Devices Are Opening New Frontiers for Product Makers & Medical Practitioners. *Health it mHealth*. www.healthitmhealth.com/wearable-devices-opening-new-frontiers-product-makers-medical-practitioners/. Accessed July 25, 2016.

Tsekleves E., A. Warland, Ch. Kilbride, I. Paraskevopoulus and D. Skordoulis. (2014). in Virtual, Augmented Reality and Serious Games in Healthcare 1. *Intelligent Systems Reference Library.* Chapter 17, edited by Minhua Ma, Lakhmi C. Jain and Paul Anderson, 68, 321–344.

Westwood, J. D., R. S. Haluck, H. M. Hoffman, G. T. Mogel, R. Phillips, R. A. Robb, and K. G. Vosburgh. (2006). Medicine Meets Virtual Reality 14, Accelerating Change in Healthcare. *Next Medical Toolkit.* IOS Press.

Part V

New Paradigm and Perspectives for Health in a Digital Age

19

The New Art of Health Care: The Hyperrealism Period

Jean-Christophe Mestres

The system must change. That is the reality. If not, in a few years the health-care system will simply implode. According to the OECD:

> Rising spending on health and long-term care will continue to put pressure on public budgets over the next decades. Starting from around 6 percent of GDP in 2006–10, the combined public health and long-term care expenditure for OECD countries is projected to reach 9.5 percent in 2060, even assuming that policies act more strongly than in the past to rein it in. Without such policy action, spending could reach 14 percent of GDP. In BRIICS countries, spending ratios will also increase significantly from the current low levels, reaching around 10 percent of GDP by 2060, unless cost-containment policies are implemented. (OECD 2013)

This will leave people with either paying a lot for simple care, or living with the disease with no care. That is not acceptable.

J.-C. Mestres (✉)
Healthcare and Life Sciences Solutions at IBM, Nice-Paris, France
e-mail: MestresJ@fr.ibm.com

© The Author(s) 2017   **347**
L. Menvielle et al. (eds.), *The Digitization of Healthcare*,
DOI 10.1057/978-1-349-95173-4_19

In reality, we can assume that, in industrialized countries, the ratio between "not cared for" versus "cared for" will be relatively low. But what will happen in emerging countries? This is a global concern and that is the reason why the World Health Organization (WHO) has initiated several programs using information and communication technologies (ICT) to avoid this situation. For example:

mHealth is the use of mobile technology to provide health care support to patients or technical support to health service providers in a direct, low-cost and engaging manner. The WHO/ITU program aims to assist governments to use mobile components to reinforce their existing national health activities to prevent, manage, and treat non-communicable diseases (NCDs) and their risk factors. (ITU and WHO 2013)

19.1 Time to Get Real

Different factors need to be examined if we are to understand the root of the problem. A number of approaches are being explored that are aimed at decreasing the number of patients and reducing costs by optimizing several factors.

19.1.1 Noncommunicable Diseases ... or Not?

Nowadays, NCDs are seen as the most significant saving opportunity in the health-care sector. According to the NCD Alliance, in 2012, NCDs represented "68 percent of global deaths, even if they are not transmissible from person to person. It is also interesting to know that more than 40 percent of NCD deaths are premature (before 70 years of age), and nearly three-quarters of NCD deaths and most premature deaths (82 percent) occur in low- and middle-income countries (LMICs). Most NCDs are preventable" (NCD Alliance 2016).[1]

But what are NCDs, and what are their root causes?

---

[1] NCD Alliance: https://ncdalliance.org/why-ncds

19.1.2   Cancer

Cancer (NCD Alliance 2016) is a leading cause of chronic disease-related death in the world; more than 30% of cancers are preventable through modification of behavior and lifestyles. In addition to the common risk factors—unhealthy diet, tobacco use, physical inactivity, and harmful use of alcohol—efforts to prevent cancer are now focusing on reducing exposure to cancer-related infections such as human papillomavirus (linked to cervical cancer), hepatitis B virus (liver cancer), and helicobacter pylori (stomach cancer), as well as exposure to environmental and occupational carcinogens.

19.1.3   Cardiovascular Disease

The morbidity and mortality associated with cardiovascular diseases (CVDs) (NCD Alliance 2016) cost some countries around 20% of health budgets; it does not have to. CVDs—including heart disease and stroke—kill more people globally than any other disease. Addressing key modifiable risk factors such as tobacco use, diet, and physical activity would mean most premature CVD deaths could be avoided, and rising mortality rates could be reduced.

19.1.4   Diabetes

Diabetes (NCD Alliance 2016) is one of the world's most prevalent NCDs and is one of the top five leading causes of death in most high-income countries. Each year, more and more people are living with this disease, which can result in life-changing complications. Despite how serious diabetes can be, around half of those with diabetes do not know they have it. Root causes can be environmental factors, nutrition problems, and lack of physical exercise.

19.1.5 Chronic Respiratory Diseases

Although breath is fundamental to life, lung health is less well recognized than other critical health indicators, such as weight and blood pressure. However, anyone who has struggled to breathe, even for a short time, knows how essential it is. Effective tobacco control is essential to any strategy for preventing lung disease (NCD Alliance 2016).[2]

19.1.6 Mental Health and Neurological Disorders

This category (NCD Alliance 2016) includes diseases and conditions such as depression and dementia. Dementia, particularly Alzheimer's disease, and depression are among the conditions affecting the brain that currently afflict millions of people worldwide, increasingly in developing countries. They are often comorbid with other NCDs. Risk factors for mental and neurological diseases include genetics, older age, tobacco use, drug and alcohol use, unhealthy diet, and physical inactivity. Environmental exposures, such as pollution and cranial injuries, also place individuals at risk. Research on prevention is still being developed, but health-promoting lifestyle choices can decrease one's risk of these diseases. A nutritious diet, avoidance of tobacco, and increased physical activity all qualify as preventive measures.

It would appear, then, that while NCDs are one of the most important causes of disease in the world, they are also among the most easily avoided, if certain factors are acted upon, such as the following:

- **Environmental conditions:** Decrease pollution factors such as chemical products (e.g., those used in intensive agriculture), non-reusable/trashed plastics (e.g., single-use plastic bags), and exposure electromagnetic frequencies (e.g., from power lines).
- **Physical exercise:** Promote physical exercise, even to the point of offering financial incentives. For example, a private insurer could

---

[2] NCD Allliance: https://ncdalliance.org/why-ncds

provide step-counting devices and offer to reduce the insurance premiums of those who reach assigned goals.

- **Healthy food:** Junk food is quick, easy, and very accessible. Therefore, it appears urgent to build barriers to such foodstuffs (e.g., by increasing taxes) and to facilitate (and/or encourage) access to healthy food (e.g., by lowering taxes on unprocessed food).
- **Addictions (drugs, tobacco, alcohol, etc.):** Addictions are another root cause of NCDs, and almost all types of addictions are well known. Many anti-addiction measures are already in place (e.g., in a majority of countries, most recreational drugs are illegal, and cigarettes and alcohol are highly taxed). Despite all these measures, however, addictions are still a reality. Therefore, it would be more helpful to focus on the factors that induce addictive behaviors, such as social conditions, lifestyle, community activities, etc.

At this point, it clearly appears that NCDs can and should be prevented. But is the remedy more expensive than the cause itself?

19.1.7 The Financial Challenge

Change is clearly needed. If the health-care system is to survive, it must be reinvented, and the way it works must change:

- The focus must extend beyond medical information. The system needs to take other elements—such as social, environmental, and familial factors—into account.
- Prevention processes need to be created and integrated into the health-care system.
- All of the information (data) that is available needs to be used in an integrated manner (i.e., not isolated or used sequentially).

However, even knowing that change is needed, it is not easy to bring about this level of change, which needs to occur at the very center of the system. This cannot be brought about by one or two actors in one or two areas; it needs to be a systemic revolution in a number of domains:

- Business processes need to be transformed to focus on preventing illness rather than curing it.
- Users (patients) need to be educated to ask for more upfront services, rather than drugs.
- Professionals need to be advisors and coaches rather than care providers.
- Payers need to transform their business model from one that is risk-based to one that is prevention-based so that the system can be financed through savings.
- Policies need to have a legal framework and incentives to support all these transformations through a comprehensive change-management process.
- The right technology needs to be available and adapted to cover all of these needs.

But, of course, these changes have a cost, so it is important to understand that every country is impacted by NCDs—including developing countries. Therefore, how can these changes be financed?

This question assumes the price of implementing change will be over and above current costs. But that assumption is false, because some solutions for reducing the number of death due to NCDs will have an almost immediate effect. Therefore, not only will the implementation costs be covered by the savings but more savings can be achieved by offering investment fuel for more long-term and costly initiatives.

The information in Table 19.1, produced by Rachel Nugent of the University of Washington, illustrates this approach (Nugent 2015). It shows how, by achieving some targets, the implementation costs are more than covered by the savings generated.

Note that this table shows only five specific targets, but hundreds or thousands could be applied. In summary, what we can say about these data is that the waste of money is so important in NCDs management that any initiative that can reduce this will be beneficial.

Table 19.1 Summary of intervention benefits and costs, and benefit per dollar

Target	Annual benefit ($ millions)[a]	Annual cost ($ millions)	Benefit per dollar spent
Aspirin therapy at the onset of acute myocardial infarction (75% coverage)	$836	$27	$31
Chronic hypertension management for medium- to high-risk patients (50% coverage)	$11,410	$500	$23
Reduction of salt content in manufactured foods by at least 30%	$12,121	$638	$19
Tobacco prices increased by 125% through taxation	$37,194	$3,548	$10
Secondary prevention of "poly drug" cardiovascular disease (70% coverage)	$13,116	$3,850	$3
Total	**$74,677**	**$8,563**	**$9**

[a]One disability-adjusted life-year (DALY) can be thought of as one lost year of "healthy" life. Authors assume one DALY averted is equal to US$1,000 (WHO, 2010: http://www.who.int/healthinfo/global_burden_disease/metrics_daly/en/).

19.1.8 The Digital Approach

To avoid the siloes described in Chapter 1, which are the result of multiple vertical applications, revolutionizing the health-care sector will require the use of proven approaches such as enterprise architecture, "a discipline for proactively and holistically leading enterprise responses to disruptive forces by identifying and analyzing the execution of change toward desired business vision and outcomes" (Gartner 2016).[3] By using enterprise architecture, the design of the solution will be horizontal, not vertical.

Having say that, the question could be, "OK, you have a vision, but what about the market? Does it support this approach?" The answer to that is both interesting and surprising; in fact, not only is the market aware of this approach but it is already promoting it.

---

[3] Gartner: http://www.gartner.com/it-glossary/enterprise-architecture-ea/

Table 19.2 Sustainable development goals

UN's sustainable development goals
1   End poverty in all its forms everywhere
2   End hunger, achieve food security and improved nutrition, and promote sustainable agriculture
3   Ensure healthy lives and promote well-being for all at all ages
4   Ensure inclusive and equitable quality education and promote lifelong learning opportunities for all
5   Achieve gender equality and empower all women and girls
6   Ensure availability and sustainable management of water and sanitation for all
7   Ensure access to affordable, reliable, sustainable, and clean energy for all
8   Promote sustained, inclusive, and sustainable economic growth, full and productive employment and decent work for all
9   Build resilient infrastructure, promote inclusive and sustainable industrialization, and foster innovation
10 Reduce inequality within and among countries
11 Make cities and human settlements inclusive, safe, resilient, and sustainable
12 Ensure sustainable consumption and production patterns
13 Take urgent action to combat climate change and its impacts
14 Conserve and sustainably use the oceans, seas, and marine resources for sustainable development
15 Protect, restore, and promote sustainable use of terrestrial ecosystems, sustainably manage forests, combat desertification, and halt and reverse land degradation and halt biodiversity loss
16 Promote peaceful and inclusive societies for sustainable development, provide access to justice for all, and build effective, accountable, and inclusive institutions at all levels
17 Strengthen the means of implementation and revitalize the global partnership for sustainable development

In 2015, one of the most important influencers within this sector, the United Nations (UN), published a new framework made up of 17 sustainable development goals (SDGs) (Table 19.2) (https://sustainabledevelopment.un.org/?menu=1300.).[4]

For the third SDG (SDG3), "Ensure healthy lives and promote well-being for all at all ages," the framework sets out nine targets and four supplemental goals (Table 19.3).

---

[4] United Nation: https://sustainabledevelopment.un.org/?menu=1300

Table 19.3 Details of sustainable development goal

Targets for sustainable development goal number 3
3.1 By 2030, reduce the global maternal mortality ratio to less than 70 per 100,000 live births
3.2 By 2030, end preventable deaths of newborns and children under 5 years of age, with all countries aiming to reduce neonatal mortality to at least as low as 12 per 1,000 live births and under-5 mortality to at least as low as 25 per 1,000 live births
3.3 By 2030, end the epidemics of AIDS, tuberculosis, malaria, and neglected tropical diseases and combat hepatitis, water-borne diseases, and other communicable diseases
3.4 By 2030, reduce by one-third premature mortality from noncommunicable diseases through prevention and treatment and promote mental health and well-being
3.5 Strengthen the prevention and treatment of substance abuse, including narcotic drug abuse and harmful use of alcohol
3.6 By 2020, halve the number of global deaths and injuries from road traffic accidents
3.7 By 2030, ensure universal access to sexual and reproductive health-care services, including for family planning, information and education, and the integration of reproductive health into national strategies and programs
3.8 Achieve universal health coverage, including financial risk protection, access to quality essential health-care services and access to safe, effective, quality, and affordable essential medicines and vaccines for all
3.9 By 2030, substantially reduce the number of deaths and illnesses from hazardous chemicals and air, water, and soil pollution and contamination
Supplemental goals
3a Strengthen the implementation of the World Health Organization Framework Convention on Tobacco Control in all countries, as appropriate
3b Support the research and development of vaccines and medicines for the communicable and noncommunicable diseases that primarily affect developing countries, provide access to affordable essential medicines and vaccines, in accordance with the Doha Declaration on the TRIPS Agreement and Public Health, which affirms the right of developing countries to use to the full the provisions in the Agreement on Trade-Related Aspects of Intellectual Property Rights regarding flexibilities to protect public health, and, in particular, provide access to medicines for all
3c Substantially increase health financing and the recruitment, development, training, and retention of the health workforce in developing countries, especially in least developed countries and small island developing states
3d Strengthen the capacity of all countries, in particular developing countries, for early warning, risk reduction, and management of national and global health risks

Now, you might be asking yourself, "Why are there no recommendations relating to technology?" Obviously, SDG3 does not include any mention of technology, nor does it promote a specific approach. Instead, the UN is relying on the agencies it works with, especially the International Telecommunication Union (ITU), to provide recommendations, standards, and tools to help governments implement a digital health program.

For example, the Digital Health Accelerator Kit will be released during the last quarter of 2016. The kit provides substantive guidelines that reflect much of what was discussed in Chapter 1:

- define what you need, including mapped technical components with final users;
- check what exists and what can be reused;
- define the gaps to understand the missing components;
- check what the best do; use commercial off-the-shelf products, or develop products using open-source tools;
- define an implementation plan, including potential extensions using "integration bus" components that can be reused in future add-ons implementations;
- deploy the solution together with end-user education; and
- take on a new service implementation.

Following the UN plan will lead to the development of integrated components able to deliver services to citizens in a sustainable manner. But, except for a few initiatives, those services will continue to be focused on treating disease, not preventing it. In other words, prevention will still not be an embedded and integrated component. How, then, do we make that happen?

19.1.9   The Prevention Approach

Prevention. It is a big word. In 2009, researchers David Katz and Ather Ali proposed the following definition for prevention in health care: "Preventive medicine encompasses both the care of individual patients, and public health practice and, as is evident in the name, focuses on the *prevention* of disease rather than *treatment,* per se" (Katz and Ali 2009).

Therefore, if we want to apply this definition in real life, it means we will have to anticipate (predict) what will happen. This requires one of two methodologies: the crystal ball (make a guess) or analytics. As you can imagine, the former is not really an option. But what does the second option really mean?

We know the health-care sector generates enormous amounts of data (see Sect. 19.1.8) that is almost impossible for doctors to manage, let alone a layperson. And, because the majority of these data are unstructured (e.g., plain text coming from reports or other medical summaries), the level of complexity is increased. Therefore, the technology has had to evolve. This has led to "analytics solutions," which fall into a number of different types or categories:

- **Reporting:** This was the purpose of the first analytics solutions to be implemented. Reporting relies mostly on structured data, that is, data coming from databases containing numbers or elements that can be easily counted. This kind of analysis provide dashboards and similar tools and is used to support a company's decisions or strategy. In the health-care sector, this method is used mainly to manage public safety in areas such as epidemiology (the study of the distribution and determinants of health-related states or events, including disease[5] (Katz 2009), and health strategy (e.g., WHO reports).
- **Understanding:** In this case, the data can be mainly structured, with some unstructured data that is easy to analyze, such as simple sentences. These are used to understand the outcomes of an event. In health care, this type of analysis often takes place after an adverse event. For example, one day, a patient develops a sudden and serious problem with liver function, and nobody can determine why. By analyzing the data, it is discovered the

---

[5] Katz & Ali (February 2009): http://www.nationalacademies.org/hmd/~/media/Files/Activity%20Files/Quality/IntegrativeMed/Preventive%20Medicine%20Integrative%20Medicine%20and%20the%20Health%20of%20the%20Public.pdf

problem is an antibiotic the patient took weeks ago for an infection not related to his liver. The data show the medication is genetically incompatible with this particular patient, causing his body to transform the drug into a weapon against the liver instead of simply fighting against the infection. This kind of analytics is interesting and important, but again works a posteriori (after the fact) rather than proactively (although having the information will certainly help prevent future problems).

- **Real-time understanding:** This is a variation of the previous category. In the health-care sector, this is mainly combined with the measurement-type data generated by medical devices. Therefore, when some patterns (described by doctors and specialists) are detected, it is possible to raise an alarm to avoid an adverse event. For example, the "Artemis project addresses a couple of significant challenges caregivers face in (neonatal intensive care) environments" (IBM), which improves survival rates because it improves the ability of clinicians to monitor ill newborns.
- **Predicting:** This analytics solution, unlike those mentioned previously, focuses mainly on unstructured data. A predictive analysis is aimed at better understanding the roots of a problem. It helps determine the profiles, factors, and other elements or reasons why a problem may occur in the medium or long term. Therefore, when an individual has a certain profile and is exposed to certain risk factors, the system can detect potential adverse outcomes in advance, enabling the physician to propose preventive action instead of waiting for the adverse event and then having to treat the patient for that.

ICT systems equipped with such tools can therefore support medical staff (doctors, nurses, social workers, etc.) to better understand their patients before, during, and after an adverse event.

19.1.10 Patient Centric or Citizen Centric?

Given what we now know about the UN's SDG3 and analytics capabilities, we need to understand how to move from a patient-centric to citizen-centric model; meaning, how do we focus on prevention, rather than treatment/cure? Therefore, to explain how technology could be used in such an environment, the following table sets out the types of solutions that could be employed to meet each SDG3 target. (Note that some of these technological solutions could be beneficial for SDG goals in other areas, such as education or environmental protection) (Table 19.4).

It is important to understand that none of these technologies focus on the analysis of individual citizen data rather than patient data; therefore, the paradigm is evolving and the sector has to evolve—or die.

Table 19.4 Technological solutions for sustainable development goal number 3 targets

Target	Technological solution
3.1 Reduce maternal mortality	Based on population profiling (analytics technologies), it is possible to define at-risk mothers (or future mothers) and use mobile applications to support them during their pregnancies. For example, in India, "a system designed to access areas untouched by the national health-care system (uses mobile phones) . . . to beep important health messages, such as reminders for pregnant women, to get their checkups done in time" (Indo-Asian News Service 2015)
3.2 End preventable deaths of newborns and children in hospitals	Real-time analysis that identifies abnormal patterns of vital signs within complex environments could alert medical staff working in neonatal intensive care units when an adverse event is imminent. Day to day, doctors and educators using mobile phone applications could educate adults and children on good practices and the risks associated with alcohol, tobacco, drugs, unprotected sex, improper nutrition, etc.). For example, in India, "ImTeCHO is an innovative mobile phone application to improve performance of ASHAs (community health workers) through better supervision, support and motivation for increasing coverage of proven maternal, newborn and child health interventions among resource-poor settings in India" (ImTeCHO 2013)

(*continued*)

Table 19.4 (continued)

Target	Technological solution
3.3 End the epidemics of AIDS, tuberculosis, etc.	Analyzing big data makes it is easier to follow epidemics and pandemics then, once the situation is understood, it becomes easier to launch targeted preventive campaigns using mobile apps as support. (Note that, in this case, "mobile apps" do not strictly mean smartphones, but can also encompass solutions that provide support through text or voice messages [see earlier solution under target 3.1])
3.4 Reduce by one-third premature mortality from NCDs	Analyzing big data, including medical and social information, makes it easier to identify risky profiles so that appropriate education and prevention programs can be put in place. For example, authorities in Senegal used this approach to encourage people to follow appropriate diets during Ramadan to avoid an increasing number of problems linked with diabetes. That program was launched thanks to the ITU/WHO "Be he@lthy be mobile" initiative
3.5 Strengthen the prevention and treatment of substance abuse	As for NCD prevention, technology can help by defining risky population profiles and then launching targeted campaigns using mobile apps
3.6 Halve the number of deaths and injuries from road traffic accidents	Although technology has resulted in an ever-increasing array of automotive security systems (emergency braking systems, intelligent airbags, etc.), security could be further enhanced through education supported by mobile apps. For example, a car's ignition system could require not only a breath test, but could also provide educational content. In this approach, technology that prevents a car from starting (because the driver has too much alcohol or drugs in their system) could then require the user to review educational content before the system can be unlocked
3.7 Ensure universal access to sexual and reproductive health care services	In terms of technological solutions, this target is closely linked to 3.1 and 3.2, where instructional systems could be put in place to educate children, and the content could be adapted to include different or more detailed information as they get older

(continued)

Table 19.4 (continued)

Target	Technological solution
3.8 Achieve universal health coverage	To support this initiative, technology could offer solutions such as the master patient index, which is a database of diverse information from different caregivers and other sources. Such a solution would enable any medical professional (based on their level of accreditation, e.g., emergency medical technician, doctor, nurse) to access relevant patient-related medical information. Some countries (such as Estonia, Canada, and Catalonia) have started to put such a system in place. However, this will need to be approached as a "global" system, in the same way the banking sector is approaching credit card data
3.9 Substantially reduce the number of deaths and illnesses from pollution	Environmental sensors in a particular geographic region can be used to capture and analyze a significant amount of data using real-time analytics. Then, populations already profiled as being at risk from a specific pollutant could be alerted (and protected) as needed.

19.2 The Race Is Underway

As we have seen, the implementation and management of the various technological approaches each have their own pluses and minuses. Next, we need to examine how the different actors in the health-care system need to evolve.

19.2.1 From Caregiver to Illness Preventer

Thanks to technology, the doctors of tomorrow will be able to better understand their patients' diseases, and they will be able to predict an individual's risk of disease if nothing is done. Thus, the doctor's job will shift from caregiver to preventer, that is, someone who is in charge of preventing illness among the population. Some organizations are already starting to recognize this. For example, the Physicians Committee for Responsible Medicine in the USA notes the following on its website: "The Physicians Committee is leading a revolution in medicine—putting a new focus on health and compassion. Our efforts are dramatically changing the way doctors treat chronic diseases . . . by putting prevention over pills." However, the work required to manage this change, which will have a huge effect on the health-care sector, is not trivial.

This new model will have to manage the following:

- **Detection:** Moving from treatment to prevention will require proactively mining the available data to detect populations at risk. Different actors would then take action as appropriate. For example, a doctor taking care of a patient could, with the patient's consent, take action aimed at preventing the patient's children from developing the same condition. At the same time, the government, obeying strict rules of confidentiality and ethics, could run analyses aimed at creating a national prevention program. And individuals who are at risk but not yet ill could, with the appropriate information, take appropriate action to maintain their health. Whatever the method of detection, however, everyone who is at risk has to be notified.
- **Notification:** In interviews conducted for this chapter, a number of general practitioners (potentially the actors in charge of managing preventive care) expressed concern regarding how to advise a *future* patient. In other words, how does one tell an individual to make an appointment for a condition he or she may develop in 10 or 20 years? There is no doubt this is a complicated situation that will need to be extensively studied, and significant educational efforts will need to be made. Governments will need to educate populations and promote the benefits of such a system. Individual citizens will need to accept the idea of being alerted. Doctors will need to change the way they think about patients. And payers in both the public and private sectors will need to be willing to pay for prevention.
- **Management:** Once the target (future patient) has been alerted, the lead preventer, such as a physician, will need to coordinate an overall prevention plan. This plan would include the services of other actors (e.g., dietician, psychologist, social worker, fitness coach), supported

by technologies that are capable of managing them. The plan would need to be reviewed and updated based on results so that services could be added or removed, as needed.

- **Evolution:** Once an individual is following a prevention plan, should there be an end to the process at some point? Or should the prevention plan be maintained (and others added) for a lifetime? The answer is not black and white and will have to be decided case by case. For example, some prevention mechanisms will focus on changing a behavior. Thus, once the new behavior is engrained, a yearly follow-up may be all that is required, with no formal appointment or interaction with professionals required.

At this stage, it is clear that the caregiving environment has to evolve and reinvent itself to fit within this new prevention paradigm. However, caregivers are not the only actors that need to change behaviors. Payers, also, have to change the way they work within the health-care economy.

19.2.2 From Risk Management to Prevention Management

Currently, there are two payer models: The public and the private.

Public payers reimburse from 0% to 100% of the costs of drugs and medical treatments. These payers follow specific rules: for this profile and that condition, the payer commits to reimburse (or not) some or all of the costs. Private payers, however, set reimbursement levels according to the amount of risk. Based on the profile of the insured (the subscriber), the risk factor is calculated and a price determined for the level of service/reimbursement that will be provided. In both cases, however, the payer assumes the majority of subscribers will not need to access the drugs or treatments, which ensures sufficient funds are available to pay for (or reimburse) the minority.

Now, however, with access to better health care and better life conditions, people are living longer. This aging of the population puts increased pressure on the health-care system, and this jeopardizes the current majority/minority model. This is why a prevention model is so important. But such a model needs data. What happens if people who are at risk are unwilling to share their data (for example, because they are ignoring prevention advice and are afraid their insurance premiums will increase)?

Just as the health care market needs to evolve, payer behavior will also need to change. The question now is, what will this new prevention model look like? While this is difficult to answer, we can imagine how an approach that focuses on prevention could be adopted by public and private payers.

19.2.3 Prevention and the Public Payer

This is the simplest to imagine since public payers are aware that financing prevention creates savings that will repay not only the amount invested but also generate sufficient savings to pay for new and better drugs and treatments. This financing capability comes from a simple equation: Investments to prevent NCDs will decrease the number of sick people. Investments will be more than covered by savings. Thus, as the number of sick people decreases, the money saved will be enough to pay the associated expenses.

19.2.4 Prevention and the Private Payer

For private payers, the paradigm is different, as they need to change their model from risk calculation to prevention management, which is not easy to accomplish. Imagine if the model were to be transformed so that subscribers enter into a "prevention contract," for example, the payers would fund prevention-related activities, making a profit margin that is based on scale (i.e., having millions of subscribers pay a set, negotiated rate). If a subscriber meets the terms of the contract (e.g., improves their level of physical fitness), the payer would still pay health-care expenses (or define a list of covered conditions. The problem with that model, of course, is the difficulty in policing attitudes. What happens to subscribers who refuse to avoid risky behavior, or who accept money for prevention-related activities, but then do not participate in them?

To avoid this, the model could, for example, incorporate risk levels that create financial incentives for following a prevention program. For example, those who refuse to follow a prevention program would face monetary penalties in the form of higher premiums. (This is not unlike current practices; smokers, for example, pay more for life insurance than nonsmokers.)

Of course this is just an example; the right balance would need to be found between the amount paid by the insured individual and the coverage offered by the insurer.

Under this model, payers could evolve toward providing prevention services instead of managing risk; however, payers will need to have the support of the government and, for that, a shift is needed. Governments, therefore, will have to reinvent their function within the health care sector, moving from a passive regulator role to one that it is more proactive (activist role).

19.2.5 From Cop to Coordinator

Currently, if we ask a government to define its role in the health-care sector, the answer is likely to be "regulator." Governments are responsible, for example, for deciding which drugs will be permitted for sale and the price that will be charged for them, the cost of each type of medical treatment, and the penalties associated with not following these regulations and laws. In other words, governments play a policing role.

By focusing on prevention, governments will still have to play that role, but they will also have to be coordinators: ensuring that everything is in the right place, for the right person, for the right need. Coordinators will need to organize services *and* create regulations and laws aimed at prevention. What would this role look like in practice?

We can expect the government's coordinator role would fall within four key areas.

19.2.6 Data Manager

A prevention model needs to include systems for collecting data and define where the data will come from. It also needs systems to analyze the information so that profiles, and the necessary services, can be created. Companies, for example, could undergo certification processes that grant them permission to manage (and combine) the resulting data. (As mentioned in Chapter 1, combining data from multiple and sometimes disparate sources—such as hospitals, doctors, and water and energy utilities—could make it possible to detect diseases such as Alzheimer's earlier. This, combined with an appropriate prevention program could, theoretically, result in a future cure for this disease.)

19.2.7 Services Manager

A complete list of services (and their prices) needs to be created and categorized, regardless whether they are public or private. Once this list is complete, governments need to identify services that will result in health-care savings (i.e., by reducing illness), what costs will be borne (or not) by the public payer, and what portion of costs will be left to private insurers (or end users).

For example, a potential diabetic (detected at risk of becoming so), could have the opportunity to take cooking classes in a public or private institution, which would be paid for by a combination of national insurance and the individual's private insurance plan. At the same time, someone with no risk of diabetes would be able to take such a class but could decide to decrease how much private insurance they purchase (because they are less at risk and therefore need less coverage).

19.2.8 Processes Manager

This is the most important part of the coordinator's role. The government needs to be in charge of identifying, assessing, coding, and validating each service. Then, each service would need to be integrated into various prevention frameworks. Each framework would require the participation of several actors (e.g., doctors, social workers, private companies) tasked with providing prevention services. The government would not define the prevention plan, nor run it (as mentioned earlier, this would be done by the preventer). Rather, the role of the government would be to provide the platform or service supporting the overall plan/approach.

19.2.9 Results Manager

Once the system is in place and operational, the role of the government is not complete, because the provided services need to be assessed and the results evaluated and analyzed. This analysis would then lead to whatever changes, additions, or updates are needed to improve results and increase efficiencies while ensuring the safety of the individual, and ensuring that their personal data is securely and ethically managed. This suggests the need for a new regulatory body (public or independent) to take on this role.

Now that we understand how the roles of health-care providers, payers, and governments need to evolve, what about the role of the person at the center of this model: the individual. How will their role change?

19.2.10 From Patient to Health Manager

The current health-care system has providers (actors providing regulation, money, or services) and consumers (the patient). But, in shifting to a prevention model, we need to understand what the individual must do to accept this new way of thinking about health care.

This new era of prevention will require the individual citizen to accept, for example, that data will have to be captured from diverse sources (including—why not—shopping data) and shared with entities such as:

- the public hub, to define the profile;
- the service hub, to define the needed services;
- the insurer(s) regarding noncompliance; and
- other actors, as needed.

Obviously, this is only an example. Rules governing the model will need to be negotiated and established between all concerned parties. Then, once an agreement is reached, citizens who want to access prevention services would need to accept the rules. Those who do not want to participate would be assigned to the "regular" health-care track. However, as that track is more expensive for the payers (greater health-care risks), there would be a surtax associated with that choice.

Placing a monetary value on health is not mercenary; it is a way to incentivize people to take care of themselves. In this model, the individual becomes the manager of their own health. Right now, many people look at health care as someone else's responsibility: if a problem occurs, the doctor will solve it, and insurance (or the government) will pay for it. That way of thinking—that model—is no longer affordable. Payers cannot continue their current practice of focusing on reimbursing ever-growing numbers of "patients" without demanding higher and higher fees or reducing the services that are covered—or both.

Each of us wants to live longer, healthier lives but, for that to happen, we need to take care of ourselves "before." Once we accept this, we will also need to accept some additional responsibilities. First, accepting the right service at the right time. Second, actively auditing the system to understand what has been performed and when. This will ensure the individual will be able to revoke the privileges of any actor that has not met its ethical obligations. (Some alarms could happen automatically, similar to what happens when a credit card company notices unusual activity on your account and contacts you to confirm the transaction.)

Without question, this shift in the health-care paradigm is necessary. Otherwise, in a few years, only people with money (the top 10% of the world's population) will be able to pay for health-care services.

Even for the lucky 10%, the outlook is not favorable. Countries that do not maintain an acceptable level of public health care will see their economies decline. Employment would fall (no need for all those medical professionals, like doctors, nurses, and pharmacists). Health insurance would cease to exist. Productivity would drop, because people would be less able to work due to poor health, further compounding economic problems.

Therefore, the decision to move to a technology-supported preventive health-care model is not optional. In fact, the technology is already there, waiting for us. To make it happen, all that is needed is the willingness of politicians, payers, medical staff, and citizens.

References

"Be He@lthy, Be Mobile: The Quiet Epidemic: Non-Communicable Diseases and How Mobile Phones Can Help," *International Telecommunication Union*, accessed August 31, 2016, http://www.itu.int/en/ITU-D/ICT-Applications/eHEALTH/Be_healthy/Pages/Be_Healthy.aspx

"Cancer," *NCD Alliance*, accessed August 31, 2016, https://ncdalliance.org/why-ncds/ncd-management/cancer.

"Cardiovascular Diseases," *NCD Alliance*, accessed August 31, 2016, https://ncdalliance.org/why-ncds/ncd-management/cardiovascular-diseases.

"Chronic Respiratory Diseases," *NCD Alliance*, accessed August 31, 2016, https://ncdalliance.org/why-ncds/ncd-management/chronic-respiratory-diseases

"Diabetes," *NCD Alliance*, accessed August 31, 2016, https://ncdalliance.org/why-ncds/ncd-management/diabetes.

"Health Topics: Epidemiology," *World Health Organization*, accessed August 31, 2016, http://www.who.int/topics/epidemiology/en.

IBM, "Achieving Small Miracles from Big Data," in *Smarter Healthcare in Canada: Redefining Value and Success*, accessed August 31, 2016, https://www.ibm.com/smarterplanet/global/files/ca__en_us__healthcare__smarter_healthcare_data_baby.pdf.

"IT Glossary: Enterprise Architecture," *Gartner*, accessed August 31, 2016, http://www.gartner.com/it-glossary/enterprise-architecture-ea/.

ITU (International Telecommunication Union) and the WHO (World Health Organization), "A Guide for Countries Joining the mHealth Program" (Geneva, 2013), accessed August 31, 2016, http://www.who.int/nmh/events/2012/mhealth_guide.pdf.

ImTeCHO, accessed August 31, 2016, http://www.imtecho.com.

Indo-Asian News Service, "Mobiles Beep Health Messages to Women in India's Villages," *Smart Cooky*, February 2, 2015, http://food.ndtv.com/health/mobiles-beep-health-messages-to-women-in-indias-villages-693604.

Katz, D. L., and A. Ali, "Preventive Medicine, Integrative Medicine & the Health of the Public, commissioned for the IOM Summit on Integrative

Medicine and the Health of the Public," *Institute of Medicine (IOM)*, *Washington, DC*, 2009, accessed August 31, 2016, http://www.nationalaca demies.org/hmd/~/media/Files/Activity%20Files/Quality/IntegrativeMed/Preventive%20Medicine%20Integrative%20Medicine%20and%20the%20Health%20of%20the%20Public.pdf.

"Medical Doctor," *Physicians Committee for Responsible Medicine*, accessed August 31, 2016, http://www.pcrm.org/about/careers/medical-doctor

"Mental Health and Neurological Disorders," *NCD Alliance*, accessed August 31, 2016, https://ncdalliance.org/why-ncds/ncd-management/mental-health-and-neurological-disorders.

"Metrics: Disability-Adjusted Life Year (DALY)," Health Statistics and Information Systems, *World Health Organization*, accessed August 31, 2016, http://www.who.int/healthinfo/global_burdendisease/metrics_daly/en/.

"NCDs," *NCD Alliance*, accessed August 31, 2016, https://ncdalliance.org/why-ncds/NCDs.

Nugent, Rachel, "Benefits and Costs of the Non-Communicable Disease Targets for the Post-2015 Development Agenda," *Copenhagen Consensus Center*, 2015, accessed August 31, 2016, http://www.copenhagenconsensus.com/sites/default/files/health_perspective_ncd_-_nugent.pdf.

OECD, "What Future for Health Spending?" *OECD Economics Department Policy Notes* June 19, 2013, accessed August 31, 2016, http://www.oecd.org/economy/health-spending.pdf.

"Sustainable Development Goals," *United Nations Division for Sustainable Development*, accessed August 31, 2016, https://sustainabledevelopment.un.org/?menu=1300.

20

Cyber Threats in the Health-Care Industry

Bertrand Monnet and Philippe Very

In addition to its numerous positive impacts, the development of information technologies in health care exposes the sector to a variety of major risks emanating from hackers, organized criminals, and terrorist organizations. In addition, the proliferation of connected devices raises specific issues and new possibilities for breaching the security of the IT systems belonging to the sector's various stakeholders. In this chapter, we examine these threats, analyze the objectives of cybercriminals, and present recommendations for preventing and dealing with cybercrime. We consider the industry at large, including providers of medical services, pharmaceutical firms, and their customers.

B. Monnet (✉)
Criminal Risk Management Chair, EDHEC Business School, Roubaix, France
e-mail: Bertrand.MONNET@edhec.edu

P. Very
Department of Strategy, EDHEC Business School, RoubaixNice, France
e-mail: Philippe.VERY@edhec.edu

© The Author(s) 2017   **371**
L. Menvielle et al. (eds.), *The Digitization of Healthcare*,
DOI 10.1057/978-1-349-95173-4_20

20.1 Cybercriminal Techniques

There are many definitions of cybercrime. We use the United Nations' (UN) definition, according to which: "cybercrime is defined as a broad range of illegal activities committed by means of, or in relation to, a computer system or network, including such crimes as illegal possession and offering or distributing information by means of a computer system or network" (United Nations 2015). While the UN definition refers to a computer system or network, current technological progress requires the definition to be extended to encompass any connected object. In the "internet of things," any object—mobile phone, household appliance, medical device—can be assigned an IP address and thus communicate using technology such as Bluetooth, radio frequency identification (RFID), or near field communication (NFC). In the health-care industry, for example, information about patients' health can flow though computers and mobile phones between doctors, patients, and hospitals; connected devices are also facilitating autonomous treatment at home. Any connected device can provide a gateway for entering a private network or developing an illicit activity focused on a target. The more connected devices, the higher the risk of security breaches.

Consequently, the health-care industry with its numerous participants and network entry-points can be particularly vulnerable. Criminal elements use diverse techniques to target organizations in the industry. Cyber security providers and auditing firms regularly publish cybercrime reports (see for instance KPMG 2015). Our focus will be on the main attacks perpetrated by elements external to the industry.

20.1.1 Intrusion

As described to the authors by an experienced hacker,[1] many companies' information systems (IS) can be penetrated using two main tactics: social engineering and by exploiting the technical weaknesses of their operating

---

[1] Interview—Paris—May 2016.

systems—particularly in the case of Windows for computers or Android for mobile phones. The first component of social engineering involves sending emails that contain malware embedded in attached documents or links to numerous employees of the targeted company (phishing) or by sending these malicious emails to employees who are specifically targeted for their level of access to the company's strategic data (spear phishing). Once the malware has been downloaded onto the employee's computer and if designed for this purpose, it can explore the parts of the IS to which the infected computer has access, and then gain access to critical data. The second component of social engineering involves scanning employees' passwords to use their access rights to penetrate the company's IS; this second technique being facilitated by a poor level of password security. Security breaches underpinned by social engineering techniques are based on human failures. The proliferation of electronic devices connected to the IS (tablets, watches, glasses, cars, etc.) makes this first technique more dangerous, especially as the employees equipped with these devices tend to be top executives.

The second way to penetrate the IS of a targeted organization is to exploit its structural weaknesses. No IS is perfect, and skilled hackers have been scanning all of them for years, to identify the weaknesses of their code-based design. They find breaches that enable them to enter a targeted IS. Once these structural security breaches—or backdoors—are identified, hackers can use them to travel inside their target without breaking the door but merely by opening it with the key they have found. They can open the door as often as they like.

20.1.2 Saturation

The second type of cyber-attack to be considered for the health-care sector involves saturating the Web interfaces of targeted organizations. Such attacks can severely disrupt operations if Internet is strategically important for the organization concerned, or if its website servers are connected to other servers that support critical data. This Denied Disposal of Services (DDOS) technique is based on simultaneously connecting thousands or millions of computers (that the criminal controls remotely) to the targeted organization's website. If the website's servers are not designed to support this many simultaneous connections, they quickly "crash" under the number of requests they try to address.

Intrusion and saturation are the main techniques employed by cybercriminals. They can be used for various purposes or types of crime. It is therefore worth understanding the objectives behind such criminal activities.

20.2 Objectives of Cybercriminals

The objectives of the various types of cybercriminals using the above techniques to gain access to an organization's IS can be classified into three main categories, according to the Monnet and Very typology (2010): destruction, predation, and competition. Some acts target specific organizations within the health-care industry.

20.2.1 Destruction

The first data to be considered here are pharmaceutical company data. The destruction of critical data, such as results of research protocols carried out on strategic future drugs and products, can severely threaten the performance and sustainability of these companies. Once cybercriminals have penetrated the IS, they can try to destroy critical data contained in accessible servers. The first potential perpetrators of this first type of data destruction are legal stakeholders and primarily competitors that may resort to these cyber techniques on isolated bases for economic reasons. Putting ethical behavior aside, it can clearly be in a pharmaceutical company's interests to destroy the added value and even the future products of a competitor by cyber-destroying its critical data. As already observed in cases of espionage—but not as yet in cases of data destruction—the attacking company does not carry out the attack itself, but tends to solicit aid from two different sources. The first source is usually a firm of specialized business and forensic intelligence consultants, which in addition to its legitimate services of data protection, can organize efficient cyber-attacks through its own internal resources or hired hackers. The second source may be the intelligence services of the attacking company's host country. There may be economic and/or political advantages for a government—American, Chinese, Russian, French, or other—in destabilizing key stakeholders in the economies of competing states, regardless of any existing diplomatic and military alliances. This form of data destruction through cyber-attack has already been observed in the nuclear and mining industry and raises an additional threat of economic warfare in which the pharmaceutical industry could prove to be a collateral victim.

In addition to data destruction, cybercrime can entail more dramatic consequences for the health-care sector, since the digitalization of this industry could potentially lead to cyber-attackers killing patients. Three possibilities are to be considered here. The first involves accessing the IS of hospitals or clinics that have digitalized the management of pharmaceutical treatments, and then modifying the data related to types or doses of drugs to be administered to targeted patients to kill them. The second one, which is rather similar, functions by taking control of patients' medical devices—insulin pumps for example—again to kill them. The third option consists of developing larger-scale intrusions, without any specific targeting of patients, to commit a new form of terrorist attack on a large number of vulnerable victims without the terrorist having to resort to any guns or explosives.

20.2.2 Predation

The digitalization of the health-care sector has greatly increased—and in some cases created—vulnerability for its stakeholders in the face of several types of criminal predation and particularly theft, which is the simplest type. Cybercriminals can access huge volumes of sometimes highly valuable data through the techniques presented above. There are two main categories of data to be considered here. The first concerns scientific and commercial data belonging to pharmaceutical companies and which can not only be destroyed but also stolen by non-ethical competitors aided by private and public sources as described above.

These acts can be qualified as espionage. The second category concerns the medical data of millions of patients, stored in servers belonging to hospitals, clinics, and public administrations. These data can be of high commercial value for companies seeking to address demands related to these patients' diseases. Community Health Systems, based in Franklin, Tennessee and an operator of 206 hospitals in 29 US states, fell victim to this kind of theft in 2014, when it had 4.5 million data items concerning American patients (details of first names, social security numbers, addresses, phone numbers, birthdates, etc.) stolen from it. Investigations proved that the theft was committed by Chinese hackers. Note also that this kind of information theft may also be valuable to non-ethical insurance companies looking to illicitly select their customers according to their health.

The second type of criminal predation liable to be augmented by health-care sector digitalization is extortion. Extortion involves the predator forcing its victim to give it money under the pressure of major threats. Hospitals, pharmaceutical companies, and other private stakeholders in the sector are already exposed to forms of physical extortion and forced to pay out millions of dollars in numerous regions controlled by criminal organizations like the Italian mafia, the Japanese Yakuza, or the Chinese Triads. However, the concept of digital extortion also needs to be considered, especially for the health-care industry. After entering a pharmaceutical company's IS, a criminal organization can copy critical data on key research programs, and threaten to release the details on the Web if the company does not pay a ransom. But the most common form of digital extortion is based on ransom wares, or in other words malwares infecting corporations' strategic servers and encrypting large volume of data. Once the data has been made inaccessible, the criminal organization demands a ransom in exchange for releasing a decryption code to the victim. This form of extortion successfully targeted the Hollywood Medical Presbyterian Center, a Los Angeles hospital, in February 2016. Ransom ware was used to encrypt data stored in the hospital's servers, thus blocking its administrative services for a week until the hospital agreed to pay a US$17,000 ransom (in bitcoin form).

In the same vein, saturation or intrusion has the potential to hinder the emergence of virtual surgery, a technology that allows specialist surgeons to control robots located on a remote site location and thus perform surgery on patients anywhere in the world. The potential exists for cybercriminals to interrupt such operations and demand ransom money.

20.2.3 Competition

Digitalization will also increase the health-care sector's vulnerability to the already-major threat of counterfeiting. Although precise estimates are clearly impossible to make, the World Health Organization considers that about 10% of the drugs sold worldwide each year are fake. This criminal economy generated an estimated US$200 billion in revenues in 2014 or the equivalent of 10–15% of the pharmaceutical industry's overall revenues (SANOFI 2015). Drug counterfeiting is extremely profitable: each US$1,000 invested in it generates US$500,000 for the criminal organizations involved. Internet plays a key role in the growth of this form of criminal competition for pharmaceutical companies. Although 60% of fake drugs are sold in emerging countries, mostly on street markets, 40% are sold in developed countries, where it is difficult for the criminal organizations to insert them into the pharmaceutical sector's legal channels. Most of the fake drugs are therefore sold on these markets through online drugstores. The growth of online drug sales is clearly dangerous for the industry: 96% of online pharmacies sell illicit drugs, either always or at times. In addition to the economic prejudice it causes, this form of criminal competition, which is accelerated by digitalization, has dramatic human consequences: in 2013, a total of 122,350 malaria patients died after taking fake drugs for the disease (SANOFI 2015).

20.2.4 Cybersecurity: Some Recommendations

Despite this dark picture of health-care industry digitalization, solutions exist to mitigate the impacts of cybercrime on the industry. Firstly, all the sector's stakeholders need to enhance and permanently update the technical protection afforded to their IS by hiring specialized IT security providers. Most of the sector's stakeholders have already moved to act on this first solution. However, it does not afford them enough protection on its own, as cybercriminals usually become capable of overriding most of these security measures.

As one weak entry point is sufficient to allow intrusion to a network, all inter-connected participants in the industry must upgrade their protection via a race to the top, so that all partners enjoy the same high level of protection. Security is not an issue for isolated participants, but for networks as a whole. An important first step for the whole of the industry is to mitigate the risks of backdoors being created in their IS. They therefore need to define and use "a less common IS" that is capable of ensuring the necessary degree of efficiency within the network.

However, the most important security measure is not technological, but strictly managerial. It relies on the sector's ability to disseminate a security culture among all of its stakeholders. Since social engineering is the most common tactic used by cybercriminals, all of the industry's employees must be informed and trained, so as to diminish the ability of hackers to enter their organization through the organization's own employees. A number of simple and fairly cheap-to-implement actions are probably the most efficient means to fight cybercrime. These may range from rules for creating and changing passwords, to guidelines for the use of social networks at work and lists of websites to avoid.

20.3 Conclusion

The exciting technological progress embraced by the health-care industry raises new security issues. The industry is particularly exposed to cyber threats thanks to its complexity and the number of organizations and individuals participating in it. In addition, the medical industry's efficiency now relies on the multiple connections that interlink the industry's participants, devices, and systems. And this vulnerability is set to remain high because, like for doping, security solutions are not invented until after a new threat is identified. In other words, hackers and other cybercriminals will always stay one step ahead of the game, thus meaning that 100% security is illusory. " . . . As we know, there are known knowns. There are things we know we know. We also know there are known unknowns. That is to say, we know there are some things we do not know. But there are also unknown unknowns, the ones we don't know we don't know" (Rumsfeld 2002).

References

Donald, Rumsfeld, US Secretary of Defense. 2002. Speech *"known unknown,"* February 12.

KPMG. 2015. *Health Care And Cyber Security: Increasing Threats Require Increased Capabilities.* http://www.kpmg-institutes.com/institutes/health care-life-sciences-institute/articles/2015/08/health-care-and-cyber-security.html

Monnet, Bertrand, and Philippe Very. 2010. *Les Nouveaux Pirates de l'Entreprise: Mafias et Terrorisme.* Paris: CNRS Editions.

SANOFI. 2015. *Report Lutte contre la contrefaçon des médicaments.* November.

United Nations. 2015. http://www.uneca.org/sites/default/files/PublicationFiles/ntis_policy_brief_1.pdf

21

Use of New Information and Communication Technologies in the Health Sector: The Legal Reason for Differences Between International and European Standards

Lina Williatte

No one would deny that new information and communication technologies are everywhere in the health-care sector today—in hospitals, clinics, and doctors' offices. Doctors are becoming increasingly connected with their patients, sometimes daily, such as when a patient needs round-the-clock medical monitoring.

However, the ongoing computerization of the sector has developed at different rates in different countries. Anglo-Saxon countries are leading the way. This is especially true in the USA where American data-processing companies are vying for lucrative contracts for the processing of health data. Meanwhile, in Europe, and in France in particular, countries are debating the consequences of restrictive regulations that make it difficult to get permission to access, process, or store patient data.

L. Williatte (✉)
Research Center C3RD (Research Centre on Relationships between Risk and Law), Department of Law, Catholic University of Lille, Lille, France
Bar of Lille, Lille, France
e-mail: Lina.WILLIATTE@univ-catholille.fr

© The Author(s) 2017   **381**
L. Menvielle et al. (eds.), *The Digitization of Healthcare*,
DOI 10.1057/978-1-349-95173-4_21

The undeniable differences between these two approaches are poorly understood by, for example, European physicians who want to undertake scientific research in the same way as their Anglo-Saxon colleagues, but who feel constrained by opaque standards. Similarly, there is the relatively recent "quantified self" movement, whose practitioners use wearable technology as a health-coaching and remote medical-coaching tool that requires accessing and sharing information. Even industrial companies and start-ups are often forced to relocate their projects because different countries impose different normative constraints.

The actors in this sector are right to denounce these fundamental differences between standards that, depending on their severity, can hinder economic competitiveness.

Nevertheless, a legal interpretation can help explain how the divergence of these normative systems is rooted in a country's legislative and policy traditions and how they approach the protection of fundamental rights.

Differences in these traditions account for the various normative frameworks that have been created for both (i) the development of "telehealth" and "eHealth" medical practices and services, and (ii) the processing and use of the data that is generated by these technologies.

21.1 Telehealth: Differing Content in Identical Legal and Regulatory Standards

An in-depth analysis of the health sectors in different nations reveals that the words used to define actions have different meanings in different countries. Therefore, even when their classification is identical, an action performed in one country may fall into a different regulatory category in another, thus rendering it non-compliant. This divergence in terminology also gives rise to diversity in normative designs. The terms telemedicine and eHealth are a good example of this problem.

21.1.1 Words Have Different Meanings in Different Countries and the Regulatory Context Is Divergent

21.1.1.1 Telehealth: One Word, Many Meanings

These days, one cannot argue with the fact that many of the terms, expressions, and words that are used to classify actions, trends, and practices related to telehealth are used indifferently and without defining their meaning.

This is evidenced by a recent study (Gallois and Rauly 2015, p. 121). The study found that while the terms telemedicine, telehealth, and eHealth are used synonymously (Crigger 2006, p. 12), in certain cases they refer to a remote medical practice and define a treatment (Chandra et al. 2013, p. 111). In other cases, they refer to the tools themselves, serving as an intermediary for a service (Kerleau and Pelletier-Fleury 2002, p. 207) or health-related e-commerce (Kirsch 2002, p. 106).

The various meanings given to these terms often have an impact on the applicable legal framework and the way in which particular actions are interpreted by legislators. To illustrate this, we will look at the example of telemedicine.

21.1.2 Telemedicine Versus eHealth: The Peculiarity of the Situation in France

21.1.2.1 Telehealth: Does It Refer to the Provision of Health Care or a Medical Action?

The two concepts of telemedicine are traditionally opposed: in developed countries, telemedicine is essentially clinical, while in developing countries, telemedicine is more informational (Simon 2013). Clinical telemedicine is understood to be "a professional activity in which physicians and other medical staff use digital telecommunication systems to perform medical procedures on patients in order to treat diseases" (Croels 2006, p. 38). Conversely, informational telemedicine is defined as "an interactive audiovisual communication service which organizes the dissemination of medical knowledge and protocols regarding the treatment of diseases and the provision of care, in order to support and improve medical practices" (quoted in Simon 2013).

21.1.2.2 The French Concept of Telemedicine

France was one of the first countries in the world to create a legal basis for the practice of telemedicine through two pieces of legislation: law 2009-879, known as the HPST (hospitals, patients, health [santé], and territories) law, which came into effect on July 21, 2009, and its October 19, 2010 implementing decree.

These two fundamental texts take a clinical approach to telemedicine, defining it as a medical action performed by a health professional using information and communication technologies. In other words, telemedicine in France refers to medical actions performed by health professionals, the efficacy of which have been recognized, thus guaranteeing the best health and safety conditions in terms of proven medical knowledge.

Other countries use a different definition, characterizing telemedicine as a "health service" that is provided using new technologies. While this difference is minimal, it is fundamental in that one refers to a medical action and the other refers to the provision of a medical service. This difference in terminology gives rise to different regulatory frameworks. In France, for example, telemedicine has its own specific legal framework while, at the European level, telemedicine falls under the more general category of eHealth.[1]

21.1.2.3 Telemedicine as a Medical Action Performed Using Information and Communications Technologies

The French concept of telemedicine defines it as a medical action performed by a health professional using information and communication technologies. This principle is confirmed by article R6316-1 of the

---

[1] This is the case in Germany. For example, see "L'e-santé en Allemagne" (www.science-alle magne.fr/fr/wp-content/uploads/2016/03/E-santé-en-Allemagne.pdf).

Code de la santé publique (CSP), which was created by the October 2010 decree. That article states that telemedicine refers to "Medical actions performed at a distance using devices enabled with information and communication technologies."

The 2010 decree also defines a number of telemedicine-related actions:

- Remote consulting: enabling medical professionals to provide patients with a remote consultation.
- Remote expertise: enabling medical professionals to contact one or more other medical professionals remotely to ask for medical information and opinions associated with the care of a patient.
- Remote medical monitoring: enabling medical professionals to remotely interpret the data resulting from the medical monitoring of a patient and, if required, to make decisions regarding the patient's care.
- Remote medical assistance: enabling one medical professional to remotely assist another health professional in performing a procedure.
- The response of a physician provided within the framework of the medical regulations (e.g., Service d'Aide Médicale d'Urgence [emergency medical assistance service]).

What is more, to be acceptable, activities within the telemedicine sector must take into account any deficiencies in health-care offerings due to the insularity and geographical isolation of the location (CSP article L6316–1). In addition, these activities must be the subject of a national program or a local contract[2] put in place with the regional health authority, such as l'Agence Régionale de Santé.

It is clear that telemedicine in France is treated by legislators as a tool that must meet patient care needs in terms of organization, continuity, permanence, and safety. It is also treated as a fundamental medical activity for which the conditions of practice must be specified and respected.

---

[2] This could be a "targets and resources" multi-year contract (contrat pluri annuel d'objectifs et de moyens [CPOM]) entered into by the director of a health establishment and a local health authority, or it could be a "health care coordination and quality-enhancement contract" (contrat d'amélioration de la qualité et de la coordination des soins [CAQCS]) between the project holder and the health insurer.

In this regard, the 2010 decree requires project holders to respect the fundamental rights of the patient and obliges health-care professionals to comply with all legal requirements relating to the practice of medicine, as provided for under public health codes and the medical code of ethics. Even if these activities have been assessed and checked by the authorities in their entirety, liabilities may arise in some cases.[3]

These regulatory constraints thus form an overall picture of telemedicine that differs from that of eHealth services.

21.1.2.4 eHealth: Providing a Service Using Information and Communication Technologies

eHealth is defined as providing a health-care service where the provider is connected to the consumer. From a wider perspective, this refers mostly to personal services associated with the information society, particularly services sold through e-commerce.

The number of possible applications are many: remote monitoring of patients being treated at home by health-care providers, remote medical advisory services, health-care information available through the Internet, and health and well-being coaching (e.g., mobile health). Because these applications are defined as services and not as medical actions, they are excluded from France's 2010 decree. Instead, they fall under the June 8, 2000 European directive known as the Electronic Commerce Directive, which was adopted in France on June 21, 2004, under a law on digital trust.[4]

Unlike the legislation that applies to telemedicine practices, the normative constraints of this directive have less to do with organizational requirements, permanence, and safety of care, and more to do with freedom of movement, ease of implementation, and the remuneration of services.

This means that the implementation of eHealth projects is easier, as there are fewer regulatory constraints. Does this mean that how the state

---

[3] This mainly pertains to civil liability resulting from injuries suffered by a patient when a standard is not complied with, or the liability of the individual health-care professional involved.

[4] The goal of this legislation was to create a legal framework overseeing the free circulation of services in the information society.

views the practice of telemedicine depends on its financial development and attractiveness? The answer is clearly yes, although it should be added that the quality of the practice and the services provided to the patient arise from these constraints. The provision of remote medical advice, for example, is a demonstration of this.

In France, the remote provision of medical advice is not covered by the 2010 decree; therefore, it does not qualify as a telemedicine activity. This is because the system does not provide protection for the customer, nor does it protect the professional providing the service.

Remote advisory services fall under the category of commercial eHealth services, which do more to protect the rights of consumers than they do the rights of patients. This is also reciprocally true for health professionals, who are categorized as service providers subject to the restrictions that apply to e-commerce.

The applicable standard therefore depends on the level of protection of the actors and those benefiting from the medical services and activities performed using information and communications technologies. As a result, normative constraints become a strategic development tool. The data-processing aspect arising from these new practices can also be used as an example.

21.2 The Regulatory Framework Covering Data

In all its various applications, telehealth services that make use of information and communication technologies intrinsically generate large amounts of data in the form of raw information concerning an activity or a specific condition at a given moment.

21.2.1 The Value of Data

The data generated by telehealth services has a certain amount of value. Some have compared data to oil: worthless in its raw form, it becomes valuable only after it is refined.[5] For example, processed data can provide valuable information about user profiles.

Once this data has been obtained and processed, it can be used to create effective and efficient marketing campaigns through the use of targeting and profiling techniques. In the health sector, data processing can provide warnings about certain diseases and can guide the public health policies of the future.

The use of this data is now at the heart of many challenges: economic, financial, and societal. But, more than any other, legal challenges impact our fundamental rights.

Personal information is one component of the individual's right to privacy. This right is one of the most highly protected in our legal systems. In particular, it is enshrined in Article 12 of the Universal Declaration on Human Rights, and included in Article 8 of the European Convention on Human Rights. In France, it is contained in Article 9 of the Civil Code and was assigned constitutional value in 1995.

The collection and processing of data is, therefore, not easy. However, a cursory glance at the applicable norms in certain countries demonstrates, once again, that the ability to "process" data depends on how a country interprets the legislation governing the right to individual privacy, and the way it prioritizes the challenges posed by (a) the data itself and (b) the added dimension of dealing with health-care data.

21.2.2 Protecting Data in a Variety of Ways While Extracting Meaning

21.2.2.1 Applicable European Standards

At the European level, the problems associated with protecting the right to privacy are covered in the recommendations issued by the Organisation for Economic Co-operation and Development (OECD)

---

[5] Comparison made by Clive Humby at the 2006 Association of National Advertisers senior marketers summit, Kellogg School of Management: http://ana.blogs.com/maestros/2006/11/data_is_the_new.html.

on September 23, 1980. These recommendations confirmed the need to harmonize the legislation implemented by the member countries to lower barriers to the free circulation of personal information.

Following this recommendation, in 1981 the Council of Europe adopted Treaty 108, which protects the privacy of individuals in terms of the automated processing of personal data. This recommendation gave rise in 1995 to the European Data Protection Directive, which became law in France on August 6, 2004, amending an earlier law from 1978.

Despite the existence of these legal measures, differing practices can still be observed in some countries. It was not until the European Union (EU) Charter of Fundamental Rights came into existence that the protection of personal data became enshrined in EU legislation.

The Treaty on the European Union and the Treaty on the Functioning of the European Union adopted the Lisbon Treaty, which was signed on December 13, 2007, at the Intergovernmental Conference in Nice. The Lisbon Treaty conferred a binding effect, the entirety of which was enshrined in the European Regulation of April 27, 2016, which concerns the protection of individuals regarding the processing and unrestricted circulation of personal data.[6]

While it is true that each member nation of the EU is now subject to the same legislation, it is also true that its interpretation within national law varies somewhat, creating disparities in its application.

21.2.2.2 Common Obligations Not Subject to Diverging Interpretation by the Member Countries

Convergent Interpretation of the Concepts

This relates mainly to the collection of data. Collection poses no problems in terms of how it is defined within the national legislation of the member countries, thus guaranteeing harmonization of application. In this case, the principles state that data can be collected only

---

[6] This regulation is directly applicable in the national legislation of the member countries and supersedes Directive 95/46/EC, which has now been ruled obsolete.

- for legitimate, predefined purposes;
- when it is relevant and up to date, and proportional to the goals of processing; and
- when it is kept only for the period required for processing.

21.2.2.3 Common Obligations That Are Subject to Interpretation by the Member Countries

These differing interpretations mainly affect the information itself and the consent given by the person whose information is being collected for processing.

The Rights of Owners to Control the Use of Their Personal Information
Considering that data is a vital component of the individual right to privacy, the European directive, and now the European regulation, require the consent of the person whose information is being collected. This consent must be informed, and the entity processing the data must inform its owner as explicitly and exhaustively as possible. If consent is not informed, then it is considered null and void, and the processing of the data is prohibited. This is exactly the point that is now under discussion.

More precisely, the discussion revolves around the rights of individuals to control their data. The challenge becomes greater the more restrictive these rights become, as the entity responsible for processing the data has greater requirements to obtain consent and to provide information. Conversely, the less restrictive these rights are, the greater freedom the processor has to collect information and make use of it.

The UK and Germany
Inconsistencies can still be seen between these countries. In the UK, as in Germany,[7] experiments such as the MyData project[8] enable users to be

---

[7] On December 15, 1983, the Constitutional Court of Germany issued an order enshrining the principle of informational self-determination in law, that is, the ability of an individual to decide, in principle, on the communication and use of personal information belonging to them.

[8] See the MyData project, www.cil.cnrs.fr/CIL/spip.php?article1645.

the managers of their own data and to negotiate the value of their information with companies.

The MyData project is intended to further the concept of open data. It posits that it is up to the person in question to decide how their data can be used. The individual is therefore considered a consumer and solely empowered to decide on the use of their data (in keeping with the principles of self-determination and empowerment). From a legal point of view, this enshrines in law the idea that individuals have a right of ownership over their data.

This idea is heavily influenced by the approach taken in the USA and undoubtedly gives data controllers more freedom to act, based on the principle that, once individuals have been properly informed about why the data will be processed, they have authorized its collection and processing and have ceded their rights over it.

France

This principle is fundamentally different from that in force in France, where data falls under individual privacy rights and, therefore, under the legal regime for subjective rights. Subjective rights are rights that are inherent to individuals; they form the basis for all rights protecting individual privacy. From a legal point of view, this is an extra-patrimonial right that the holder cannot waive or cede to another. This means that, even if the holder has given permission for their data to be used, the individual still has the right to withdraw consent at any time. If this right is infringed, the data-processing controller may be held liable.

21.2.2.4 Differences That Need to Be Mitigated in View of the European Regulation Adopted in 2016

The difference in these approaches means the severity of restrictions differs widely, depending on the country where one is located. However, with the adoption of the 2016 European General Data Protection Regulation, which strengthens the rights of individuals and facilitates the exercising of these rights, these differences may be mitigated, at least for the member countries of the EU.

The regulation requires that an individual's consent or refusal be obtained after they have been provided with clear, understandable, and easily accessible information about the use of their data. It is up to the data controller to prove that it has obtained consent, and the regulation requires that this proof be unambiguously demonstrable.

These same controllers must put in place all of the technical and organizational measures required to protect personal information by default during the design of the product or service (privacy by design).

If these obligations are breached and an individual suffers material or moral damages as a result, they have the right to claim compensation for these damages from the data controller.

Lastly, the inclusion in the regulation of the right to portability of personal information may lead to the French approach being adopted, making data an offshoot of the private lives of individuals. In that case, the goal would be to give everyone the right to recover the data they have provided in a way that makes it easily reusable and, if required, the right to transfer it to a third party afterwards. This approach implies that the individual remains the owner of the data and never cedes their rights over it.

While the European regulation obliges the member countries to use the same design to protect personal data within the EU, there remain several diverging aspects to be resolved at the international level, particularly regarding the legal status of connected objects (devices) that generate data.

21.2.3 Processing of Health-Care Data: A Fundamental Challenge Subject to a Variety of Normative Constraints

21.2.3.1 Health-Care Data: Processing Is Strictly Regulated

Both in Europe and abroad, health-care data is classified as being sensitive, which is why, in principle, its processing is not authorized. This is only "in principle," as *sensu largo* (broad) interpretations of the concept suggest that, once again, there are biases that may prevent all individuals from being guaranteed the same level of protection for their health data. To illustrate this concept, we could use the examples of connected objects and mobile applications dedicated to well-being and health.

21.2.3.2 The Problems Associated with Connected Objects

The connected objects that are now used in health-care environments represent a real legal challenge given the invasive nature of the data collected and its legal classification. Currently, the legal classification of the data obtained with connected tools is under scrutiny because the legal distinction between "health" and "well-being" data is weak.

The World Health Organization (WHO) defines health as being a state of complete physical, mental, and social well-being, not simply an absence of disease or infirmity (WHO 1994). Both European and international standards on the protection of personal information clearly distinguish between "health" data, which is classified as being sensitive and the processing of which is prohibited, with exceptions, and "well-being" data, the processing of which is authorized under certain conditions.

The example of connected weigh scales illustrates this point. Such scales are traditionally used to weigh something or someone. In the context of connected objects, this purpose may satisfy a number of needs. For example, they may be used by a person to monitor their weight. In that hypothesis, the data generated will be collected and protected as personal information. Conversely, the scales may be used to check a person's weight while monitoring a certain medical pathology. In that case, the health information collected would be classified as sensitive data.

21.2.3.3 Distinguishing Between Personal Information and Health Data Using the Applicable Regulations in an Individual Country

Personal information and health data are therefore covered by different legal systems. Personal information can be collected as long as the fundamental principles of protection are respected.[9] Health data can be collected only under a restrictive set of conditions[10] and with the permission of the national regulatory body[11] for the territory where the collection and processing take place.

Given the differing normative constraints to which the two categories of data are subject, manufacturers of a connected object may be sorely tempted to state, before it is marketed, that the object is purely for well-being purposes and absolutely not for health purposes. This temptation exists in all territories, but new modalities of regulation are emerging to address this issue. The first such initiatives have been implemented across the Atlantic, particularly in the USA.

21.2.3.4 The Example of the USA

In the USA, the processing of health data in the medical sector is governed by the Health Insurance Portability and Accountability Act (HIPAA) of 1996. This federal law requires the US Food and Drug Administration (FDA) to create guidelines for the regulation of connected devices and mobile applications.

Given its mandate and the context in which data is collected, the FDA decided in September 2013 that its guidelines would not include mobile applications that enable people to record, follow up, or make individual decisions. Conversely, when the data is likely to be presented to the public

---

[9] In particular, this is provided for under France's 1978 law on computers and liberties. That law covered the following aspects: prior provision of accurate information; explicit consent; that the data must have a legitimate and predefined purpose, be relevant and up to date, and have a limited conservation time; and that appropriate security measures to protect the data be in place.

[10] Article 8 II of the law on computers and liberties specifies that the conditions for the collecting and processing of data are to be monitored by the Commission nationale de l'informatique et des libertés, particularly regarding: security and information; treatment required to safeguard human life; treatments carried out by physicians or biologists for preventive medical purposes, medical diagnostics, and administration of care and treatment; medical research; public interest; the processing of data that has been anonymized; and the handling of assessments of health-care practices.

[11] In France, this is the Commission nationale de l'informatique et des libertés (CNIL) (national commission on computers and liberties).

(e.g., for use in diagnostics and prevention), the FDA reserves the right to revise its decision, even a posteriori (later).

At the same time, the FDA's mandate also involves raising awareness within target publics and making recommendations to developers of mobile applications, for example, requiring them to obtain explicit consent from the user when health data is collected, and to provide clear information on how it will be used.

A code of conduct for handling information belonging to users of mobile applications is currently in the test phase. Those covered by the code of conduct will be required to publish a notice detailing their practices for protecting personal information. Simplified labels will be used to inform consumers about the categories of data being processed and who will receive the data (CNIL 2014).

21.2.3.5 The Situation in Europe

In Europe, the legislation that applies to medical devices is used as the basis for regulations governing connected objects and mobile applications.[12] It is up to the manufacturer to follow the assessment procedures regarding the conformity of medical devices so as to identify the risks of non-conformity and, therefore, the procedure to be followed with the appropriate authorities. (In France, this is the Agence Nationale de Sécurité du Médicament et des Produits de Santé [ANSM] [National Agency for the Safety of Medicines and Health Products]).

However, this legislation contains no special provisions to protect the data collected by devices, which has resulted in a number of self-regulation initiatives. The same is true in Germany, which has successfully developed a quality label for health applications that is available to the public. It has also developed a code of conduct that requires compliance with a set of fundamental regulations regarding the protection of data and that limits the use of data to the purpose of the application (CNIL 2014).

---

[12] Directive 90/385/EEC applies to active implantable medical devices, 93/42/EEC applies to medical devices, and 98/79/EEC applies to in-vitro diagnostic medical devices.

In France, legislators gave the ANSM responsibility for developing the French guidelines. In doing so, the agency decided that controls apply if the application or device collecting the data is capable of assisting health professionals in making a diagnosis. Unfortunately, the manufacturer must voluntarily classify its software as forming part of a medical device; if it does not, the controls do not apply (Serma Ingenierie 2016).

21.3 Conclusion

21.3.1 An Impact Study Needs to Be Conducted That Examines How Domestic "Digital Markets" Legislation Affects a Country's Economic Development

It should be noted that the legislation that applies to new health technologies still needs to evolve to better protect the fundamental rights of individuals and to guarantee harmonization of regulatory constraints for entrepreneurs. These are the constraints that have been accused of handicapping the future economic development of those countries that are committed to the protection of fundamental rights; however, this allegation, which has been presented as evidence by many, has never been scientifically demonstrated.

It would be useful to conduct a study on the economic impacts of normative constraints on the development of markets associated with telehealth. If such a study were to verify the detrimental economic effects of these constraints, then being forced to choose between economic benefit and protecting the rights of individuals would not represent a solution. The ideal situation would be international harmonization that guarantees equality of both rights and opportunities.

References

Chandra, A., C.E. Pettry, and D.P. Paul. "Telemedicine from a Macromarketing Viewpoint: A Critical Evaluation with Proposed Licensing Strategies," In *Government Policy and Program Impacts on Technology Development, Transfer* and *Commercialization, International Perspectives,* ed. Kimball P. Marshall et al. (New York: Routledge, 2013), 111–136.

CNIL. "Le corps, nouvel objet connecté du 'quantified self' à la M-santé: les nouveaux territoires de la mise en données du monde," *Cahiers IP, Innovation & Prospective,* no. 2 (May, 2014): 45–48.

Cons. "Const," *Official Journal,* no. 95–352 DC (January 18, 1995). January 21, 1995.

Council of Europe Treaty Series no. 108. "Signed in Strasbourg, France," January 28, 1981.

Crigger, B. "E-medicine: Policy to Shape the Future of Health Care," *Hastings Center Report* 36, no. 1 (2006): 12–13. doi: 10.1353/hcr.2006.0006.

Croels, M., "Le droit des obligations à l'épreuve de la telemedicine," *Presses Universitaires d'Aix-Marseille* (2006): 38, quoted in P. Simon, "La télémédecine ce n'est pas du e-commerce," *Association Nationale de Telemédecine* and the *Ordre national des médecins* (November 22, 2013): www.automesure.com/library/pdf/telemedecine_e-commerce_2013.pdf.

European Union. "Charter of Fundamental Rights of the European Union," December 18, 2000, C 364/1.

European Union Regulation 2016/679. *Official Journal of the European Union,* no. L119 (May 4, 2016): 1.

Gallois, F., and A. Rauly, "Télémédecine et comparaison des systèmes de santé: questionnements méthodologiques" (paper presented at Colloque international Recherche & Régulation, Paris, France, June 10–12, 2015).

Kerleau, M., and N. Pelletier-Fleury. "Restructuring of the Health Care System and the Diffusion of Telemedicine," *The European Journal of Health Economics* 3, no. 3 (September 2002): 207–214, doi: 10.1007/s10198-002-0131-8.

Kirsch, G. "The Business of eHealth," *Journal of Medical Marketing: Device, Diagnostic and Pharmaceutical Marketing* 2, no. 2 (January 1, 2002): 106–110, doi: 10.1057/palgrave.jmm.5040062.

"Law no. 2004–801 of August 6, 2004 on the protection of individuals with regards to the processing of personal information, amending law no. 78–17 of January 6, 1978 on computers, files and liberties," *Journal officiel de la République française,* no. 182 (August 7, 2004). 14063.

Loi no. 2010–1229 *Official Journal,* no. 0245 (October 21, 2010).

Serma Ingenierie, Study on Safety of Medical Devices Software (France, 2016). http://ansm.sante.fr/var/ansm_site/storage/original/application/1f3c81fac07 d6e659075a332c5d00431.pdf.

Simon, P. "La télémédecine ce n'est pas du e-commerce," *Association Nationale de Telemédecine and the Ordre national des médecins* (November 22, 2013): www.automesure.com/library/pdf/ telemedecine_e-commerce_2013.pdf.

"Treaty on European Union and the Treaty on the Functioning of the European Union," *Official Journal*, no. C326 (October 26, 2012): 001–0390.

World Health Organization, "The Declaration on the Promotion of Patients' Rights in Europe," (presented at the WHO European Consultation on the Rights of Patients, Amsterdam, June 28, 1994).

22

What Ethics for Telemedicine?

Alain Loute and Jean-Philippe Cobbaut

The development mode of digital technology innovations in the health-care field has been qualified by some as "hyperactive inaction," which refers to an anarchic multiplication of experimentations and tools resulting in a certain inability to set up useful, desired, and sustainable products (Rialle et al. 2014, our translation). Actually, the development of such a field as telemedicine sparks the emergence of new techniques, new practices, and new organizations. It simultaneously involves new challenges regarding security, the respect for individual rights, the way medical activity is organized, together with economic and access challenges, as well as eventual public policy ones.

Through the example of telemedicine and of the related French regulations, we would like to show, from an ethical point of view, in

A. Loute (✉) · J.-P. Cobbaut
Center for Medical Ethics, ETHICS (Experiments, Transhumanism, Human Interactions, Care & Society – EA 7446), Catholic University of Lille, Lille, France
e-mail: alain.loute@univ-catholille.fr;
Jean-Philippe.COBBAUT@univ-catholille.fr

© The Author(s) 2017
L. Menvielle et al. (eds.), *The Digitization of Healthcare*,
DOI 10.1057/978-1-349-95173-4_22

399

what way the development of telemedicine requires a *reflexive governance* (Lenoble and Maesschalck 2011) permitting to match the various challenges induced by that developing field.

Although telemedicine has already been granted recognition through the August 13, 2004/2004–810 law related to the reform of the state health insurance, its true recognition results from the HPST law (Hospital, Patients, Health and Territory July 21, 2009 law), which recognizes and defines this practice. In the course of the following year, the October 19, 2010 decree states the characteristics required by the regulation of the practice. It defines its outlines, sets out the rules to be complied with regard to the patient and specifies the framework within which telemedicine projects have to be organized in agreement with regional authorities.

This framework is now very controversial and we believe that it reveals the challenges of a normatively controlled development of telemedicine. In this contribution, we would like to raise the question of a telemedicine ethics. Does telemedicine raise new ethical questions? Generally speaking, does the emergence of digitalization technology involve a new way of considering ethics, deontology, or the law in the field of health care?

Our reflection here will not be empirical: We are not analyzing a concrete telemedicine project. Neither are we giving any comprehensive list of the possible ethical challenges of telemedicine. Our questioning will be mainly methodological and epistemological: *How* should the ethical question be formulated regarding this development?

22.1 A Few Telemedicine Development Challenges

As a first point, we will try to identify the major lines of the questioning raised by the deployment of telemedicine, with no pretentions to being exhaustive. These lines are more or less directly linked to the technology through which this deployment is made possible. Others are related to the insertion of that technology into medical practice and more besides, namely related to the territorial redeployment permitted by those new devices. The deployment of those projects raises security issues, access concerns, as well as questions related to the transformation of the medical relationship.

22.1.1 Challenges Directly Related to Information Technologies

The use of digital technology is likely to give rise to several issues "directly" linked to the technique itself, such as security, the respect for private life, and the protection of data property. The notion of "directly related to technology" is to be relativized in so far as the technological aspect will never be freed from social aspects. The fact that we always have to make do with "socio-technical devices" in that field will be a major connecting thread throughout this contribution.

22.1.1.1 Security Concerns with Telemedicine Systems

Even though telemedicine relies on advanced and high-precision technologies, we should not minimize the fact that telemedicine devices rely on a relatively complex technical infrastructure which may include one or several quality internet connections, computers, cameras, screens, software programs, and medical devices that have to be adapted, compatible, and high-performance ones altogether. Each of the items included in the system, as well as the whole system itself, have to operate optimally to ensure the quality and sustainability of health-care deliveries. Thus, the functionality, quality, and security of the technical system are the minimal requirements for the implementation of telemedicine. The fulfillment of those first requirements is likely to raise all the more complex questions regarding coordination and responsibilities as these devices are seen as performing articulations between technical objects and human organizations.

22.1.1.2 Private Life and Personal Data Protection

Then, since what can be defined as socio-technical devices are widely relying on information and communication technologies, patients' confidentiality, and privacy questions are obviously raised. For some authors, the evolutions of the medical practice such as telemedicine "generate inevitable threats to privacy and medical confidentiality" (Béranger et al. 2012, p. 87, our translation). These authors remind us that "any IT system is violable—all the more so as it is connected to a network" (Béranger et al. 2012, p. 88, our translation).

22.1.1.3 The Data Property Question

Finally, and as an extension of the questions related to the protection of private life, the accumulation of data permitted by those devices raises the question of the property and use of the data, for instance for research purposes. There again, the question cannot be seen as fully new but its intensity and spatial dimension together with the multiplication of the actors involved in those systems will undoubtedly raise questions specifically pertaining to this field.

22.1.2 Impact on the Health-Care Relationship

The specificity of those devices (intensity of the technical presence, virtual relationship, multiplication of actors) are likely to transform the health-care relationship. Telemedicine may not bring fundamental alterations to the health-care relationship but it will transform a certain number of procedures in such a way that they will induce several challenges.

22.1.2.1 Is Medicine Being Dehumanized?

Many criticisms in the related literature evoke "the fear of human care and support being dehumanized" (Rialle et al. 2014, p. 135, our translation), the fear of a "depersonalization" of medicine. Let us first make it clear that some ethical approaches would see the cause of that dehumanization in the technique itself. Indeed, those approaches emphasize an opposition between the technical medical gesture (cure) and a caring gesture (care) performed without any preset measurement or protocol. Besides, according to Mark Coeckelbergh, "technology has always mediated care practices" (Coeckelbergh 2013) Medical practices have always been both a technical and human compound likely to have dehumanizing effects as well as humanizing ones. The complexity of those systems is undoubtedly likely to multiply those effects which may rather originate from the technique itself or even from its use. Truth be told, we should rather say it comes from some sort of articulation between both. Then the major challenge mainly lies in our capacity to identify those effects and challenges. To this end, the emergence of questions about those techniques has to be made possible. In that respect, a full series of questions can be identified, which will obviously be raised throughout the deployment of those systems:

> Any physician knows the importance of body language, bearings and hesitations during a face-to-face consultation. Telecom links and terminal units can only transmit and reproduce non-verbal messages imperfectly. Neither can they reproduce the numerous factors contributing to the ambiance in a healthcare room (people's breathing, smells, the quality of the air, draughts, the participants' stress), or what is going on beyond the scope of the cameras or microphones. (Parizel et al. 2013, p. 466, our translation)

In his work, *Télémédecine, Enjeux et pratiques*, Pierre Simon emphasizes that "the climate of confidence that sets up between a patient and their physician during their first meeting is based on the warmth of a direct face-to-face relationship, which can only be reproduced by a videoconference distance consultation" (Simon 2015, p. 79, our translation). This is the reason why, according to him, a teleconsultation cannot substitute for a face-to-face primary consultation, except if it is justified in the interest of the patient. Telemedicine thus urges to rethink the conditions of the building up and sustainability of the confidence-based bonds between a physician and their patient.

According to some approaches, the relationship established by telemedicine seems to even question the possibility of a therapeutic relationship. According to Pierre Simon, again, the reason why the development of psychiatric teleconsultations has not been the same in France as in other countries is to be seen in "the mark left in French approaches in psychiatry by the influence of Pr. Jacques Lacan, a Freudian psychiatrist and psychoanalyst. According to psychoanalysts, the face-to-face contact is indispensable, which excludes any psychiatric care solution in which the physician speaks to their patient through a videoconference system" (Simon 2015, p. 50–51, our translation).

The recent opinion of the European Group on Ethics in Science and New Technologies (EGE)—*The Ethical Implications of New Health Technologies and Citizen Participation* (opinion n°29), puts forward the ambivalent effects of those new technologies (p. 31): On the one hand, they establish novel possibilities for sick persons and patients to exchange and share experiences; on the other hand, information technologies are likely to transform a rich and diversified experience into pieces of information that are transmittable but isolated and disconnected from the person's social context and biography.

22.1.2.2   Participation, Empowerment, or Responsibilization?

The EGE puts forward other impacts of those technologies on the health-care relationship. One of the key ideas of their opinion is that digital care new technologies contribute toward a "participatory turn" in the health-care field: Patients are participants in their own care continuum. They even mention an *empowerment* of the patient. Some eHealth applications or systems enable the patients to get an easier access to their medical data and to better control them. Telemedicine is likely to broaden some sick persons' range of possible options. Thus, some chronic care patients may be able to stay at home, while hospitalization would have been the only option. One may even think that on the basis of the data that the patient will get in real time, he or she will be able to make certain decision concerning his/her treatment.

But the patient's "empowerment" may also result in their excessive "responsibilization," which means that the responsibility of their situation may be more and more incumbent to them. Thus, "GEE warns against a deviation of health-related autonomy," "which either corresponds to a more general transfer of the public health services' responsibility towards individuals or let them bear the responsibility inherent in the risk as well as the regulating capacity, and which would eventually pave the way for lower standards and quality of the care delivered" (European Group on Ethics in Science and New Technologies 2015, p. 68).

This risk is relatively hard to control. However, the way the French regulation is set up reveals this issue. Indeed, the October-2010 decree[1] includes two sections: one referring to the patient's participation in those plans and the other one concerning their implementation and organization. This decree shows the need for what currently relies on the concept of governance, that is, "the setting up and running of institutions" (considered not so much as "organizations" but rather as the laws of the game), defining the various actors and their prerogatives in a cooperation to the benefit of the community as well as in the resolution of conflicts that are likely to occur.[2] A governance of those plans requires both to make a participation of the concerned actors—namely patients—possible and a capacity to take into account the questions raised within the scope of the "lifetime" of those telemedicine plans permitting to correct the issues faced, and even to revise the regulation framework by taking the purposes of that kind of plans into consideration. Such an approach could undoubtedly make up for a response

---

[1] Décret n°2010–1229 du 19 octobre 2010 relatif à la télémédecine, *JORF* n° 02045 du 21 octobre (2010).

[2] Groupe de travail n°5, *Renforcement de la contribution de l'Europe à la gouvernance mondiale*, Rapport du Groupe, Pilote: R. Madelin, mai (2001).

both to the deviation consisting in over-responsibilizing the patients and to the dichotomy between telemedicine plans and more traditional medical practices which may induce discriminating effects.

22.1.3   Toward a Territorial Justice for Health Care?

In the current difficult economic context, with the decreasing number of physicians and their geographical distribution over the territory being sometimes far from optimal, with the growing demand in health care due to the aging population and the increase in chronic diseases, the questions of the access to health care and of its equity are more and more acutely raised. Telemedicine can be a response to this situation in terms of quality, efficiency, and equity altogether.

In a way, telemedicine represents a real possibility to redeploy the health-care system. That redeployment raises a full series of questions: What health-care distributive justice can be expected with technologies such as telemedicine? Can the fact of responding to a "medical desert" situation by just implementing a telemedicine system be considered as an equitable response to unequally treated areas and territories in terms of a health-care offer? How can the digital exclusion issue be avoided? How can the "digital divide" factor (regarding gender social backgrounds, ages...) be abolished? How can quality, efficiency, and justice be altogether guaranteed in telemedicine projects? The deployment of telemedicine definitely raises questions in terms of distributive justice.

The specificity of the questioning in this respect lies certainly in the entanglement of the questionings related to equity and access to health care with those regarding security, quality, and efficiency, all those questions being raised by an evolution which, according to some people, changes the way to do medicine completely. Considering these challenges, we understand why the French 2010-decree envisages to formalize telemedicine projects by contract with the public authorities. As a matter of fact, one may realize that this decree more generally reflects the various questions that we have raised here, including security, health-care relationship, and equity. In spite of the number and diversity of the questions raised by telemedicine, is it still possible to consider that the development of telemedicine raises novel ethical questions? Does the development of telemedicine require a renewed approach of ethics and regulation?

22.2 What Response from Ethics?

As seen above, the law seems to take the questions raised by the development of telemedicine into account to a large extent. In France the 2009-law and its application decree define telemedicine, state the rules to be complied with by its specific health-care relationship, and makes allowance for those questions through a kind of contractualization tending to ensure a balanced deployment of this new medical practice procedure. Likewise, the deontological codes and bioethical principles seem to provide responses to the questions we have raised below. According to several authors, telemedicine would not require a new definition of ethical principles or of the deontological code which may need to be reinterpreted at the very most.

So, according to Pierre Simon,

> clinical telemedicine is a medical activity. It refers to ethical principles stated in the Code de la Santé Publique (public health code) which has integrated the deontological code and the decree concerning telemedicine. Four pillars of medical ethics apply to clinical telemedicine: the benevolence principle, the non-maleficence principle, the justice principle and the respect for the patient's autonomy. (. . .) The telemedicine activity is a medical activity as any other one and therefore does not require the implementation of a specific judicial system. The French national council of the medical order (Conseil National de l'Ordre des Médecins— CNOM) considered, in 2009, that the practice of telemedicine could refer to the Code of medical deontology. (Simon 2015, p. 111, our translation)

Actually, the French National Council of the Medical Order (CNOM) stipulate, in their 2009 recommendations regarding telemedicine, that "the patients' rights are imperative with telemedicine just as they are with the current healthcare framework" (Conseil National de l'Ordre des Médecins 2009, our translation). Likewise, "the physicians' obligations within the context of telemedicine practices results from the application of the common rules of medical deontology. However, these rules acquire a new dimension due to the necessity for their interpretation to be stipulated in this application" (Conseil National de l'Ordre des Médecins 2009, p. 10). The CNOM's position is then clear: "The use of information and communication technologies in the exercise of telemedicine does not justify a specific provision in the code of medical deontology since all the principles in force regarding the usual form of medical practice remain relevant and apply" (Conseil National de l'Ordre des Médecins 2009, p. 12).

The European Council of Medical Orders emphasizes in their turn that the use of information and communication technologies within the exercise of telemedicine does not impose specific provisions either in the medical deontology codes of the member states of the European Union or in the European chart of medical ethics since the ethical and deontological principles in force remain relevant and apply to that medical practice.

In an article entitled *"Ethique, jurisprudence et télémédecine"* (Ethics, jurisprudence and telemedicine), Jean-Louis Arné seems to have the same approach: "Telemedicine must comply with the ethical and jurisprudential rules stated in the code of deontology which manages the medical act on the whole (. . .). Physicians' general duties, as stated in the code of deontology, must apply to telemedicine (. . .)." However, he admits that "a new technology should not necessarily generate a new legal or ethical theory. It may yet lead to a redefinition or a new clarification of the preexisting principles, in order to adapt them to the new situations induced by the emerging technology" (Arné 2014, p. 124, our translation). Among the specificities induced by telemedicine, Jean-Louis Arné points out the following:

- The specificity of information and consent-related questions induced by telemedicine
- The traceability of the medical report
- Specific responsibility-related questions, particularly the duties and responsibilities induced by technology, etc.

22.3 Limits of the Principlist Approach

How should the various views mentioned above be envisaged? It is clear that the major principles of bioethics find their application in front of the various challenges induced by the development of telemedicine, a brief outline of which has been presented in this article. These challenges have been identified within the scope of the development of modern medicine. As maintained by their promoters (Beauchamp and Childress 2001), they find their origin in contemporary morals (and somewhat recapitulate the history of the ethical line of thought by joining the consideration of an adequacy, a patient-centered, and a plurality principles) but they are also related to the major polarities of the medical practice (respect for the patient, health-care quality and humaneness, as well as the fact that any care delivery is to fit within the scope of a system aiming at matching the needs of the whole population equitably).

Even if these principles may reveal some orientations that converge with Hippocratic medicine principles, they definitely emerge from the contemporary society in which the central ethical challenge is to join efficiency and respect for the individual, all of which being considered from an individual (autonomy) or a collective (justice) point of view. Here are the definite cardinal challenges of medicine.

Does this mean that there is nothing new under the sun? To start with, as seen above, the ethics of principles clearly originates from a contemporary situation. This reveals in itself a form of the topicality of this ethics permitting to explain its relevance as regards medicine. Does it mean we should not go any further? No, it does not. Because principlism somewhat bears the mark of what constitutes the current criticism against this paradigm. Indeed, if the principles are relevant today, it is because they bear the mark of their contextual characteristic or, in other words, because they depend on the circumstances of justice. To put it even differently, today's core issue of ethics or of the regulation is *application*. The current major criticisms against principlism are precisely about the application modes of the principles: How to arbitrate between those principles? According to what method? Who is to apply those principles? All those questions not only show the incomplete characteristic of the principlist approach but also, above all, the obliteration of the contextual challenges and of the consecutive evolution of those contextual dimensions through this approach or through the various regulation modes it inspires. The sector called *clinical ethics*, as a sector of excellence for the application of ethics to clinical situations, clearly reveals that problematics as related to the application and to the conditions of application. This problematics has given rise to an abundant literature in the field of ethical foundations as well as in the way clinical ethics is practiced (Doucet 1996; Cobbaut 2007).

Besides, in the problematics we are dealing with, the evolution imparted by telemedicine to the medical practice alters the medical practice context and modes rather substantially. In that respect, we find the very recent report produced by the Conseil National du Numérique (French National Council for Digital Technologies) "Health, a social good in a digital society" very significant (Conseil National du Numérique 2015). According to the authors of the report, the new uses of digital technology change the traditional patterns drastically and give rise to new possibilities, whether it be a more democratized health-care system and patients' better empowerment or to an individualization and increased health social inequalities as well as to a commodification of health care endangering our universal and solidarity-based health social pattern. In the context of a more and more extensive access to knowledge, actors, and infrastructures together with individualized innovative health services leading to patients' increased responsibility and greater power over their health, health becomes a social good more than it has ever been, as well as the object of a political, social, and economic project requiring a three-front fight for the activation of health fundamental rights, for the reassertion of solidarity and universality values and the creation of spaces allowing each individual to be a tributary and a stake-holder of health as a social good.

According to this report, these perspectives are made possible in so far as the importance of information and of the matter of access to information, together with the new ways to cure and to take care

are taken into account (Conseil National du Numérique 2015, p. 98 and following). The point is not only to integrate the new temporality induced by digital medicine and leading to a more preventive, predictive, and individualized medicine but also to get to a networking medicine (Conseil National du Numérique 2015, p. 105) that requires to experiment new cooperative medicine methods mobilizing the health-care staff, the persons cared for, as well as the natural caregivers and requiring both a human support and new fields of expertise.

The perspectives launched by this report urge to think about a new way to envisage the governance of that development (Conseil National du Numérique 2015, p. 7). The report actually insists on the fact that "the conservation of the principles of our health pattern (quality, solidarity, universality) relies on our ability to turn digital technology into a leverage in the service of a consistent and ambitious political, social and economic project" (Conseil National du Numérique 2015, p. 8, our translation) relying on the determination of "the conditions for a management of health as a common good (Ostrom 1990) of which each individual is a tributary and depositary" (Conseil National du Numérique 2015, p. 9, our translation). The report thus comes into line with the notion of governance in as much as it opens to a pragmatic turn promoting the aspect of a cooperative action induced in the networking process and based essentially on the new possibilities to compare, exchange, and exert a mutual control in the search for solutions (Lenoble and Maesschalck 2011). Governance must refer to a type of action conducted by the society on itself, mediatized by the transformation of the collective relation to the norm, or, to put it differently, to an approach focused on the involvement power of the various actors concerned in their cooperation to a representation of the common good, that is, to making a living-together world possible (2014).

In the case of telemedicine, such an ethical and political governance certainly requires to pay attention to the technical object itself, to the temporality of its processes and to the many actors involved in those processes. We would like to conclude this article with the consideration of those aspects which, in our views, constitute major challenges around which a reflection is to be conducted on a reflexive governance of telemedicine and with regard to which the inadequacy of principlism seems to be obvious.

22.4 Methodological Marks for a Reflexive Governance of Telemedicine

22.4.1 Taking the Technical Object into Account

First of all, we do find essential to integrate the technical object itself into the reflection on an ethical and political governance of telemedicine. Indeed, according to many authors, technical objects are not neutral instruments which would just be the support of our actions. According to such a view, the technical object is likely to be approached only indirectly, through the new obligations to which it may give rise or the redistribution of the responsibilities it may involve among healthcare actors. Yet, for many authors, technical objects are far from being neutral or passive instruments. They rather represent true "mediators of our actions." For Bruno Latour, norms "are delegated" to systems which impose moral involvements through their own structure and the way they operate. Some authors even pretend that certain values are "incarnated" in the design of technical devices: "the values of a design-team members, even those who have not had a say in top level decisions, often shape a project in significant ways as it moves through the design process. Beliefs and commitments, and ethnic, economic, and disciplinary training and education, may frame their perspectives, preferences, and design tendencies, resulting eventually in features that affects the values embodied in particular system" (Flanagan et al. 2008). Going beyond principlism by taking a broader account of the contextual conditions required by the application of an ethics of telemedicine first relies on a consideration of the values that the technical object can materialize.

22.4.2   Taking the Temporality of the Development of a Telemedicine Project into Account

A second methodological precept that we feel is important to express is to be careful of the temporal dimension of the ethical assessment that can be conducted on the practice of telemedicine and that is likely to be overshadowed by the focalization on just the deontological code of medicine and the four medical ethics principles. As Xavier Guchet emphasizes it in his book about nanotechnologies, technical mediations are characterized by a non-topicality aspect: "Technical mediation inscribes the non-topicality of a past but also of a future into human communities" (Guchet 2014, p. 21, our translation). Talking about the non-topicality of techniques means referring to the fact that they open, make way for temporalities other than the temporality of the present of our interactions. Indeed, "techniques always bring with themselves the world in which they will make sense" (Guchet 2014, p. 22, our translation). They give birth to the power to transform reality.

It is thus essential not to confine oneself to an ethical judgment that would be limited to the *present* of a medical procedure. One should both take its consequences into account and feel concerned by the *downstream* part of the project but also consider the way the object is being designed, that is, the upstream part of the project.

Opening the reflection on the upstream process of a telemedicine project is the point because, as mentioned by Andrew Feenberg technique is characterized by a form of "interpretative flexibility." It may be submitted to interpretation forms in the same way as a poetical writing or a work of art. To put it differently, "technical functions are not pregiven but are discovered in the course of development and use" (Feenberg 1999, p. 86). It necessarily follows that "there are always viable technical alternatives that might have been developed in place of the successful one" (Feenberg 1999, p. 10). Making a telemedicine ethics effective thus implies the opening of a refereeing procedure between the principles of bioethics concerning the temporality of technical developments.

Opening the reflection on the downstream process of a telemedicine project. According to the philosophers of technology, it is important to consider the fact that a technique shapes the world into which it is inserted. But the effects are not directly visible. They often remain unspotted before the *aftermath* they provoke and on the basis of which ethical views are established. The point is then also to organize an "ethical reflection in the future," despite the real methodological and epistemological difficulty of an anticipation of the effects of a technique. More fundamentally, some authors have drawn our attention on the fact that new technologies are part of a real "techno-scientific promise-based regime," to quote the words used by Pierre-Benoît Joly in one of his articles (Joly 2010). Today's technological innovation takes place in a promise-based economy structuring all actors' expectations. Many speeches produced along with the scientific development suggest a staging of the evolution of technologies. *Roadmaps* anticipate the capacities of technologies and those scenarios can be seen as strategies aiming at "confiscating from citizens the mastery of the time in which the problems arose" (Guchet 2014, p. 19, our translation). This opening onto the future may then take the form of imposed "*scenarios*" which, rather than opening to a reflection about the potentiality of the technical development, are more likely to *naturalize* the technological development.

22.4.3 Taking the Multitude of Actors into Account

Finally, the opening onto whether the downstream or the upstream side of a telemedicine procedure necessarily requires to consider the related actors. A multitude of actors are involved in all the various stages of the development of a telemedicine project: industrial actors, health-care professionals, patients, public authority representatives, etc. Does not the development of an ethical reflection on telemedicine, in terms of security, accessibility, or of the alteration of the medical relationship, imply the consideration of the plurality and diversity of the actors concerned by a telemedicine project? Can this reflection be conducted without involving those actors in some way or other? Besides, an author such as Pierre Simon, stipulates that "telemedicine is not a therapeutic innovation. *It is an innovation within the organization of care*" (Simon 2015, p. 129, our translation). This point is a reminder of how telemedicine ethics must always be understood as an "organizational ethics" too.

In this article, we have concerned ourselves with some of the ethical challenges of the development of telemedicine by showing that if the law, the code of medical deontology and the principles of medical ethics delimit the legitimate framework within which telemedicine must be exerted, the matter concerning the application of that deontological framework or of the principles at the heart of medical ethics cannot be approached satisfactorily on the sole basis of a principlist methodology. Principlism overshadows many of the contextual challenges involved in the application of a telemedicine ethics. In our views, overstepping those limits seems to require the development of a telemedicine project and a commitment of telemedicine actors.

References

Arné, J. L. "Ethique, jurisprudence et télémédecine," *Bulletin De L'académie Nationale De Médecine* 198(1) 2014: 119–130, 124.

Beauchamp, T. L., and J. F. Childress. *Principles of Biomedical Ethics*. Oxford: Oxford University Press, 2001.

Béranger, J., H. Servy, P. Le Coz, and P. Tervé. "Télémédecine sous X ? Pourquoi prolonger cette protection individuelle historique?," *Les Tribunes De La Santé* 35(2) 2012: 83–96.

Cobbaut, J.-Ph. Bioéthique et réflexivité, Thèse de doctorat, Université Catholique de Louvain, 2007, 317 p.

Coeckelbergh, M. "E-care as craftsmanship: virtuous work, skilled engagement, and information technology in health care," *Medicine Health Care and Philosophy* 16(4) 2013: 807–816.

Conseil National de l'Ordre des Médecins *Télémédecine, Les préconisations du Conseil National de l'Ordre des Médecins*, 2009: 9, 2010, https://www.conseil-national.medecin.fr/sites/default/files/telemedecine2009.pdf.

Conseil National du Numérique, La santé, Bien commun de la société numérique, Rapport remis à la Ministre des Affaires Sociales, de la Santé et des Droits des femmes, octobre 2015.

Décret n°2010–1229 du 19 octobre 2010 relatif à la télémédecine, *JORF* n° 02045 du 21 octobre 2010.

Doucet, H. *Au pays de la bioéthique, L'éthique biomédicale aux Etats-Unis*. Genève: Labor et Fides, 1996.

European Group on Ethics in Science and New Technologies, *Ethics of New Health Technologies and Citizen Participation*, Opinion 29, 2015, https://ec. europa.eu/research/ege/pdf/opinion-29_ege.pdf#view=fit&pagemode= none.

Feenberg, A. *Questioning Technology*. London/New York: Routledge, 1999.

Flanagan, M., D. C. Howe, and H. Nissenbaum (2008). Embodying Values in Technology: Theory and Practice, in J. Van Den Hoven and J. Weckert, *Information Technology and Moral Philosophy*, 335, Cambridge: Cambridge University Press.

Groupe de travail n°5 *Renforcement de la contribution de l'Europe à la gouvernance mondiale*. Rapport du Groupe, Pilote: R. Madelin, mai, 2001.

Guchet, X. *Philosophie des nanotechnologies*. Paris: Hermann, 2014.

Joly, P-B. "On the Economics of Techno-scientific Promises," In *Débordements. Mélanges offerts à Michel Callon*, ed. Madeleine Akrich *et alii*. (Paris: Presse des Mines, 2010), 203–222.

Lenoble, J., and M. Maesschalck, *Démocratie, droit et gouvernance*, Sherbrooke, Les éditions Revue de Droit à l'Universté de Sherbrooke, 2011, 396 p.

Maesschalck, M. *La cause du sujet*. Brussels: Peter Lang, 2014, 255 p.

Ostrom, E. *Governing the Commons. The Evolution of Institutions for Collective Action*. New York: Cambridge University Press, 1990, 280 p.

Parizel, E., P. Marrel, and R. Wallstein "La télémédecine en questions," *Études* 419 2013: 461–472.

Rialle, V, P Rumeau, C Ollivet, J Sablier, and C. Hervé "Télémédecine et gérontechnologie pour la maladie d'Alzheimer: Nécessité d'un pilotage international par l'éthique," *Journal International De Bioéthique*, 25(3), 2014: 127–145.

Simon, P. *Télémédecine, Enjeux et pratiques*. Brignais: Le Coudrier, 2015.

23

The New Paradigms of Connected Health—What Impacts and Effects on Organizational Models of Care Structures?

Pierre Simon

23.1 Introduction

Our health-care system changes paradigms with the digital revolution. First, communication between the different health stakeholders is faster and can become more frequent. There are more territorial or regional boundaries. Co-operation between health professionals is done as much on a national basis as an international one. The democratization of the Internet in the 2000s as well as the arrival of the first smartphone in 2007 have gradually changed citizens' behaviour vis-à-vis their health. Connected health increasingly integrates into traditional medicine and requires that health professionals review their method of communication with patients, on the one hand, and on the other hand, to innovate in organizations and professional practices to optimize the coordination of care and promote knowledge sharing. Digital health increases professional skills and knowledge of patients. It thus allows for organizations

P. Simon (✉)
Past-President of the French Society of TeleMedicine (SFT), Paris, France
e-mail: pierre.simon22@gmail.com

© The Author(s) 2017
L. Menvielle et al. (eds.), *The Digitization of Healthcare*,
DOI 10.1057/978-1-349-95173-4_23

to innovate how they deliver health care and to better understand the demand for care of patients with chronic diseases. Medicine of the twenty-first century will be more personalized than that of the twentieth century, thanks to digital health care.

23.2 Background: The Gradual Onset of Health-Connected Concepts

Connected health designates all areas where information and communications technology (ICT) are put at the disposal of health services, a concept defined by the World Health Organization (WHO) in 1945 as: "[health is] a state of complete, physical, well-being, mental and social well-being and not merely the absence of disease or infirmity." The tools and support of connected health are the subject of a very promising market, where we find video conferencing systems, robots, tele-health platforms, mobile or Web health applications, connected objects, to name a few examples. All these devices and connected health objects enable remote communication, measure and/or analyse a person's activities or parameters with regard to their welfare or care.

23.2.1 Telemedicine

Most developed countries have begun practising telemedicine since the early 2000s with the advent of the democratization of the Internet. The USA, Canada, Norway and France were pioneers in this area.

In 1920, *the USA* was the first to develop a solution for medical tele-assistance for medical situations occurring on commercial boats as well as trans-Atlantic voyages. This solution used a telephone link. In 1950, the first image transfer occurred in Philadelphia. In 1955, the Psychiatric Institute of Nebraska was endowed with a closed-circuit television network and in 1959, offered the first psychiatric tele-consultation. In 1964, a bilateral link was established with the Norfolk Hospital, also located in Nebraska, but 180 km away. In 1967, a Medical Liaison link in telemedicine was created between the Boston Airport and the Massachusetts General hospital to deliver care to airport employees and travellers in transit. In 1973, the USA organized the first international congress of telemedicine with the conclusion that the technology was not yet sufficiently developed to allow an acceptable telemedicine practice. These technological problems were partly resolved in the 1980s, which allowed the development of telemedicine in the USA.

While five telemedicine development programmes were already recorded in 1990, their number increased to 110 in 1995 and surpassed 800 by 2007. The programme launched by the US Department of Health at the beginning of the 1990s, included four types of applications: teleconsultation in isolated areas, particularly rural areas, continuing medical education, medical IT and tele-robotics. These three applications fall within informative tele-health or telemedicine. Clinical telemedicine has grown rapidly in rural hospitals. The most frequent applications were tele-cardiology and orthopaedics.

Presently, more than 40 US states use telemedicine and the related programmes cover more than 70 health-care networks. Tele-consultation using the Internet has greatly expanded, thanks to the MyMD health-care programme, for example, which offers anyone the opportunity to access a tele-consultation 24 hours a day, 7 days a week, for $4 per minute. The service prioritizes those consultations which are considered urgent.

Canada developed telemedicine in the mid-1980s. Considering the size of its territory, a video-conference solution was adopted by health authorities, which connected the provinces.

In 1995, government of New Brunswick launched a vast development project for cardiology telemedicine (remote monitoring of cardiac insufficiencies at home), in nephrology (remote monitoring of dialysis patients in satellite areas), emergency care (specialized tele-consultations before an eventual transfer to a referred hospital), paediatrics, psychiatry and radiology. The province, as well as the federal government, financed this programme and followed its realization. In Québec, the catastrophic health condition of Inuits living in the Far North was a powerful stimulator for the development of telemedicine at the beginning of the

1990s. Most video conferencing systems have been developed for obstetrics, paediatrics and paediatric cardiology. The paediatric tele-cardiology network, established in 1992, brought together 18 paediatric cardiologists in four university hospitals and three surgical referral centres. In 1998, the four university hospitals in Québec were linked to the 32 general hospitals of the Quebec tele-health children's network. A remote monitoring network for diabetic retinopathy for retinography was set up at the University of Montreal during the same time. Similarly, in 1998, a socio-sanitary tele-communications network (RSST), totally secure, and serving 36 sites, was set up.

The reform of the health system in the early 2000s led to the creation of four large health regions (integrated, academic health regions or RUIS) and 95 local health services networks and social services (RLSSSS). This reform allowed telemedicine to have one, single point of entry regarding their projects and funding at the university hospital responsible in that region.

Norway developed telemedicine at the end of the 1980s. In 1987, it established a research and expertise centre for integrated care and telemedicine (*Nasjonalt senter for Samhandling og Telemedisin* or *NST, Norwegian Centre for Integrated Care and Telemedicine*) which its mission being to collect, produce and disseminate knowledge on telemedicine services, both in Norway and internationally. The *NST* centre also had to ensure the proper integration of telemedicine services in the Norwegian health system. The NST has become an internationally recognized organization, referenced by the WHO. The Tromsø (*Tromsø Telemedicine Laboratory* or *TTL*) centre was created in 2006 to develop basic research on technological innovations and health caregivers. These two structures are designed to help improve the production of care and reduce the growing financial burden of the Norwegian health system.

Since its creation, the *NST* has developed a multi-disciplinary approach, which includes medical, technological, statistical, sociological and economic. Its employees are experts in medicine, technology and social sciences. Its activities are divided into three main areas: co-operation with the hospital, e-learning and technology solutions for patients. *NST*'s annual budget was 8 million Euros in 2011, have of which was provided by the Norwegian State and half by external funding and grants from the WHO, the European Commission, industries, etc.

Several telemedicine projects have marked the *NST*'s action, such as the FUNNKe project. This pilot project has been the main objective of implementing telemedicine services in northern Norway and the results were to ensure the deployment of other telemedicine projects on a national level. This project was in line with the national strategy on eHealth and with the 2009 "Coordination Reform." From an organizational point of view, the FUNNKe project is characterized by the establishment of a telemedicine service platform dedicated to the health sector in order to foster interdisciplinary co-operation. Among the services offered is the transmission of lab analysis results, tele-dialysis and remote, dermatology consultations. For now, the development of telemedicine in Norway is limited to isolated regions in the Great North and the western part of the country.

During this same period in Norway, at the end of the 1980s, telemedicine was developed in the midi-Pyrenees region *of France*, following the initiative of Professor Louis Lareng, anaesthesiologist at the University Hospital in Toulouse. This visionary medical doctor, who created the EMS in 1969, founded the European Telemedicine Institute in 1989 and initiated new medical practices between the Toulouse University Hospital and health establishments in the midi-Pyrenees region. He set up specialized tele-consultations between the Rangueil Hospital in Toulouse and Rodez Combarel Hospital, thus allowing patients access to specialized care in remote areas and avoiding transferring to the University Hospital if it was not necessary. The experiment was then extended to all public and private institutions in the region (more than 60 in 2009). Specialized tele-experts and tele-consultations were managed both technically and medically, by the Toulouse University Hospital telemedicine service by a public interest group (PIG). The midi-Pyrenees telemedicine GIP thus has the largest and oldest French experience in tele-consultation and tele-expertise between health institutions and prisons, as well as in tele-neuroradiology. The record of over 20 years of operation has shown convincing results, which include the 50% of transfers to the Toulouse University Hospital.

Telemedicine has been practised in France since the mid-1990s. As in most countries, it was developed in the hospitals. It was in 1999 that the minister in charge of health became interested in telemedicine. DHOS sent a circular to the directors of the regional hospital agencies (RHA) encouraging them to develop telemedicine solutions between hospitals in order to create a new dynamic between those in a same health region. This desire is reflected in the Territory of Hospital Groupings (GHT), created in January 2016 by the health modernization law, which included a shared territory medical project to be structured by telemedicine in order to create a progressive health-care programme for people in the territory: the right care in the right place and at the right price [1].

Clinical and informative telemedicine was defined by the WHO in 1998.

"*Clinical telemedicine* is a professional activity which implements a means of digital communication which allows doctors and other medical staff to perform remote, medical procedures for patients."

"*Informative telemedicine* is an interactive, audio-visual, communication service that organizes the dissemination of medical knowledge and care protocols for the sick and their care in order to support and improve medical activity."

In other words, clinical telemedicine corresponds to medical practice at a distance through technological means, while informative telemedicine refers to the dissemination of knowledge and information to improve medical activity through these means. These two forms of telemedicine are not subject to the same rules and regulations. Informative telemedicine services benefits are governed by the competition law, which falls under the European directives of 1998 and 2000 regarding e-commerce [2, 3]; clinical telemedicine practices fall within the national health law, which is specific to each state.

23.2.2 eHealth

If telemedicine is clinical medicine practised from a distance by medical health professionals, eHealth and tele-health in Europe refers to commercial services in health information systems which correspond to informative telemedicine.

The concept of eHealth was introduced by English IT [4] specialists to replace telemedicine, resulting in national eHealth based on the economic logic of e-commerce. France launched the "e-Health 2000" plan in 1999, with endowed public funds of 25 million Euros. The plan was to develop a new health system through the use of the Internet and wireline and wireless networks. This public funding helped industrial investment with regard to the connected tools, most of which favoured the circulation of medical data, especially in emergencies. This first French eHealth plan failed for several reasons, including the lack of sustainable funding, the non-involvement of health professionals in the construction and especially the non-inclusion of the French, clinical, medical culture [5]. In addition to this analysis, the report advocated a vision of clinical medicine upon which its development should be based on the academic practices of health professionals rather than on a hypothetical change that these digital tools would bring about.

In 2009, industrial environments dealing with digital health and health information systems wanted a new approach to eHealth and tele-health. The desire to development an industrial logic, they requested that the Prime Minister prepare a second report to launch "an eco-friendly five-year plan for the deployment of tele-health in France". Written by a computer expert, the plan was submitted to the Minister of Health in late 2009 [6], a recognized leader in developing telemedicine, the only application of connected health included in the Code of Public Health. Very quickly, in January 2011, the public authorities launched the national deployment of telemedicine strategy, which was ratified by the Cabinet on June 9, 2011. This strategy targeted the improvement of access to care in the metropolis and overseas for cutting imagery for thrombolysis in acute ischemic stroke, for psychiatric and dermatological care for prisoners, for home care of chronic patients (heart failure, kidney failure, respiratory failure, diabetes) in order to prevent inevitable hospitalizations, to encourage specialized consultations in medical-social establishments, especially for handicapped persons.

Digital can positively impact the public health sectors: more efficient operation of health facilities and primary care facilities, better management of medical consultations in primary care and hospitalization days in the health facilities, prevention of any medical oversights regarding consultations by generating automatic reminders by email or SMS. Various software programmes today manage the availability of hospital beds in a health region according to the pathologies, which ensures a more appropriate management of patients. Efficiency may increase 20 to 30% in a digital hospital as compared to a conventional hospital [7].

23.2.3 The Example of Digital Applied to the Epidemiology of Infectious Diseases

The consequences of international trade and travel on the dynamics of infectious diseases are of interest to researchers today. In a world of "nomads," where more than one and a half million travellers are in the air at all times, viruses have more opportunities to be spread worldwide by migrating with business or leisure travellers, thus contributing to the development of new, infectious epidemics, which occur more frequently. The increasing connectivity of our world promotes the transmission of viruses . . . . In addition, the introduction of new travel destinations to places previously "disconnected", also contributes to this dissemination and anchoring of the pathogen. For example, air transportation between South America, Africa and Southeast Asia, now interconnects the continental tropics, where the presence of infectious diseases is very high and where transmission of pathogens lasts throughout the year. In addition, the increase in the volume of world travel via sea freight and air cargo can spread contaminated, commercial products or accidentally introduce new infectious disease carriers such as mosquitoes.

Despite the importance of geographical location to the epidemiology of infectious diseases, the effects of global mobility on genetic diversity and molecular evolution of pathogens are underestimated and are only now being understood. The host mobility patterns can be particularly important for RNA viruses. Even if they do not survive for long outside of their environment, there are genetic mutations. Viruses rapidly change and are able to quickly adapt to modify vector specificity or sensitivity to drugs or immune responses.

Several technological solutions have emerged over the last decade and have stimulated research in this area. First was the advent of geolocation systems, which were less expensive, mobile and adaptable to epidemiological studies that assess the impact of infectious diseases and their prevalence in the population, especially when combined with geographic information systems and electronic communication. In addition, a lot of data (e.g., high-resolution satellite images) representing environmental, infrastructural and socio-economic variables are now available which is capable of determining the dynamics of the viral disease. Particular importance is given to new perspectives of human mobility generated by the analysis of data sets that describe the overall context of travel and the number of passengers, ticket movements, calls from mobile phones, etc. The treatment of this data by powerful analysers has the ability to understand human mobility. It has been used to track the mobility of populations due to disasters and predict the dynamics of infectious diseases as well as to plan for strategies to eliminate the diseases. At the same time as the geolocation progress of diseases, the sequence analysis of viral genes has progressed considerably. Thus, the pathogen genomes are now more likely to be collected with the sampling locations and dates of the samples. More than 100,000 virus sequences are accessible for the most-studied viruses, such as HIV1 and Influenza A (human influenza). Powerful computers are able to analyse this data. A digital epidemiology is being born, based on health-connected data. The use of digital tools has allowed us to better understand the Ebola epidemic, and the evolution of epidemics related to Chikungunya or those of the HIV1 epidemic [8].

23.2.4 Mobile Health and Connected Devices

Defined in 2005 as the use of emerging, mobile communications in public health by Prof. Robert Istepanian [9], the term "Mobile Health" (m-health) is used to describe the practice of medicine using mobile communication technology: mobile phones, tablet computers and PDAs (personal digital assistants), etc. While these technologies have existed for twenty years, it was the emergence of the smartphone in 2007 that helped develop this new concept of mobile health, which currently has tens of millions of health-connected objects and mobile applications worldwide.

Hundreds of mobile health projects have emerged in Africa and South Asia over the past decade in order to improve health in the following situations: monitoring or pregnant women, support for people with AIDS in order that they participate more in their treatment, monitoring of epidemics, etc. In African countries, the Gustav-Praekelt Foundation of South Africa supported many projects [10]. Ten years after its marketing, the smartphone is widely distributed throughout the world and represents an essential tool for developing mobile digital health.

In 2015, there were over 150 million health-connected devices and mobile applications worldwide. The question of reliability and safety of these devices and applications arises in every country. The authorities would like to entrust to an independent company the evaluation of these mobile health tools. The question is important, as shown in the recent study of mobile applications in calculating insulin doses in patients with diabetes [11]. The authors conducted a systematic review of all mobile, ultra-dose insulin calculators distributed on the market in English and which are available on iOS and Android. In 2014, 46 calculators were available and evaluated. The calculation of the ultra-rapid insulin dose to be injected is made based on the estimated intake of dietary carbohydrates and blood glucose measurement prior to a meal. The results of this study show that 59% of 46 mobile applications reported a clinical non-liability clause in case of error; only 30% knew the formula. Even worse, most involved a risk of error in the result display, which can induce deterioration in the patient's health rather than improving it. Of the 46 applications, a single one, running on iOS, was validated without any error risk to the patient [11].

23.3 The Main Evolutions of the Health System in the Twenty-First Century

The emergence of these new paradigms since the early 2000s challenges traditional health system organizations. The new health-connected paradigms strengthen organizations and traditional business practices that were previously insufficient, particularly in the management of patients with chronic diseases. They can also help to create new practices and professional organizations, including more personalized medicine. The health-care offer has evolved with the coming of the digital age. While the usual public health programmes take into account the need to care for a population seeking adequate offers via health care, health and welfare institutions, and primary care facilities, connected health, especially mobile, develops new approaches vis-à-vis health populations. This application does not always correspond to a care need, but may fall under the wishes of the citizens to better protect their health and prevent disease by controlling upstream risks. Figure 23.1 summarizes the new paradigms that impact our health system.

23.3.1 The Evolution of Health Demand in the Population

Citizens' handling of their own care is probably the thing that has changed the most in the health-care system at the beginning of the twenty-first century. The health system of the twentieth century was inefficient in the field of prevention of chronic, degenerative diseases, especially cardiovascular. Environmental risk factors for these diseases often amplify the generic predisposition, which has been clarified by numerous epidemiological studies. The commercialization of the first smartphone launched the concept of mobile health. Many connected

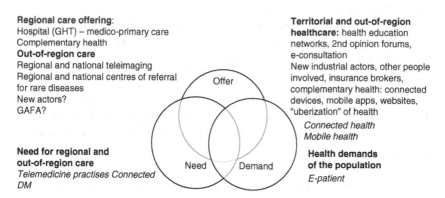

Fig. 23.1 The new paradigms which have impacted our twenty-first-century health system (GAFA: Google, Apple, Facebook, Amazon)

devices and mobile applications were developed to propose a new approach to health, base, on particular, on personal quantification of certain parameters, such as physical activity to improve their well-being and prevent or master the disease risk factors of cardiovascular disease, for example. The measurement of daily physical activity with a pedometer connected to a smartphone and a mobile application measuring daily calorie and weight loss enable people to master some of the cardiovascular risk factors. If physical activity produces beneficial effects on a patient's weight and blood pressure, the sustainability of the positive effects of this physical activity on blood pressure control has not been demonstrated [12].

In the twenty-first century, a society characterized by a need to "immediacy," a greater number of citizens want to access health information in time. So much so, that many countries are trying to respond by developing forums for custom, medical e-consultations [13]. This new medical practice is intended to guide the caller in their primary care plan. A doctor from an e-consultation forum allows a first filter on demand and may direct the patient to the nearest medical facility in case of an emergency or be able to reassure the patient, give health advice or prescribe a medication which will be sent directly to the pharmacist nearest the place where the caller is located. The personalized medical e-consultation helps prevent unjustified visits to the emergency room and ensures greater fluidity in primary care consultations.

With the use of connected devices and mobile health applications, the patient becomes an "e-patient," that is to say, a proactive actor of his health. He can communicate with health-care professionals via email or SMS and health professionals can communicate in the same way with the patient as part of a secure relationship, as is the case in France [14]. These digital tools are used to monitor post-operative patients [15] or patients with chronic diseases, in addition to face-to-face consultations [16]. However, in an exhaustive literature review published in 2012, no clinical impact was demonstrated by the use of e-mail in the coordination of care between health professionals and patients [17].

23.3.2 The Care Needed Is Increasing in the Chronic Disease Era

In the mid-1980s, the prevalence of chronic, degenerative diseases has become greater than that of acute diseases. Longer life expectancy in developed countries is associated with chronic, degenerative diseases. Life expectancy beyond 65 years of age has increased on all continents and the number of people affected will double by 2050 [18]. Chronic diseases are increasing the need for care and, consequently, the State's health expenditure, including those related to [19] hospitalizations. Finally, urbanization generates growth in areas where there is a little number of public services available, including the presence of doctors. In France in 2015, nearly 80% of the population lived in urban areas, representing 21.5% of the surface of the national territory [20].

It is in this societal context that connected-health tools appeared on the market in the early 2000s. Telemedicine then developed in order to improve access to care, primarily in rural areas where most elderly people with chronic diseases live [5]; the intended goal is to create new care organizations to improve the management of patients with chronic diseases, to keep them at home as long as possible or in alternative (for dependent elderly and nursing homes), through tele-monitoring that prevents complications and hospitalizations.

Clinical telemedicine is intended to complement the traditional medical expense due to new medical practices such as tele-consultation, tele-expertise, medical helpline, medical monitoring and personal medical e-consultations [21]. In late 2008, the European Commission asked member States to define telemedicine and the conditions for its inclusion in their national law. France, who wanted to develop practices in this area, has followed this recommendation and created, July 21, 2009, the Hospital, Patients, Health and Territory Law (HPST) as well as the October 19, 2010, decree to implement it. New health-care organizations can thus be implemented.

Tele-consultation by medical specialists in nursing homes and with the elderly and disabled, allows them to avoid some difficult transfers. It complements the face-to-face support when it comes to regular monitoring of chronic diseases. It also applied to monitoring, particularly for common chronic and complex wounds in these institutions [22]. It is also recommended for remote areas, with no doctor nearby, provided it be planned and organized in conjunction with the medical centre where the doctor is. Tele-consultation may not be suitable for emergency situations that usually require a physical examination. Finally, it must first be done by consultation, exceptionally, for any telemedicine practise, as the patient must first give their consent after being informed of the benefits and risks of this practice. Tele-consultations, which are organized by some private forums, are more a matter of personal medical e-consultation than a real tele-consultation, especially when it comes to a caller with a chronic illness and the forum doctor does not have access to their medical file.

Tele-expertise is probably the activity which will structure new medical organizations the most. Medicine has achieved a level of scientific complexity over the years, which partly explains the phenomenon of medical specialization, even hyper specialization, which has been prominent over the last thirty years.

Tele-expertise in primary care is used to prevent the patient from having to travel to where the specialist is. The attending physician directly consults his specialist colleague on the basis of the medical file or elements of a transferred image which is accompanied by clinical information (transfer of a skin lesion photo, an electrocardiogram, etc.). This way of proceeding is what the new generation of general practitioners wants during their internship and they have become accustomed to working this way when consulting their hospital colleagues about their patients. For primary care, getting advice quickly facilitates the coordination of care and avoids a break in continuity. Young doctors realized that telemedicine allowed them to bypass waiting times which could be several months. The tele-expertise with the expert saves time, enhances the role of the doctor and strengthens interprofessional co-operation. In addition, knowledge sharing between GPs and specialists has the advantage of mutually improving skills. This is the learning function of telemedicine. Doctors practising in aggregate (multi-professional nursing homes or health centres) or individual practices are now in favour of these tele-expertises in areas such as dermatology, cardiology, nephrology and neurology.

The practice of regular tele-expertise, or even daily, between public and private health facilities, is an inevitable organizational change to improve the care of patients in a health area or region. The practice of tele-expertise between institutions allows a better management of a patient's hospitalization and avoids unnecessary transfers to the hospital or referral centre, in 50% of cases, in addition to correcting one out of every five lost opportunities [23]. It also enables emergency services to avoid certain hospitalizations, especially those in need of a specialist's opinion. With tele-expertise, the advice comes at the cost of 14 or 28 euros, depending on the service, rather than 2,000 or 3,000 euros for two or three days of hospitalization. The tele-expertise requested of specialists by emergency physicians in small health facilities provides a first, expert opinion, the development of a therapeutic programme, the recommendation not to hospitalize the patient or to transfer the patient, as well as set up an outpatient consultation.

The tele-stroke inter-institutional programme has provided emergency facilities services with a telemedicine device that can be used for other specialized tele-expertises. In the hospital sector, specialists of the institution chosen must incorporate into their services time for this service in order to be able to offer it to smaller, regional establishments. The 135 Hospital Groups Territory (GHT) created in France on July 1, 2016, by the law modernizing health [24] to replace the 850 public health institutions, will develop a medical project which will be shared by all its members. Telemedicine will facilitate the medical operation between member GHT institutions.

Tele-radiology, which is the second possibility, targets a second opinion with a radiologist imagery specialist. The French Society of Radiology believes that a specialist in radiology, who is authorized to give a second opinion, must meet at least two criteria in a list of expertise. In addition, the expert radiologist must perform in connection with or belong to a referral centre.

Remote medical monitoring complements the tele-monitoring service which manufacturers who market forums offer as well as connected medical devices (DMC). The doctor may follow certain clinical indicators and/or biological factors in patients with chronic diseases. The forums and tele-monitoring of DMCs can be versatile and integrate several indicators that allow the doctor to make the most appropriate choice for monitoring the patient. It is preferable that these DMC forums take into account the fact that a patient can accumulate several chronic pathologies during aging.

Asynchronous tele-monitoring corresponds to the collection of clinical data (automatically or by the patient) which is analysed by the attending physician in real-time (a few days or weeks) or at the next face-to-face consultation. This monitoring method, which has been used the most during the past decade, has shown no significant impact on morbidity and mortality of patients with chronic diseases, especially in patients who are tele-followed at home for heart failure [25, 26]. Several studies have now shown that the most severe patients, frequently hospitalized, benefit more from tele-monitoring systems than stable patients. The asynchronous nature of the monitoring and the absence of disease severity criteria are the two factors that explain the randomized controlled study results that show no significant difference between home treatment by monitoring and decision-making using care via regular consultations [27].

Synchronous medical tele-monitoring is for patients who have one or more severe chronic diseases causing frequent hospitalizations. It requires an operational monitoring forum 24 hours a day, seven days a week. Most large, clinical studies which are randomly controlled with regard to tele-monitoring in heart failure patients, use this type of remote monitoring that is, immediate intervention of a health professional in case of severe alarm [28], and incorporate the most severe forms of the disease [29].

Medical tele-assistance concerns mostly non-medical, health professionals (pharmacists, paramedics) who participate in a structured course of care through telemedicine, under the responsibility of a medical, health professional. Medical Helpline allows a doctor, a midwife or a dentist, to help a non-medical professional from a distance. This activity is the translation of telemedicine for co-operation between health professionals in a chronically ill patient care treatment. Here are some examples.

Many small public health establishments, who retain emergency services and cutting-edge imaging equipment, no longer have permanent radiology care 24 hours a day, 7 days a week, especially at night and on the weekends. They must use a local or regional tele-radiology centre or a national, private radiology company. With no radiologist onsite, the electro radiology technician works alone, possibly assisted by an emergency room doctor for various intravenous injections. He may also benefit from a radiologist's teleassistance in needed; the benefit coming from either the continuity of care in tele-radiology or the radiology department to which the electro radiology technician is attached. Remote assistance for the electro radiology technician by the radiologist doctor for realization of scan or MRI need rooms equiped with visio conferencing systems.

Tele-ultrasound, whatever the specialty (cardiology, obstetrics, gastroenterology, urology, etc.), requires that the physician specialist in sonography tele-assist a paramedic trained in the handling of the ultrasound probe. The interpretation of an ultrasound examination should be done in real time. It is "sonographer dependent," which requires that the "call centre agent" be particularly well-trained. The same organization characterizes the cardiac tele-consultation with tele-cardiography.

Dialysis patients in remote units of dialysis centres where there are nephrologists can benefit from remote monitoring and remote assistance. These satellite units are equipped with a tele-dialysis system and are supervised by dialysis nurses. They may need the nephrologist's hotline number at the beginning of treatment (puncture difficulty, vascular access, etc.) or other issues which may arise (blood pressure falls, cramps). During the medical tele-consultation at the end of the session, the doctor may tele-assist the nurse, if needed, for example, during the dressing of a chronic wound.

Patients who have had an ischemic stroke (cardiovascular arrest) may benefit from thrombolysis after discussion via tele-expertise with a vascular neurologist. In this situation, once the brain image has been analysed, and the results are known, the nurse request assistance via tele-assistance with the neurologist for the drug injection.

With regard to the monitoring of chronic and complex wounds, the intervention of a medical expert in chronic wounds may be necessary. This can be achieved through tele-consultation. In this case, the doctor tele-assists the nurse, who is with the patient and performs the care.

23.3.3 Health-Care Offers Are Diversified for More Personalized Medicine

Health-care facilities and primary care settings that traditionally offer health care accomplish organizational change through digital technology. This is the case in France when the "digital hospital" was launched in 2013 in the public sector.

The "Haute autorité de Santé" (HAS) and the Ministry of Health encouraged the modernization of hospital information systems (HIS) and developed a certificate for hospitals based on twenty-seven indicators. The certification criteria pertain to both the foundations of the hospital information systems as well as on thematic areas such as patient identification, at all stages of the procedure, respect of privacy, the prescription for samples of laboratory tests, the transportation conditions, the transmission of results or drug delivery. Even more specific criteria are targeted such as IS security and SI disaster recovery plan, management and computerization of medical management, organization and operating room IS built at HIS [30]. Alongside these traditional care offerings, a new offer based on the digital industry to expand the management of patients at home with chronic disease appeared. Close management of these patients through the use of connected objects and mobile health applications was now possible. This is called the "uberization" of health care [31].

Obviously, twenty-first-century medicine will be more technologically advanced that the twentieth century and doctors should participate in the co-construction of new technological solutions with engineers in order that the actual benefit to the patient be regularly assessed and maintained.

All semantic efforts to define another twenty-first-century medicine are intended to replace the "curative" group, which was prevalent in the last century, dominated by the fight against infectious diseases. It should, nevertheless, be remembered that this collective, curative medicine has helped increase life expectancy up to fifty years in the twentieth century. Twenty-first-century medicine, or 5P medicine, is based on the high hopes of even an even faster progression for life expectancy, which the digital age in connected-health and genomics (Fig. 23.2).

In 2013, Leroy Hood defined personalized medicine as "4P medicine" [32], with its four, main attributes: personalized because it takes into account the genetic profile or protein of an individual; preventive because it takes into account health problems focusing on wellness, not illness; predictive because it targets the most-appropriate treatment for the patient who is trying to avoid drug reactions, and finally, participatory because it allows patients to be more responsible for their health and the care they receive.

Digital age medicine should be an evidence-based medical service for patients, particularly when based on connected health and telemedicine.

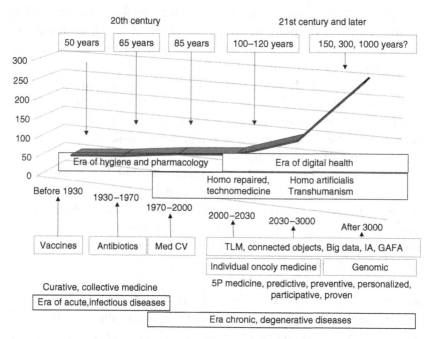

Fig. 23.2 Transition from collective curative medicine towards personalized, predictive, preventive, participatory and proven medicine (5P medicine)

This is known as 5P medicine. Telemedicine facilitates personalized, participatory, predictive and preventive medicine. Medical evidence must remain the common thread of any medical course. Predictive medicine unquestionably raises hopes, but it will take years of research before man "with no genetic risk of disease" can expect to live for hundreds of years by attaining the age of transhumanism.

23.4 Conclusions

Nearly 20 years after the definition of telemedicine by WHO, telemedicine and connected-health structure the new paradigms of medicine of the twenty-first century. There will be no questioning of this development of the health system as it improves access to care and provides medical service to patients, particularly those with chronic, degenerative diseases related to aging. The efficiency of these news organizations is demonstrated in numerous scientific studies. Well-controlled, clinical telemedicine will continue to attract patients and health professionals, especially younger generations of doctors who will be more likely to integrate the digital revolution in their practice.

Informative and clinical telemedicine complement and feed upon each other. Industrial/physician co-management is required for remote monitoring of chronic diseases in the home, which brings a better service to patients. They, alone, enable the digital businesses to gain a better understanding of this new market.

What does the future hold for connected health? No doubt, it will contribute to the development of increasingly personalized medicine. Social scientists are beginning to explore new behaviours of patients as well as health professionals, induced by these new practices. Can the very nature of medicine change? This is unlikely because it would mean the end of scientific medicine based on evidence.

Consumption of digital health goods (such as applications and connected-health objects), reflects the desire of users to better take care of themselves using these new tools. It is very different from the difficult and risky practice of medicine whose scientific complexity continues to grow. The analytical computer that processes hundreds of millions of health data (big data) is already born. It can help reduce this complexity and enable a more personalized approach. It will promote the development of predictive and preventive medicine. The telemedicine clinic is the heir of scientific medicine. This is why these practices should always be for the benefit of patients and based on scientific data.

References

[1] LAW n° 2016-41 dated 26 January 2016 regarding the modernization of our healthcare system. https://www.legifrance.gouv.fr/eli/loi/2016/1/26/AFSX1418355L/jo.

[2] Directive 98/34/CE from the European Parliament and the 22 June 1998 Council. http://eur-lex.europa.eu/LexUriServ/LexUriServ.do?uri=CONSLEG:1998L0034:20070101:fr:PDF.

[3] Directive 2000/31/CE from the European parliament and the 8 June 2000 Council regarding certain legal aspects of the information society services, in particular, electronic commerce in the internal market ("directive on electronic commerce"). http://eur-lex.europa.eu/LexUriServ/LexUriServ.do?uri=OJ:L:2000:178:0001:0016:FR:PDF.

[4] Mitchell, J. Increasing the cost-effectiveness of telemedicine by embracing e-health, *J Telemed Telecare*, 6(Suppl. 1) 2000, S16–S19.

[5] Pierre Simon et Dominique Acker. La place de la télémédecine dans l'organisation des soins. Direction Générale de l'Offre de Soins (DGOS), Ministère de la santé, novembre 2008. http://www.sante.gouv.fr/IMG/pdf/Rapport_final_Telemedecine.pdf.

[6] Pierre Lasbordes la télésanté: un nouvel atout au service de notre bien-être, novembre 2009. http://technosens.fr/files/2009-11-Rapport_Telesante_Lasbordes.pdf.

[7] http://www.sante.gouv.fr/programme-hopital-numerique.html.

[8] Pybus, O. G., A. j. Tatem, and P. Lemey. Virus evolution and transmission in an ever more connected world. *Proc Biol Sci.* 2015 December 22, 282(1821), 20142878.

[9] Istepanian, R., Swamy Laxminarayan, and Pattichis, S. Constantinos Eds 2005 *M-Health: Emerging Mobile Health Systems*. Springer. ISBN 978-0387-26558-2.

[10] Fondation Gustav-PRAEKELT http://blog.praekeltfoundation.org/.

[11] Huckvale, K., S. Adomaviciute, Prieto Jt, Leow Mk, and J. Car Smartphone apps for calculating insulin dose: A systematic assessment, *BMC Med* 2015 May 6; 13.

[12] Bravata, D. M., C. Smith-Spangler, V. Sundaram, A. L. Gienger, N. Lin, R. Lewis, C. D. Stave, I. Olkin, and J. R. Sirard Using pedometers to increase physical activity and improve health: A systematic review, *JAMA* November 21, 2007 298(19), 2296–2304.

[13] Simon, P. La place du téléconseil médical personnalisé dans les pratiques de télémédecine, *European Research in Telemedicine—La Recherche européenne en télémédecine* 4(3) 2015, 71–80., http://dx.doi.org/10. 1016/j.eurtel.2015.07.003.

[14] La messagerie sécurisée de santé. Réunion des industriels. *ASIPsanté*, 20 novembre 2012. http://esante.gouv.fr/actus/services/la-messagerie-securi see-de-sante-mss-au-coeur-de-la-journee-nationale-des-industriels.

[15] Cota, A., M. Tarchala, C. Parent-Harvey, V. Engel, G. Berry, R. Reindl, and E. J. Harvey Review of 5.5 Years' Experience Using E-mail-Based Telemedicine to Deliver Orthopedic Care to Remote Communities. *Telemed J E Health.* June 23, 2016. [Epub ahead of print].

[16] Viedma-Guiard, E., P. Agüero, L. Crespo-Araico, C. Estévez-Fraga, G. Sánchez-Díez, J. L. López-Sendón, I. Aviles-Olmos, G. García-Ribas, M. L. Palacios Romero, Vallejo J Masjuan, and J. C. Martínez-Castrillo Alonso-Cánovas A. Use of e-mail for Parkinson's disease consultations: Are answers just a clic away? *Neurologia* July 26, 2016 S0213–4853(16) 30096-2, doi: 10.1016/j.nrl.2016.05.020. [Epub ahead of print].

[17] Atherton, H., P. Sawmynaden, Sheikh A., A. Majeed, and J. Car Email for clinical communication between patients/caregivers and healthcare professionals, *Cochrane Database Syst Rev* 2012 November 14, 11, CD007978, doi: 10.1002/14651858.CD007978.pub2. Review.

[18] GBD 2013 DALYs and HALE Collaborators, Global, regional, and national disability-adjusted life years (DALYs) for 306 diseases and injuries and healthy life expectancy (HALE) for 188 countries, 1990-2013: Quantifying the epidemiological transition, *Lancet* November 28, 2015 386(10009), 2145–2191, doi: 10.1016/S0140-6736(15)61340-X. Epub August 2015, 28.

[19] Thorpe, K. E. Treated disease prevalence and spending per treated case drove most of the growth in health care spending in 1987–2009, *Health Aff (Millwood).* 2013 May, 32(5), 851–858, doi: 10.1377/ hlthaff.2012.0391.

[20] La France et ses territoires, édition 2015, Institut national de la statistique et des études (Insee). http://www.insee.fr/fr/ffc/docs_ffc/FST15.pdf.

[21] Simon, Pierre *La télémédecine, enjeux et pratiques* (Lyon, Le Coudrier 2015), 47–70.

[22] Blanchére, J. P., and A. Dompmartin The latest developments in telemedicine applied to wound care, *Soins Gérontologie* 101 mai–juin, 2013, 38–40.

[23] Simon, Pierre *La télémédecine, enjeux et pratiques* (Lyon, Le Coudrier 2015), 55–60.

[24] Loi 2016-41 du 26 janvier 2016 de modernisation de notre système de santé. https://www.legifrance.gouv.fr/affichTexte.do;jsessionid=E9B55DD91B17C3D94BEF36E18138547E.tpdila22v_3?cidTexte=JORFTEXT000031912641&categorieLien=id.

[25] Chaudhry, S. I., J. A. Mattera, J. P. Curtis, J. A. Spertus, J. Herrin, Z. Lin, C. O. Phillips, B. V. Hodshon, L. S. Cooper, and H. M. Krumholz "Telemonitoring in patients with heart failure," *The New England Journal of Medicine* 363(24) Décember 2010, 2301–2309.

[26] Koehler, F., S. Winkler, M. Schieber, U. Sechtem, K. Stangl, M. Böhm, H. Boll, G. Baumann, M. Honold, K. Koehler, G. Gelbrich, B. A. Kirwan, and S. D. Anker Telemedical interventional monitoring in heart failure investigators. Impact of remote telemedical management on mortality and hospitalizations in ambulatory patients with chronic heart failure: The telemedical interventional monitoring in heart failure study, *Circulation* 123(17) mai 2011, 1873–1880.

[27] Steventon, A. et al., Effect of telehealth on use of secondary care and mortality: Findings from the WSD cluster randomised trial, *British Medical Journal* 344, juin 2012, 3874–3892.

[28] Black, J. T., P. S. Romano, B. Sadeghi, A. D. Auerbach, T. G. Ganiats, S. Greenfield, S. H. Kaplan, and M. K. Ong BEAT-HF Research Group A remote monitoring and telephone nurse coaching intervention to reduce readmissions among patients with heart failure: Study protocol for the Better Effectiveness After Transition—Heart Failure (BEAT-HF) randomized controlled trial, *Trials* 15 avr. 2014, 124–130.

[29] Kotooka, N., M. Asaka, Y. Sato, Y. Kinugasa, K. Nochioka, A. Mizuno, D. Nagatomo, D. Mine, Y. Yamada, K. Eguchi, H. Hanaoka, T. Inomata, Y. Fukumoto, K. Yamamoto, H. Tsutsui, T. Masuyama, M. Kitakaze, T. Inoue, H. Shimokawa, S. Momomura, Y. Seino, and K. Node HOMES-HF study investigators "Home telemonitoring study for Japanese patients with heart failure (HOMES-HF): protocol for a multicentre randomised controlled

trial," *BMJ Open* June 20, 2013 3(6), e002972, doi: 10.1136/bmjopen-2013-002972.

[30] Mise en œuvre du programme hôpital numérique par les établissements. http://social-sante.gouv.fr/systeme-de-sante-et-medico-social/e-sante/sih/hopital-numerique/article/mise-en-oeuvre-du-programme-hopital-numerique-par-les-etablissements-de-sante.

[31] Normand, Alexis Ubérisation de la santé: réconcilions le médecin et l'ingénieur. *Le Monde*, 1er avril 2016. http://www.lemonde.fr/idees/article/2016/04/01/uberisation-de-la-sante-reconcilions-le-medecin-et-l-ingenieur_4894073_3232.html.

[32] Hood, L. Systems biology and p4 medicine: past, present, and future. *Rambam Maimonides Med J* 4(2) April 30, 2013, e0012, doi: 10.5041/RMMJ.10112. Print 2013 April.

Conclusion

Uses related to connected health increase at a steady pace, leading to encouraging prospects concerning information exchanges between patients, doctors, and caregivers, and enabling researchers to get a refined collect of medical information, which is necessary to better understand diseases and patient's psychological state. As a background of the digitalization of health, it involves a meaningful paradigm shift that is in process and that initiates a deep questioning on how to do, practise and position into a market both for professional caregivers and manufacturers. Are the Google, Apple, Facebook, Amazon (GAFAs)[1] on the way to merge into the health sector that is in a reorganization process, interfering in the value chain to become a future key player in the medical field if mastering and having a key skill? It is not done yet, but if it is so, new power relations could appear. This "healthcare digitalization" is inevitably going to make actors related to the health field reconsider the ways they do and practice while focusing on patients, the major concern, and for which digital technology should produce an advantage, not dehumanization.

---

[1] Google, Apple, Facebook, Amazon.

© The Author(s) 2017
L. Menvielle et al. (eds.), *The Digitization of Healthcare*,
DOI 10.1057/978-1-349-95173-4

The digital technology emergence in the health sector will have impacts on current business models and on the reorganization of health financing systems and division of powers between public and private area (particularly health and mutual insurances). Digital solutions provided by eHealth appear in a particular context in which the major Western countries—but not only—may be wondering about economic future and sustainability of current medical systems. The balance between the desire to maintain access to health care for the greatest number of people and the need to strive to reduce the deficits of the health system, identifies connected health as a way to partly respond to these issues. A skilled integration of those technologies also represents a relevant solution with regard to deployment of access care solutions for populations affected by lack of medical services for both developed and emerging countries. In this regard, several programs under the World Health Organization (WHO) and the International Telecommunication Union[2] (ITU) carried out experiments in developing countries to take advantage of eHealth and mHealth to meet patients located in the most remote rural areas in the world.

Due to the digitalization of health care, medical practice is reviewed. From current medicine that provides medical and post-traumatic treatments, we will shift to a medicine that focuses on prevention and customization. Computerized solutions based on the processing of big data are issues that will be an integral part of medicine in the future. Calculating capabilities, integration of artificial intelligence such as those proposed by actors including Microsoft or IBM, will get a better handle of diseases and anticipate treatments. The issue of this type of solution concerns warning signal detections of diseases to provide the best therapeutics, and thus reducing costs related to health expenditures at the same time. Growth of knowledge concerning DNA sequencing will contribute to strengthen this personalized medicine over the coming years.

---

[2] Specialized agency of the WHO that is responsible for issues that concern information and communication technologies.

The practice of medicine is evolving and this transformation made by the health sector leads to a great support of practices and organizational structures. The digitalization of health not only involves to implement digital solutions but it also involves, and above all, to support general practitioners, medical specialists, and caregivers in the future medical sphere. Dr. Google or Dr. Watson will never substitute medical practitioners. They are used as an aid that should be wisely used for the well-being of the sick and for the improvement of their treatment conditions. We must not confuse commercial success of certain health apps or connected objects with medical efficacy. The connected health field is complicated and cannot become a marketing tool used by any manufacturer searching for new business opportunities, particularly in the mHealth field where there are hundreds of thousands of offers with highly heterogeneous contents.

Legal context remains quite vague, however, in a number of countries, there is a set of measures that can be mobilized to partly help connected health development, particularly mHealth and health connected objects. Both Europe and the USA have established regulations on protection of personal data, for example, but they prove to be insufficient and they place too much faith in private organizations for the implementation of labelling systems of those health solutions. The European Union strives to open up the debate on this delicate topic with the firm intention to strengthen the protection of personal data and to extend it to all types of information related to individuals' mental or physical health and also to all types of health-care service delivery.

Besides this aspect related to the protection of personal data, manufacturers can implement solutions that are as safe as possible. For hackers and especially for criminal networks, this field is prolific for those organizations. Plenty of apps, health solutions, and health connected objects do not guarantee the protection of personal data: a defect in securing communications, data that are easily identifiable . . . so many flaws allowing people with dishonest intentions to take advantage of this information. Because of the fact that health data is extremely lucrative regarding cybercrime and, because of the strong digitalization of solutions brought to market, health data can become the new Eldorado for cyber criminals if nothing is done. To solve those security and protection problems related to health data, actors of the digital and health sectors are basing their hopes on solutions such as blockchain. This data storage and transmission technology, which is transparent, secure, and considered as reliable and untouchable, will certainly be an important part of this eHealth era and be a major part in digital health systems and solutions over the coming years.

In this digital evolution, is the user informed or simply aware of the use of personal data? Is he aware of the commitments and risks that use of health app and connected objects can lead him or the exploitation that can be done? Which level of transparency should it take to reassure both users and patients while maintaining company competitiveness? Regarding the increase of trackers, to whom does data belong to and where does the limits of privacy protection of the users of those solutions are?

The use of those digital tools allows us as well to focus on new relationships that are developed between patients and doctors. Internet has become a medium to democratize medical knowledge. Community platforms that were created are a good way to restore a social link that might have been broken by disease. It is also a good way for patients to discuss among themselves about their pathology, to better understand it and to be back on their feet from a psychological standpoint. Those community platforms are genuine privileged spaces for both the sick and the family caregivers that wish to capture and understand diseases through those spaces. Doctors have created spaces to generate more collaborative and efficient groups to implement medical protocols or share their expertise. The main medical and pharmaceutical institutions make the transition to digital technology as well to be closer to patients and their families.

eHealth is a field that has good prospects. Solutions provided, particularly those concerning help with treatments and integration of artificial intelligence, are significant advances. The digital technology has allowed to broadening the huge range of opportunities. Almost 15 years ago, Professor Marescaux carried out the Lindberg operation in performing surgery at more than 6,000 km from its patient. From now on, the medicine field through the numerical technology tries to be accessible for everyone and this is how we should consider it. It must in no way replace medical practitioners or caregivers, but must be considered as a tool that support the well-being of people both physically and mentally. It is important to remember that digital solutions must be available to many people as possible for both Western and emerging countries where access to medicine turns out to be an unbounded complexity.

Index

© The Author(s) 2017
L. Menvielle et al. (eds.), *The Digitization of Healthcare*,
DOI 10.1057/978-1-349-95173-4

Printed in the United States
By Bookmasters